Praise for *Finding The Midline*

"**Finally! I have been teaching** using Bill's early manuscripts in my yoga trainings for over three years. Now I have an actual book to hand my students! This is an immeasurably valuable asset for any yoga student trying to learn Tantra, and a one-of-a-kind *must have* for any yoga teacher training or intensive!"

—MADHURI MARTIN, Founder of ShamMa Yoga (Boulder, Colorado)

"**In a city where you can't** throw a rock without hitting a yoga instructor like myself, Bill's book stands out as a real life meditation, observation, and participation in 'awakening'. Bill takes ancient yoga teachings and philosophy and applies them to life, in an applicable, intelligent, and—often times—whimsical way. I think Bill's humility and underlying gratitude help us all to connect a bit more deeply to our own hearts and to 'wake up' to the beauty of life. I have to say it.... A breath of fresh air."

—BILLY POTOCNIK, Yoga Instructor and Realtor (Denver, Colorado)

"**Bill weaves his personal story** and deep knowledge to create an accessible, human, and humorous book -- an invitation to make the incredible wisdom of yoga available to us all and, as he powerfully illustrates, through the limitless possibilities in our daily lives. This book is a worthy investment for us all toward deepening our engagement with life."

—JOE SOMA, MA, MS, LPC, therapist, teacher, trainer (Boulder, Colorado)

"**Bill has pieced togeth** knowledge in a most down-to-earth manner, yet witho the teachings. This is the type of book you will want to ytime you lose track of why you were born and what it

—COLLYN R. BROWN, Acupuncturist and Kundalini Yoga Teacher
(The Berkshires, Massachusetts)

"**What a great book** for the everyday person! If you are looking for that balance in your life, this book will challenge you to make the changes necessary to live a richer, fuller life. Through a unique combination of experiences, philosophy, and yoga, Bill Dorigan opens your mind to the many crossroads that we face daily. Regardless of your profession, habits, or background, the tools provided throughout this book will undoubtedly make you a stronger, healthier person. A must read for the life-long learner."

—KEN BURDETTE, High School Principal (Denver, Colorado)

Life is offering you a rich experience—can you pause
long enough to feel it? Can you be still long enough
to see, to feel, Life's hand beckoning to you?

In the pause, listen to the song of your heart.
In the space between breaths, between thoughts,
can you hear how much your heart longs to reach out
and accept the invitation, that beckoning hand?

You're now in Midline—the place of *Madya*—
the Heart of all things.

My wish is that you find the courage to answer
your heart's song—the song Life asks you to sing
and needs you to sing.

Finding the Midline

How yoga helps a trial lawyer make friends and connect to Spirit

the Midline

Bill Dorigan

with Judyth Hill

LuHen Publications
Winter Park, Colorado

LuHen Publications, LLC
PO Box 3284
Winter Park, CO 80482

Editors:
Lesley DuTemple
  lesleydutemple.com
Judyth Hill
  judythhill.com

Cover and interior design:
Laura Smyth
  smythtypedesign.com

ISBN 978-0-9893812-0-8

Printed in the United States.

To purchase books in quantity please contact the
publisher directly: info@findingthemidline.com

CONTENTS

Acknowledgements

I'm having a great life. I lead a life that is meaningful and full of rich and valued relation-ships. I laugh a lot. But it wasn't always this way. I've done well, enjoyed myself, made some good friends, and had jobs that accomplished things significant to my community. Yet, something was always missing and it wasn't until I found yoga that the missing pieces came together. I write this book as an expression of gratitude to all the people who helped me discover yoga and weave it into my life.

I also thank those people who helped me do an extraordinary thing—devote a decade of my life to my passion for yoga philosophy and its practices. Thanks to the efforts and gen-erosity of others, I've been privileged to have the time and resources necessary to commit myself for a number of years to the study of yoga philosophy and consistent engagement in its practices.

This book is my way of giving back and sharing what I've learned. It's not easy to find the time or money to sit at the feet of the top scholars in the world, buy and read the books recommended by these scholars, complete a Masters' Degree, and train with the top yoga teachers all over the country and even outside the United States. I was able to do so in large part due to the rewarding opportunities given me by my former law partners in Minnesota and, later, the generosity and support of attorneys I worked for after moving to Colorado: Scott Sullan, Ron Sandgrund, and Russell Yates. I thank them all.

Despite this foundation, my interest in yoga would not have gone very far without the guidance of Emma Addison, certified Iyengar Yoga teacher, and Dr. Priscilla Herbison, my advisor in graduate school. Together they helped me create a unique and fascinating cur-riculum correlating the wisdom of western behavioral psychology with yoga philosophy. In addition, Emma took me, a total novice, and with kindness and humor, began to mold my body into something that could actually do a pose or two.

Scholar and professor, Dr. Douglas R. Brooks, one of the most stimulating and entertain-ing lecturers I've ever encountered, hooked me on the non-dualist Tantric yoga philoso-phy I discuss in this book. What is "non-dualist Tantric" philosophy, you ask? The answer is in this book. Years ago I stumbled into a lecture where Dr. Brooks was speaking on the *Ramayana,* a famous and fascinating Indian epic. But for that encounter, I might have gone off in a different philosophical direction. Dr. Brooks changed that. After listening to him I decided I had to learn all I could about this form of yoga philosophy and I had to keep studying with him: he was that good. The experience was like watching *The Daily Show* for the first time and just knowing you'd be watching it as much as possible for years to come. I knew I had found a spiritual and intellectual home in this philosophy.

In my home state of Colorado, I began studying with yoga teacher Madhuri Martin. She came highly recommended as somebody steeped in this philosophy I was suddenly so hungry to explore. Madhuri took me under her wing and I studied regularly with her, learning so much through her masterful classes, trainings, and workshops. Over time, as my study of non-dualist Tantric philosophy deepened, she asked me to give lectures to her students. I did so on a number of occasions. When necessary, she politely but firmly challenged me on my interpretations of what I was learning. On numerous occasions she took time out from her busy schedule to answer questions about the most esoteric yoga subjects. Madhuri eventually encouraged me to write a book about what I'd learned. This is the book. Without her encouragement and support there was no way I would have undertaken this task. I owe her a huge debt of gratitude for all her support, which continues to this day.

Once I began writing this book, there were certain people who stuck with me, and one way or another, supported me through its completion. Particular thanks to Murray Greene, Ellin Todd, and Roger Pressman for their kindness, patience, and persistence in making sure I finished what I started. Thanks, too, for their friendship.

It was also Madhuri who introduced me to Judyth Hill, the poet, writing teacher, editor, and coach extraordinaire who helped me present this philosophy in an understandable and enjoyable way. When I first began working with her I tried to get a chapter past her about driving over Berthoud Pass in Colorado, calling the drive "pretty." "PRETTY???? Oy!!" she responded, after reading that description; "Looks like there's some work to do." So, if you read something in this book that flows like nectar, thank Judyth. If it sounds like a legal brief, it's likely I ignored one of her edits.

I owe Judyth a debt of gratitude that extends far beyond the technical help that has made this book so much more readable—those tastes of honey you'll find in the language. Judyth took the time to read between the lines, sensing when I was holding something back, refusing to share. On those occasions she would prod me to consider going deeper, to drop down and explore what I really was feeling and share from those experiences. As a result of her constant vigilance, there are stories in this book that were truly cathartic for me, truly liberating and healing. She coaxed these experiences and stories from me so that this book would have a greater chance of moving the reader. As a secondary benefit, the ice cream on top of the hot apple pie, so to speak, she greatly enriched my life. How do you thank somebody for that?

I am also grateful to yoga teacher John Friend. I spent several years attending his workshops around the country, and digging deeper into the yoga philosophy first introduced to me by Dr. Brooks. Thanks again to my former law partners for this; how many lawyers of pre-retirement age get to do things like follow yoga teachers around? I was able to freely ask John questions and discuss yoga philosophy with him. I learned so much about yoga philosophy from him and I thank him for that. I was also able to experience first hand the brilliance of his teaching methodology, the way yoga poses can be taught and practiced to maximize the opportunity to create positive neural linkages; i.e., make us feel better about ourselves. John's way of joining, or yoking the philosophy with teaching poses is a true gift to our world.

I'm not done thanking Madhuri, I guess. Once she takes you under her wing, there's no end! She introduced me to Sally Kempton, formerly Swami Durgananda, a top meditation and spiritual teacher. Over these years I've greatly benefited from Sally's lectures, her books, her on-line meditation courses, and occasional private conversations. She probably doesn't realize it, but her voice is so calm, peaceful, and full of Grace as we say in yoga, that sometimes I just queue up one of her recorded classes. The sound of her voice alone makes me feel like I'm on a beach in Hawaii with all the bills paid and no meetings scheduled.

I also wish to thank Dr. Paul Muller-Ortega, a Tantric scholar and meditation teacher. I've studied with Paul for some time now and thank him for his kindness and incredible gift of explaining this philosophy. I owe Dr. Muller-Ortega a tremendous debt of gratitude: I learned my daily meditation practice from him. As you will read, the meditation practice he teaches is like getting a free pass to the top five bakeries and ice cream shops in New York City AND Paris, only sweeter and with no weight gain! I also wish to thank him, as well as Dr. Brooks, for teaching me a true appreciation for *Mantra*, a practice I hadn't paid much attention to for years until studying with these great teachers.

In addition, I thank other teachers who helped me understand this philosophy. I've learned so much from Colorado yoga teachers Cindy Lusk and Jaime and Justin Allison and value their support. I owe Cindy Lusk a big thank you for all her efforts to mentor me on my path to become certified as a yoga teacher. She never gave up and always made me feel I was the best teacher in the world, even when I made the most basic mistakes. Her tireless encouragement has helped change my life because it allowed me to eventually become a teacher. If that hadn't happened, I would have never met the many incredible students I've had over the years, each of whom has touched my heart in a special way and made me a better person for knowing them.

As I trained to become a certified teacher, and even now, the teacher trainings, on-line courses, and yoga immersions offered by Colorado yoga teacher Amy Ippoliti are incredible sources of information on how this philosophy has value in our day-to-day lives. Time after time as I studied to become certified, Amy asked us to read the philosophy, whether it was Patanjali, the *Gunas*, the *Tattvas*, or some other subject, and then break it down into how it mattered to us in our interaction with family, friends, or co-workers. Those were invaluable, stimulating conversations. Thanks, also, to yoga teacher Desiree Rumbaugh for being...Desiree. Take a workshop with her if this book moves you to study yoga and you'll see what I mean about "being Desiree."

I thank Joe Soma, MA, MS, CHT, LPC, a professor in transpersonal counseling psychology, for helping me with the behavioral science information in this book. From my graduate work, I had the sense that John Friend's teaching methodology, with its focus on using heart-oriented themes and instructions to help strengthen students' positive psychological makeup, was a true gift to yoga and society. I wanted somebody trained in behavior to verify for me that my understanding was supported by the science. Joe was kind enough to do this for me, and for you. I also wish to thank author and yoga teacher Lesley DuTemple for her ongoing encouragement and assistance with editorial advice that helped me find my direction in writing and completing this book. Thanks, too, to Ken Burdette and Lisa Rockers for their helpful suggestions that I found invaluable.

As I said, my life is good. Nobody, in my view, gets to this place in life without help. I'll never be able to repay my parents, my grandmother and my Aunt Irene for what they did for me, molding me into somebody capable of making it in the world. I thank my sister, Patti, for being a friend. I thank all my friends, particularly Bill, Jerry, Marie, Joyce, Carly, Donna, and Jim. These are people who have helped me see the best of myself.

I'm forever grateful to my ex-wife, Cyndi, and her husband, Chuck, who have for years behaved with style and class in our common relationship with my son Jeff, always putting Jeff first so that he and I could have a relationship. I'm grateful to Jeff and his wife, Caitlin, for their support of my pursuit of yoga. I'm grateful to my grandkids, Lucy and Henry, who call me "Grandpa Yogi" or "Yogi" for short. They are a constant light of inspiration. Finally, I'm also grateful to Jeff for putting up with me for so many years, giving me chance after chance to be a good dad. Beyond all else, it has been my desire to make him proud of me that keeps me on the yoga path, the path I share in this book.

One final note: I want you to know that the philosophy I discuss in this book is my personal assimilation of the many hours of classes, lectures, reading and conversations with all these teachers, as well as others. I provide my experience and understanding of what I've read and heard, as opposed to a reiteration of any one teacher's particular point of view. Yoga's helped me to achieve a life well lived, rich and satisfying, and this is the perspective I offer to you, and for having this book in your hand and accepting my gift of these teachings…I thank you!

Note to Readers

This book explores the ways yoga practices and philosophy can greatly enrich your life, fill it with meaning, deepen your relationships, and, if you are on a spiritual path, help you find clarity on whatever path you've chosen.

That's great, but what if you don't want to do yoga poses? What if putting your leg behind your head is just not your thing?

Don't worry—this book is exactly for you, intentionally written so you can apply the lessons of yoga in your life without ever having to balance on one foot, or do a Down Dog.

You will notice that most of the chapters are very short, limited to one particular aspect of yoga practice or philosophy. Each chapter starts with a story meant to be entertaining. The purpose of the story is to capture the essence of the yoga practice or philosophical teaching in a personal way, pertinent to your life. And you'll notice very few of the stories have anything to do with a yoga pose. Some of the stories involve me learning a life-lesson; some of the stories involve others showing what a well-lived life looks like in action. The stories are intended to apply to us in our daily lives, regardless of our occupation or whether or not we practice yoga poses.

Following each story is a short discussion of the practice or teaching highlighted in the chapter. Then, at the end of each chapter is a very short practice that invites you to focus your attention on a special aspect of the chapter and help you assimilate the lesson of the chapter. Each practice usually takes no more than a minute or so.

Introduction

I wonder if you've ever had a wild night like the one I'm about to describe to you. Even now, as I look back on it, it is still amazing.

It was around Thanksgiving in my sophomore year of high school, back in Hammond, Indiana, a very "urban" city bordering on the south side of Chicago. It had been a pretty good year up to that point. I had made the varsity football team, a tough thing to do in our conference, particularly because we were the defending Indiana State Football Champions. I got to play in every game and we made it all the way to the state championship game. Unfortunately, we lost, but we were proud of what we'd accomplished and were excited about the next season.

With some newfound popularity, no doubt due in large part to being a varsity football player, I lined up a date with Linda, the apple of my eye. She was not just any apple; we're talking Fuji, Cameo, or Honeycrisp here. Linda was a cheerleader and went on to be Homecoming Queen when we were seniors, which gives you a hint of the kind of apple I'm talking about: beautiful and a sweetheart.

Anyway, I had a date with Linda for a basketball game during Thanksgiving weekend. Our high school basketball team wasn't too shabby either, and, regardless of what team we were playing, it was a big game. One thing about Indiana high school basketball, there are no insignificant games.

I didn't have a car, always a problem for high school sophomores, but I solved that problem since one of my new friends from varsity football, Ralph, had a car and wanted to double date. Unfortunately, he had no date. Ralph and I were a match made in heaven because I was good friends with Carole, a friend from junior high, and Ralph really wanted to go out with her. The only problem was that Carole had spent all of junior high dating my closest friend, Jim. They'd broken up and Jim had started to date, so I didn't think too long and hard about it; I fixed up Carole with Ralph. This was to be my first date with Linda and I didn't want to miss out because I didn't have a car. Plus, Ralph was cool, knew all the kids in high school, and was somebody I wanted to hang out with.

Game night arrived. Ralph picked me up and we met Carole and Linda at the Civic Center, a 4,500-seat arena that my high school filled for basketball games. Like I said, basketball is a big deal in Indiana. Sometime during the game I had to go to the restroom. On the way back to my seat I ran into Jim in the stairwell. Remember him—my best friend whose recently former girl friend is now with Ralph, thanks to me?

Did I mention that Jim had also made the varsity football team that year? Did I mention that he was already 6'3" and 225 pounds of muscle? In fact, if it's possible to have negative body fat, that was Jim. Just like Linda would eventually become Homecoming Queen, Jim would eventually become All-State as a football lineman. He was not somebody to trifle with.

As we passed each other we both said, "Hi." Then, abruptly, Jim stops and turns to me and asks: "Did you fix Carole up with Ralph like I just heard?" I said, somewhat meekly because I can already see that Jim isn't too pleased: "Yes, but…" Well, just as the "but" came out of my mouth, Jim's fist went into my left eye. BAM!—and I do mean BAM!! Did I mention that Jim and I had lifted weights together almost every day since Seventh Grade so we would be strong and make the varsity? To tweak me, Jim would spot me in bench presses, wait until I did my last repetition, and then lift the bar and do some cheat curls. For those of you that lift weights; enough said. For those of you that don't, translation: this guy was powerful.

Neither of us was a stranger to street fights but I was so far out of my league, it was unbelievable. I yelled at him and made noise so I'd attract the cops who were always on duty, while at the same time clutching, grabbing, and doing whatever I could to stay away from those incredibly strong fists and stay on my feet. In just a few moments the cops came, broke us up, and we went our separate ways. Back then; if they had sent folks to jail for this kind of stuff, they'd have to add ten stories to the jailhouse.

That wasn't the end of the evening. In fact, it was just the beginning. I still had my date.

After the game we left and grabbed some high quality cuisine at a local drive-through, likely one with Golden Arches. Ralph and I really knew how to impress the ladies. Then, off we went looking for a place to "park." None of us, I suspect, planned that anything major would occur, but parking to talk sounded like the thing to do. All of us had curfews and we didn't have much time anyway.

Ralph succeeded in finding the only empty field within the greater Chicago metropolis. We pulled into it and turned off the car. Linda and I talked and I think that is what was going on in the front seat as well. I suppose it doesn't matter because Ralph and Carole eventually married each other and are still married today, 48 years later! I guess they liked each other.

After a short while we started the car and Ralph began to back out. Only the car wouldn't move. We were stuck in mud. Our car had managed to find the only muddy place in Lake County, Indiana. Not good. We had fifteen minutes until curfew.

This was back when there were no cell phones. So, Ralph took off running to find a place with a phone so we could call a tow truck. Wisely, he also took Linda and Carole's home numbers and called to tell everybody's parents we'd be late; we were stuck in mud. I bet the parents were excited to hear that. Eventually a tow truck showed up, got us out, and we drove the girls home.

Since this was my first date with Linda, I had not met her parents. I got to meet them that night, a good two hours after curfew. To really make the experience a total fun night, I got an added bonus when I walked Linda through her front door. In addition to her parents, I got to meet Ed, her big brother, as in BIG. He was the All-State Defensive End from the preceding year's state champ team, home from just finishing his first college football season, well-fed on turkey to boot. I apologized to both of them profusely but, of course, they were distracted. Why? By now I had a black eye, a classic shiner the size of Jim's fist, about the size of a nice steak, which I could have used about then, to put on the black eye.

I did my best to explain to Linda's dad that I was a good guy and babbled whatever else could come out of my future lawyer's mouth to try to get him to let me date his daughter again. All the while, Ed is looking at me with a look that said: "I'm not worried about my little sister's conduct—her choice in guys, perhaps—but thanks for the entertainment watching you explain this." What a great way to start Thanksgiving break! Apparently my explanation bought me additional dates and Linda and I went on to date for quite awhile. Though we eventually broke up, she remains a friend.

That's a great story, right? I'm not quite done. You're probably wondering why I would tell you a story about a fistfight and getting stuck in the mud as an introduction to a yoga book. Let me continue and I'll get to the yoga. Although, as you'll see when you read this book, life is all yoga.

There's still one more set of parents to worry about—mine. I get home and when I walk in the door there is my father, a large, tough Irishman who expected me home two hours earlier. I had no excuses in that house for being late. However, before I could get my story out my dad sees the black eye and says: "What happened to you?" I started to tell him and he stops me mid-sentence and roars at me: "You did WHAT? You fixed Jim's girlfriend up with somebody else? What the hell is wrong with you? That's your best friend. That's the guy who's had your back since you were a kid. How could you do that?" My dad was shocked. Even my mother was stunned that I would fix somebody up with Jim's recent ex. All she could do was look at me in disgust, mutter "Oy" and leave the room.

My father sat me down and lectured me that nothing, "Nothing!" was more important than being loyal to those close to you. I told him that I hadn't realized Jim would care because he was dating again and my father shut me up, telling me it was my job to know it would hurt Jim's feelings because he was my friend. It was my job to understand him. It was all pretty black or white with my dad. He went on that it was my job to protect my friends where I could and not be a source of further pain to them. My dad acknowledged that he knew I wanted to make new friends, such as Ralph, but that was no excuse for turning my back on Jim.

My dad concluded by telling me I had a lot to learn about how to be a man and how to be a friend. He said it was up to me whether I had the guts to do what was necessary to be the kind of friend somebody would want to have around. So far, he said, I hadn't shown that I had. He ordered me up to my room, shaking his head, and muttering, "If he hadn't kicked your ass, I would have."

Wow, and ouch! What a night.

I tell you this story as an introduction to yoga because the lesson my dad imparted to me that night teaches perhaps the most vital lessons I've learned from yoga. Ultimately, yoga is about helping us create a life of meaning and relationships in this world. Regardless of our religious beliefs, we know that we are here on this planet for only a short time, at least in this particular body. Do we want that time to be full, rich, and satisfying? Do we want to die surrounded by friends and the knowledge that we mattered while we were here? If the answer is "Yes," then this book is for you.

To create such a life we must learn to be awake to the feelings of others and what is going on around us. At the same time, we have to be fully awake to what is going on inside us— our feelings and our motivations. Finally, we have to be awake to how our actions impact others. If we learn these lessons, our life will be jam-packed until the last breath with hot apple pie and ice cream.

This book provides you with information you need to set your path for that full, rich and satisfying life I just described. How?

This is a book about finding Midlines and connecting to Spirit. I doubt if very many of you reading this Introduction picked up this book because you wanted to find a Midline. What is that, anyway? And do I even want a Midline if I find it? Maybe you picked up the book thinking it's a yoga book, so finding a Midline must involve learning how to balance on one foot or maybe, in a handstand. But that isn't what the Midlines in this book are about.

A Midline is wherever and whenever God whispers an invitation to step outside our comfort zone and embrace the potential of that moment. A Midline is whenever Spirit beckons us to cast aside the fears and insecurities holding us back in order to more fully engage in the gift of our life. A Midline is where we courageously choose to take the risks necessary to create a richer sweeter life of meaning and engagement, a life full of relationships that we treasure and savor.

What Midlines did I face that night? There were several. When I saw the hurt look on Jim's face I could have apologized right then, telling him what a jerk I was for disregarding his feelings for Carole, still so raw and painful. That would have required me to admit to myself that I had selfishly put aside Jim's feelings just so I could find a way to gain access to a car for my date.

That was the first real Midline of that night. It takes bravery to confront our own foibles, own them, and then shift our behavior. It was far easier for me to take on Jim, one of the toughest street fighters in our city, than to engage in the honest introspective work I needed to be a true friend. Life will always present Midlines to us. If we want a life of friendship and intimacy, we will have to look inside ourselves and do what it takes to be a true friend, a supportive partner, a good parent, and a meaningful member of our community.

The second Midline was my father's challenge to me to "be a man," and stand up for things important to me instead of selling myself out for convenience and expediency.

Midlines come in all shapes and sizes, and if you run away from one, another shows up soon after. I failed to be a friend to Jim, but I've passed the big test, the gauntlet my dad threw down. At the time I didn't have a clue what it meant to let my friend down but I've become the person my dad challenged me to be.

Finally, this book is about connecting to Spirit. You may have picked up this book because you feel an urge to more intimately connect to God. You've heard enough about yoga to suspect that practicing yoga and learning about its philosophy might be just the ticket. It is. Trust me, I'm a trial lawyer and if I can intimately connect to God through yoga, the likelihood is sky high that you can too.

Yoga helps us to deeply connect to God, or Spirit. God exists in each of us, in every place, and in every moment. The lessons of yoga philosophy, and its practices, provide a pathway for the type of intimate closeness to God that so many of us seek. When life presents you with a Midline, yoga will help you address it. This is what yoga is ultimately all about. I've studied it, devoted myself to it, and hunger to share it with you out of gratitude for the life it has given me. Have fun reading!

PART I

What's a Midline?
Why do I want to find one?
And, by the way, I've been looking for
Spirit forever—where do I look?

CHAPTER 1
Time to wake up

A messenger from my hotel burst into the courtroom and handed me a note. I was trying a very high-profile case: a construction product liability trial against an international chemical company, and I represented a number of clients from around the country claiming property damage in the millions of dollars.

I knew the note was serious by the way he rushed in. I opened and scanned the contents quickly: my father had suffered a stroke and was in the hospital in Chicago. The note was from my uncle, his brother, and told me I needed to get to Chicago right away. The Judge asked if there was something wrong and we took a recess. After telling everyone about the message I made arrangements with the judge and my partners for how the case would continue in my absence and caught a plane to Chicago.

On the flight from Denver to Chicago my mind filled with thoughts of my father. We didn't have much of a relationship, partly because I was always busy, but mostly because I resented him. All I could remember was how strict he had been with me, constantly pushing me for better grades, never satisfied with my athletic performance, never approving of my friends or anything I did. The more I thought about him, the more angry I became and, sad to say, I even felt annoyed having to take time off from this trial because of him. This was the biggest case of my career and here he was, once again, inserting himself into my life.

I took a cab from the airport to the hospital, feeling bitter. I got to the hospital, found his room and paused outside the door. I took some deep breaths to calm myself. No matter what I felt, I wasn't going to dump my anger and hostility on him. When I opened the door and stepped into his room, I was shocked at what I saw. Instead of the big, tough and hard-edged Irishman I had grown up with, I saw a tired, frail, sad-looking and frightened man with a tube in his throat. The man I remembered as well over six feet tall and towering over me, didn't look like he weighed even 100 pounds.

It was all I could do to say hello. Looking at him lying there, all my anger, bitterness, and resentment evaporated. Before I knew it I started telling him all about the trial. I told him how the national press was covering the progress every day, usually on the front pages. I told him plaintiffs from around the country had hired me because they knew I would do a good job. They knew I had the discipline to gather and read all the documents needed to win. They knew I would master all the important facts, including sophisticated science, engineering, and construction issues.

As I continued it suddenly dawned on me. These very skills and traits were the results of the way my dad had raised me. The very experiences that had made me so angry with him for so many years were the experiences that had sculpted me into a talented, disciplined and strong man. My brain suddenly made the connection: he kept me away from certain friends to keep me out of trouble. He made me study so someday I would be a success, a partner in a major national law firm handling complicated cases on a national stage. He had never expressed satisfaction with my grades or anything else I did because he always wanted me to try harder. He wanted me to be forever reliable, forever curious, forever hungry to be the best.

He hadn't been trying to create a buddy; he'd tried to mold a responsible man. By this time I too was the father of a son and I could see my father's motivations were just the same as mine with my own son. We both wanted the world for our boys and both did what we thought was best at the time, even when it created rifts in our relationships.

As I stood there putting two and two together a wave of appreciation swept through me for all the habits he had willed me to develop. I was so overwhelmed with gratitude there was no space left for anger. It was as if gratitude and anger couldn't co-exist in me at the same time. Free from anger I was able to do something I had never done before: I thanked my father. I told him my ability to handle such a large case came out of his efforts to keep me on track when I was growing up. I told him his influence had instilled in me the very traits needed to do my job and do it well. His commitment to me had enabled me to create a life of financial success. I thanked him for the times he kept me out of trouble. I thanked him for being a good dad.

As I told my father these things, tears welled up in his eyes and I felt moved to yet another new experience. For the first time I could remember, I felt love for him and told him so. My father, who couldn't talk because of the tube in his throat, raised his hand, pointed at his heart and then pointed at me, as if to tell me he loved me too. This was something I don't remember ever hearing him say to me.

From there, I was off to the races. I started jabbering about all the things we would do when he got out of the hospital. He'd never seen my son play football or ice hockey, and my dad was a big fan of both. We lived in different states and I'd never invited him to visit. I guess he was too proud to invite himself or maybe I'd made him feel that unwelcome. I told him he had to come see Jeff play. I was so proud of my son and I knew my dad would be bursting at the seams watching Jeff carry a ball, skate with the puck, or smack somebody off their feet. I knew my father loved dogs so I told him I would get him a dog. Since I had a big house and yard, he could even come live with me. My dad smiled and nodded in agreement as I went on and on.

That night was the last conversation I had with my father. He died without ever leaving the hospital, without ever seeing his grandson play, and without our getting another moment together.

This is a book about yoga; what does this story have to do with yoga?

It has everything to do with yoga. Yoga is more than practicing the physical poses. Yoga is a pathway to a full and meaningful life. Yoga practices awaken us to the gift that is our life. Through yoga practices we learn how to identify and embrace our own unique potential, our capabilities and talents, and offer them in a way that brings contentment, meaning and a sense of engagement and accomplishment to our lives. By living this way we deepen and enrich our existing relationships and create new ones. Yoga practices help us wake up and become aware of the amazing possibilities waiting for us.

With my father, I woke up only to discover what I had missed. I had been asleep, wrapped in anger and resentment. I was too busy to get to know my dad, too sure I had been right all those years and he had been wrong. In my certainty I was right, I missed the chance to experience something so precious and yet for many of us so rare—a close, loving relationship with a father.

The way I had interacted with my father before that night was the same way I interacted with everyone: harshly judging, keeping distance, and putting up barriers. Now, here I was, an adult and a father myself, and for the first time I recognized my entire life was slipping by with no chance to enjoy what it has to offer unless I could somehow change these habits. The way I conducted my relationship with my son looked all too much like the way I had behaved with my dad.

Accepting the gift of life includes creating a life filled with passion, joy, commitment, fun and play, rain and sunshine, a football spinning just right … whatever is our unique version of happiness and fulfillment. Here I was, finally recognizing I had a father that cared for me, and the second I let go of my old assumptions and glimpsed what was available to me, he's gone. The moment I realized I had in my life a fascinating, funny, and bright person to hang out with, I lose him. Instead of going off with him to watch football and hockey games, I'm signing release papers so they can turn off the machines keeping him alive.

As painful as that experience was for me, it was a major break-through in my life, a shake-up, waking me to what I was missing. I finally worked up the courage to take off the iron plating surrounding my heart that for years had been preventing me from having meaningful relationships with anyone. If I hadn't connected with my father that night, if the circumstances had not been just right for me to take off the armor protecting my heart, I might have lost forever the chance to let myself become vulnerable. This is the kind of vulnerability we all must have if we are ever going to really experience love and connection in our lives.

Life's most worthwhile and richest offerings exist in Midlines, those moments when life invites us to choose a potentially rich experience where something so special, so enduring, can happen to grant our life greater meaning.

A Midline is the opportunity to develop a new relationship or take it to a deeper level. A Midline is the offer of a new job or career, a new interest that brings us joy, or the chance to fulfill a lifelong dream. A Midline is the chance to learn something about ourselves we didn't know, or have been afraid to confront. Maybe we find out we are loveable, influential, or brilliant; conversely, maybe we find out we aren't as loveable, influential or brilliant as we thought. But maybe we see, as I did with my dad, a way to change, to have another chance at fulfilling our potential for a juicy and loving life.

A Midline is also those occasions when fairness and integrity call us to stand up for something we know is right, even at the expense of ridicule or exclusion from our social group.

Yoga practices, including a regular meditation practice, and the study of yoga philosophy, help us identify, understand, and transform aspects of ourselves that hold us back from stepping into Midline. We come face to face with our insecurities, our fears, the need to be right, anger, prejudices, greed, and other attitudes that disconnect us from others. Whether I'm practicing yoga poses, meditating, or reading something uplifting, the disruptive emotions can ultimately give way to feelings of peace, intimacy, spiritual and emotional depth, and unfettered joy. These are the feelings that I'd rather have, the types of feelings I associate with a life of well-being,

These positive emotions are our birthrights, yet many of us are imprisoned by our own fears and inner demons, refusing to make the choices that allow us access to this birthright. Yoga teaches us to transmute these emotions into positive, even valuable, influences in our life. Every time we take the risk of reaching out for the opportunity presented by a Midline, we move closer to reclaiming our spiritual birthright, a life of passionate curiosity, simple delight, of love given and returned, and a deeply intimate and continuous love affair with our always amazing, enthralling world.

Midlines appear both as a time and a place, available to us whenever, wherever, and however we wake up to the spirit inside us. My personal belief is this spirit inside each of us is part of a larger Spirit: God to many of us. Midline is where we make a connection between our own spirit and that greater Spirit that connects us all. We can make this connection at any time because this opportunity to make connection is available to us in every moment of every day.

I wish I had begun yoga practices and studied its philosophy long before that last night with my dad. Every time he called me to say hello, a Midline arose. Every time somebody asked me: "When did you last see your father?" a Midline offered itself. Each time I shied away, imprisoned by emotions I hadn't had the courage to explore and understand. I know that often in my life, I let those emotions dictate my choices to step away from the Midlines, to step away from love. My marriage was a Midline, but I chose to run from it rather than risk fully opening my heart.

I've learned to watch for Midlines now and meet them head on. I have been blessed to have the chance to do things differently with my own son—children are great teachers— and this has gifted me with the relationship we have now, that I value more than anything. I've admitted mistakes to people in my life, and in doing so, forged bonds of friendship that I treasure. I've taken risks of rejection and have been rewarded with new friends who enrich my life.

We are invited to step into Midline every time we make connection with another human being. We are invited to step into Midline every time we pause and remember to notice and enjoy the moment, connecting to Spirit through the gift of our senses.

I've also learned over the years there is no better way to cultivate the capacity to find and hold the Midlines of life than through the lessons of yoga. Yoga has deepened my awareness of what is going on around me as well as inside me. Yoga has taught me to look beyond the distractions to see the potency in each moment. I now welcome opportunities for relationships; instead of letting them slip away because I feel unworthy or afraid. I trust that the people and events I encounter are connected to me through Spirit. I embrace opportunities to make my dreams come true. I seek them.

Yoga has taught me to be excited to be alive, excited about not only my future but also the way each moment beckons with intriguing possibilities. This is a great way to live. Living like this is our way to Spirit, our way to fulfill the promise that is each of us.

This book is a road map, a how-to and a why-to based on the hard-won lessons of my own life. It shows you how to recognize and successfully navigate the Midlines that appear in your own life, those moments when life invites you to step outside your comfort zone and embrace the potential of the moment. This book helps you set your own personal GPS toward love, happiness, meaning, and engagement. In finding yoga, I found my path to Spirit. These stories are my heartfelt offering to you, that your own path will be a bit easier and sweeter. ■

A MIDLINE PRACTICE

Think of somebody in your life who has helped you in some way, perhaps a parent, a teacher, or even a stranger. Take a moment and allow yourself to find gratitude for this person.

CHAPTER 2
What life can look like when we do wake up

I want to share an interesting story. I don't know if I have all the facts right, but, in any event, it's a good story about a man with spirit. It is about a man who had a dream. This wasn't just any man. This man had achieved a great deal of success in his chosen field and was well known and highly respected. In the midst of his popularity, he had an idea, something that spoke to him and aroused his passion. He began to devote his time to this idea, using his assets and resources to bring it into a reality.

Unfortunately, almost everybody thought his idea was ridiculous. Even his wife and business-partner brother pleaded with him to stop his silliness. His peers in the business world called his idea "folly." Despite his success and reputation, he had a very hard time raising money to complete the project. Eventually, though, his passion and commitment won out and the dream became a reality.

The man was Walt Disney and the dream was *Snow White*.

Snow White became the most successful motion picture of 1938. Walt Disney went on to receive more Academy Award nominations and awards than anybody else in history. *Snow White* became one of the best-selling movies of all time. With profits from this "folly," Disney studios expanded its capacity, enabling it to produce such wildly popular movies as *Pinocchio, Fantasia, Dumbo, Bambi, Alice in Wonderland, Cinderella, Peter Pan,* and *Mary Poppins*, to name just a few. Based upon these successes, Mr. Disney's legacy expanded to include *The Little Mermaid, Beauty and the Beast*, and *Toy Story,* among many others, as well as theme parks on both U.S. coasts attended with joy by millions of people from all over the world every year.

Imagine what the world would be like if Walt Disney had listened to all the naysayers. Imagine the hurt and discouragement he must have felt to have a dream he cared about so deeply, so readily and emphatically dismissed, even by his loved ones? What was it like to be the object of such ridicule, to pick up a newspaper and read about "Disney's Folly?" How easy would it have been to give up? How simple life would have been for him if he hadn't taken the risk to follow his heart.

Think what your own world would be like if Walt Disney had given up, had not taken that risk. I know my life would not be as rich. I just returned from visiting my granddaughter, Lucy, and I bet I read her *Mermaid* stories at least five times, with *Beauty and the Beast* a close second. She even put on her "Ariel" outfit. How many millions of people have been made at least a little bit happier because Walt Disney honored a voice inside him that told him his idea was worthwhile and he should keep going? How many people, like my granddaughter, have begun to cultivate their own creative capacity and ability to dream because of Mr. Disney's genius, courage and persistence? How much have we all benefited because Walt Disney listened to the voice of Spirit, ignoring the naysayers by stepping into Midline?

Fortunately for us, Walt Disney had the courage and self-presence to listen to his heart. Casting aside whatever fears, hurt, or insecurities he may have felt, he met Midline head-on, choosing to make his dream, *Snow White*, a reality. We all face challenges in which we are tempted to play it safe, ignoring our spirit, listening to others who would have us do so. How many times do we let our own dreams fade into oblivion? How many of us have hopes and dreams but we let opportunities slip by because we are afraid of rejection, looking silly, or because we feel unworthy? Or do we let ourselves get so emotionally beaten by the advice of others that we give up dreaming entirely? Do we get caught up in life's pressures and stresses to the point we forget to even check in with that part of ourselves where dreams are made?

Dreams don't die; they can only be hidden from our view. Our capacity to dream can never be extinguished. Walt Disney's desire to fully express himself was so powerful no amount of humiliation and disapproval could squelch it. The same is true for us. The same Spirit resides in each of us.

Here's the fun part: the study and practices of yoga awakens us to that Spirit. Where we have forgotten our creative fire, yoga helps us find it. Where we have completely given up, yoga can re-kindle our flame. We each have within us unique strengths that long to be expressed. Yoga helps us awaken to and remember those strengths. When we do so, and make up our minds to engage them in our lives, whether at work or play, our whole life becomes filled with meaning.

Who would have thought, years ago, that I would have found such pleasure and satisfaction teaching yoga? Who knew? Coaching football, sure, but a trial lawyer teaching yoga? This is what happens when we awaken to the songs in our heart. For me, Walt wrote some of the sheet music for my songs.

Leaders in the field of positive psychology have identified elements or markers that identify a life well-lived—the kind of life we all would like to look back upon and say: "YES, that was a great ride." It is certainly how I intend to look back on my life. Don't you want that, too?

In his book *Flourish,* Dr. Martin Seligman, a former president of the American Psychological Association (1998), and Director of the Positive Psychology Center at the Ivy League's University of Pennsylvania, identifies five elements of a life of well-being: 1) positive emotion; 2) engagement; 3) meaning; 4) positive relationships; and 5) accomplishment, that together evidence a life that is flourishing.[1] These five elements serve as guideposts for finding Midline, connecting to Spirit.

Walt Disney certainly represents the flourishing life Dr. Seligman outlines. You're probably thinking: "But, that was the great Walt Disney, a famous man with resources. It's easier for people like that to express their spirit; he invented Mickey Mouse." That may or may not be true; I don't know. However, I don't have to look past my own family to see inspiring examples of people that have created a meaningful life out of a vision fueled by their own particular dreams.

My daughter-in-law Caitlin found herself in Los Angeles when a family emergency required she move there. This was a totally unexpected change of life plans. Graduate school was out of the picture, at least for quite awhile. But, instead of meekly going along with life's curve ball, Caitlin decided to express her creativity in the entertainment industry, specifically, to be in the movies or on television. Never mind that thousands upon thousands of other people with the same exact dream were also living in Los Angeles. Undaunted (well, there was some daunting), she plugged away, facing rejection after rejection.

Caitlin studied, she volunteered, and she took numerous part-time jobs because she still had bills to pay. Yet despite all that effort, nothing seemed to pan out. Every day she was told she was not quite "this" or not quite "that." Then, one day, things did pan out. She was in a television show and then another one, and a movie, and then another one. There was something in her spirit that wouldn't quit. That something is in each of us. It is a spirit that yoga helps us find.

Caitlin's brother is another example of spirit. He was a personal trainer of the stars, one of those guys actors hire to get buffed out for a movie, or get lean and mean for a television show. One day, while skydiving, his parachute lost its air and he plummeted to earth. Miraculously, he survived and is now a paraplegic. For many of us, that would be an end to our dreams. Not for Jeremy. When he is not training others or competing in a triathlon or some other event, he is traveling all over the world inspiring others with disabilities how to fully experience life. Both Caitlin and Jeremy overcame the challenges life threw at them and, instead, accepted the invitation of Midline to find new ways to create lives of meaning.

Yoga not only teaches us to value and seek the same qualities of a life of well-being that Dr. Seligman identifies, it also teaches us practices that can make that life a reality. Yoga gives us a blueprint to identify the innate energies inside each of us that vibrate with a longing to be expressed. And we learn to pay attention to those energies and to skillfully express them in our daily lives. We learn to step into life's Midlines and, by doing so, connect to Spirit. The lessons of yoga teach us how to find the Divine meaning in our lives. The Midlines are there, waiting for all of us. ■

A MIDLINE PRACTICE

What did you want to be when you grew up? Sit for a few minutes and visualize what your life today might look like if you had pursued that vision.

CHAPTER 3
We can make a change

My calls to my secretary, Carol, kept going directly to her voicemail. Furious, I slammed down the phone and stormed into her office. Even though I could see she was on a rare personal call, I ignored her privacy, pacing impatiently in front of her. Who cares whatever personal problem she might be dealing with!

Despite my obnoxious behavior, Carol looked up at me and smiled. She lifted a finger, silently and politely asking me to give her just a moment. I responded by a sharp, edgy exhale, bursting with anger and frustration. Seeing this, Carol quickly said goodbye and hung up the phone. She apologized, telling me that a dear aunt, a woman who helped raise her, had just survived an emergency life-threatening surgery. Carol was checking to make sure things were going to be okay.

I recoiled, hit by a shock wave of humiliation. My face burning with shame, I mumbled an apology, turned, and walked quickly back to my office. I shut the door and sat down at my desk. How could I be so insensitive to somebody else's feelings?

To this day I have no idea what I needed from Carol that I thought was so important. But, I'll never forget the hurt look on her face. I'll also never forget how I felt as I sat at my desk in my office that day. I was a successful trial attorney with a lifestyle to match. Yet despite these facts, I constantly felt almost strangled by stress. Even the most trivial items had become earth shattering, requiring immediate action. As I sat at my desk I acknowledged this was not the first time I had shown such disregard toward people. Far from it.

Not only was I ashamed of myself, I was afraid. What kind of man could so frequently discount other people? How could I treat someone with so little respect, no matter what crisis I thought needed to be handled? I knew I was also treating my friends and family this way.

These anxiety-ridden outbursts weren't limited to the office. I couldn't drive in traffic without irritation. I was constantly impatient. In conversations, I never let anybody else finish a sentence before I interrupted. I was short with store clerks. I didn't return smiles from strangers. Much of my day was spent with an elevated heart rate caused by my reaction to some perceived irritant. I was the epitome of the "Type A" businessman courting a stroke.

I realized that I didn't like this man at my desk. Even more, I felt that if my son, Jeff, were to see me behave like this, he would be ashamed of me. That thought really stung.

Something had to change. But what? And how?

Let's fast-forward just a few years from that scene in my law office, years during which I'd studied yoga and developed a regular yoga practice. One afternoon I was roaming through a bookstore, relaxed and looking for nothing in particular. I "people-watched," taking in everybody I could see. I scanned the shelves, my attention casually drifting wherever a book title prompted it to go.

While I stood there, happily browsing, a young store clerk walked hurriedly by with a pile of books in her arms. She slammed into me, and then continued to a shelf across the room. To add aggravation to insult, I was carrying a cup of hot coffee and the coffee spilled all over my shirt. Despite this rough collision, the clerk didn't stop or even slow down to acknowledge she had hit me. It was as if I wasn't there, like I was invisible.

I felt a surge of anger roar up within me. My face became flushed, my breath quickened, my muscles tensed, and my heart started to race. How could somebody treat me that way? As I stood there, angry, my shirt sopping wet, my initial reaction was to lash out. I wanted to shout at her or otherwise get in her face. Next I decided I would go to her supervisor and get her fired, telling myself it was my duty to keep the store free of such insensitive clerks. Actually, I just wanted to get even.

However, before I could yell at her or find somebody to fire her, I began to calm down. My breath and pulse slowed. The anger diminished and my body relaxed. This took just a few moments and the change was radical. I looked at the clerk. By now she was placing her heavy load of books onto the shelves. Her face was strained, tense. Her body language was tight. She looked so unhappy. I found myself wondering what could be going on in her life. What would cause her to care so little about slamming into a customer in the store? She seemed beyond caring.

As I looked at her, I knew that whatever troubles she had, they would only get worse if I went to her supervisor or talked to her when she was in this frame of mind. I remembered when I had been rude and insensitive to others, when nothing but my own needs seemed to matter; certainly not the feelings of people around me. My stomping around huffing and puffing in front of my secretary trying to force her off the phone is but one example. And yet, time and again, the people around me had given me another chance. I looked at the sad, tense store clerk and felt compassion.

So, rather than causing further disruption to her life, I returned the favors others had given me. I went to the bathroom and washed myself off. Soon, I was back in the bookshelves, lost in wherever my imagination took me.

What happened to the stressed-out, insensitive guy who steamrolled right over his secretary? Where was the man who let his anger and resentment prevent him from ever really knowing his father?

I was finally waking up to what I was missing in life. The one thing I know with certainty is that I am only going to be on this planet for a finite period of time. How am I going to use that time? So far, I'd made a bunch of money but not very many friends. I'd accumulated a lot of cool stuff but few invitations from people to visit them. I wanted to experience what I was missing. I wanted to reawaken to my dreams and even create more of them. And if this were going to happen, I would have to slow down enough so my emotions didn't get in the way.

I began to wake up after losing my dad, but now it was time to slow down and fully engage the world and myself. You need space to recognize life's Midlines, those moments where you can hold on to destructive patterns of behavior, or take a risk and break free. The reward for taking those risks, of course, is a life of never-ending dazzling and wondrous experiences.

How did I figure these things out and get out of my own way? I'd begun studying and practicing yoga and learning to slow down and recognize Midlines. If our mind is racing or so full of conflicting emotions we're going to miss the invitations Midlines offer. How can we hear the Voice of Spirit if we are too distracted to listen? ∎

A MIDLINE PRACTICE
The next time you feel yourself thinking a negative thought, whether it is about a person or a situation, simply notice that you are doing so.

PART II

Western behavioral science: meet yoga

CHAPTER 4
Getting our mind un-hijacked

Once I got out of my own way, opportunities and Midlines were everywhere. My growing interest in spirituality prompted me to take a tour of Machu Picchu with Dan Millman, the author of *The Way of the Peaceful Warrior*.[2]

Signing up for this trip was a Midline that changed my life. Part of me wanted to keep the status quo, afraid what might happen once I opened the door to exploring my interest in Spirit. What habits would I have to give up? What would I find out about myself that would require changing? I signed up for this trip because I was beginning to realize I had a choice. I could choose to experience life fully. To that end, I figured it was time to literally travel "to the mountain top," in this case the sacred places of Peru.

During our time in Peru we did self-actualization exercises, yoga, shaman rituals, and toured beautiful, mystical, and sacred sites. Our voyage culminated with a night spent atop Machu Picchu. We each were invited to find our own private place to meditate or just sit and take in the sounds of the wind and the river raging way down below in the valley. That night was an unforgettable experience.

Throughout the trip, Dan was generous with his time and talked privately with each of us as we wished. I told him about my experiences as a lawyer, my yoga practice, and that I was learning to slow down and become more relaxed. And, as a result, I felt a burning curiosity to connect to something bigger than me. I felt a larger energy and wanted to connect to it and find my role in it. I told him that this was the underlying inspiration for taking this trip with him. I also asked his advice about this awakening and wondered what he might suggest.

Dan suggested I think about graduate school and look for a program that would allow me to pursue whatever subjects interested me. He cautioned that rather than enroll in a particular field of study, with pre-selected coursework, the idea was to choose or even create a curriculum responsive to my particular interests. Doing this, Dan said, would help me to get in touch with my own unique voice and, in doing so, a direction for my future would appear.

This made sense to me so, following his advice, I enrolled in a graduate program to study behavior and the philosophy of yoga and obtained my Masters in Human Development from St. Mary's University (Minnesota) in 2005. My course of study focused on finding a correlation between yoga philosophy and western behavioral psychology, and included the subject of mindfulness and how mindfulness practices taught through yoga can influence the brain and behavior.

My graduate work included study of a diverse group of scholars ranging from William James to Dr. Daniel Goleman; Dr. Rollo May to Thich Nhat Hanh; the Dalai Lama to Dr. Daniel Siegel. I not only studied behavior from both Eastern and Western perspectives; I also studied meditation, chanting, shamanism, and, of course, yoga, its history, philosophy and practices. All the while I continued my personal yoga and meditation practices.

One book that resonated with me was *Emotional Intelligence* by Dr. Daniel Goleman.[3] It explains in layman's language what happens inside us when we are exposed to new experiences, whether stressful or pleasant. It went a long way towards helping me understand why my life as a lawyer was a perfect breeding ground for non-skillful, knee-jerk emotional behavior. I saw that learning through therapy the reasons for some of my emotional responses to situations wasn't enough. That understanding alone wouldn't prevent my emotions from running my life and blocking my ability to hear my own spirit speaking to me. Dr. Goleman's book showed me I would need to learn and engage in practices that could change old patterns of behavior. My yoga practices were doing that.

Dr. Goleman described how, to protect ourselves, we as a species from prehistoric times through today have used automatic responses that allow us to sense danger and react to it in a way that keeps us safe.[4] If a person pausing at a pond failed to react to the sound of a branch snapping behind him, he might likely end up as some animal's dinner. This automatic response system meant the difference between life and death. Even nowadays, we still have to pay attention to our environment; when walking through warm, rocky dry places we better pay attention to the sound of a rattle or else risk a dangerous and painful snakebite. We jump when somebody startles us. This system of automatic response is called our fight-or-flight mechanism.[5]

A sometimes-unfortunate byproduct of having such a system is that it not only protects us from danger but also plays a role in how we react in our every day encounters with others.[6] This explained my actions with my secretary. My pattern was to react to every little stress in my law practice with the same emotions my ancestors had when saber-toothed tigers jumped in front of them on the path to the waterhole. My nervous system was apparently unable to distinguish the extent of a threat and so an automatic reaction, passed down through the genes from caveman times, took over. When I couldn't reach my secretary by phone, at some level deep within me I reacted to that situation with the same degree of anxiety as if a stranger was pointing a gun at me and demanding my money.

How does this system work within us? In response to some perceived threat fear causes the brain to release a flood of hormones that puts us on a high alert, causing us to become edgy and focused on the perceived threat so we can protect ourselves.[7] That is what I felt like all the time as a trial lawyer—I was in a constant state of alert. There were so many deadlines; so many times I had to defend against motions to dismiss my clients' cases. If someone didn't pick up his or her phone right away, I went ballistic![8] Every day I was edgy, jumpy, and never able to relax.

When we feel threatened, even if just by too much stress at work or home we experience what Dr. Goleman calls "neural hijackings" in which the brain reacts to what it believes to be an emergency by preparing us to respond to what we think is a serious threat.[9] This hijacking occurs in an instant, before the rest of our brain gets a chance to consider the most appropriate reaction.[10] This works fine when there really is a threat, such as somebody on a bike swerving in front of our car.

The problem is this system can also view a situation as an emergency when it is not. When that happens, the automatic fight-or-flight part of the brain, perceiving an emergency, hijacks us, forcing us into a precipitous reaction all out of proportion to the actual event. Sometimes, even the littlest thing can push us to seriously overreact. To this day, when I watch an episode of *Law and Order* and the bad guy's lawyer hands the prosecutor the little blue paper containing a motion to dismiss the case, my own heart rate spikes, my muscles tense, and I squeeze my popcorn bowl tighter! It reminds me too much of my own personal legal experiences.

The more I read about this internal alarm system, the more I thought: "This isn't good." This described my life and I was tired of living this way. Compounding the problem, I found out that we store memories of past threatening situations throughout our body and they can remain stored there for life. Our brain is so efficient that if we encounter a new situation that looks even the slightest bit like the memory of a past threat, our brain will associate the new situation with the memory of the past, seemingly similar, threat. The brain, in a fraction of an instant, will mistakenly think we are being threatened again and put us into immediate protective mode, hijacking us into acting in a way we, only moments later, regret.[11] Isn't that great! My secretary doesn't pick up my call right away and my reaction is as if I just overslept for the bar exam and have ten minutes to get to St. Paul—a 45 minute trip when there's no traffic; and it's rush hour.

There are even more potential pitfalls. Once we experience a strong emotion, particularly anger, our habits and patterns of thought can keep this emotional response alive for hours and even days. This can lower our threshold for neural hijacking by the next experience, making us even more likely to lose it tomorrow, with the next response likely to be even more severe.[12] So that grudge I choose to keep alive is keeping me in "grudge mode" all the time. That can't help win friends and it can't be good for my health.

Learning this, it wasn't hard to see how living a life of stress, without any practices designed to mitigate the pressure, acted just like a teakettle. The pressure builds and builds until it has to be released. This made my system vulnerable, maintaining a constant high state of alert. I continually felt like I was clinging to a rope above a river full of crocodiles.

The lessons from yoga were helping. I was learning to relax, which allowed me to rebuild my resilience for reaction to stress. For an hour or so each day I paused the constant chatter in my mind, even if it was just to check out the alignment of my feet and hands in the various poses or to pay attention to my breath. Similarly, I slowed down and began to pay attention to other things I did throughout the day, whether it was taking a walk, making dinner, or talking with friends. I was giving my system a chance to learn to relax and enjoy the moment.

Meditation also gave me time each day to focus on a *Mantra* or my breath, rather than chase after every prattling thought that entered my mind. Everything was no longer life or death. I wasn't under attack just because somebody objected to a deposition question I asked. I was learning new habits and—Glory be!—I was becoming a nicer guy. ∎

A MIDLINE PRACTICE

Think of a time when, out of an emotional response, you spoke or acted in haste and later determined that you had misread the situation. Did you wish you hadn't spoken or acted so quickly?

CHAPTER 5
Sweet memories

Many people have heard about the magic of Machu Picchu, former "Lost City of the Incas" in the Andes mountain chain in Peru. I'd certainly heard of its mystical energy and wondered what that was all about. I was hungry for a spiritual connection of some sort and thought that if ever I was going to get a taste of such a thing, why not go right to the place with all the vibe? I can tell you, as high as my expectations were, they were exceeded beyond my wildest dreams.

My tour with Dan Millman included people from all over the world, Russia, Europe, South America, and the U.S. Machu Picchu is a deeply sacred place, built somewhere around 1450 C.E. It sits high up in the mountains, above the Urubamba River, with steep cliffs and mountain peaks rising above the lost city.

The evening we were to spend on the mountain, we met with Dan and our other tour leaders as the sun went down. Then we each went our separate ways, to meditate in whatever form we knew. I quietly left the others, looking for some solitude. I found a private place, climbed off the path and discovered an old stone perch, perhaps part of a stairway or a fence of some sort. I sat and made myself comfortable.

By this time it was dark and the moon cast a soft, clouded light. I could feel a gentle breeze on my face as I listened to the roaring river below and a soft whispering of the wind blowing through the mountains. I began to meditate, never dreaming I was about to have one of the most amazing experiences of my life.

Eyes closed, I sat for just a short while and then I heard a woman giggling. I looked down at the path about fifteen feet below me and watched as a man and woman walked hand in hand along the path, passing underneath where I sat. Just as I started to watch them, a voice right next to me suddenly said in a low but incredibly powerful voice: "Keep meditating." Who the heck is that? I turned my head and in the now moonlit night I saw a man sitting about two feet away, side by side with me. He was staring straight ahead, a blanket wrapped around him. He was older than me, strong looking, with a sharp nose. "He looks just like an Incan!" I thought.

I said: "Who are you?" and, without looking at me, he answered: "Meditate." I then realized, even though it looked like I could reach out and touch him, he wasn't really there.

But…he was there. Sitting next to me was this presence as real to me as the couple on the path, the stone I sat upon, or the moonlit night.

I turned my head, closed my eyes, and began my meditation again. Suddenly in my mind's eyes, my old high school friend Jim floated into my "vision." I asked Jim what had happened to him: "Did you really drown like they say?" He answered by nodding his head. Jim had been the toughest guy I'd ever met, 6'3" and 225 pounds of raw muscle, and, in my mind, incapable of falling out of a canoe and drowning. That's what I told him: "No way! How could YOU drown?" He smiled at me and said: "It happens, man, be careful." Then he was gone.

Others floated into my consciousness: former teachers, my grandmother, friends; all people who had passed on. Each had something kind to say. At some point in this endless stream of visits from loved ones who had passed, my father showed up. He told me he was checking in and was proud of me. Following him came my mother. She told me that she, too, was really proud of me and wished she'd told me so earlier. Then, off she went. Shocked and scared, I opened my eyes. I looked to my right and the man was still there. He turned his head this time to look at me, smiled, and said: "Keep meditating." Then, he was gone.

I continued to meditate, overwhelmed with emotion: I felt totally immersed in love. I don't know that I've ever felt so protected, so cared for, so safe as I was in those moments. For lack of a better term, I felt so "held." I couldn't stop the tears from flowing; tears of love, gratitude, and a peaceful feeling beyond anything I've ever experienced before or after. I walked back and joined the group as we came together to head back to our buses.

What was that all about?

My graduate work has helped me have some understanding. It may well be that the energy of each of us continues in our world even after we pass on. Maybe there really are spirits, the Spirit in each of us that truly is eternal, existing in a giant network of circuitry, able to engage us from time to time for whatever reason.

I suspect that is true; here is another explanation that we now know is true from work done by specialists in behavior. Drs. Thomas Lewis, Fari Amini, and Richard Lannon, three psychiatrists and professors at the University of California, San Francisco School of Medicine write that the brain can link whatever we are experiencing in the moment to our memories similar to the current experience.[13] Not long after this occurrence at Machu Picchu it hit me who the old, strong man next to me was; it was my grandfather, a tough, determined man who had loved me and made me the center of his life when he was alive. I went back and looked at old pictures of him, big nose, powerful face and all!

My grandfather died when I was six, but, before he died, he instilled in me a sense that I was special, brilliant, capable, and any number of other great qualities I had forgotten over the years. Yet, the memory of this wonderful man and his support for me had not gone away; it sat deep inside me waiting to be summoned back into my consciousness. Perhaps, the stimulus of the retreat with Dan Millman, Dan's kindness, the Shamanic rituals, the music, the nature of the people on the retreat, as well as the energy of the location, all operated to stir those memories, and they showed up in the meditation.

The people who came to "visit" were all very special to me and in each case were telling me what I think I already knew but hadn't dealt with. They had connected me to my memories. That night offered a Midline, an invitation to connect to and embrace the warm, positive memories inside me, inspiring me to view myself as a brilliant shining light of potential.

What a magical night! My grandfather, one way or another, along with Jim, my parents, and a few others, all decided if I was going to wake up to life, maybe it was time for a little nudge. Whether ghosts exist or not, I know there really is a wellspring of everything we need for a successful life living inside us, waiting to be summoned into service, encouraging us to Midline. I had wanted mystical connection to Spirit, and this was getting pretty mystical! ■

A MIDLINE PRACTICE

Think of somebody from your past about whom you are particularly fond. Spend a few minutes with your eyes closed and think about that person. Pay attention to any feelings that arise.

CHAPTER 6
Focus on what matters

My experience at Machu Picchu is an example of how a meditation practice awakens us to knowing we are unique and special, capable of being loved and loving others. Meditation, however, was not the only yoga practice helping me wake up, slow down, and enjoy life with far more regularity. The yoga classes themselves, the classes in which we do the poses, also were having a tremendous effect.

Instinctively, I gravitated toward yoga classes in which the teachers focused on positive reinforcement, regardless of the school of yoga. Sometimes the teachers began each class with a story or reading, teaching a character trait such as gratitude, courage, kindness, or compassion. These teachers made me feel good about myself even before we started doing the poses. Often, during the class, these teachers used images and ideas from the story or reading to direct us in some of the poses. This further instilled those qualities in me because I could sometimes feel those character attributes inside me as I did the pose, expressing them with my body.

Here's an example. I was taking a class from Marley at a local Denver studio, CorePower Yoga—Stapleton. We were doing a pose called "Warrior II" (*Virabhadrasana* II), a pose where the front leg is bent to a square and both arms extend in opposite directions. Marley wanted us to reach a bit farther, put more stretch into the arms. To encourage us to do so, she told us to remember somebody we really cared for who had died or perhaps lived far away.

She asked that we pretend that person was standing in front of us and all we had to do is just reach a tiny...bit...more...and we could touch their face, showing with our touch how much we loved them. I had recently lost somebody in my life and I reached and reached, eventually extending out of my heart to gently "touch" the vision of my departed friend's face. I felt the love and gratitude Marley had invited us to experience and those feelings fueled my pose.

How could practicing yoga this way with such great teachers not have an effect on me? I was learning how to connect to my own feelings as well as honor others and myself. Teachers regularly asked me to "open to" my own unique beauty, my courage, my gratitude, my compassion, and many other amazing qualities I hadn't paid any attention to. Before my mind could protest: "I'm not beautiful," "I'm not special," the teachers would tell me to "embrace" the positive qualities, "honor" them, "share" them, "celebrate" them, or any number of other pose instructions that infused within me these very qualities.

These teachers were not only putting my body into a position that felt good and free, they were coaxing my mind and spirit into working through the negative messages I had allowed to take over in my system. The dominance of these negative messages was being replaced with messages of self-honor, love, and other wonderful attitudes that make life rich. And I was taking those lessons off my mat, treating people with greater kindness, courtesy and attention, which, in turn, created positive new experiences for my storehouse of memories.

Again, Dr. Goleman's *Emotional Intelligence* provides important clues to this process. When we are happy, he writes, there is an increased activity in the brain center that inhibits negative feelings and worry.[14] Just as negative emotions can build within the brain, positive emotions cause positive reactions inside us.[15] When we experience affirmative feelings such as happiness or gratitude, we create an internal environment that not only counteracts the power of anger and fear but also creates the possibility of having these good feelings again and again: to get neurologically un-jacked, so to speak.

If we give our brain enough positive input, we can actually change our overall mental outlook. Dr. Daniel Siegel, clinical professor of psychiatry at UCLA's School of Medicine and also Co–Director of the UCLA Mindful Awareness Research Center, writes in *The Mindful Brain,* that every time we have an experience, neural firing occurs that can grow new connections in the brain or strengthen already existing connections.[16] We can do this by simply directing our focus on whatever constructive image or thought we wish to strengthen in the mind or create for the first time.[17]

This helped explain to me why each time I did a yoga class and contemplated a productive message or heart quality such as kindness, I was imprinting the message or quality more deeply within me. Quite possibly I was linking that quality to a long-forgotten memory. Even better: when memories link together, they develop a collective power, making them easier to access.

My yoga practice, with its upbeat, heart-opening themes and instruction, was "working me." Being told I was "loving" and "courageous" over and over, was causing my brain to re-pattern itself by finding evidence inside me, memories that I was, lo and behold, loving and courageous. Even when I took yoga classes in which the teacher didn't utilize such positive messaging, I set an intention based on this upbeat and nurturing approach and used the intention to influence my poses in the class. When I practiced yoga at home, by myself, or even when I went for runs, long walks, hikes, or skied, I did the same, using positive language in communication with myself.

This is an important component of Midline. Midline isn't just about overcoming voices of doubt and gloom. Sometimes the most profound Midlines are those that challenge us to accept our greatness. Engaging in practices that connect us to memories of how special we are is crucial to living a flourishing life. The more often we focus on a particular memory, the more likely it is that our brain will turn to that memory, and similar memories linked to it, on a regular basis.[18] With enough practice, this new growth becomes a habit.[19] It makes sense, then, that the more we contemplate or repeat positive words and images, such as empathy, or compassion, such character traits become habits that lead to deeper and richer relationships.

Attitude is important! When yoga or other activities are practiced with this type of positive mindfulness, it not only lessens the likelihood of our brain being hijacked, it also helps us forge a stronger affirmative self-image. A powerful self-image allows us to turn to the questions: Who am I? What's my role in the world? How can I offer who I am in a way that both celebrates my spirit and serves the Spirit that I believe connects all of us? Where are the Midlines? How can I cultivate the spaciousness to find them and the courage to step into them, accepting life's invitations to a more fruitful, meaningful and rich experience on this planet? ■

A MIDLINE PRACTICE

Before meeting a friend for dinner, a walk, or any other social purpose, spend a moment remembering why you like this person's company. Allow yourself to feel the appreciation you have for this person. Then, when you greet your friend, see if you can transmit some of that appreciation through your handshake, hug, kiss or whatever appropriate greeting you choose to give.

PART III

What does Spirit look like?

CHAPTER 7
*Lights and mirrors—*Prakasha and Vimarsha

I met a man at a yoga class fundraiser in Winter Park, Colorado held to help pay some of the medical bills of one of our local teachers. The room was jammed by the time I arrived so I went to the very back row. We came to a standing position at the front of our mats; feet pointing forward, arms at our side, bodies upright and alert. People were looking around, adjusting their clothes, and slowly bringing their attention to the teacher. I was one of those people looking around, and noticed a man in the front row. Because he was tall, his upper body was in my line of vision.

As the teacher spoke to us and asked us to set our intention for the practice, this man stood motionless and solid in a stance that told me he was ready to offer his practice fully to our friend. When we raised our arms overhead in our warm up, his arms flowed smoothly and powerfully as he reached to the sky. Even in this simple movement his posture and actions were strong and purposeful.

We moved through poses and, while I paid attention to my own practice, I continued to catch this man's movements out of the corner of my eye. When we transitioned into a series of standing poses I couldn't help but be impressed by how much poise and elegance he put into his poses. His obvious strength and refinement made me want to honor my friend all the more through my own poses. As a result, I went even deeper into my own practice.

At some point I finally caught a glimpse of this man from the waist down. He only had one leg! This man, whose powerful, dynamic and poetic practice had inspired me to be stronger and more refined in my own practice, was doing all this on only one leg! After class I introduced myself. His name was Mark. I told him how much his practice had inspired me. He said he had worked and saved so he could come to Winter Park to train at the National Sports Center for the Disabled ("NSCD") in hopes of making the national ski team. He said yoga was an essential part of his training, helping him to learn the discipline, balance and body awareness necessary to succeed.

Afterwards, I thought about what I'd learned from him. The excuses I used to explain why my yoga practice hadn't advanced as much as I wanted were just that—excuses. In fact, I saw that many of my excuses for not having accomplished more of my life's dreams had lost their credibility as well. I hadn't always summoned up enough courage or commitment to make my dreams come true. Watching Mark was a revelation to me as to how I, too, could fully embrace and then celebrate my own spirit, creating a more spectacular life.

I tell this story to illustrate the process of *Prakasha and Vimarsha,* a process essential for connecting to Spirit and living in Midline.[20] The Sanskrit term *Prakasha* refers to the pure light of Spirit, present at each and every level of creation, including each of us.[21] As part of Spirit, we, too, are this light. Whether we are aware of it or not, we each have within us a unique combination of strengths which hold great potential. We are each capable of creating a meaningful life for ourselves and inspiring others as Mark inspired me. That is our light.

For this potential to manifest, we must not only be aware of our light, we must also accept Midline's invitation to fully and bravely reflect upon its potency: Who are we? What can we do with ourselves? What can we create in the world, given our own unique gifts? How can we craft an amazing and meaningful life?

To engage in this reflection we have a complimentary power called *Vimarsha. Vimarsha* refers to the capacity for Spirit to reflect upon its light and then give it meaning.[22] *Vimarsha* allows us to discern, label and identify potential, whether our own or that of another. This is how we collectively create a greater world. How does it work in our lives?

My son and his wife took my grandkids to the climbing gym. My five-year old granddaughter, Lucy, harnessed up and began to climb. My three-year old grandson, Henry, had never seen a climbing wall and had little concept of climbing until he watched his sister. Then, having seen this fun new thing his sister was doing, he decided he had to climb as well. Up he went.

Lucy's example, her light, inspired and created a whole new activity for Henry to enjoy. His whole worldview expanded. This is what we can do for each other every day, create new experiences, new worlds, expanded relationships, for each other.

Just like we can't see our own face without a mirror, we are unable to see all of own potential except through interaction with others. When we interact we become the mirror for each other, offering a glimpse of what we are capable of being but can't see without the mirror held up by someone else right in front of our face. For example, I never really saw myself as a lawyer until a friend, Bruce, told me in college that he thought I'd be a great lawyer and he gave me reasons why he thought so. His comments, his mirroring, made me look at myself in a completely different way. I ended up going to law school, in part based on that feedback. His mirroring reflected my light.

A vital component of this philosophy is that we all have something to offer that can inspire others in some way. When we figure out what that is and find a way to share those gifts through our work, our hobbies, or just the way we carry ourselves, we are offering our light to others. Others, seeing that light, as I saw Mark's light, may become inspired to emulate what they see in us. Perhaps after watching us, they choose to learn a new skill, like Henry watching Lucy at the climbing wall, and instantly becoming a climber. Maybe they learn to play a musical instrument they heard us play. Or, maybe they decide to treat other people more kindly after watching us do so. We are each constantly shining out our light and receiving reflections back. This is how we create a world of greater harmony, both for ourselves and for others. Very simply, we awaken each other. ∎

A MIDLINE PRACTICE

In a conversation with a friend, co-worker, or family member, find something appropriate and fitting to tell that person about how much you appreciate one of their special qualities, their sense of humor, their dependability, their competence, or something else that is true about them for which you are grateful. Be their mirror.

CHAPTER 8
Is Spirit a He, a She, or both?— Shiva *and* Shakti

Many of us question what this "something bigger" than us, this Spirit, looks like. As a result, we may turn to various religions that offer answers. Sometimes the answers just lead to more questions. For example, imagine how tough it was for a young Catholic boy like me to follow the logic of why, if somebody ate a hamburger on Friday, he went to Hell. Then one day the Church changed its mind. As I sat there the following Friday with a now spiritually "legal" hamburger sitting in front of me, I recall thinking: "What if God changes His mind again? How can I be sure my priest heard the new rule correctly?" It took awhile for me to feel safe eating the hamburger!

I remember sitting in church every Sunday and numerous "holy days of obligation," days we were required to go to church, and staring up at the ceiling in our church. On the ceiling I saw a painting of a man who looked like an angry Charlton Heston in the movie *The Ten Commandments*. I remember asking the nuns why God was so angry and the answers were, to say the least, a bit hard to follow. For years that image of a fuming Heston was my personal image of God. His personality (God was definitely a "He") was a mixture of power, fury, vengefulness and perhaps a wee bit of grudging tolerance, as long as I did what I was supposed to do each day. I wasn't "feeling the love."

Down deep most of us are like I was as a little boy, looking up at the church ceiling and being filled with wonder. As little kids we could see Spirit's hand in everything and we naturally wondered about Spirit. My wondering eventually led me to return to school, getting my Master's in Human Development. I found a way to weave into my program some study of what I called "mysticism"—the study of personal experiences with God. I was curious about God, or Spirit, and what it might be like to really know Him or Her.

My advisor, Dr. Priscilla Herbison, told me that I already was tackling a pretty substantial course of study but that we would look for ways to explore mysticism as I worked my way through my graduate work. Proving Dan Millman's advice prophetic, my coursework led me to the study of yoga philosophy and practices. Before long, I had found my study of mysticism; I had found a path to Spirit.

In studying yoga philosophy I've found possible answers to questions that have puzzled me all these years: who is God, what does He or She expect, if anything, and how do I fit into this world in relationship to God? The philosophy I write about in this book is based on my understanding of various schools of thought considered part of a non-dualist, Tantric tradition. Each school has its own particular viewpoint and this is my personal assimilation of my studies of certain of those viewpoints, rather than an attempt to explain any particular school's philosophy.

Yoga philosophy often refers to God or Spirit as *Shiva,* representing the masculine energy of Spirit. *Shakti* refers to the feminine, creative energy of Spirit. They co-exist as one. There is a beautiful creation story in this philosophy that tells us Spirit created the Universe through a beautiful dance of these energies, *Shiva* and *Shakti*, the Divine Couple.

I'm reminded of this creation story when I watch my son and his wife prepare a large meal. Jeff invites people over and Caitlin typically chooses the menu. They both go off in different directions gathering the food needed to fill the recipes, then return and, together, make the meal. Caitlin starts the soup, and then runs after Henry. Jeff adds ingredients at the appropriate time. They both set the table, both welcome the guests, and both serve. Who created and made the meal? My own Divine Couple! Who eats the meal and is smart enough to stay out of the kitchen? Me.

Spirit's creation continues every day. That is why it is easy to find Spirit. It is easy because everyone and everything is Spirit. Because of this, every moment offers Midline, the opportunity to sense Spirit's presence; a chance to find and partake of the Divine potency of what is taking place right then. If we wake up to that fact, or at least play with the idea that such might be the case, then the world becomes a far more interesting place. Midlines pop up every moment because every moment is an invitation to an encounter and connection to God. As a Catholic boy yearning to connect to God, finding the mystical just became a no-brainer!

Regardless of your own particular spiritual viewpoint, as you read this book I ask that you keep the vision of this happy dancing Divine Couple, *Shiva* and *Shakti*, in mind. No matter what your own personal spiritual beliefs, there are valuable insights in this philosophy that can lead each of us to a fuller, richer life in which we too dance in the Midlines, embracing Spirit. ∎

A MIDLINE PRACTICE

Recall a work project in which the final product became better because you invited somebody to help you, or you were invited to help them.

CHAPTER 9
Spirit's attributes—the telltale signs

I like to think of the Statue of Liberty in New York as millions have seen it; a shining light of possibility. As immigrants arrived on our shores, looking for opportunities, the Statue of Liberty represented a chance to fulfill their hopes and dreams for a better life. For many, such as my family, this country offered the prospect that, with hard work and some luck, there was no end to what the future might hold. This is what I see when we talk about *Shiva's* light.

For those arriving on our shores, their visions were as diverse as the people on the ships. Some saw the chance of opening a small shop, selling whatever products made sense for them; perhaps a flower shop like my dad's family. My father's family came from Ireland and opened a successful flower shop in Chicago. I wasn't surprised, then, when on one of my many trips to Ireland I visited two crusty, tough old Dorigan relatives deep in the countryside and the first thing they showed me was a beautiful rose garden, creating a corridor along their road.

Others, as they approached our shores, had different visions, perhaps a bakery or a tailor shop. More than a few hearty souls likely planned to continue to the Wild West, hoping to strike it rich mining for gold or silver. Still others knew there were jobs in the coalmines or the factories. But each saw a chance to pursue their own particular vision of what a good life looked like.

When I reflect on the wide-ranging visions of these people, I think of the dance of *Shiva* and *Shakti*. I consider *Shiva* as a shining light of possibility and *Shakti* as the unlimited creative energy of that light. Like them, we can choose to create our world out of the light of our dreams. For each of these newly arriving immigrants, as they sailed into our country under the glowing, welcoming torch held aloft by the Statue of Liberty, their dream was the "light" that drew them to our shores. Their imagination and the courageous application of their strengths was the creative fire that forged their new lives. These energies are at play for us: they operate as we create our world through the imaginative dance of this Divine Couple, a dance with no limits to its creative potency. The dance of *Shiva* and *Shakti* represents the ability of each of us to awaken in each other something we can't otherwise see in ourselves.

Shiva is considered to be Spirit alive within each of us as a force connecting us to each other.[23] *Shiva* exists as eternal Truth, unlimited by space or time.[24] The essential nature of *Shiva* is good, "auspicious," a word understood to mean "benevolent."[25]

Shakti is *Shiva*'s creative mirror, the power that brought each of us into existence.[26] In this non-dualist story of creation, *Shiva*, through *Shakti*'s mirror, sees the reflected unlimited potential forms of every person or thing yet to be created. Our entire world is created from this reflective process. Spirit looked into the mirror, saw me, and was thus inspired to create me. He saw you, and...here you are! Similarly, Spirit saw in the mirror the reflection of oceans, mountains, valleys, flowers, horses, elephants, trees, flowers, and, perhaps most important, chocolate chip cookies.

This dance of creative freedom is a major underpinning of the yoga philosophy in this book. It is also a key teaching in understanding how to spot Midline when it appears, as an inviting light beckoning us to reflect and then take the risk to create something meaningful.

To make the most optimal use of Spirit's invitation, a use that most enriches our lives, it is helpful to know that Spirit, *Shiva* and *Shakti*, has a number of key attributes, which constitute Spirit's "essence," all existing concurrently. In this book I will discuss seven: 1) *Ananda*—delight of creative expression; 2) *Shri*—benevolence, creative power; 3) *Svatantrya*—ultimate freedom; 4) *Purnatva*—fullness, peace; 5) *Sat*—truth; 6) *Chit*—self-awareness; and 7) *Spanda*—pulsation; vibration; polarity of energies.

Why pay attention to Spirit's key attributes? Because this is a book about connecting to Spirit, finding those places, the Midlines, in which deeper and deeper connection is offered. So we should understand what we are looking for. What does Spirit look like in full bloom? Also, because we are each Spirit in embodied form, by understanding these attributes, the essence of Spirit, we understand our own essence. Our ability to connect to Spirit within us grows.

In order to live a life as Spirit in our human form, we study these attributes and try to reflect them in our behavior. We seek to become these attributes. We become joy; we become benevolence. We live a life that is satisfying, a life of freedom of our heart, freedom to express our own inner truth. We inspire and serve others. When we are able to do this we achieve a flourishing life, a life filled with positive emotion, engagement, meaning, valuable relationships, and a sense of accomplishment.[27] And it is important that we pay attention to those aspects of Spirit that are challenging for us: these may be exactly the paths we need to fulfill our life's promise.

You can see why I find this philosophy so uplifting and appealing. When we view the entire world as an expression of God, we can't help but immediately place value on every person we meet. We begin to find Spirit in ourselves, in our thoughts, emotions, and conduct. We each have our own Divine imprint, something special about each of us that can enhance the world and bring us pleasure in its expression. My teacher, Dr. Paul Muller-Ortega,[28] challenged us to awaken to our particular imprint, embrace it, and then seek to make it our default way of viewing ourselves; i.e., to see ourselves first and foremost as this Divine imprint. We don't stop there. We then seek to find the Divine imprint in every other person, every animal, every plant, every event, everything. No matter what happens, including the tragic, we seek Spirit even as we fully experience the pain of the tragedy or the joy of the moment. ∎

A MIDLINE PRACTICE
Think of something you enjoy doing.

CHAPTER 10
Blissful engagement—Ananda

I recently spent Christmas back East visiting my son Jeff and his wife and kids. My former wife, Cyndi, Jeff's mom, was there as well. I could tell the minute she walked in the door because I heard her laughter and the kids' cheering her arrival. Before long she had my granddaughter playing some Christmas songs on the new piano keyboard. Cyndi had labeled the keys with a letter representing each note and then prepared "sheet music" with the letters. Lucy was able to follow the "sheet music" and play the songs. I don't know who laughed louder or longer, Lucy or Cyndi.

Later, Cyndi went into the living room with Henry and, before long she had stripped the cushions off the big chair and sofa and created bridges for Henry to run his trucks over and under. Again, both of them were squealing with delight. Come to think of it, she had all of us laughing and this was just within the first hour of her visit.

That made me think back to another example of how Cyndi can bring warmth and light to the room, in this case, ironically, an ice arena. She remarried when Jeff our son was ten, marrying Chuck, who lived in a small town of about 4,500 people, two and one-half hours southwest of Minneapolis. I didn't know Chuck at all and I didn't know Windom, his town. Jeff moved with Cyndi to Windom and tried out for the youth ice hockey team. He was a good player and made the team. He called to tell me how excited he was and invited me to the first game with his new team the following Saturday. It was a home game and I told him I would be there.

On the way down to Windom I felt nervous about going to this new place and meeting not only Chuck but also most of the town. Ice hockey on a Saturday afternoon in a small Minnesota town is a very big deal! And this was Chuck's town, they already knew Cyndi and had adopted her, and I was the "ex." Since I was the "ex," I assumed that the town's people had already concluded I was some sort of jerk. I didn't know how Chuck would treat me and, even though Cyndi assured me he was a nice guy, I was more than a bit afraid. This was the man who my son was going to live with every day. He held in his hands a great deal of influence as to how much time I would get to spend with Jeff in the future. Jeff was a vital part of my life and the thought of no longer spending time with him on a regular basis was heart breaking to contemplate. So I was feeling more than a little anxiety as I walked in to the ice arena.

Anyway, I walk into this huge ice arena, thinking: you guys have THIS for a town of only 4,500! I no sooner walked to the front of the stands when a large guy stands up and shouts "Hey Bill: over here," waving at me to join him. It was Chuck. Sitting next to him was Cyndi. They had a blanket stretched across the bleacher seat and they spread it out for me to join them. Chuck shook my hand, asked me how the drive was, and then introduced me to the people from town sitting around them.

Almost immediately my fears were calmed. This man who could have made it hard to see my son over the next eight years, or even spend time in the town, was doing everything he could to make sure the relationship between Jeff and me was nurtured and allowed to flourish. He made sure I felt welcome.

Some of that response, I've since learned, was simply Chuck. If you have to get divorced and have your son live with another man, he is the guy. He has become, over the years, somebody I consider a friend. My son's life was greatly enhanced by living with him. However, part of that response was due to Cyndi. She is in the business of creating relationship. Her greatest joy is inspiring laughter and harmony in those relationships. She creates happy people (if, unlike me, you let her have a chance). When it comes to building relationships, particularly those involving her son, Cyndi never misses Midline. She always makes choices that foster deeper connection and honor her most precious relationships.

I tell this story because I think Cyndi exemplifies the first attribute of Spirit, *Ananda*, the delight of creative expression. Cyndi loves people and it gives her great joy when she can help them be happy. When we describe the attributes of Spirit, we talk about *Ananda* in terms of God's creative delight in making our world, creating the world for the sheer pleasure and joy of it.

For our part, we can experience this same joy every time we recognize our special, individual spirit and then creatively embrace and offer it in celebration and in service to others, recognizing our connection to each other.[29] I'm not saying that simply expressing ourselves can't bring joy. But I have concluded that my own highest joy, like Cyndi's, seems to come from serving our connection to Spirit; i.e., to each other.

Each of us can experience delight in being alive. Sally Kempton, a meditation expert, points out that our ability to be happy is possible because this happiness is already within us.[30] She says that things outside us aren't what make us happy. Rather, extrinsic things simply trigger the happiness that is already part of our nature.[31]

I don't know about you, but I've lived much of my life trying to reach goals purely for the sake of being able to brag about it, to acquire more stuff, or otherwise try to make a great impression or gain approval. To know that this striving is not only unnecessary but, even when successful, feels good only because it is a reminder of the innate joy already inside us, is an amazing revelation. If you want to connect to Spirit all you have to do is listen to the song inside you telling you what makes you happy and then sing that song. This happiness is always there and can be accessed whenever you choose.[32]

Reminding ourselves of this innate joy helps us thrive in Midlines, those places when the challenges of life offer us a chance to be something greater, to creatively express ourselves as even more amazing than we were the moment before. Challenges of life are actually Midlines.

Midlines appear constantly throughout each day. They are present whenever Spirit offers us an invitation to confront ourselves by overcoming whatever holds us back; maybe feelings of fear, jealousy, unworthiness, political correctness, whatever. When we overcome such feelings, taking a risk for something more profound in our life, we step into Spirit.[33]

It is the taking of the risk that constitutes Midline, even if we aren't successful. I say that because in the very taking of the risk we overcome the voices of doubt. Doing so makes those voices less capable of interfering with our lives in the future.

In his discussion of the five markers of a life of well-being, a life that flourishes, Dr. Seligman refers to the first marker, positive emotions as the "pleasant life," and says that this pleasant life consists of feelings such as joy, pleasure, ecstasy, comfort, and warmth.[34] These are the same definitions we use to describe *Ananda*: "joy," "delight," and "bliss." *Ananda* comes when we think beyond our own gratification.

Dr. Seligman acknowledges that true happiness involves not just joy but also meaning, serving some purpose and feeling engaged in the doing.[35] He describes "engagement" as being absorbed in the flow of an engrossing activity that heavily taps into our thoughts and emotions.[36] We learn in yoga philosophy that while we innately possess an inner joy, the greatest joy comes from awakening to our own strengths and then expressing them in creative and meaningful ways.

As a trial lawyer, I had a hard time seeing how I was creating much joy or beauty when I sued or defended people or corporations, even though I was truly engaged in what I was doing, feeling a tremendous personal satisfaction in doing my job well. How is this *Ananda*? Dr. Seligman's work helps answer that question. It was clear that I loved that work. I experienced joy in solving the puzzles that presented themselves as we put the cases together. I now realize that an important additional factor in my sense of satisfaction was that the job had meaning. Since I was helping my clients, I felt a strong sense of purpose.

What is "meaning" in this context? Our ultimate joy requires that we use our key strengths, whether in a job, hobby, or as a volunteer, in a way that advances values such as knowledge or goodness.[37] Dr. Seligman writes about police, fire fighters, and national service as examples of people who use their gifts to bring goodness to the world.[38]

It occurs to me that the world needs a sense of structure, something we can generally count on as we move through life, making choices and pursuing our dreams. In yoga, this sense of order is called *Dharma*, one of a number of definitions of that word. We rely on some sense of organization and predictability in the world so that each of us can have an opportunity to flourish. We cannot have beauty, love, or peace in the world without such forms of service that honor and seek to preserve societal structures, including the provision of some likelihood of fairness.

In many ways, as a trial lawyer, I've been like a policeman, stepping in when a corporation sells a harmful product or steals a patented idea or, in other cases, when I defended a corporation when it was unfairly accused. I've heard my teachers say that the notions of beauty, love and peace also include the creation or restoration of harmony to the world. That feels right to me. It helps explain the sense of joy I get when I am engaged in a complicated legal problem. I am in fact engaged in something that uses my particular talents in a way that helps assure order in the community. I am engaged in something that is meaningful. I am experiencing *Ananda* just as Cyndi does when she brings laughter into the room. ∎

A MIDLINE PRACTICE

Notice what you really enjoy doing, what makes you laugh, what makes the time fly. Think about how to incorporate more of those things into your life.

CHAPTER 11
Is it really all good? How about trying?—Shri

I was in Costa Rica at a yoga retreat and became friends with Alejandro who owned several businesses in that country. We talked about the health care debate in the United States. Alejandro said he was required to pay a very significant percentage of his income in taxes to help provide health care coverage for everybody in the country. I'll never forget the look on his face when I asked if it bothered him to pay so much more into the health care system than he would ever personally take back out for his own care. I could tell that he had a hard time even processing my question.

After a minute Alejandro figured out what I was asking and replied that he was not the least bit bothered. "For me," he said, "it's an honor. I am blessed to be able to provide." In the United States, Alejandro would get to keep substantially more of his income; he would not have to pay in to a universal coverage system. But he felt satisfaction in contributing to the health and well-being of his country's citizens who were not as financially blessed as he.

Alejandro's response is an example of the concept of *Shri*, a second attribute of Spirit. *Shri*, among other things, is abundance, the capacity of the Universe to provide for each of us. We forget that this is our nature. So often we tend to view the world from the perspective of scarcity. We feel that there is just enough for us and we are reluctant to share.

Much of our political discourse revolves around the issue of taxes. We fight against any program that helps other people if it means we might have to pay more in taxes. Our fear of paying more in taxes is so great that we fall vulnerable to any argument that fans the flame of that fear. As a result, we forget our most core values. I know people who are generous with others and who would never, if faced with such a situation, allow a stranger injured in front of them to suffer in the streets without medical care, even if they had to pay out of their own pocket. Yet, absent such an emergency, when confronted in a conversation about having to pay for somebody else's health care, they become angry at such a notion.

We forget it is our intrinsic nature to be *Shri*; good, generous, and kind, a reflection of the abundance of Spirit's benevolent nature. So, unless we practice these attitudes and behaviors, this essential aspect of our very being atrophies. We miss Midline's invitations to relationship and opportunities to serve, to live with meaning, because, having lost touch with our own generous heart, we immediately assume others are acting out of scarcity as well.

Soon our entire community contracts: roads fall apart, schools get overcrowded, and people who are sick cannot find care.

We cut more and more essential services just to feed the bottomless pit of greed that exists in the vacuum created when *Shri* is ignored. Sure, we wake up when it is our own loved one who falls victim to a system fueled by scarcity, unable to find health care, no police or fire protection in an emergency, or unable to find well-educated employees for our business because we've laid off so many teachers over the years. If we remember that our essential nature is to share our blessings, no "wake-up" call is needed.

If life is intrinsically good, then why is there evil? Certainly, some people suffer from chemical imbalances or mental disease that can lead to conduct we consider evil. However, for most of us, I suggest a different explanation. Human beings forget their innate goodness and do things that might be considered bad or evil. We rationalize our behavior, choosing to act in ways that serve only our private interests regardless of how it might hurt others. Even when we behave this way we are still, at our essence, *Shri*. We have simply lost track of who we are, playing Russian Roulette with life, betting that we can get by without a true participation in each other's welfare.

Because *Shri* is a creative energy, yoga philosophy teaches us to look for that which creates more joy, goodness, beauty, love, freedom and accord. Not everything that happens to us feels good or makes us happy. Even in those cases, yoga teaches us to seek to find the learning experience in everything that comes our way.

My active lifestyle really suffered as it became obvious that I needed a hip replacement. Not only had I cut back on my physical activities, I had turned into a grump. The surgery and recovery taught me an incredible lesson of empathy for others in pain, many of them in far worse shape than me. I've better learned how to work with my students, to be kinder, more understanding, more willing to share so others wouldn't have to undergo the same pain as me. I look at how much money I spent for various forms of body work to ease the aches and what it cost me even with insurance to do the surgery and I realize that many people don't have the luxury of taking care of themselves like I do. Understanding the principle of *Shri* has allowed me to look for and find the *Shri* in this event, and be grateful for my own healing, and the blessing of helping others.

If a loved one passes, we mourn and then we honor that person by living in a way that expresses and shares the beauty and grace of their life: the qualities we loved. It tragedy strikes, we deal with it as best we can, grieve, embrace our anger, but then look for a lesson. We can dialogue in our imaginations with our pain; we learn to go towards the hurt, rather than avoid and deny. Then, however, we move on. We create more light. Everything we experience is an invitation to a more exquisite and harmonious experience in this body while on this planet. Everything, especially those events that challenge us emotionally, is a chance to step into Midline where we find Spirit.

As an example of *Shri* in our everyday world, think back to Mark, the skier from the yoga workshop. He uses his disability as a tool for creating beauty and inspiring others. There was probably no person in the room moving with more elegance, more power, and more passion, than him. I don't know of anybody who lives with more dedication to creating what he wants out of himself. A few of my friends and I talked later and agreed that when we remember Mark we add a bit more juice to whatever we are doing as we, too, seek to be *Shri*. And, of course, when I think of *Shri* I remember my Costa Rican friend who intuitively understands that sharing his blessings honors himself and honors God. ■

A MIDLINE PRACTICE

Remember a time when you were disappointed about something. Look for some lesson in the disappointment that you can now use to make your life richer.

CHAPTER 12
It can be easy to be Shri!

I want to discuss *Shri* a bit more. After all, with *Shri* the whole idea is that there is always more! I remember one morning, living in the woods outside my small mountain town, waking up and feeling really lonely. It was one of our relatively few dark, overcast days and that added to my gloom. Feeling sorry for myself I drove into town. I was out of coffee at home, adding to my dour mood.

I walked in to the Safeway and stopped at the Starbucks counter. The woman behind the counter smiled brightly at me and said "Good morning!" In that moment she made me feel like I was the most important person in the world. My whole mood shifted. All of a sudden I felt her cheerfulness and it made me happy. Her smile forced the corners of my mouth to turn up into, yes, an actual, genuine smile. As I left the store, I noticed again how beautiful it is where I live and how happy I was to be alive.

The point of this story is that *Shri* isn't measured by how magnificent an act might be. We can create *Shri* with even the smallest act. While we all agree that people like Beethoven, Monet, and Ella Fitzgerald added beauty and happiness to the world on a very large scale, so too, do each of us add *Shri* to the world. We do so by the simplest of gestures, gestures nobody may ever see or hear about.

Consider the people you see when you go grocery shopping. If you pay any attention at all, you will notice some people look sad or lonely, the same way I felt when I went in to my Safeway that overcast morning. By saying "Hello" as you pass each other, you may be the first person that whole day or even that whole week that acknowledged them. I can remember times when a smile from a stranger, or a barista, brought me back from the emotional dumpster. This is *Shri*. It expands our collective consciousness, our collective greatness and potential, and the quality of our lives. It feels great simply being nice.

How can we think of *Shri* in our everyday lives? Swami Chidvilasananda (Gurumayi) reminds us that Shri is not only beauty and abundance but also dignity.[39] Do we move through our day with dignity? Do we treat others with dignity? Do we seek to create an air of dignity by what we say or write? I think one of the pleasures of teaching yoga is the opportunity to see the care with which the students choose their clothes for class. The color combinations and the styles are their personal expressions of a beauty inside. I think of President Obama during the 2010 State of the Union speech being interrupted when a representative yelled out "You lie!" during his speech. The President responded with dignity, even though the interruption was extraordinarily insulting.

Life is full of moments when the temptation is to take a lower road, to respond to a situation with less than our best. These moments are Midlines, offering us an opportunity to make more harmony instead of diminishing Spirit. Yoga reminds us that regardless of the circumstance, we can act with the highest honor for each other and all material things, including the planet itself. When we speak, we can ask ourselves if what we are saying is true, necessary and kind. Even if what we want to say meets those tests, we can then ask: is this the right time to say it? When we engage in relationships with others, we can choose to act in the way that honors them. The tone of voice we use, the way we look at someone, and the way we interact with others all have an impact. Therefore, we seek to act and speak artfully.

These are all aspects of *Shri*, habits of mindfulness that guide us in our actions with our families, workplace and community. This is how we become the type of person that people look forward to spending time with, eagerly anticipating our visits, emails or phone calls. We bring smiles to the faces of people simply by entering a room. We become the lift in somebody's day. We not only find Midlines, we create Midlines in our own lives and the lives of those with whom we interact. We not only find Spirit, we are Spirit. ■

A MIDLINE PRACTICE
Smile at somebody in the grocery store.

CHAPTER 13
Freedom's just another word for nothing left to lose—Svatantrya

I remember going to a party during law school. I was with my wife, Cyndi, who was pregnant. I drank too much and Cyndi drove us home. Along the way, she looked at me and gently said something to this effect: "Good party, wasn't it? I really like those people." I agreed with her, but then she went on: "There's something you might want to think about. You are going to be a dad soon; you've told me that you want to be a good dad, and I know you do. Maybe it might be time to start looking at whether you need to drink so much. Think about what kind of example you want to be for our little boy (we knew we were having a boy by then)." I listened to her and while part of me resisted, I knew she was right.

At that moment I had a choice. I could have chosen to become angry at her, rationalizing that I didn't really have a problem: it was just law school pressures; I'll stop once our son is born. Then I could continue to drink as much as I wanted. Alternatively, I could have chosen to examine the drinking and make a choice to create the type of man I wanted to be.

I took what Cyndi said seriously and decided to figure out why I tended to party too much. I found the courage to dissolve those habits and patterns that caused me to go over the edge with alcohol. I eventually created a different guy, the same man I had been, but with a healthier approach to drinking. I used my freedom to choose something worthwhile. I chose to be the best father I could be. I stepped into Midline, rejecting old, comfortable behaviors and selecting a course of action that would bring out the best in me.

The freedom to make choices, *Svantantrya,* is a third attribute of Spirit. *Svatantrya* means autonomy[40] and the ultimate freedom to create. Just as Spirit has the freedom to create Itself in any form It chooses, so too did I had the choice to create what kind of father, husband, and man I wanted to be.[41] Yoga philosophy teaches that it was out of this freedom that Spirit created us. It is this same freedom that allows us in each moment to create our future, one choice at a time.

When Cyndi spoke to me about my drinking, I was fortunate enough to make a wise choice. However, I did have the freedom to make a different choice that would ultimately have been harmful to my family and me. Midline invited me to turn away from the gratification of behaving like I wasn't responsible for anyone else but myself. Instead, I moved into adulthood and parenthood with greater clarity.

Yoga philosophy teaches that we have freedom to choose paths that bring us either closer to Spirit or farther away: into Midline or away. We make these choices every day, whether by the people we pick to spend time with, the activities we undertake, or the attitudes we cultivate. We make these choices when we choose to act out of scarcity or, alternatively when we choose to act out of abundance and kindness, no matter the circumstance.

Because we are free, we can always make choices that end up harming others, whether by damaging their reputation through gossip or innuendo, acting dishonestly in order to satisfy our short-term needs for gratification, or otherwise taking advantage of another's slip ups just so we can look good in comparison. I've learned that when I behave this way I'm not being free at all, even when I think I am expressing my freedom. Instead, I am a captive of ego. A truly free person doesn't need group approval of something that diminishes harmony. So, when I engage in that type of behavior out of a perceived notion that I am simply expressing my freedom, I know that I'm feeding myself a line of—you fill in the blank.

Any time I act contrary to the other attributes of Spirit, that is a red flag to me that I am in that moment shackled to ego, imprisoned by a false bill of goods I've sold myself for a momentary indulgence. I know in these cases that I will not be feeling any true joy in the long run from my behavior. I will not be feeling the satisfaction of legitimate and meaningful self-expression. I know that I have acted contrary to Spirit, turned away from Midline. ■

A MIDLINE PRACTICE

Think of a choice you've made that enriched your life.

CHAPTER 14
Scratching the itch—Purnatva

I've heard it said that our dark side or shadow side is the portal to our soul. I read that in at least one book by author and psychotherapist, Thomas Moore, as well as in other books. By this I refer to those parts of us that sit so deeply within our subconscious that we either don't know they exist or, when they appear, we refuse to acknowledge them. In any event, this always struck me as an important point to remember when I'm frustrated with myself over some mistake or aspect of my personality. I know that on more than one occasion somebody has complained to me that I am way too intense. My intensity puts them off. Whenever I hear this I walk away, feeling down about myself.

This intensity may be part of my shadow side. I can be overbearing, impatient, and rude. However, when I remember the phrase that our "dark side is the portal to our soul" I calm down. I remember that my very intensity, when applied in my legal profession, has served many people quite well. This intensity drove me to dig deeper into the facts of my cases, finding important evidence that others hadn't found. The intensity caused me to think of arguments to help my clients when they seemed beyond help. My passion for politics, although boring to some and too intense for others, comes from a compassionate and caring heart, a heart that wants the world to be kind. My intense curiosity to learn leads me to study with great teachers. My desire to be a good dad has, at least occasionally, made me a good dad.

This brings us to a *Purnatva*, the fourth attribute of Spirit, which means fullness or peace. When we know and appreciate who we are, including our quirks, there is a feeling of completeness and a natural state of peace, or *Shanti*. Often we forget that we are already a unique manifestation of Spirit and, instead, worry about trying to do everything right in order to satisfy others. Since no human being can ever "please all of the people all of the time" or live a life free of mistakes, these kinds of attitudes inevitably feed feelings of separateness and unworthiness.

In contrast, a feeling of peace arises when we remember our essence, our own Divine imprint; i.e., our own unique package of strengths, and look for how to be engaged in offering them in a meaningful way. This offering leads to connection to others. Out of this sense of connection it is much more difficult to be jealous, envious, or resentful for the things others have. We learn to value what we are and what we have, not crave what the other guy has. We become genuinely pleased for our neighbor's good fortune. From that perspective we are able to see the abundance within the world and in our lives.

Embracing all aspects of our personality is a challenge. I can't tell you the number of times I spent the day taking depositions, literally forcing reluctant, angry defendants to finally admit to deceptive or negligent acts that had harmed my client. That is tough, stress-filled work. Sometimes I then went out that evening, only to be told by somebody I just met that I need to lighten up. Immediately I would feel bad about myself, thinking I was not fit to be around other people socially.

It took me a long time to cut myself some slack and recognize that this intensity was a valuable part of me. I would have loved to just flip a switch turning myself into somebody fun to be around before going out for the evening. I just didn't know how. We often get down on ourselves over some mistake or habit. This causes us to focus exclusively on what we perceive to be a shortcoming. We become mired in self-reproach. When that happens we need to treat ourselves with the same patience and understanding that we might give others. This is Midline work; having the courage to fight through the negative messaging that unfortunately can arise so easily.

Eventually through yoga I learned a number of ways to calm down and give myself a break, emotionally. One of the most important lessons was learning how to honor the person I am and stop feeling ashamed because I get so wired up. While learning practices to slow down and become spacious were key to becoming a more relaxed social companion, learning how to view myself with tenderness and appreciation was crucial. I learned that all parts of me were manifestations of Spirit. These lessons taught me to appreciate that I am a Divine package, a beautiful expression of Spirit in wrapping paper that not everyone will fall in love with.

We don't ignore how we affect other people or take a free pass with our behavior. While we are accepting of who we are as a person, we at the same time recognize that who we are is an evolving, expanding light of potential. Out of this recognition we engage in practices that cultivate that potential: we become our own garden, and we tend to our blooming, and to our weeds with equal tenderness and love.

It is critical that we balance the sense of fullness with the energy of *Iccha Shakti*, our desire to fully know and express ourselves. *Iccha Shakti* is always at play within us, always vibrating with desire to expand our expression in the world, to explore the boundaries of what we are capable of being. This impulse is different from saying that what we have and who we are is insufficient. This is different from the Type A personality who is never satisfied and is constantly chasing the carrot in order to fill an empty hole inside them, a hole that exists because of the lack of self-study, self-knowledge, and self-acceptance.

We can be happy with ourselves yet still desire to more fully cultivate our own special gifts. We need engagement to have a life of well-being, using our highest strengths and talents in a way that meets what the world is asking of us.[42] We learn to find a way to fully acknowledge all aspects of ourselves and recruit our entire being into how we live our life, utilizing our shadow and our light while recognizing that it is all light. As we become more attuned to all aspects of our personality, and view ourselves with compassion and understanding, we become free to offer ourselves fully, no longer bound by episodes of self-directed anger and concerns over disapproval. Only then, in this self-actualized form, are we best able to live the type of life that recognizes and welcomes the Midlines. ■

A MIDLINE PRACTICE

Think of a time when you did something that you or somebody else labeled as a mistake but where your motivation came out of trying to create something positive; i.e., make a friend or fix a problem. Cut yourself some slack.

CHAPTER 15
What is our truth—Sat?

I was getting some bodywork from Bricks, a top body worker in Denver. He's a New York lad who brings that great New York energy to his conversations, making a visit to him always interesting. And don't count on the music necessarily being "spa" music. You might hear Massive Reggae in the background, or you might hear who knows what; it's always good tunes when you visit Bricks. And, he's a genuine healer. I limp into his office and when I walk out, it's like I'm sixteen.

Since I'd known Bricks for a fair amount of time, I decided one day to ask him what he thought was my most positive quality. I know that seems like a strange question, particularly coming from someone like me who is focusing so much on being content with my own unique character. Here's why I wanted to know: I am very curious about who I am and what I am capable of creating in this world. Perhaps you are already asking yourself these questions. I also know I'm not the best judge of my own potential. Just as it is impossible for us to see the nose on our face without a mirror, I've learned we can't see all of our greatness without the mirror of others, reflecting back our potential based on what they know of us.

For me, then, it is worthwhile to look for feedback from others: what do they see that I might be missing? Try it sometime. Ask your business partner how she or he thinks you could be of greater value. It's a risk, a Midline. You may get some grumbling, non–helpful response. If you pick the wrong partner, or the wrong time or place, you might even receive a stinging insult. On the other hand, you might hear something positive and inspiring.

Consider the experience I had one time when I tried this tactic. One of my senior law partners said: "You're funny. You're personable. The clients find you refreshingly different and intriguing because they don't know karate people. They don't know former college football players. Invite people out for lunch and dinner more. You'll make friends and we'll get more work." Wow... I didn't know! More free lunches and dinners, more friends, more income; I could live with that. Or, ask your wife or husband what they would love to see more of from you. Or, ask your kids. If you pick the right time and place, you will get some interesting feedback and quite likely clues on enriching not only the relationship but your life in general. If you have the nerve, it's pretty cool.

There is a freedom that comes from admitting your faults and coming to peace with yourself that you are an okay person. It is out of this freedom that I am able to do things like ask Bricks and carefully selected others what special qualities they see in me. I knew Bricks would be honest and I also knew that he is the kind of person that would give me a meaningful answer, not a response intended only to make me feel good. If there was something about me he admired, he'd tell me; if not, he'd tell me.

Bricks surprised me with his answer. Without even a moment's hesitation he said: "You're really generous." "Bricks," I said, "no way. I don't give you very big tips; they're pretty average." He responded by telling me that it wasn't money he was talking about. He then described something I had done for him and some other people quite some time ago. He told me that I never asked for anything in return for what I'd done, and it was obvious that I hadn't expecting something in return. He said it was clear to him and his friends that I just wanted to give a service and he hadn't forgotten it.

That led to a discussion about generosity. Bricks said that, to him, it isn't about money. Many people, Bricks said, will write a check but few people give of their time. Giving of your time, in his view, indicates a generosity of the heart and that is what he meant when he told me I was generous.

I thanked him and added his comments to what I call my own personal wellspring. My wellspring is a storehouse of memories that I tap into from time to time to remind me who I am. Generosity was a quality I was proud to add to the wellspring. It joined "sense of humor;" I think I am funny. I also work hard and don't quit. I have a creative, quick mind. These are beliefs I have about myself that reside in my wellspring.

I mention the wellspring as an introduction to the next of the seven attributes, *Sat. Sat* is Spirit's attribute of being the foundation of all beings,[43] an "eternal truth," and the ultimate Reality.[44] What do these concepts of "eternal," "truth," and "reality" mean to us in our human bodies? Certainly our bodies die, so how can we as humans claim the attribute of being eternal? We make mistakes, so how can we claim to be truth or an ultimate reality? I sometimes feel ignored or not relevant; how can I be a foundation for anyone?

Spiritual teacher Sally Kempton discusses this very point. She teaches that this attribute of eternal truth or reality applies to us as humans because we are made up of our experiences; memories that never leave us and are always present to serve us. These memories are our foundation.[45] We have our own truth that stays with us always. She refers to *Sat* as a Self that is always present.[46] This Self stays with us as we age and thus provides a context for our entire life, always available to us awake or asleep.[47]

When we are faced with obstacles, we can always return to our memories, education and training, in order to help us determine how to act. This Self is Spirit residing in us, along with each of Spirit's attributes. We are love and joy. We are complete. We are free to choose how to experience life. This sense of Spirit within us never leaves us, even if we forget that it is there.

In addition to my memories and experiences, my wellspring is a collection of those things about myself that I know to be true. I turn to this wellspring to remind me of who I am and also my finest points, those things I can be most proud of. In times when I'm down, or feel the need for a booster shot of confidence, I can turn to this wellspring. When I take the risk of insult or rejection in order to explore how others see me, I create the opportunity, as I did with Bricks, to make this wellspring even more potent. I'm generous; that's yet another example of how Spirit is present in me, and another gift I can share with others.

Speaking of times when I'm feeling down: what if I make a mistake and the wellspring doesn't have a ready feel-good message for me? How can I be Spirit even if I goof up? Rabbi David Aaron addresses this question in *The Secret Life Of God*.[48] When asked how God could be both perfect and imperfect, he explains that perfection is "dynamic" in that it is always growing.[49] In each moment we are, like Spirit, complete and perfect, yet with potential to expand. We are created with our gifts and talents as well as our shadow sides. Learning to use our shadow side in a way that is beneficial is an example of a dynamic expansion of Spirit.

Sometimes we get so upset with our behavior that we just want to give up. We wonder if we can ever change. However, just like Spirit, in each moment we have the opportunity to create a new person, dissolving those attitudes or habits that no longer serve us as we create a more skillful version of ourselves. Every time we act in a way that disappoints us, we have the opportunity to step into a giant Midline. We have the chance to learn from the experience instead of becoming lost in self-reproach. We can become even more perfect based on how we respond to our imperfection. In fact, the imperfection was itself perfect, because it was the catalyst for our growth. This is how we create the life of well-being that is our promise.[50] ■

A MIDLINE PRACTICE

Ask somebody you know well and trust, to share with you something about you they really appreciate.

CHAPTER 16
Who am I, exactly?—Chit

I didn't know any lawyers when I was in college but, from what I had seen, mostly on television shows and in the movies, lawyers were different from me. They seemed to be bright, articulate and powerful advocates for their clients. I didn't see me as having any of those traits. I was surprised, then, when my high-school friend Bruce suggested I go to law school. When I protested he told me I was silly. He said I had every one of those skills and that was the very reason he felt I would be a good lawyer.

I thought long and hard about his suggestion and I started to see what he was talking about. I was able to quickly piece together solutions to problems, so long as they didn't involve math! I received good grades on written work I handed in. When there was trouble, I was often the person who stepped in and talked people into relaxing and backing away from escalation. Thanks to Bruce serving as a mirror, I was able to see me—my light—in a different way. Maybe I could be a lawyer after all.

My lawyer light has shined pretty brightly over the years. I did well in law school, serving as Research Editor for the Law Review and writing several academic articles that have been published. If you ever have trouble falling asleep, consider finding a copy of my first published article. It was a spellbinding discussion about the relationship of Section Seven of the Clayton Antitrust Act and bank holding companies. As intrigued as you might now be with that subject, you won't learn much about it reading my article; you will be snoozing within two minutes. But I digress.

After graduating I began my law practice and worked for some high profile firms. It's been a great career. I learned so many things from so many people. Importantly, over time I learned what I was particularly good at and, conversely, where I was not so skilled. For example, I felt like nobody could piece together a puzzle (a case) from so many seemingly unconnected pieces like me.

On the other hand, watching some of my partners try a lawsuit showed me what a real trial lawyer's skills looked like. I was already a good legal writer but I worked with and against partners and associates who taught me what true legal writing is all about. My career put me in daily contact with some of the top trial attorneys in the country and, as a result, I was able to see the wide range of gifts these individuals possessed.

Part of what makes some law firms so successful is the ability to weave all their talent into a powerful representation of their clients. Over years of law practice I learned to appreciate my strengths and turn them to an advantage. The ability to master complicated statutory schemes, for example, resulted in doing work that was fun and lucrative. Instead of worrying about being somebody I was not, I focused on cultivating my particular skills. I played a role, as part of a team, in cases that not only served our clients but also were helpful to the community.

"Team" is an important word. We all can quickly see how in sports it's not only acceptable but actually necessary that each member of the team use their own special talent. Can you imagine, for example, what a problem the respective teams would have if the New York Giants' Eli Manning decided he wanted to play middle linebacker, or if top hockey goalie Ryan Miller of the Buffalo Sabers insisted on playing center?

Why, then, can't we see this important point as it relates to ourselves? We each have our own special combination of things we are good at and other things that, well, are not so good. This is what brings harmony in the community; when people can recognize and value the worth of their own talents and, without jealousy or envy toward others, offer them as part of a cooperative package toward meaningful ends. Just like Spirit, each of us has the gift of self-awareness, the ability to awaken to our own unique skills and, in doing so, remember that each of us is part of a shared whole that is bigger than us and which needs our contribution for true harmony to exist and for excellence to expand.

This ability to reflect on our true nature is the next of the seven attributes of the Divine, *Chit* (self-awareness). *Chit* means an unlimited intelligence with a capacity for unbounded creativity.[51] This is a handy attribute to have if you are God and decide to create a world, or two or three. What does it mean for us as humans? *Chit* commonly means self-awareness, the ability to awaken and remember, or otherwise recognize our particular strengths as well as our connection to the shared whole as part of Spirit. We are aware of what is special about us—our light—and we know our own ability to serve as mirrors for others so they can see their own potential. We recall that in each moment we are co-creating the world, each of us in our own way and through our interactions with each other.

The interaction of *Chit* and *Sat* connects us to our own truth, which includes our personal experiences in life, our strengths, and our remembrance of our nature as part of Spirit. When my friend Bruce suggested I become a lawyer, I awakened to that potential within me. I started to think about it, and could see myself using my talent, the gifts Bruce brought to my attention, and how I could enjoy a life in which I served the community through the exercise of those gifts. This awakening helped illuminate my path, answering some of my questions of who I am and where I fit in.

I imagine this interaction of *Chit* and *Sat* is part of what must have driven Walt Disney when he recognized he had a very special idea that could heighten the joy of millions. I suspect it was this recognition that helped him to keep going in the face of so much rejection and ridicule. His self-awareness helped him overcome such negativity and step into Midline.

Our self-awareness not only makes us aware of who we are but also reminds us we are part of something bigger than just us. Dr. Seligman, after years of research into the subject of happiness, writes that our deepest joy comes from finding how, each day, to offer our strengths in a way that serves others.[52] He writes of the real value for each of us in taking the time to identify what we are good at and then figuring out a way to use our skills in service of something larger than just our own needs. Such self-study is the practice of *Chit,* self-awareness. ∎

A MIDLINE PRACTICE

Tell somebody something you really appreciate about them in a way that will help them see their own value and deepen their own self-awareness.

CHAPTER 17
It's in the doing—Satchitananda

When I first moved to Denver my friend Jim talked me into going to a yoga class. Our teacher was Emma, and she immediately made me feel welcome. The class was fun, even though I couldn't do most of the poses in any way close to the form of the other students. Much later, when I decided to focus on yoga philosophy in grad school my advisor told me I needed to find a mentor. I immediately went to Emma because of her deep commitment to yoga and its philosophy. It was easy to sell Emma as a mentor to my advisor. In addition to being certified in the Iyengar tradition, for years Emma has made a practice of regularly visiting India to study with the Iyengars. Emma agreed and together we crafted a course of study that easily met my advisor's approval.

Over the years I've continued to attend Emma's classes when I can. It is not unusual to walk in and find other local yoga teachers in class such as Julieta, now herself a highly regarded yoga teacher. We are all there to learn from Emma or perhaps just be around her. People who are committed to their practice gravitate to Emma, not only because we would learn something but also because her classes are a blast.

I remember one time when we were doing handstands against the wall, Emma could be heard saying: "Shins together for Julieta!" and "Straighten the left arm for Bill Dorigan." Julieta is, today, probably the "Goddess of Handstands;" but this was years ago. Emma sometimes even stops in the middle of teaching a pose and asks how certain other teachers might cue a pose. She does this because she is not only an amazing teacher; she is forever the student. Ego doesn't prevent her from learning everything she can. She easily meets Midline's invitation of putting aside concern about what others might think in order to increase her knowledge and value as a teacher.

Emma represents an example of *Satchitananda,* a description of Spirit's nature of *Sat* (truth), *Chit* (self-awareness) and *Ananda* (bliss) viewed collectively. These three combined attributes of Spirit are part of our true nature as well.[53] We experience *Satchitananda* in our own lives by finding our own personal truth and then celebrating that truth in a meaningful way. We do this when, like Emma, we answer Midline's invitation to courageously explore who we are, acknowledge our gifts, and then commit our lives to creating more connection in the world through that offering. When we live this way we find real happiness.

Emma does this every day. She understands that yoga is her love and so she has dedicated her life to teaching it in a way that serves her students. Whenever I attend her class I learn something about myself. I challenge myself and yet, when I leave, I find that I like myself more. I'm a bit nicer, a bit kinder, a bit more inclined to treat people well. This is because Emma is living and teaching out of her true nature, *Satchitananda*.

Without this awakening, we simply move through life like a ship without a compass, or rudder, with a constant dull vibration in our hull indicating that the ship is not firing on all cylinders or drifting without a port-of-call. To still that dull vibration and find our destination we need to be aware of what makes us feel fulfilled. Then we need to find a way to live a life in which we are engaged in doing those things.

Linking our awareness of our strengths with a meaningful use of those strengths is what brings us *Ananda*. It is easy to find superficial happiness if all we do is gratify our every desire, even if it is at the expense of others. Behavioral psychology teaches us, however, that the greatest joy arises when we embrace our signature skills and then live a life that engages those skills in service of something bigger than ourselves.[54]

Noted psychologist Dr. Rollo May wrote that the highest level of emotional health arises in a creative process through which we "enlarge human consciousness" in our own unique way, by expressing who we are in our work and daily lives.[55] Dr. May emphasizes that we experience joy when we actualize our potential through our engagement in such activities.[56] He concludes that the ultimate joy occurs when we can find meaning in what we manifest, creating harmony and connection in our relationships and the world.[57]

When I first heard this I was skeptical. It sounded to me like some sort of spiritual concoction created to help keep us in line. If somebody feels they would be happier driving a Porsche, why not just steal one? If we feel desire for somebody physically, why not just say whatever we need to say to get that desire satisfied, even if it is dishonest? However, my personal life experience teaches me that living that way leaves us incomplete and even empty. I write this at age 64. I've had a Porsche—two of them, actually, one bright red with the whale tail. I've flown first class to extraordinary destinations, lived in large homes, worn amazing clothes, and dined in elegant Parisian restaurants. Yet here I am at this age thinking primarily about what I can do to make a difference.

I don't think about the Porsche or the great restaurants much but I regularly and fondly recall a smile on someone's face when I made them laugh. I remember when I've helped somebody feel more confident. Instead of focusing on how much more I can gratify myself, I find myself asking questions such as: How can I make this life worth something? What can I do so that other people's lives are at least a bit better off because I was here on the planet for a short while? I don't ask myself these questions because I need to earn my way into Heaven. I'm not all that certain there is such a place and, if there is, I feel I've done what I need to do to gain entry. Rather, I ask these questions of myself because I believe it is my true nature to want to serve in some way that utilizes the blessings I've been given. This is my *Satchitananda*.

How do we create this joyous life of meaning when we are barely making ends meet, often working more than one job to provide for our families? Not everybody can be like Emma, finding a job we truly love and which provides obvious value to others. The message seems clear: even if it is through volunteer work, we need to identify our strengths and then creatively find ways to express these strengths in some way that serves a purpose, by serving our family, community or society in general.

We don't have to be grandiose about it. One example immediately comes to mind. My friends Lisa and Chris, and their high school son Christopher, used one of their Sundays, normally a much deserved weekend break from work and school, to go to Colorado Springs and volunteer at the Catholic Charities center set up to help fire victims. They enriched their lives by offering their spare time to distribute clothing to people who had lost everything in the fires. That is Spirit in action; the type of action that, according to both yoga philosophy and modern behavioral psychology, brings real joy, *Satchitananda*. ▪

A MIDLINE PRACTICE

Think about somebody you know who has found a way to use their skills and talents, whether in a job, through a hobby, or volunteering, in a way that seems to be satisfying to them and serves the community.

CHAPTER 18
The real meaning of "give and take"—Spanda

I listened to a radio talk show, hosted by David Sirota, discussing how society continues to impose more and more demands on our kids, further restricting their opportunities to relax and enjoy life. He was referring at least in part to the mandatory testing that requires teachers to spend so much time "teaching to the test" rather than using class time for discussion and expansion of the capacity to think. Either Mr. Sirota or his guest commented that "the metabolism of our culture" has increased so much that there is hardly time for any of us, including school children, to find space to contemplate, assimilate thoughts, and tie concepts together.

I think this concern is spot-on. When will kids have time to contemplate what they've learned and figure out how it applies in their lives? How will they develop the skills necessary to make moral and ethical distinctions? When will they have time for fun?

I like the phrase "metabolism of our culture." In their conversation, Mr. Sirota and his guest discussed how we all are increasingly bombarded with information from the media and the Internet. While obtaining more information is a gift, that gift has value only if we can process the information in a way that makes it useful. By useful I mean that we are able to absorb the information and use it to lead a life that is flourishing. If we can't assimilate information fully, we become overwhelmed, and the energy we put back out into the world may not be as productive as we would like. We need to pause and create a space between taking in information and then acting upon it. By doing so we are best able to live in Midline, processing information presented by Midline's opportunity, and then formulating a response that best serves Spirit.

When we have a new experience we take in new information. Ideally, we then contemplate the experience. What did we learn? How might this latest experience guide us in the future, if at all? After we've assimilated our latest experience, we are then able to view and act in the world just a bit differently, if we choose, because of that work of contemplation and assimilation. This internal contemplation and assimilation can be considered a contractive energy. What we do with the product of that contemplation and assimilation, how we act in the world based on this process, can be considered an expansive energy.

This contraction and expansion relates to a seventh attribute of Spirit, *Spanda*. In addition to the energies of contraction and expansion, *Spanda* also can mean a pulsation or vibration between contrasting or polar energies, as well as an opening and a closing, such as the opening and closing of an opportunity, a Midline.[58] We engage Spirit through *Spanda*, much like a game of hide and seek. Each experience gives us a chance to learn something we knew little or nothing about, an experience of Spirit seemingly hiding from us. We create greater knowledge of Spirit where there was ignorance.[59]

The universe was initially created through the throb of *Spanda,* the dance of *Shiva* and *Shakti* we've discussed. This creative and vibrating energy exists in every particle of the universe today.[60] *Shiva* is universal consciousness and the power that connects all things. The contrasting energy of *Shakti* energizes this consciousness and power through the reflective spark of creation. This interaction, or *Spanda*, between the two different or polarized energies of *Shiva* and *Shakti* is how Spirit expands in the world and how we expand our own spirit.

We experience the vibration of contrary energies every day. Nature offers us the polar energies of the sun and moon, dark and light, day and night, the tides, and the seasons. In our own body we have the pulsation of our heartbeat, as well as the inhalation and exhalation of the breath. In life we have up and down, opening and closing, growth and decay, male and female, vertical and horizontal, active and passive, happiness and suffering, and freedom and bondage. Taking it even further, we have polarity of ideas: differences on the role of government, budget priorities, and whether to go to war. We have the dynamics of yes and no, for and against, inaction and action. We have acceptance or rejection of Midline's invitations to greater possibility.

This interaction between polar opposites occurs in every moment and requires us to make choices. We have to make a choice between "yes" and "no." If I say: "yes" to becoming a serious marathon runner, I guarantee you that I am saying "no" to becoming a champion in karate. While I develop tremendous endurance running mile after mile, I also tighten my hamstrings to the point where I'm lucky if I can kick above my knee. Although I can run for hours, my fast-twitch fibers, necessary for fighting, move at the pace of a calendar turning from one month to the next. I've made these choices in the course of my life and so I can attest to the process of "yes" and "no."

Every choice has a consequence, and these consequences go far beyond issues such as what sport or activity we undertake. Our choices create our world. Some people who study and teach yoga say that our greatest joy comes from this creative freedom to choose. In my experience, our greatest joy comes from something more—the feelings we experience when our exercise of choice creates something more beautiful, more harmonious.

This is why, as David Sirota and his guest suggests, we must learn to slow down the metabolism of our culture. We need to create enough quiet time in our day so that we contemplate and assimilate. Only when we take this time can we fully recognize the invitations life gives us to step into Midline, making choices that best serve our family and ourselves. Only in this way do we exercise real freedom, the freedom of choosing to manifest ourselves in a way that best reflects who we are and in a way that honors and grows Spirit. Otherwise, we are contracting and expanding all over the place, but not out of a freedom based on wisdom. Instead, we are acting as a prisoner of emotional forces we don't even recognize.

This is why I find the practices I learn through yoga to be so valuable. Even if I am only able to spend a few minutes on my mat, the process of aligning my hands, feet, muscles and joints is a contemplative act that slows me down and builds a capacity to assimilate. Meditation, if even just for fifteen minutes a day, has a profound impact on my ability to access and process the huge amount of information I've taken in. One of my friends finds these quiet moments when he takes the dog for a walk. Another friend processes her day sitting in her chair, cat in her lap, listening to soft, classical music. All these practices create space in the mind where contemplation can occur.

There is *Spanda* in every experience we have. This is so because in every experience the world is offering us something and we have the opportunity to evaluate how, and if, we choose to respond. We learn through practices to make time for quiet so that we can heighten this ability to recognize and evaluate. This is *Spanda* as I choose to understand it, bringing life's experiences from the outside world into our heart, and then, after mindful reflection, offering from our heart back out to the outside world.[61] ■

A MIDLINE PRACTICE

Pick a routine task you have to do, such as making the bed, shaving or putting on make up, putting on your clothes, writing a grocery list, packing a lunch, or making coffee or tea. Do the task slowly, being aware of every movement of your body, including your breathing, as you do so.

CHAPTER 19
The Spanda *of relationship*

Years ago I competed in martial arts tournaments, specifically point-fighting, a form of karate in which we wear pads and engage in full contact fighting. One point is awarded for a hand strike that lands and two points for a kick that finds its way home. As an aside, in some states, kicks to the groin were allowed. In Minnesota, my home base at the time, such kicks were banned. Trust me: when you compete in this type of karate, it is good to check the rules of the state in which you are fighting. You only forget to check once!

Anyway, I trained at a highly competitive school that included several nationally ranked fighters. My primary training and sparring partner was Reggie, a man about ten years younger than me. Reggie was a rising top fighter. He was really fast, really talented, and trained hard. It seemed to me he was nothing but fast-twitch muscle fibers, able to bring his back foot from the floor to my eyebrow before my brain could register that he had even moved. And I wasn't slow. We trained together constantly. Training with him made me a serious competitor, sharpening my reflexes and techniques way beyond anything I had experienced before.

We enjoyed each other's company and became good friends. One time we traveled together to Europe and took time off to visit the Musee D'Orsay, a world famous museum known for its collection of impressionist art. While we were there we came upon a beautiful painting by Degas. This particular painting included a single ballerina seemingly lost in thought, standing slightly off-stage. I had studied that painting in my college art history course and immediately launched into an explanation to Reggie of what we could "see" in this painting. Reggie listened politely and took in everything I had to say. I finished and turned to walk away. Reggie softly said: "Thanks. Now let me tell you what I see."

I stopped, more than a bit surprised that he had something to add after my learned pontification. I thought to myself: "Wait a minute, here I am a guy who went to college and studied this stuff and Reggie is a guy who hasn't had any of this background. What could he offer me?" Anyway, out of courtesy to my friend, I stopped and listened. Reggie proceeded to share his impressions from the painting, impressions so emotionally moving and clearly suggested by the painting, yet impressions I'd never heard nor read about and certainly hadn't considered.

That was a huge learning experience and a Midline for me. In addition to coming face to face with all my biased and limiting ways of viewing the world, I learned from Reggie to see the world in a more extended way. The more time I spent with Reggie, the more I learned to see the world not just from my perspective but also from his point of view, a point of view informed by experiences growing up significantly different from mine. My time with Reggie in effect helped create a new, broader-minded me.

One on one relationship provides amazing potential for us to learn more about many things: the world, other people and ourselves. Relationships can deepen and enrich our experience on this planet. In fact, to truly find ourselves we have to engage with more than ourselves.[62] We invite the unfamiliar into our lives, exploring diversity because it is in the unknown that greater possibility exists.[63] By getting to know Reggie, I was not only learning more about somebody other than me, I was learning about different ways to view the world. In this process I was, myself, becoming "more" with respect to my understanding of how the world works and how I could participate in and experience it more fully. In turn, it was this greatly expanded viewpoint that I offered to my son as he grew up.

Engaging the unknown and expanding our relationships is risky, but the way to the Midline comes by overcoming our own fears and other limiting attitudes and stepping into the risks of the unknown. Reggie and I had much in common but were also very different from each other in terms of our backgrounds. By spending so much time with him I learned from these differences. My relationship with him broadened my ability to connect to others because I now realized that it is in the very differences that a potential for richer experiences exist. Once we start viewing each other this way, it becomes easy to see that people who may appear different from us are not threats to who we are. Rather, they are clues to what we can become.[64]

Modern behavioral psychologists recognize the *Spanda* of relationships, the ongoing mirroring we do for each other; the vibratory interaction we experience every day. I find Dr. Seligman's discussion of "positive relationships" to correlate with the energy of *Spanda*. He believes the solitary life is not optimal because our greatest happiness, joy, meaning, and pride of accomplishment occur around other people.[65]

This view on the importance of personal relationship to a life of well-being is echoed by noted author and psychology professor, Dr. Mihaly Csikszentmihalyi, who wrote that true quality of life requires not only finding a full, meaningful engagement or flow in our work, but also in our relations with other people.[66] Dr. Csikszentmihalyi adds that we are programmed as human beings to seek relationship and that where we can find harmony in those relationships, we increase the quality of our life experience.[67]

Spirit offers Herself to us in the countless and diverse forms of this world. Whenever we meet somebody new, there is an invitation to step into Midline. We risk being hurt or rejected, but the potential reward is a new and valuable friendship. It is out of these relationships that we learn more about ourselves and our worldview expands. When I got to know Reggie, and see the world a little bit from his perspective, I was given just such an opportunity. I was invited through my relationship with him to savor the world from a completely different mindset, seeing things I had missed and learning things that otherwise would have passed me by. This is how the *Spanda* of relationships can work. ■

A MIDLINE PRACTICE

The next time you attend a business or social function, take time to get to know somebody who normally you would not pay attention to, somebody who appears particularly uninteresting to you.

PART IV

A Road Map Of the Outer World—
The Tattvas

A. The Creation Story—
Who, What, and Why?

CHAPTER 20
A roadmap to Spirit—the Tattvas

As I write this, my grandson, Henry, is three years old. On a recent trip to Boston to see the family, I was amazed at how captivated he was with virtually every kind of truck. No matter what he was doing, if a fire engine, an ambulance, or a garbage truck drove by he dropped what he was doing, jumping up and down, vibrating with excitement, urging us to watch. Then, he would stare, rapturously, long after the vehicle was out of view. He was fascinated.

My son Jeff, Henry's dad, takes the train to work. The train station is close by; so we sometimes go down to meet the train when Jeff comes home. Henry is just as excited with trains as he is with trucks. In fact, on those occasions when the Amtrak train comes roaring through the commuter station, Henry is beside himself with excitement. I have to check to see if he is levitating!

I noticed that Henry's attention isn't limited to trucks and trains. Whenever a person walks by who is a different color, or otherwise looks or acts a bit out of the ordinary, Henry's attention is drawn right away to that person. He watches them, totally absorbed, until they are gone, or until something else unusual comes along.

I have a theory as to what is behind Henry's fascination with trucks and the variety of people Henry sees. Henry is drawn to people and things that are different from what he is familiar with. Trucks and trains are different from cars. It is the same with people. Some people stand out in their differences, either by skin color, size, mannerisms, or attire. Henry is curious about difference. He wants to explore it. Difference makes him excited. He is curious about the world.

I use this story about Henry's curiosity to introduce the *Tattvas*. What are the *Tattvas*? *Tattvas* are considered to be the cosmology of the universe, answering the questions of why and how the entire universe, including you and me, was created and how it is organized.[68] The *Tattvas* are categories of the many diverse ways Spirit is expressed in the material world, providing us a roadmap for how to view the world in such a way as to connect most skillfully and meaningfully with that universe and to Spirit.[69]

Understanding this roadmap of the *Tattvas* is critical to living in Midline, living a life that flourishes through its connection with Spirit. Midline is that moment when God offers an invitation to us to step outside our comfort zone and embrace the potential of the moment.

Through the *Tattvas* we develop the capacity to recognize that offer, transcend our fears and insecurities, and respond to God's invitation. Through the *Tattvas* we learn to explore each experience, play with it, try it on for size if we are so inclined, or say "no thanks" if the risks look too great or potentially harmful.[70] We can always walk away, having deepened what we know about the world by our exploration.[71] If we understand and weave the *Tattvas* into our lives, we can better attain that life of well-being that modern psychology and ancient teachings agree we seek.

When I think about it, Henry's passion for exploring difference illustrates exactly what the *Tattvas* invite us to do—use our curiosity and imagination not only to find greater enjoyment in our life but also to find Spirit as She is expressed in the vast diversity of our planet. Little kids naturally are curious about differences because it is our nature as humans to explore diversity and find the fascinating, to find the next great possibility. We seek inspiration for our dreams to help us formulate who we wish to be.

Somewhere on the way to adulthood, we stop being so curious. Far too often we step outside on a beautiful day, and instead of pausing to enjoy the day, we immediately look down at our phone to Twitter, text, or check for email. In those moments we turn a blind eye toward the invitations offered by the unfamiliar. An elephant could walk by, we might not notice. But kids notice. It's their nature. And so, of course, it is our nature. Studying and practicing with the *Tattvas* returns us to that nature. The *Tattvas* teach us the value of paying attention to the world around us, as well as our own senses. In doing so, they teach us how to find the Midlines in our lives.

The word *"Tattva"* technically means "that-ness" and is commonly translated to mean "principle," "reality," "truth," or "category of existence." Each category is simply a different form of Spirit. For example, each of us in our embodied form is considered a unique form of Spirit, although we exist in a reduced, more limited form based upon our own particular capabilities and limitations.[72] So, too, every other material form in this world, the animals, the plants, the mountains, the oceans, even the weather, are all manifestations of Spirit. Each of the primary elements: the boundlessness of space, as well as the earth, water, fire, and air, is considered to be different expressions of Spirit.

In summary, everyone and everything is an expression of Spirit. The *Tattvas* teach us how to locate Spirit everywhere. This makes me want to pay attention: to wake-up, to be *curious* about the world that is available to me every day. After all, if I am on a quest for Spirit, I had better pay attention to the innumerable expressions of Spirit all around me. ■

A MIDLINE PRACTICE

Spend a few minutes people-watching and notice how different one person looks from the next in terms of facial appearance, height, weight, and mannerisms.

CHAPTER 21
Out of nothing arises you and me—why?

I had a college roommate named Pete. Pete was a big football player and one of the nicest people I ever met. Everybody loved him. His energy was like a magnet. We could walk in to the Student Union and before you knew it, people would be moving all around at their table so he could have a seat. And, in the next minute, the table would be surrounded with even more men and women drawn to him.

I remember one night at our dorm when two guys he didn't even know squared off outside to fight each other. Pete was walking out the door with his girl friend and he stopped when he saw them. He walked right into the middle and said something to the effect of "Guys, guys, guys. It's Friday night. Do you know how many women are at the Union looking to meet a guy? How about you go with us over there right now. I'll buy you a beer and if, later, you still want to fight, I'll take you both on." Who could fight after that? Who could turn down a free beer, maybe a date, and then have to fight Pete?

More than once when I had nothing to do on a Saturday night Pete and his girl friend would take me over to the Union, stop the first group of women we saw and ask them to go out with us. It worked every time. As soon as they saw that they could hang out with Pete, I suddenly looked pretty good to them! Pete was fun, he was kind, he was generous, and he made everybody happier to be around him. He was a leader who showed us how to treat each other and have fun.

Right after college Pete joined the Marines. He was sent to Viet Nam and, leading a patrol, was killed. What a painful lesson of the shocking suddenness with which life can turn from laughter to stunning sadness. When we experience this ourselves or hear stories about such tragedies, we can't help but ask: "Why?" I still wonder almost every day why guys like Pete are taken from us, how it can be that good people, beloved to many, have their lives cut short.

The *Tattvas* offer some possible and hopeful ways of dealing with such questions. Through the *Tattvas*, the template for understanding each other and our world, we learn how to engage all that the world throws at us, the good and the bad, the funny and the sad. The *Tattvas* remind us each person or situation that comes across our path might be an opportunity to more fully appreciate our time on the planet and the people and experiences we encounter.

I want to tell a bit of the history of the *Tattvas*. As you read this discussion, recognize that the creation story charted by the *Tattvas* is a beautiful metaphor for how, deep inside each of us, exists a dream and desire to fully express ourselves in the world, to make our own personal mark. We know from studying documents that date as far back as 1,500 B.C.E., that people expressed their wonderment about life: "Why and how was the world created?" "If there is a Divine creator, how are we as humans related to that creator?" "What does He or She want from us, if anything?"

These early thinkers speculated that before any creation of our universe took place, an Absolute Reality existed in solitude and in chaos as a formless dark energy, often called *Rta,* meaning "universal order."[73] *Rta* had a sense of His own existence and began at some point to ask the question "Who am I?"[74] Book 10; Hymn 129 of the *Rig Veda* describes this energy and its creative power as existing before any matter, space, sky, night or day, light or dark, before anything.[75] Out of this nothingness arose an impulse of desire; a longing to "be." The poets of the time noted this impulse as the beginning of existence.[76] It is always the poets who notice things, isn't it?

I find this hymn provocative and beautiful at the same time. It brings me solace for our loss of Pete. While there is no doubt that, had he lived, his life would have been amazing, he chose to live even his few short years as a full expression of his desire to experience life: with humor, passion, and zest for life. He took his gift of life and played with it fully. This hymn suggests to me that there is a Creator, an existence within the chaos that was and is always there, waiting to manifest, wanting to live, to exist. More importantly, maybe this Creator wants me to get the message that His vehicle for living is me; it is you; it was Pete. While there may be no plan for what that will look like; that is part of the brilliance of creation—we get to create the plan.

If, in fact, there is a Creator and the primary rationale for creating each of us is to fully experience what life has to offer, or even if there is not, then all of a sudden I no longer feel sorry or sad about Pete. Today he inspires me to live a life as fully as he did. We don't know if there will be a tomorrow. ■

A MIDLINE PRACTICE

Is there somebody in your life that really matters to you but you haven't spoken with him or her in awhile? Before moving on with your day, pick up the phone and call them, or email or write them, to let them know you are thinking of them.

CHAPTER 22
Elvis points out God

Last summer I took a hike at the top of the Continental Divide, leaving from a base at Rollins Pass, which is 11,660 feet in elevation. From the pass I climbed and began to hike along the Divide, heading north, with amazing views in all directions. There were red, yellow, and purple wildflowers everywhere I looked, spread out along the green grass high above timberline. Rock formations were everywhere. I could look down and west at the Winter Park ski runs, all emerald in the summer sun. The scenery was breathtaking. The air was crisp and clean. The more my senses took in, the more alive I felt. I sensed a feeling of inner peace, like I had "come home." I hadn't just connected to Spirit. I was Spirit.

Unbidden, the lyrics of Elvis Presley's song *If I Can Dream* started playing in my head. He sings about a dream of a land where we all get along and we all can live in hope. As the lyrics played inside me I started to feel Elvis' voice beckon my own dreams for others and myself, including a dream that we can each live a meaningful and happy life. It was as if Elvis had reached out and touched my heart. I felt so alive and ready to do whatever it would take to make my dreams come true; to help create an environment where we all have a chance to make our dreams a reality.

This is what happens to us when we slow down and take time to truly connect to the simple offerings of our world. I wasn't sitting in meditation, doing a yoga pose, or reciting a *Mantra*; I was taking a walk. It is through connection to the experiences life offers, whether in our relationships with other people or by coming vibrantly attentive to our senses as we go about our day, that we further invite our visions to become realities. This is one reason I so appreciate the *Tattvas*. Their teachings show us how to recognize and embrace all the offerings of Spirit that exist in everything and everyone around us.

To better understand how we can use the *Tattvas*, it helps to contrast the viewpoint I discuss in this book with that of a more classical philosophy. For example, early Samkhya philosophy, around 200 C.E., recognized 25 categories of existence, or *Tattvas*, with one of them, the true Self or Spirit, referred to as *Purusha*. The other 24 categories are collectively considered *Prakriti*, or "matter."

We, as humans, are considered *Prakriti*, or matter just like the earth, water, fire, the air and space. A number of such philosophies consider all matter, including us, as separate from Spirit. For these reasons models such as the Samkhya metaphysical model are considered a dualist model, consisting of two distinct aspects: Spirit, *Purusha*, and then everything else, *Prakriti*. There is a God, but It is not us. In some forms of this dualist viewpoint people are even taught to squelch their thoughts, feelings or any other attachment to the material world because the material world is not Spirit. That being the case, the world serves only as a distraction in any attempt to find Spirit. In fact, in some cases life itself is viewed as a prison, keeping us in bondage, separate from Spirit.

I can tell you, when Elvis and I did our hike on Rollins Pass, that experience didn't feel like being in prison. My experiences hanging out with Pete and his friends in college didn't feel like being in prison. It was fun and free. I felt alive and happy, existing as Spirit. When I get off a ski lift at 11,000 or more feet and look out over miles and miles of mountains, woods, and nature, and breathe in the crisp air, I am Spirit. When I play with my grand-kids, Spirit is in the room. My soul soars in these experiences. In fact, it is in these experiences where connection to Spirit becomes easiest.

Obviously, way back when, this idea that our time on earth is a literal "life-sentence" must have felt a bit confusing. So, a revolution occurred sometime around the 7TH or 8TH Century. A group known as Theists, believing there is a personal God who is active in the organization of the universe, developed an additional eleven *Tattvas*.[77] They believed that the 25 *Tattva* model did not sufficiently explain Spirit's role in the world or our relationship with God. This separation between people, nature, and God apparently didn't jive with their experiences.

Think about what these people must have felt. You spend a day going on a picnic to a beautiful lake, walking through picturesque woods, full of vibrant aromas and eye-catching foliage. You lie on a blanket, drink delicious wine, eat some tasty grapes, and listen to birds singing and a nearby waterfall dancing over some rocks. The day eventually ends and you go back home. THAT was prison? No way! The very imbibing in these sensory pleasures felt like a deepened connection to God.

Not surprisingly, an expanded 36 *Tattva* model appeared somewhere around that time. This expanded model sought to accommodate a view of Spirit's presence in the material world. The viewpoint expressed by that model, based on what is considered a "non-dualist" philosophy, holds that Spirit exists as every category of existence: you, me, the animals, the plants, the earth and the sky—everything. Every aspect of our picnic is considered Spirit, from the wine to the tasty cake I didn't even mention.

Since Spirit can be found everywhere and in everything, the goal is to learn to use each category of the *Tattvas* to fully appreciate our day-to-day experiences. To accomplish this, we necessarily must learn to value diversity, the full array of God's offerings to each of us. Think back to my story about my sparring partner, Reggie. By learning from our differences, I developed a more expanded way of viewing the world, thus, making it easier for me to connect to Spirit. Up on the mountain, because of what I'd learned about exploring difference, I was able to tap into Spirit in the form of nature, with a bit of help from Elvis.

Rather than seeking Spirit by separating ourselves from life's experiences, we use the *Tattvas* as a technology for finding Spirit in every form of the material world. Spirit will remain hidden or concealed from us unless we are curious enough and open enough to explore the diversity of life, those persons and things we don't already know.[78] If we stick just to what we already know, our understanding of Spirit is accordingly limited. While it is risky to explore life this way, stepping out of our comfort zone, each time we face that risk is Midline, the chance to connect to Spirit on an even deeper level.

Maybe now you can see what I mean about my grandson Henry's curiosity about all things different and new. Unhampered by bias and judgments, kids recognize that Spirit exists in everything. So it is no surprise that every time something shows up in their day that looks a bit different, they are hungry to explore it. They know, intuitively, that by exploring difference they are connecting to Spirit. This, again, is a reason why I appreciate the lessons of yoga. They bring me back to being like a little kid. Wandering along the mountaintop with Elvis was like being in a candy store with an unlimited budget and a thumbs-up from the dentist. ■

A MIDLINE PRACTICE

Go to a large grocery store, and stand in the middle of the aisles of produce. Spend a few minutes taking in the seemingly endless varieties of fruits, vegetables and flowers on display. Notice the different shapes, the rainbow of colors. Imagine the tastes and enjoy the fragrances.

CHAPTER 23
Kids—the role models for how we can create our lives

I just spent some time with my two grandkids. It was fun watching them take on different roles, depending on what toys they were playing with or whatever else inspired them in the moment. They have innumerable sets of blocks, for example, and they can come up with all forms of architecture when they play with the blocks. They build a tower, and then knock it down. They build a fort, then knock that down and build something else totally different and new.

At some point Lucy gets up and starts painting. Another time she'll put clothes on a doll. These dolls come equipped for travel all over the world: ski trips, biking, hiking, formal dining. Henry plays with his trucks. One minute he is picking up garbage in the garbage truck. The next moment he is putting out a fire with a fire truck. Lucy can be the Little Mermaid, a ballerina, and then, before we know it, a concert pianist. Henry then quickly becomes a drummer. Henry, for his part, can be an EMT and then a hockey player. They are forever creating and re-creating themselves in response to whatever magic they feel in the moment.

There is no end to kids' imagination. We are just the same as these little kids, except we've grown up and lost sight of the magic of imagining what we can create with our lives. Midline offers us a moment of fun and we back away, afraid to look silly. However, that magic is still there; it is our basic nature. That brings me back to my questions about why God made us, and how we can connect to God. A beautiful aspect of non-dual Tantric philosophy is that it suggests answers to these questions that remind us of that magic kids feel daily. It encourages us to re-awaken to the magic.

Spirit created the world in response to feelings of desire, curiosity, a sense of wonder, and the joy of expression. The *Tattvas* explain how this expression takes shape in the world; step by step from God to the ground we walk on. At the very top of the *Kashmir Shaivism* chart of the 36 Tattvas of Tantric Cosmology, Table 1, is *Paramshiva*. *Paramshiva* is considered to be the Supreme Lord[79] or Supreme Auspiciousness.[80] If you're looking to connect to Spirit, here's where it starts!

TATTVA CHART

Paramshiva

Shiva   Shakti

Sadashiva   Isvara   Suddhavidya
(Iccha)   (Jnana)   (Kriya)

Psychical *Tattvas*

Maya

Kala Kanchuka – limits power to act
Vidya Kanchuka – limits power to know
Raga Kanchuka – limits sense of feeling complete
Niyati Kanchuka – limits sense of cause and effect
Kala Kanchuka – limits our perspective of time

Physical *Tattvas*

Purusha   Prakriti

Buddhi – understanding; intellect
Ahamkara – ego
Manas – mind

Jnanendriyas (Sensory organs)	Karmendriyas (Action organs)
Ears	Arms/hands
Eyes	Legs/feet
Nose	Mouth
Tongue	Genitals
Skin	Excretory

Tanmatras (Subtle elements)	Mahabhutas (Gross elements)
Smell	Earth
Taste	Water
Sight	Fire
Touch	Air
Sound	Space

The term "Auspiciousness" indicates that the foundational nature of Spirit is goodness. While we are free to act in ways that are not considered good, our nature is to make more beauty and harmony, even if we have to do so out of tragedy or loss. The word *Paramshiva* is derived from *Param* which means "Supreme," and *Siva* which means "the Auspicious One" and is traditionally associated with kindness and friendliness.[81]

Kashmir Shaivites view *Paramshiva* as the highest source of benevolence.[82] This fits with my life's experiences. I find that any time I act selfishly, serving my personal interests but at the sacrifice of somebody else, I'm ultimately bothered by that choice. For awhile I can create a story around my choice which rationalizes my self-indulgent behavior, but in moments of meditation or other quiet times, if I'm honest with myself, I know that I've acted contrary to my true nature. Yoga practices, particularly meditation, bring us real freedom by piercing through the layers of our rationalizing stories into our true essence, where we remember our connection to each other and how we diminish that connection by selfish behavior.

How does the process of creation occur? How does *Paramshiva* show up as our neighbor's dog or us? Imagine Spirit, whether we call Her *Rta*, God, *Paramshiva*, or whatever name works for us, holding a mirror in which She can see Her reflection, Her shining light of potential. When Spirit sees Her reflection, She sees unlimited possibilities. For the reasons I've stated (to play, to explore, to express), Spirit decides to split Her energy into many different forms, with each form being a unique and diverse, although limited, expression of Spirit.

Just like the innumerable ways my grandkids can play act, assuming numerous roles while still being Lucy and Henry, Spirit, too, elects to take on an endless stream of roles. Spirit, out of a desire to fully enjoy Her power to make different expressions of music, created Mozart, Beethoven, Pavarotti, Elvis, and Bob Dylan. Each is Spirit just as Henry is a drummer or an EMT, but is also Henry. In order to experience the playfulness of physical form, Spirit created Michael Jordan, Mikhail Baryshnikov, and Wayne Gretzky, as well as lions, cobras, and moose. In order to satisfy Her taste buds, Spirit created chocolate, strawberries, endless varieties of wines, and pizza. To fully explore Her creative potential, Spirit created Monet, Rembrandt, and Redon; but also computer chips and ibuprofen.

This non-dualist understanding of the *Tattvas* teaches us that the way Spirit creates our universe is the very same process we can employ every day to create our own world. Spirit is creating through us. Just like my grandkids, we can use our imagination and gifts to manifest a life of magic. ▪

A MIDLINE PRACTICE

Take a walk down any urban or suburban street. Notice the various ways the designers expressed themselves in the shapes of each house or building. Even if the street you select happens to be one where the buildings all look the same, notice the assorted ways the occupants have decorated the windows or landscaped the properties.

CHAPTER 24
Let's dance!

In the 1930's and 40's there was a great dance team, Fred Astaire and Ginger Rogers. They made movies together and are one of the top dance partnerships of all time. They were playful, emotional, creative and energetic: spinning, waltzing, dipping, sliding, and singing their way into the hearts of moviegoers everywhere. Part of their on-screen appeal was the way they charmed, courted, and inspired each other.[83] Even though it was a movie, they appeared to totally love what they were doing and their passion came through to audiences.[84]

This reminds me of the dance between *Shiva* and *Shakti,* the next steps on the *Tattva* journey, Table 1. *Shiva* exists as the beacon of what can be, and *Shakti* is the creative energy that reflects that potential back to *Shiva*. This dance results in the manifestation of you, me—everything in our world. Together, like Ginger Rogers and Fred Astaire, the delightfully creative power of *Shakti* spins and weaves with *Shiva's* shining light of unlimited promise. Together, they dance our world into a rousing existence. It is out of this process that creation occurs. The feeling that arises spontaneously from this creation is joy, *Ananda*.

I can only imagine what a sheer, inventive blast it must have been for both of them when Fred Astaire and Ginger Rogers got together to create their artistry. Just as in the creation story, these two gifted dancers must have constantly reflected each other's light back to the other, urging and coaxing each other into ever more spectacular spontaneous creative expression with each step. Each time they danced it was *Spanda*, a give and take in which one served as yin to the other's yang.

They drew out of each other even more amazing originality than either could individually imagine might exist. They extracted from the other their highest potential. How much easier it would be for all of us to recognize and step into the invitations of Midline if we had such relationships in our lives, relationships gently coaxing us to take the risk of enjoying the moment, constantly mirroring for us our potential.

This Divine dance is ongoing in our daily lives. Just as Fred and Ginger created new dance steps constantly, we too have the capacity to re-fashion our world each day based on our experiences and the choices we make. Throughout the day we stand across from a Fred or Ginger and they encourage us to find our greatest potential. They invite us to dance. Mark the disabled skier invited me to dance through his courage and demeanor. Lucy invited Henry to dance when she showed him how to climb a wall. My friend Bruce invited me to dance when he told me I could be a good lawyer. When I teach yoga, I'm not only teaching poses, I'm teaching my students how to dance with their promise. When you serve in relationship with others, as a friend, a parent, a teacher, a partner, a spouse, as somebody's boss or co-worker, you can encourage greatness from all those around you.

When we appreciate this process of *Prakasha* and *Vimarsha* in our lives, we start to get it that anybody at any given moment can be our Fred or Ginger. We then immediately view them as somebody not only to respect but also somebody to be nurtured because we have a vested interest in their full expression in life. They are the mirrors for our light; the very persons who might in any moment encourage us to a greater expression of ourselves.

Wouldn't it be great if the very first things we thought of when we interacted with another was this: "How can I inspire this person in this moment?" or "What is it about this person that makes meeting them just now such a gift?" That would really spice up our dancing. ■

A MIDLINE PRACTICE

The very next time you interact with a co-worker or, if you work alone, another human being, find a way to compliment that person about something, however simple.

CHAPTER 25
Why would Michael leave a perfectly good career to play baseball?— Sadashiva Tattva and Iccha Shakti

When my son was a senior in high school he was named one of Minnesota's top 25 college football recruits. We were thrilled. Numerous colleges contacted him to attend their school. However, he really wanted to play both college ice hockey and football. That made his choice difficult because most big schools had no interest in extending a scholarship to a student who was going to play both of those sports: the seasons overlapped too much, among other reasons. In addition, Jeff was over 6'3"and while 205 to 210 pounds made for a nice-sized, quick hockey player, it limited his potential in football. His frame could handle 230 pounds or more, making him a possibility for linebacker, a tight end, or other positions, but that could slow him down as hockey player. Nonetheless, he found a college that told him he could play both sports.

Off he went to college. He enrolled in a big time Division 1 school and eagerly spent the summer getting in condition for both sports. Cyndi and I tried one more time to convince him he was biting off way too much and should just stick to his favorite sport, hockey. He acknowledged that, but said he would never be happy if he didn't at least try to compete at the major college level as a football player to find out how good he really was. He was willing to undertake huge hardship and stress to find out the answer to that question.

If that weren't enough, one day I visited him out east to see a football game and as we walked by the indoor facility where the varsity rowing teams sometimes practiced, he said he wanted to try that sport. He was serious. We looked at each other and, after a minute, we both laughed; when would he find the time or the energy? Fortunately, even Jeff decided that enough was enough.

I share this story to illustrate the next step in the *Tattvas—Sadashiva,* which means "always *Shiva.*"[85] This is the point when *Shiva* sees a reflection from *Shakti* that plants the seeds of what could be created out of their dance. *Shiva* now becomes aware not only of himself but also the possibility of an "other," an object other than Him. Within this awareness is the potential of creation.[86] This reminds me of Jeff as he walked by the rowing facility. For just a moment *Shakti*'s energy planted within him the vision of a rowing career. Knowing him, he saw himself in the Olympics, rowing hard for the U.S.A.

At this level of the *Tattvas,* the desire to "be" pulsates so loudly and strongly that it cannot be ignored. The questions for Spirit, though, are: with unlimited choices, what to create, where to begin? What to choose? The same is true for us. Jeff went off to college and wanted to play so many different sports. Which ones? This was also true with decisions about what major to pursue. Should he be an engineer or architect, or lawyer? Should he remodel homes? These were all options he considered based on his desires.

The very act of going off to college and pondering his future was a response to the creative spark inside him, revealing to him a glimpse of the kind of life he could create. He hadn't created that life yet but in an instant he could see endless possibilities for his future. He was at the stage of his life beginning the process of turning an "I" into a "this"—his future and his role in the world.[87] These are some of the most significant Midline issues we deal with in our lives, making the choices of how to express ourselves in the world, how to create for ourselves a life of meaning and significance.

The energy associated with *Sadashiva* is called *Iccha Shakti. Iccha* means willpower or desire. Here, just like my son when he started college, Spirit has a sense of wonder and a desire to fully know Itself.[88] Because we are each manifestations of Spirit, we also have the energy of *Iccha Shakti,* existing as our desire to experience our own potential.[89]

Because of *Iccha Shakti* we all, down deep, want to know what we are made of; how we stack up. I see it in little kids, particularly my grandkids as they went through the "Terrible Twos" (or is it Threes?). They insisted on getting into the car seat without help, and threw a conniption if you tried to help. Then and now they want to "be." They want to experience their independence and express who they are. This urge isn't just for little kids or young people finishing high school. This energy is always with us.

It shouldn't be surprising that once we find success in our job or whatever other venture we undertake, we will begin to hear a subtle voice whispering to us that there might be "something more" or "something different" we could be doing with ourselves. That voice is the spark of *Iccha Shakti* enticingly whispering: "That's great; what's next?" "That woman playing the piano sounded amazing; I bet you can learn to play like that." "Tell your boss about this great idea you have to expand your role in the company." "You can run a marathon." "Of course you can be a teacher!"

Acknowledging that spark and then taking the risk, to explore being an even greater presence in the world, is one way we step into the Midlines of life. This is how we build a life that truly flourishes and is filled with meaning.

Remember the famous basketball player, Michael Jordan? He was certainly one of the greatest players of all time. For some seemingly inexplicable reason, he decided to become a pro baseball player. People couldn't understand why a person who was at the pinnacle of his sport would go off in a different direction. They thought something must be wrong with him. Jordan gave as his reason the fact that he had lost his desire to play basketball. He left the NBA and signed a contract with the Chicago White Sox baseball team. He was sent to the minor leagues and after a short, not-too-glamorous stab at baseball, returned to the NBA, where he again became a prominent star.

I don't know Michael Jordan at all, so I don't know what went on inside him when he made these choices. Even though he was one of the greatest basketball players ever, and I mean ever, I suspect that deep down he had some unanswered questions. I wonder if what really motivated Michael Jordan was his desire to find out if he could play baseball at as high a level as he played basketball. How good of an athlete was he? Did he have what it takes? In any event, he had the courage to step into Midline and find out, risking looking foolish in order to fully explore his potential.

There is a wonder and joy in seeing what we are capable of manifesting or even finding the courage to try. It is important that we be aware of that urge inside us and, as we can and where we can, do something about it. Spirit beckons us to live life fully and not hold back. Spirit calls us to Midline. ■

▌ A MIDLINE PRACTICE

Without regard to practicalities, such as income, education, training, or time, ponder for a few minutes what career you would really enjoy other than the one you have now.

CHAPTER 26
Things are getting clearer— Isvara Tattva *and* Jhana Shakti

I've had some great teachers. One who comes to mind is my high school English teacher Carol Fisher. I remember when she asked us to read and discuss some Robert Frost poems, including "Stopping by the Woods on a Snowy Evening." One of the first questions she asked us was why the horse and owner would stop by the woods that night? Why would they do that when there were promises to keep and miles to go before sleep? To us, the obvious answers included: "So the horse could relieve itself." or, "To case the house out."

However, even back then, as we were sitting there giving silly answers, my mind was dying to understand what she really wanted, what Frost may have meant. I could see vague, blurry forms of answers lurking in my brain but I couldn't quite get any answer to come clear, even as I tried and tried to put substance to those hazy forms.

Ms. Fisher moved around the room, prodding us with hints. Eventually we started to look at this poem differently. She slowly coaxed us into a serious discussion where no interpretation was too silly or too out there to be considered. I remember how much fun we all had that day. For me, the vague answers started to take on more and more shape. We moved on to "The Road Not Taken," and immediately we all turned to that poem, completely engaged and excited to see where it took us.

Egos aside, all that mattered to us was our opportunity to delve deeply into Frost's words and see what they might mean: "Why the sigh?" "Why did taking the road less traveled make all the difference?" Ms. Fisher had us totally hooked. I wish we had pictures of what our faces looked like, all excited and screwed up in thought, as we each sought to put some "meat on the bones" of those answers sitting just a touch out of reach inside our active minds.

This story helps illustrate the next place on the *Tattva* chart, Table 1, "*Isvara*," which means "Lordship." Like a landowner looking out over the landscape of his vast property, Spirit's vague image of "other" begins to come into clearer focus.[90] Now, at the level of *Isvara Tattva*, the fuzzy picture of the future starts to become a bit clearer as Spirit begins to perceive a picture of what can become real, what can be created out of Spirit's unlimited power and vision.[91]

See how this parallels our own life's journey? My son gravitated more towards a liberal arts program, beginning to see his future lay in that direction. After one year of success playing football, he dropped that sport and stuck with hockey, in time becoming one of his college ice hockey team captains. Today he is a businessman and continues to play hockey. The fuzzy vision of his future that he held as a freshman began to take on particular shapes.

The energy of *Isvara* is called *Jhana Shakti*, the energy of knowledge, because as our vision moves from fuzzy to some level of clarity, as we start to see where we fit and how we might contribute, we associate this increased clarity with the attainment of knowledge. Where things were fuzzy, we now have some clarity of where we can go with our lives. We now identify ourselves with the world.[92]

This is part of the gift Ms. Fisher gave us and the gift we can give each other. She helped us move from the stage in our lives when we knew we had potential but didn't know what to make of our potential. She enriched us by teaching us how to think and view the world. We learned that the world offered subtleties and nuances that mattered. Our curiosity was triggered. She taught us how to face Midline head on by creating an environment in which we didn't worry about looking silly or sounding dumb. The more wild our interpretation of poetry the more fun we all had, the more we reveled in creative thought.

We were some of the luckiest students in the world to have had classes with Ms. Fisher because that time with her made the rest of our lives fuller, richer, and deeper. We saw the world as possibility and we hungered to gather as much knowledge about it as we could.

This is part of the beauty of this philosophy and the reason it brings so much hope to our lives and to the world. We can do for each other what Ms. Fisher did for her students and what college did for my son. We can help each other find clarity of purpose and focus for our dreams and aspirations. We can teach each other how to find the Midlines of life and have the courage to step into them. That would be a life of meaning. ∎

A MIDLINE PRACTICE

Pretend that you are a home stager hired to get your house ready to sell for maximum dollar. In your mind's eye, re-do the living room and a bedroom to properly stage the house to sell.

CHAPTER 27
Making things happen—
Suddhavidya Tattva and Kriya Shakti

I remember a woman, Mary, who used to come to my yoga class every Wednesday. She was middle-aged and held a clerical position within a big group at a large company in its Denver office. When I first met her she told me she wanted to build up her strength and fitness. I also learned over time that her divorce had sapped much of her self-confidence. In response, I carefully structured my class sequences to help build her strength. Mary came to class every week and also started a home practice so that she could meet her goals. Initially, she couldn't lower herself to the floor from a pushup position without being on her knees. Gradually, as she continued to come to class and practice at home, she gained strength and was able to easily do pushups in proper form. Over time, her arm balances became stronger and she didn't have to modify them.

One day we had a snowstorm and the driving conditions were terrible. Mary was the only person who showed up for class. I suggested to her after she had warmed up that it might be time for her to do her first assisted handstand. She said she was afraid but as long as I spotted her, she would try. I stood against the wall while she got ready and then we took her to the Down Dog position. I held her hips and had her spring up against the wall. Up she went. She was so strong that I moved a hand to the top of her feet, giving her more and more of her own weight and feeling of freedom. She then found a place of balance and I slid my hand away, ready to take her hips if necessary.

At that moment I told her to look back at the mirror on the opposite wall, which she could see between her arms. I said: "Who's that balancing in handstand?" She squealed with laughter and I brought her down. She continued to laugh, then started to cry and gave me a giant hug and said "Thank you so much."

Not long after Mary came to class and said that she had some good news and some bad news. I asked her to give me the good news first. She said that earlier in the week her boss called her in to his office and told her that over the last year she had become a powerful leader in her group. He said that he didn't know what she had "done to herself" but that everybody was impressed. Because of that, the company had decided to promote her to a regional group leader, a promotion that came with a very big raise. Mary was beaming. I congratulated her and then asked her for the bad news. She replied that the bad news was that the promotion required her to move to another state, so she wouldn't be able to come to my class anymore.

A couple of months later Mary sent me a card thanking me for helping her find her own inner strength through building her outer strength. She said that she had tried other ways to get stronger, both inside and out, but that somehow my class had resonated with her "just right." I was really touched by her words.

A major goal in my life for some time now has been to become a nicer, kinder man. Since practicing and studying yoga had been such a great way to move in that direction I figured learning to teach yoga would be even better. I tried hard to learn as much as I could about teaching and, along the way, I found that I really cared about my students. I truly wanted them to be happy and successful. As I read Mary's card over and over I discovered something I hadn't realized. From her words I saw that just as Mary had transformed herself into a strong leader, I, too, was transforming. I was becoming the very nicer and kinder man I had set my sights on creating. We had both embraced Midline; stepping out of familiar old patterns to realize more of life's potential.

This story helps explain the next step of creation, *Suddhavidya,* or pure knowledge. At this level of creation Spirit's vision of how to manifest in the world has come into a sharp focus. Spirit sees the objects of Her creation, the "other," but also sees the unity of Herself with that creation; She sees both as One.[93] My clear vision and commitment to Mary's potential resulted in a manifestation of potential for both of us.

Suddhavidya Tattva is associated with the energy of *Kriya Shakti,* the power of doing. It is a step in which we take the clarity of knowing what to do with ourselves and put it into action. My son's college experience, a time for discovery, helped him create a life in which he is now a family man and an important member of his community. He earned an MBA and holds a management position at his place of business. Ms. Fisher's students have made her proud. Mary became a leader.

This step is referred to as "pure" knowledge because at this stage of the creation myth, God's actions are solely in furtherance of creating objects in harmony with Her own true nature. This is true because God or Spirit recognizes that She is each of the very objects She creates. Spirit is creating more of Himself/Herself with each one of us. In this philosophy Spirit is both a He and a She, and every time I refer to Spirit as He, She, or It, we both know that we mean this Larger Thought.

It would be great if we all lived as if we were pure Spirit, viewing everyone and everything as simply a different version of us, intrigued by the differences. However, this isn't reality for most of us. We forget this true nature and, instead, perceive the world as separate from us, separate from Spirit.[94] ∎

A MIDLINE PRACTICE

Spend a few minutes thinking about a co-worker or friend who you believe is living with unrealized potential. Think what that potential would look like if encouraged to blossom.

CHAPTER 28
The desire to create knows no bounds—
Iccha, Jhana, and Kriya

There is a tiny restaurant in Winter Park that primarily sells hot dogs and bratwurst, although it turns out a yummy hamburger as well. The owner is a man named Matt and the restaurant is Fraser Valley Hot Dogs. I use the word "restaurant" loosely because it is a tiny, one-room place. You walk in the door and immediately to the right are the cash register and a little cooking area. There's room for about five people to sit down.

Falling in love with this restaurant is pretty easy to do. First of all, when you walk in the door, if you've ever been there before, Matt will likely greet you by your first name or will say something to you to let you know he remembers you and is happy you're there. I walked in one time and Matt immediately asked me how my trip to Boston went. I had traveled to Boston for Christmas but didn't remember telling him I was going. Yet, he remembered and even asked me if I had been able to skate with my son, since he knew I had wanted to do that on the trip.

As I understand it, Matt started out running a summer hot dog stand from a cart in a parking lot along Highway 40. He sold great food, treated people well, and dreamed about opening a year-round, inside restaurant. Not only has he brought that dream into fruition, he may be on national television because the word has gotten out. I can't wait to see the show and I guess I'd better go get a "Bison Chipotle Cheese Brat" so I can congratulate him in person.

Matt's success story is a real-world example of the way the three energies of *Iccha, Jhana,* and *Kriya Shakti* work together. *Iccha Shakti,* our willpower or desire "to be," is a primal urge. We constantly desire to express ourselves, just like Matt wanted to move from one vision, the hot dog stand, to the bigger vision of the restaurant. Once we focus on what we wish to create, we gather the knowledge necessary to make it happen. This is *Jhana Shakti.* We study and observe, and we apply ourselves. We make choices that most align with becoming that which our dream demands of us and society asks of us.

For Matt to have become so successful he not only learned the craft of making his food; he also learned the art of treating customers well so that they would want to return. He learned the art of business. He also has learned the art of living in Midline, how to recognize the potential in each moment and get out of his own way in order to manifest his dream. If we wish to manifest our dreams, we similarly need to figure out how to align in our workplace and with our family, friends and community to make those desires come true.

Finally, we put our efforts and study into action. Matt expanded his business and now the door may be opening for even more possibility. This is *Kriya Shakti*.

This interaction or cycle of *Iccha, Jhana, and Kriya Shakti* constantly repeats itself. Our nature is expansive, longing to be more, to explore the horizon, even as we enjoy our current place in life. Even after achieving success we will be prodded by that burning desire to create even more. We look inside ourselves and ask questions such as: What else can I be? How deep can I go? How richly can I taste life? Remember Michael Jordan turning to baseball? Matt's expansion from the relatively safe summer-only hot dog stand to the year-round restaurant is another example. So, once we've put out into the world the final product of our dream, we will cycle from our *Kriya* or action back to *Iccha Shakti*.

Again, as I noted earlier, this isn't type A behavior. This is our true nature. This is how our whole world becomes richer. Think of Walt Disney and how much more magic he brought to every one of us by not resting in his own success. It's our nature to fully express ourselves and, in doing so, honoring Spirit. We're the "other" Spirit saw in the mirror. ■

A MIDLINE PRACTICE

Remember sitting down and asking yourself what career you would like to have, other than your current job, if there were no practical limitations? Now ask yourself what would be one thing you could do now to get closer to that career down the road.

PART IV

A Road Map Of the Outer World— The Tattvas

B. Where's Spirit hiding?

CHAPTER 29
It's all an "illusion"—Maya

When I graduated from junior high school, I entered a big, urban high school as a sophomore and tried out for the football team. The high school, Hammond High School in Hammond, Indiana, was the defending state football champion with many of its players returning from the previous seasons. So, "good luck" making the team! The school was large and there were literally a couple hundred kids trying out for football. The varsity regulars and subs practiced at one end of the fields. The rest of us, the freshman, sophomores like me, and those juniors not likely to see playing time, practiced at the other end.

The second afternoon of the two-per-day football practices, a kid ran down to our group and told me the coaches wanted me to come up to where the varsity was practicing. I sprinted up and the coaches, including the legendary head coach Bernie Krueger, gathered around me and asked me where I was from and how had I learned to do the long snap so well. The long snap is the pass from the center through his legs to the punter or to the holder for extra points and field goals. I told him that Jim, the all-state center who had just graduated off the state champ team the year before, lived in my neighborhood and made me learn how to snap so I could make the team.

The rest of the afternoon I practiced with the varsity and soon became the first-string long-snapper. This meant that I would enter the games to snap the ball on every punt, every extra point and every field goal. It also automatically made me the third-string center overall because the school only traveled to away games with three "strings" of players, in my case three centers. Because we were a strong team, again ranked Number 1 in the state, I was guaranteed playing time because the team was always way ahead in most games, allowing subs a chance to play.

After that practice Coach Krueger called me into his office and standing there was this tall muscular guy from the varsity. Coach introduced him as Acie, whom I knew to be one of the returning varsity players from the state champion team. Coach said that now that I was on the varsity, I was moving to the varsity locker room and Acie was there to escort me. Acie and I walked up to the locker room and he showed me my locker, right next to his. Standing on the other side of my locker was another very large guy. He introduced himself as Hayward, (another of the returning players who had played on the state champion team), and, from that day on I felt like I had two good friends. They showed me the ropes and made me feel accepted and like I belonged. Pertinent to this story, both Acie and Hayward are black.

Both Acie and Hayward graduated before me but while we were in school together they made my time in high school, both on the field and in the hallways, welcoming and rewarding. I had been more than a bit intimidated about going to a big school with such a diverse population but these two teammates showed me that we were all just young men in high school trying to get along, discover ourselves, win at sports, and find a way to get dates.

In my senior year, thanks to Coach Krueger and football, I ended up with a choice of colleges to attend. I again was intimidated, thinking that there was no way I could make it through college. It would be way too difficult. One day, after the Augustana College (Illinois) coach came to visit us at our high school and really impressed us, Acie showed up at our school. He was attending Augustana, had made the varsity football team, and was doing well academically. He felt at home there, even though it was far away from our familiar neighborhoods.

I didn't know anything about Augustana College but I did know and trust Acie. If he said I would be okay there, that was enough for me. So, I signed up and so did my teammates Ralph and Chief, as well as Rico, a quarterback from a neighboring rival high school. Not only did we feel comfortable at Augustana, we all graduated. I met my wife there, Jeff's mom. Acie didn't do too badly either—he graduated, got married, teaches at the college level, and had a son who went on to play pro basketball in the NBA. Not bad for some urban kids.

I think about how my life's course was guided in no small way by the kindness and mentoring of a couple of guys who simply treated me like just another guy, never seeing me as somebody separate from them because of the difference in our skin color. We each ignored the outward appearance of "difference" to accept Midline's invitation to relationship.

I use this story to introduce the concept of *Maya*, the next step on the *Tattva* chart. As you look at the *Tattva* chart in Table 1, *Maya* is the place where Spirit is now preparing to separate into the many diverse forms of our universe, including you, me, Acie, Rico, Chief, as well as elephants and giraffes, horses and cows, daisies and daffodils, spruce and aspen trees, strawberries and grapes—everything.

On the *Tattva* chart we are now stepping down from *Suddhavidya* into *Maya*. By way of short review, at the level of *Suddhavidya* Spirit sees the concept of "others" as simply part of Itself, as the endless, different ways Spirit can express Itself. There is no separation, only unity and connection. That is why the level of *Suddhavidya* level is called "pure knowledge." When we view the world as Spirit, we aren't fooled by the many languages, cultures, races, gender preferences and whatever other "isms" operate to keep us at odds with each other. We, as pure Spirit, simply see pure Spirit. We see with "pure knowledge." We don't see a white guy; we see a teammate.

Maya is often translated as "illusion." However, I learned to view *Maya* as the power that creates difference in the universe. As we've seen, in some philosophies the material world is truly viewed as an illusion, not spiritually real, with the goal being to disengage from the material world to find Spirit inside us. However, in the non-dual Tantric philosophy I discuss, the material world is very real, with everything an expression of Spirit. We see through racial, cultural and ethnic differences because we know that we are each simply and beautifully an alternative way of God expressing Itself.

We are each another fun dance step in *Shiva* and *Shakti's* ongoing dance. And we can waltz, tango, line dance or two-step ourselves into Midline because the differences of *Maya* are gifts of endless choices and opportunities. ■

A MIDLINE PRACTICE

Visit an ice cream store and ask to sample three different flavors that appeal to you before buying a cone or dish. Take a minute to appreciate each of the three flavors, recognizing that they are each pretty delicious even while being different.

CHAPTER 30
Difference is "us"

I spent a few moments taking in the amazing scenery one morning on the last day of a visit to Costa Rica. I felt the sweet hint of rain in the air as I gazed out across the bright green hillsides toward the mountains, admiring a sky with starkly varying shades of blue. I once more enjoyed the gardens filled with banana trees, purple orchids, and brilliant red and yellow Parrot Flowers. Even though the air hinted of rain, the sun shined brightly as if to remind me to make the most of that very moment. This may sound strange coming from a lawyer, but that moment made me feel like God was reminding me that I don't have to wait to go to Heaven, it's here right now, everywhere I look. All I have to do is take a minute to open my eyes.

I flew back to Colorado and by the end of the day was sitting in my upstairs home office staring out at a completely different scene: snow covered mountains and valley below—equally beautiful to me, but dramatically different from Costa Rica. Where in the morning I had enjoyed the lush, warm scene I just described, by nightfall I stared out at expanses of towering green lodge pole pines laden with snow, as well as aspens, now stripped bare for winter. I knew that if I waited, moose would walk through my line of sight and perhaps settle on my back hill for a snooze. Although wholly distinctive from my Costa Rican morning, it was, to me, just as stunning, just as heavenly.

Snow started to fall so I went downstairs, opened a bottle of Merlot, started a fire in the big stone fireplace and watched the snow gently falling through the trees while night settled in. As I sipped my wine I again felt connected to Spirit, and whispered a prayer of gratitude to my teachers that they had taught me to slow down and learn how to experience the "Heaven on Earth" that constantly surrounds us.

Spirit, through *Maya*, reveals itself in all the diversity of our world, including not only nature, but also the different types of people we see each day. All that it takes for us to find Spirit is to pay attention. Each person has a special Divine imprint, a unique package of qualities often hidden from view. Unless we make an attempt to find this imprint in others, it may well remain concealed from us. However, if we view people with curiosity, aware that they have something dynamic to offer, that something often will be revealed if we give it a chance.

I used to go to parties or social gatherings and immediately find the people with whom I felt comfortable. If I didn't know anybody, I would find people who looked and dressed like the people I typically hang out with. I felt safe doing this. I didn't have to open myself up to the risk of being rejected by people I didn't know. Eventually, however, I learned that this approach kept me mired in being the same old me. If I wanted to expand my horizons, sharpen my personality, learn new things, and create more connections with people, I had to take the risk of exploring new relationships. This is an example of Midline, taking a risk to possibly create a richer experience.

Now I make it a point to meet someone who would normally be off my radar. It never fails that this person reveals something intriguing, often hidden, but waiting to be revealed to anybody who takes the trouble to get to know him or her. This is the process by which Spirit, once the material world comes into form, is able to express Himself in so many ways. This is the process of *Maya*.

Maya as like a game of hide-and-seek,[95] in that Spirit hides within the infinite forms He creates—trees, flowers, snow, thunderstorms, as well as people like you and me—waiting for us to find Him. Through an understanding of the *Tattvas* we learn that Spirit is never really concealed at all. Each category of the *Tattvas* tells us right where to look.

Unfortunately, too many people are captured by the nature of *Maya*, the illusion that because we are look different, practice a different religion, or live a different lifestyle, for example, that we are truly separate from each other. This viewpoint is the real illusion since we are in fact not separate from each other at all. We are each Spirit, simply cloaked in different forms. The lesson from *Maya* is to treat difference as an invitation to come closer to God. We learn to celebrate difference rather than run from it.

Maya is the vehicle by which we can, through curiosity, relationships, and interactions with each other, begin to get a greater sense of Spirit and, therefore, our true nature. We can explore diversity with a child-like inquisitiveness, searching for the Divine revelation within each other. We can marvel at somebody else's special skill, instead of envying it, because we know that this is just another form of God.

What makes us forget that we are all expressions of Spirit? The *Kanchukas*, the next step on the *Tattva* chart, are the five cloaks by which Spirit conceals Itself from us in our every-day lives. ■

A MIDLINE PRACTICE
Introduce yourself to a neighbor you've yet to meet and spend a few minutes getting to know each other.

CHAPTER 31
A handy tool to find Spirit—the Kanchukas

Years ago, when I first met my friend Bill I didn't care for him. He irritated the heck out of me. He spoke in a really loud voice and was quick to offer his opinions, even when he hadn't been asked. It wasn't clear to me how much education he had. He seemed nothing like me and I usually tried to ignore him. Gradually, however, as I came to know him, I saw him in new ways. Like me, he had gravitated to this group of people because of his deep spiritual interest. His loudness was simply the result of being hard-of-hearing. He wasn't trying to shout over us at all; in fact, he was shy. As for education, he was more educated than most of us. There was quite a bit concealed in this package that was Bill, at least concealed from me at first.

I remember one Saturday morning when we were all sitting around a coffee shop. One of our friends was complaining about the way her boyfriend treated her. This had gone on for a couple of months, ever since she had first announced that she was dating this man. Suddenly, and I'll tone down the language, Bill shouted something to the effect of: "For God's sake, would you dump the bastard or else stop whining about him every week? Please do something to put us all out of our misery!"

This woman initially looked like somebody had slapped her. The whole coffee shop became silent. We looked at Bill a bit aghast; I say "a bit" because this was not unusual for him. Also, every single one of us felt the same way he did. We were beyond tired of hearing our friend complain about this guy and wanted her to break up with him and find somebody who would treat her well. The difference was that Bill had the guts to say something.

After a moment or two of stunned silence, our friend looked at Bill and thanked him, telling us that she knew this guy was bad news but was afraid nobody else would want her. We spent some time telling her how great she was and that she would be sure to find somebody else much more suitable if she would give herself a chance. She did break up with this man, found somebody else, and is now happily sailing along through life. She is living the vision of her life we all could see but she could not, until Bill spoke up.

This is how Bill has been as long as I've known him, revealing Spirit at every turn. He offers his opinions because he has experienced many things in his life and genuinely wants to use that experience to help others.

I remember another time when my son was trying to decide what to do about playing more ice hockey; should he turn pro or should he go to grad school? He had a chance to play professionally, but he also had some strong reasons for not doing so, not the least of which was a torn shoulder that would require surgery. I, however, kept pushing him to turn pro. One day Bill took me aside and said: "You know, you have to leave your kid alone. Is it Jeff's interests that you're thinking about or is it just your desire to tell everybody your kid is a pro hockey player? He's smart enough to figure out what's best for him; why don't you put your ego aside and let him?"

Ouch! Bill was spot on. I'm sure my other friends felt the same way, but nobody else had the nerve to look me in the eye and tell me what they saw. I backed off from trying to impose a choice on my son, one of the wisest things I've ever done. This also represented a great example of successfully navigating Midline. Out of a desire to nurture my relationship with my son I was able to look deep within myself in response to Bill's advice and see where my ego was getting in the way of that relationship. Of course, for Bill, Midline was much easier to navigate because his desire to express himself as Spirit, to serve his friends, was so strong that there were few risks he wouldn't take to make that happen.

Over time I sought Bill out more and more. I eventually found Bill to be one of the most caring, kind, interesting and thoughtful men I'd ever met. When one of us was in trouble or really hurting, he was always there. He could step into any situation and help resolve it, somehow bringing laughter into the process. In short, he was everything I wanted to become as a man. He was Spirit big time, hidden from me behind layers of apparent hard edges and my propensity to judge others.

I mention Bill to lead off a discussion of the *Kanchukas*, the five ways Spirit, through the power of *Maya*, steps down into diversification in order to make our world. This is how Spirit makes the "others" manifest in our material world.

In the myth of creation, Spirit uses these five *Kanchukas* to conceal Herself through all the diverse forms on our planet. Mark Dyczkowski, in his book, *Doctrine of Vibration*,[96] explains how Spirit hides Her five primary powers through the *Kanchukas*. These primary powers are: 1) the unlimited ability to act; 2) unlimited knowledge; 3) an essence of fullness or completeness; 4) freedom from the natural law of cause and effect; and 5) eternality (freedom from the operation of time). These limitations are often called the five cloaks or veils that can hide Spirit from us.

The *Kanchukas* initially operated to cloak my ability to find Spirit in Bill when I first met him. Initially, I found that I wasn't in control; I felt powerless when he was around. The group didn't pay much attention to me, the highly educated and successful lawyer from the famous firm. They hung on every word Bill had to say but mustered only routine courtesy when I spoke. Even worse, when I did butt in and offer my opinion, it generally turned out that I was way off base, with no clue whatsoever about the bigger picture. Bill, on the other hand, was always right on, cutting through the problem and finding the response that served our friends. Finally, to add insult to injury, he called me out on my limitations, and that frightened me. "Me? There's something about me that could use some improvement? I don't want to hear that!"

Second, because I didn't try to get to know him for some time, his attributes, the things about him that made him so special, remained hidden from me. Here was a truly great human being walking around but my refusal to get to know him blinded me to what he was really like. I limited my chance to connect to him and this group of friends through my limited knowledge of Bill's depth.

Third, my own lack of fullness, my sense of inadequacy as a man's man whenever I was around him kept me from seeing his true nature. I think I was flat-out jealous. I felt incomplete, not because of his efforts to make me feel that way but rather, because he represented so much of what I could be if I would overcome my own sense of inadequacy.

Fourth, for some time I created a rift between us because of my refusal to get to know him and give him a chance. I occasionally pushed him away out of my own sense of envy. This, again, blocked me from connecting with a person who would eventually become a valued friend. It also limited my ability to connect with our group of friends because I remained blind to my own social shortcomings. What a great example of cause and effect.

Eventually the passage of time removed the cloaks that prevented me from seeing Bill as Spirit. He hadn't come in the package I expected so it took time for our relationship to develop. Also, over time, I became much more of what I respected in him, in no small part due to being around him so much and learning from those experiences.

As this example shows, the *Kanchukas* operate to cloak Spirit, distracting us from what is really right in front of us. We can only do so much, so we should stop living under the illusion that we can control everything. We very seldom know all the facts in any particular situation, so we learn to avoid jumping to conclusions. We sometimes feel inadequate. But, knowing we each have our own set of strengths, and that none of us can be perfect, removes the burden of having to always be the star of the show. And we can't know the ramifications down the road of what we do. As a result, we keep in mind the law of cause and effect, spending more time considering the long-term possible effects of what we are about to say or do. Finally, we can't predict how something that seems a problem today will turn out over time, so we learn to sometimes just let go.

Being aware of our natural-born limitations, represented by the *Kanchukas*, helps us make wiser choices in our lives. By acknowledging these limitations, we open the door to Spirit. We become available to Midline. ■

A MIDLINE PRACTICE
Can you think of a person in your life you initially didn't care for or paid no attention to but now you're happy to know them?

CHAPTER 32
We really can do anything!—Kala Kanchuka

I recall the Viet Nam protests of the 1960's and early 1970's. Clearly no single person or small groups were able to stop the war. I remember how over time we became more and more enraged as our friends and family members kept dying or came home wounded and disabled. We knew there was no good reason. The government kept talking to us like we were children and that only further fueled our anger. Eventually, this anger and frustration, when collectively engaged, was transmuted into an overwhelming energy forcing an end to the war. The protestors, most of whom started with a sense of frustration over their lack of power to make a change, united collectively and brought about this important result. By being in touch with their initial feelings of frustration and seeming impotence, they connected to each other and, through that connection transmuted these feelings into the omnipotence of Spirit.

Like the Viet Nam war protestors seeking to end that war, we can find connection with others to bring about that which we as individuals cannot accomplish. We see this all the time. When a large river floods, no single person can prevent the river from overflowing into the town. However, many people filling sandbags can stop the flood. In countries where enough citizens decide to provide for the health of their neighbors, affordable health care is available for everyone.

This brings us to the first *Kanchuka*, called *Kala*. Here Spirit' omnipotence, *Kriya Shakti*, Its unlimited power to do anything, is limited in us. As a human, I can't do everything. I can't play violin like Isaac Stern or hockey like Wayne Gretzky. I can't pick room colors like the designers on HGTV or, you name it, many other things people do so well. This is the result of Spirit manifesting in the world in my particular body. While there are many things I can do, it is true that I am limited. Unfortunately, if I kid myself that I can do anything I want, I may try to control everything around me. Believe me, I've tried. Inevitably, this can only result in disappointment, frustration, and anger. Such emotions often cause us to act in inappropriate ways.

I think this may be a clue as to why we guys have the rap of refusing to ask for directions. We all react the very same way if somebody suggests we look at a map or stop for help at the gas station: "No way!" It's not just about trying to impress our wife or date. I think we have this built-in insistence that, in the clutch, we are Superman—we really can do anything. I have to admit I've become lost in places where nobody could become lost.

But, ask somebody for directions? Not a chance! Eventually, I meekly give up, pull in to a gas station and make an inquiry, and get pointed in the right direction.

By recognizing that we can't possibly do everything, we can use this realization as a tool for positive action. While we acknowledge that we are indeed limited in some ways as to what we can accomplish individually, we can also remember that we are all part of something larger than just us. We are all Spirit, and Spirit has no such limitations because, collectively, we can accomplish way more than we can as individuals. Our capacity to create change becomes far stronger because it draws upon the cumulative capacity of everyone else.

We can also use the knowledge of our limitations to effect personal change. Once we acknowledge that we are limited, we become free to explore what changes we can make in our life which are within our power. I mentioned my student Mary and her lack of physical strength and low level of self-confidence. She made a commitment to do something about this situation. Through practicing yoga she developed her outer body strength and discovered an inner strength and character. As she discovered this inner strength she began to carry herself with that recognition and her leadership skills quickly became apparent to her bosses.

From all my conversations with Mary I believe that what motivated her to begin her serious yoga study was an acknowledgement that while she felt powerless, she knew there was something she could do about it. She could explore who she was and how she fit in the world. Rather than try to force any outcome, she had the patience and dedication to explore and peel away the clouds shrouding her particular greatness. This was an important Midline for Mary; courageously recognizing her lack of strength and self-confidence, setting a course for change, and then following through, giving her greater access to life's possibilities. ■

▌ A MIDLINE PRACTICE

Remember a project, whether at work, at home, or in the community, which succeeded because you worked with others.

CHAPTER 33
It's good to admit we don't know—
Vidya Kanchuka

When we become aware that we don't know something, it is a gift. It makes us explore and learn. Think, for example, of all the advances in science that grew out of researchers admitting that they didn't know something. In 1895 a German physicist named Wilhelm Roentgen accidentally discovered X-rays while he was conducting experiments on another project. He won the Nobel Prize in Physics in 1901 for this discovery. A biologist from Scotland accidently discovered the life-saving antibiotic penicillin while working on something else. The 2011 Nobel Prize in Physics went to three men who discovered that the expansion of the Universe might be speeding up, whatever that means.

In each of these cases, and in many more, important discoveries are made because people understand that their knowledge is limited. Because they are able to recognize that fact, and because they are curious and hungry to expand their knowledge, we are all better off. This is why it is important to understand the powers of the *Kanchukas*. By our very nature, because we are limited expressions of Spirit, we cannot know everything. But, if we can step into Midline by recognizing that limitation, we become free to look for and embrace new ideas and opportunities. By just admitting the obvious, we can't know everything; we take our egos off the hook. We are then open to explore and grow.

This brings us to the next *Kanchuka,* called *Vidya,* Table 1. Here Spirit reduces Its unlimited knowledge, *Jhana Shakti,* into limited knowledge. We can only know so much. If I studied to be a lawyer, I can't likely know how to be a doctor. Even as a lawyer, if I specialize in litigation, I probably shouldn't be doing your taxes. We seek out the top orthopedic surgeon to fix our broken arm, but don't want her replacing our heart valve. Similarly, each of us, no matter how well traveled and educated, have only a finite amount of knowledge and experiences.

We may get upset with ourselves, feeling we don't know anything, or even that we are stupid. We then feel incomplete and separate from others. Because of ego and the desire to look good, we may speak or act anyway, with only limited knowledge. This leads to mistakes: We misinterpret. We fail to communicate. We "put our foot in our mouth." We judge unfairly. Such behavior inevitably leads to the very separation we fear.

This *Kanchuka* is a gift because it can open us to learning something new and different, increasing our knowledge base. This, in turn, gives us a broader perspective from which to enjoy our world and also makes us more interesting to be around. Acknowledging that our understanding of something is limited leads to great results, as demonstrated by the scientists I described at the beginning of this chapter. We seek out answers. Like the scientists, our curiosity is what leads us to discovery. We find Spirit where we never thought to look. Simply admitting that we can't know everything makes it far more likely we will recognize Midline and welcome its invitations. ■

A MIDLINE PRACTICE

Do you know more today about how to do your job well than the first day you started it?

CHAPTER 34
Don't suppress the itch—Raga Kanchuka

I remember a girlfriend of mine, Jane, who, after watching me struggle with some job frustrations, said to me one day: "Why don't you open your own firm? Those clients don't care what firm you are in. They like and trust you." I had never considered doing that. I gave her all sorts of reasons why opening my own firm wouldn't work and she answered me, excuse for excuse, showing me why I could do it. Jane's loving prodding eventually got through, showing me things I hadn't realized. The clients who had hired our firm for this particular product liability case, while impressed with the firm, had really hired me. They liked me. They trusted me. I knew the case better than anybody. She was right.

Jane's comments rekindled in me a long-dormant desire to manifest myself fully, be top dog, in charge, and find out if I was as talented as I thought I was. Although I chose not to leave the firm at that time, the conversation opened doors I later was able to walk through. Also, my attitude changed once I was back in touch with my ability to create something different if I wanted to. I felt free because I knew my choice to stay with the firm was freely made and not made from anger, fear, resentment, envy or other emotions that lull us into sometimes making really lousy choices.

This brings us to the third *Kanchuka,* called *Raga. Raga* can hide from us our *Iccha Shakti,* our willpower and our desire to make our mark in the world. We may have a sense that something holds us back from chasing our dreams and making them a reality. We feel like we are stuck in situations and can't figure out what to do. Unfortunately, over time, if we constantly ignore our dreams we will begin to feel empty and unworthy. We can become depressed. We may even give up dreaming, using all our energy just to make it through the day.

I wasn't happy in my old law firm. I had, over the years, made things tough for myself because of my ego and failure to appreciate how things I said and did affected people, alienating some. Over time I felt my spirit slowly being strangled, my vision of myself as a significant member of an important firm, my vision of myself as a meaningful person, dying a slow but seemingly sure death. It was pretty awful. I wanted out of there but because of my spirit's malaise; I couldn't visualize any other alternative.

What Jane did for me was open my eyes to possibilities I hadn't had the energy or courage to even consider; I could leave and start my own firm. I had the means to do so. Awakening to these facts, my spirit soared like a jet rocketing off into the sky. My *Iccha Shakti,* my desire to be everything Spirit made possible for me when I was born was rocking, no longer hidden by my funk.

Think of a time in your life when you found yourself in a job or a relationship that you knew wasn't serving you but, like me, you no longer believed in yourself enough to make a change. So, you stayed. Perhaps you are in that situation now or you have a friend who is in that spot. This *Kanchuka* teaches us that circumstances inherent to being a human being can result in our feeling overwhelmed. We lose track of our dreams and the power we have to make those dreams come true. Society often cooperates to squelch our dreams. Friends, trying to say the right thing, wishing to keep the status quo, or simply reflecting their own lack of confidence, are always there, it seems, to talk us out of taking some step that might improve our lives. It seems like every time we find Midline in life, there is always somebody willing to help us stand pat in our fear while the opportunity slips away.

Hopes and dreams don't die; they are simply hidden. We learn from this *Kanchuka* that even though we feel down and without hope, the dreams are still there, waiting to be awakened. The very fact that we feel so low is a suggestion from Spirit that it is time to do some work; to dig deep and figure out why we've forgotten our greatness. This is a reason why Dr. Seligman's advice is so important: we have to learn our special strengths so that we can find the means to use them in a way that brings meaning back to our hearts. We do so perhaps by using those strengths as a volunteer or in a hobby, if a job change isn't possible. We start making plans for the future when circumstances might be more favorable to change. Accomplishing anything of value by using our strengths will help snap us out of our downer mood.

Not all situations are easily resolvable, but the lessons of yoga prepare us to take advantage of resolutions as they arise, even creating our own resolutions. Just like we remember to breathe or place our hands or feet a certain way, we remember to connect with those friends who, like my girlfriend, mirror back our potential, reflecting back to us our light, the light we've turned away from. Meditation cultivates the skills we need to become aware; so that when life presents an opportunity we recognize it. Our brain makes the connections we need to spot opportunity and then access the courage to reach out and grab that opportunity, launching our jet, our spirit, into the sky. ■

▌A MIDLINE PRACTICE
Ask a friend to describe their future dream vacation.

CHAPTER 35
We have to really pay attention—Niyati Kanchuka

I want to return to my story about Jane, the girlfriend who opened my eyes to the fact that I was a good lawyer who could succeed if I went out on my own. As I mentioned, I chose at the time to stay in Minneapolis with my law firm. There were a number of valid reasons for doing so and I'm glad I did. It is a great firm and we handled interesting cases. However, once Jane was able to get me to see my light, my ability to succeed as a lawyer without being part of my large law firm, departure became inevitable. A few years later I was invited to move to Denver to help a former partner of mine who had himself moved and opened his own law firm. I decided to step into Midline and take the chance to join him. This choice proved to be a crucial positive change in my life.

After a short while I opened my own practice. I soon took on a major client, the State of Colorado. I was hired to serve as Special Trial Counsel by the Colorado Attorney General to put together the State's damages model in its lawsuit against the tobacco industry, as well as its racketeering claims against the industry. My last assignment in my old law firm in Minneapolis had been working on the team representing the State of Minnesota and a large, private health insurance carrier in their claims against the same tobacco companies. I had been involved with document review and then preparing and defending certain of our clients in depositions. So, my addition to the Colorado case was a natural.

I worked on the Colorado tobacco case until it settled and then went to work for an old friend, Scott Sullan. Scott's firm handled plaintiff's construction claims and he and his partners, Ron Sandgrund and Curt Sullan, offered me an interesting proposition. They agreed to pay me a small but fair salary, with benefits, but also offered to pay me additional and potentially substantial compensation based on performance which included increasing the client base.

This was a big risk, of course, a Midline, because at the same time I was considering a safer financial offer from another firm that paid a solid, but traditional form of compensation to handle cases for already-existing clients. Thanks to Jane, I had the confidence to accept Scott's offer. I stayed with Scott and his firm for six years and it was a success for me far beyond anything I had ever dreamed. Everything good Jane told me could happen if I took such a risk happened, only more so.

This experience gave me the courage to take an even deeper look at my doubts about myself. I wanted to find out how else I was avoiding the Midlines of life now that I had experienced the reward of stepping into Midline a few times, including my move to Colorado and working for Scott. I signed up for the Landmark Education personal development courses, taking their basic and advanced courses. I accepted the opportunity afforded by these courses to dive into a greater understanding of who I was and what games I played to keep from being everything I could be.

As I learned more and more about myself, my whole world opened up. Eventually I discovered yoga and its practices. None of this would have happened if Jane hadn't had the wisdom and courage to talk to me about my potential as a lawyer. She set into motion a chain of events that has led to significant personal transformation. Jane's intercession into my life continues to pay dividends, likely far beyond anything she ever imagined.

This story illustrates how we never know the effects our actions may cause down the road. We fail to see these effects due to the cloaking of *Niyati Kanchuka,* the fourth *Kanchuka.* This *Kanchuka* hides from us our appreciation of our creative potential. We fail to appreciate the reality that we are creating the world around us with everything we say or do, regardless of whether we intend some of the consequences of our speech and actions. Just because we have forgotten our innate ability to construct a world of our choosing doesn't mean that we aren't still constructing that world, impacting others as well by what we do or don't do. Simply put, we are affecting others whether we know it or not. This is the danger of this *Kanchuka.*

As with each *Kanchuka,* once we remember that we are being cloaked in this way, this *Kanchuka* becomes a great gift. We then remember to act mindfully, increasing the likelihood that what we create with our words and actions will be of our liking. We also remember that when we act mindfully, treat strangers well, are generous with our blessings and grateful to those who bestowed them, we are creating a world filled with the predictable results of such behavior—more mindfulness, kindness, generosity, and gratitude. It's a giant spiritual Duh!

This *Kanchuka* teaches us to pay attention to what we do and say. Once we accept the fact that we will have an impact beyond the immediate moment, we become more sensitive to the effects of our behavior on others, the planet, and even on ourselves. Often we have no idea what will eventually happen as a result of what we say or do. When we smile at a stranger, we may be catching that person in a moment of despondency and our warmth pulls them out of it. Maybe we praise somebody at work for a job well done at just the moment they were thinking of quitting because they didn't feel valuable and appreciated.

I want to say one more thing about cause and effect. This lesson comes from the *Bhagavad-Gita*. Krishna teaches that there are ramifications even when we don't act. "Inaction is action." Consider my story about Jane and my desire to leave the law firm. Had she not bothered to share her thoughts about my abilities, the positive changes I've experienced in my life might not have happened; certainly not in the way they've unfolded. Her inaction would have had ramifications.

Think of the movie *It's a Wonderful Life* in which the angel Clarence takes Jimmy Stewart's character, George Bailey, on a tour of what things would have been like for the people of Bedford Falls had George never been born. George learns how much his conduct over the years changed things for the better for so many people. Clarence gave George the gift of seeing life as Spirit, with the veil of *Niyati Kanchuka* lifted. Thanks to the movie, we all received the gift of seeing a classic example of the law of cause and effect; we got to see exactly how Bedford Falls benefited from Bailey's life and, conversely, the suffering that would have occurred if George had not been born. All our lives would be so much better if we would remember the import of this *Kanchuka*. ■

A MIDLINE PRACTICE
Remember a time when you were feeling down and somebody said something to you that lifted your spirits.

CHAPTER 36

"Fifty years from now you'll never know the difference"—Kala Kanchuka

Have you been in a relationship that you think is everything you ever wanted? We dream about a life forever with this person. Then, for whatever reason, the relationship ends. We are heartbroken and just know that we will never find another partner. So, in that moment in time, and for so long as we let those thoughts imprison us, we are miserable. I remember wasting an entire summer pining away because a girl friend broke up with me.

When all my friends were out every night having a great time, dancing at the Union Bar in Minneapolis, hanging out at the lake, or whatever else we did to keep busy and laughing, I sat at home and moped. I was certain my life might as well be over. This was before the advent of television reality shows. Too bad: I could have made millions being filmed in a series called "Co-Dependency: Twin City Style." Eventually I got over it, after firmly solidifying the college fund for my therapist's young children.

For most of us we eventually do get over it. As my wonderful father-in-law was fond of saying: "Fifty years from now you'll never know the difference." He was right. The catastrophe of the break-up, viewed years later, often turns out to have been a lucky event. We never know for sure in any one moment what life will look like down the road, how things might evolve.

I remember, years ago, when I ran with a group every day at lunch. We would leave our respective clubs, meet at the bridge by the Mississippi River in St. Paul, and then run along the river, usually about six miles. Most of these people ran marathons and so I started training with them to run a marathon myself. My law partner, David, the one who I joined in Denver years later, thought we were crazy running so much. However, he wanted to be in shape and really liked the people who made up this group. So, he reluctantly joined us so he could hang out with this group every day. He made it clear, though, that he would never run a marathon or any of those other long races: that was just "silly."

Years later, David became one of our local premier ultra-marathoners, finishing the famous Western State's 100 Endurance Run a couple of times, as well as numerous other long-distance challenges. These are very serious runs, folks! You aren't just running 100 miles; that's easy for these people. You are running those miles up and down mountains, over rocks, through streams, and sometimes around bears or mountain lions. The races are not casual endeavors.

I remember one time when David fell down at around mile seven of the Leadville (Colorado) 100, cutting his knee badly. When asked after he finished the whole race why he didn't drop out, he joked that he thought about it but realized he "only had another 93 miles to go," so he might as well finish. We used to tease him about how he had made fun of us running those "ridiculous" six-mile runs every day; how "nuts" we were to run that far. After the passage of time he no longer thought that long races were silly.

This leads us to a discussion of the final *Kanchuka*, *Kala Kanchuka*. This *Kanchuka* reminds us that, unlike *Shiva*, we are not eternal. As humans, we view every experience within the context of our immediate time frame; our life has a beginning and it will have an end. Everything is linear to us. We don't see the bigger picture, how things will eventually shake out not only for the world but also for us. We make choices, say things, and do things all based on our perception of what we are experiencing in that moment and how we think it will affect our future based on our notion of time.

This *Kanchuka* teaches us to remember that how things look today is simply that, how they look today. Tomorrow this same event may turn out to have consequences different from the gloom we predict today. Bill, the guy I meet at a gathering of mutual friends and can't stand turns out to be one of my dearest friends. The break-up of a relationship today, although painful, makes us available to meet that perfect soul mate that will walk into our life tomorrow; or, at least it allows us to watch more football and hockey without having to share the remote.

How can we create a life full of *Chit-Ananda* (the bliss of recognizing our true nature and co-participating in making the world more melodious) when we are constantly dealing with the reality that we have limited power, limited knowledge, often feel inadequate, can't possibly predict what harm we might be causing, and have no long-term sense of context? Good grief! Yoga philosophy responds in part by teaching us about the Five Divine Acts of *Shiva* (*Panca-Krtya*), or five cosmic actions. Through these Five Acts in each moment we can fine-tune the direction of our life to become an increasingly more artful expression of Spirit. ■

A MIDLINE PRACTICE

Think back to a project you worked on that seemed to take forever, or a social engagement you didn't enjoy and thought would never end and how you thought time was standing still.

CHAPTER 37
The Five Acts of Shiva; *a must-see play*

Yoga and its practices, particularly doing the poses and meditation, have been a major resource for me. These practices have helped me shift my behavior; allowing me, a hyped-up, self-absorbed trial lawyer, to actually make some friends. I even get invitations to family events. Imagine that!

Initially I was drawn to counseling because I wasn't happy. At the time it didn't occur to me to think how I was affecting others; the world was all about me. The world was good to me, yet there was this constant undercurrent of dissatisfaction. I had no idea what was going on, so I figured therapy would help. I had the good fortune of working with some very competent therapists. I also took self-actualization courses. In addition, I gathered and read all sorts of self-help books, at one time no doubt owning the largest selection of self-help books west of the Mississippi River. (I'm guessing somebody in Berkeley has me beat).

Through all this work I began to better understand why I wasn't as happy as I thought I should be. I also saw, particularly as a result of the courses I took, what a pain I could be to others. This fact was verified often when I would run into conflicts in the workplace arising from how I treated people. Eventually, I began to see how the two issues went hand-in-hand: my lack of happiness and the way I interacted with others.

The point of telling you all this is that things can change. As a result of what I learned in the therapy and trainings, and after witnessing the carnage I left in my wake in various work and personal relationships, I decided that I was going to recreate myself. We hear all the time about people doing this and I can tell you that we really can transform ourselves, to borrow a phrase often applied to such efforts.

How does that happen? We learn this process by understanding the Five Divine Acts of *Shiva (Panca-Krtya)*, or five cosmic actions.

What is the *Panca-Krtya*? We find mention in *Sutra* 10 of the *Pratyabhijnahrdayam*, a key Tantric text dating from somewhere around 1025 C.E., written by Kshemaraja.[97] The first of the Five Acts is creation (*Srsti*), birth: when Spirit chooses to step into manifestation by creating the diverse forms that make up our world, including us, that moment when we are born.[98] In the figurative sense it means anytime we wake up and decide we want to make a change, no matter how small that change.

The second of the Five Divine Acts of *Shiva* is Sustenance (*Sthiti*), or our day-to-day, steady living.[99] Just as the world is held together by various energies, such as gravity and other esoteric physics stuff I know nothing about, our personal world is sustained by the habits and patterns of how we live. Do we always hang out with the same people? Do we do the same things over and over, even though we know that we will get the same unwelcome results? Yoga practices, including meditation, and mindfulness in all our activities, are a particularly good way to help us identify our patterns of behavior so we know where tweaks are needed. In some cases, such as mine, therapy can help us identify these patterns.

The Third Divine Act is Dissolution (*Samhara*), or dying.[100] In addition to referring to death, in our day to day lives this refers to those moments we choose to take action to shift some pattern of behavior, an attitude or bias. It refers to any choice we make that moves us into new patterns that better serve us. This dissolution is a necessary step to Midline. For example, as soon as we choose to deal with suppressed emotions about a parent, the turmoil and confusion that we've allowed to coalesce around those feelings and interfere with our life begins to die. This death leaves room for a new attitude and, in a way, a whole new person to be born.

The Fourth and Fifth Divine Acts of *Shiva* are concealment (*Vilaya*) and revelation (*Anugraha*).[101] At the Absolute level, Spirit chooses to conceal its true nature through the cloaks and veils of *Maya* and the *Kanchukas*. For us, revelation occurs whenever we awaken to the Spirit concealed within us, another person, or an event.

I woke up to what a great friend Bill could be once I took time to get to know him. While it is easy to imagine Spirit revealing itself in such nice ways, Spirit sometimes reveals itself in ways that are not nice at all. Spirit revealed itself in devastating hurricanes, not only by their fury, but also by the compassionate, generous and kind response of thousands of people who rush to help. Spirit reveals Itself by displays of random, seemingly inexplicable violence as well as the courage and strength of those who respond by helping to rebuild.

In every moment we have the opportunity to create and re-create ourselves. We have in every moment the opportunity to step into Midline when we summon our courage, like the victims of natural disasters, to rebuild ourselves. We undergo this process when we recognize a desire to make some change in ourselves that opens the door to a sweeter, more fulfilling life. As painful as introspection might be, we eventually realize remaining isolated because of our behavior, in the long run, will be even more painful. ■

▌ A MIDLINE PRACTICE

Bring to mind a time you decided to make a change, however tiny, in how you were living so as to make your life richer.

CHAPTER 38
Why can't I hear my heart?—Malas

A number of years ago, I received an email from a friend inviting me to her home for a party. I was in a bit of a funk at the time. Being in this bad mood, I immediately thought to myself: "Oh, she really doesn't want ME there...I'm a boring pain and she would be happier if I don't show up." I figured she was just asking me as a courtesy. I decided I would hit "reply" and give her some lame excuse about why I couldn't go to the party.

As soon as I thought these things, however, another part of my brain started pointing out the flaws in that idea. I knew I was feeling down and wondered if that might be coloring my reaction. Also, this was my friend and she always treated me well and seemed happy to have me around.

So, why in the world was I thinking that she didn't want me at the party? It was the impact of the deeply rooted residents living inside us known in yoga as the *Malas,* energies that can make us feel unworthy, inadequate, and separate from everybody else. Despite my friend's efforts to help me feel welcome and important, these feelings were so strong that they almost took over when I received the party invitation.

The word *Mala* is found in *Sutra* 9 of the *Pratyabhijnahrdayam,* a key Kashmir Shaivite text. It teaches that the *Malas* are like dust or film blanketing our heart. One of the results of being embodied in our limited form is that we can lose ourselves. Our sense of worthiness, self-esteem and connection to others becomes hidden or blanketed by the limitations that come with the program, our body/mind, when we are born. When Spirit splits off into so many diverse forms, becoming each of us, we don't bring with us Spirit's unlimited ability to do everything or know everything. As a result, we can become frustrated, experiencing fear, anger, depression, and insecurity. We feel unworthy and separate from others.

When we attend a party and somebody glamorous or really funny turns the crowd's attention away from us and towards them, we might feel down and disconnected. We want to slink away and hide, perhaps with a feeling that we don't belong. In situations like that, our ability to see connection to others is blanketed, hidden from us. In such a case we may feel unworthy or separate from everyone else. This is how I was feeling when I considered my friend's party invitation.

There are three *Malas*. While not *Tattvas*, I include them in this discussion because they operate as additional coverings of our heart, ways we can forget connection. We've met the first one: *Anava-Mala*. *Anava-Mala* is a feeling of being incomplete, inadequate, or imperfect.[102] We experience a lack of self-esteem: "She doesn't want me at her party!" "Nobody wants me around!" We dwell on what we perceive to be our inadequacies. [103] We feel separate from everyone.

The second of the three *Malas* is *Mayiya-Mala*. *Mayiya-Mala* causes us to view ourselves as different.[104] Failing to see everything as simply a different version of Spirit, we fall into patterns of judging everyone in comparison to us. We label everyone and everything as "good" or "bad" based on our worldview, as if the world revolves only around us. It doesn't take much to imagine how viewing everybody and everything this way actually does create separation. Who wants to hang out with somebody who is always evaluating us and judging us based solely on whether we serve their self-interest or not.

Getting back to the party invitation, fortunately I figured out what was going on inside me before I hit the "reply" key. I had the courage to step into Midline, examining the source of my feelings and then making a choice that fostered greater relationship in my life.

I changed my response to tell my friend I would be coming to the party. Had I not, I would have made it a "*Mala* trifecta." I would have fallen prey to all three *Malas*, including the third Mala, *Karma-Mala*. With this *Mala* we tend to allow ego to govern our actions. Influenced by our feelings of unworthiness or separation, we act with the false sense that we can do anything and control everything in an effort to alleviate these feelings. Had I decided to reject the party invitation, it would have been out of the twin feelings of inadequacy and separation. Had I acted on these feelings of unworthiness and separation, I would have begun a process that would have actually led to separation.[105]

Like everything else in this wonderful Tantric philosophy, even the *Malas* can be tools for connection to Spirit. For example, the feeling of unworthiness of *Anava-Mala* inspires us to do things to prove our worthiness. As unhealthy as that sounds, out of feelings of unworthiness we might spend years and years learning about ourselves, studying, meditating, seeking counseling, reading, or any number of other self-improvement activities. We do all this out of a desire to be worthy and to find connection with others.

These efforts, in turn, often result in deeper and more meaningful relationships and life experiences, adding joy to our lives. In fact, this is exactly one of the primary motivations that has resulted in whatever positive changes I've made in my life. Out of a longing to feel worthwhile, I've worked hard and my life is richer as a result.

Similarly, out of *Mayiya-Mala*, a feeling of separation, we may study people if for no other reason than a desire to fit in. In time, and in part because we are constantly contrasting ourselves to others, we may start to see that these "others" are fascinating and well worth getting to know. At a minimum, we find that they, like us, have the same basic desires and needs as we all do. In many cases, this observation of others can lead to connections that enhance our lives. ■

A MIDLINE PRACTICE

Have you ever chosen to reject a social or business invitation or opportunity because you felt unworthy?

CHAPTER 39
The candy store of life—the Rasas

I talk about curiosity quite a bit. I do so because life is like a candy store; there are so many things to explore and wonder about. I've become hooked on television channel HGTV. There are shows about re-doing backyards, loving or listing your home, fixing up a bathroom, turning a basement into a family room, tearing out an outdated kitchen; you name it. "Property Brothers" is one of my favorites. Twin brothers find run-down, dumpy houses and turn them into beautiful homes made to order for their clients. The brothers find out what the couple wants in a home, locates different properties, prepares alternative fix-up designs, including choices of furniture and décor, and the couple gets to select among the different but exciting alternatives. They are in the candy store of home shopping!

Maybe my favorite HGTV show is "House Hunters International." The other night a couple was looking for a home in Sweden. Later, two guys were searching for a getaway in Mexico, followed by a woman from Canada looking for a place in Belize. I love this show because I am searching for a getaway, as well as new places to visit, and the choices are endless. I've put Mexico and Belize on my "must visit" list, and Sweden, although a bit cold for me, would no doubt be worth a trip.

I think a reason I like these shows so much is because they arouse my curiosity. I love watching the variety of creative designs and the extraordinary diversity of so many places around the world. Curiosity is vital to us because it prompts us to explore new things, meet new people, visit new places and otherwise expand our experiences in the world. This is how we find more of Spirit, because Spirit is everywhere and in everything. A value of gathering experiences from so many sources is that our experiences and memories inform how we view and respond to new situations.

Yoga philosophy has yet another tool for helping us connect to Spirit. This tool is called the *Rasas. Rasa* is a term that means: "taste" or "essence," and refers to our basic moods.[106] Gurumayi calls the *Rasas* the various flavors of life.[107] Everything in life has a different flavor or taste to it. In this book I use the term to refer to emotional "taste," how something makes us feel.

I learned from Dr. Douglas Brooks that the *Rasas,* while not part of the *Tattvas,* can be viewed as tools for helping us navigate the *Tattvas* in our quest for finding Spirit.

There are nine different *rasas*, or flavors of emotions:

Shanta Rasa (Peace): This *Rasa* refers to feelings of calmness, fulfillment, contentment, and relaxation.

Karuna Rasa (Compassion): This *Rasa* refers to feelings of pity, empathy, and a light sadness.

Vibhatsa Rasa (Disgust): This *Rasa* defines refers to feelings of repugnance, self-loathing, and heavy depression.

Shringara Rasa (Love): This *Rasa* refers to feelings of erotic love, desire, devotion, divine beauty, and admiration.

Vira Rasa (Courage): This *Rasa* refers to feelings of heroism, confidence, pride, and fiery disappointment.

Raudra Rasa (Anger): This *Rasa* refers to feelings of fury, irritation, violence, and hostile rage.

Hasya Rasa (Joy): This *Rasa* refers to feelings of humor, comic happiness, satire, sarcasm, and exuberance.

Adbhuta Rasa (Wonder): This *Rasa* refers to feelings of curiosity, astonishment, and the thrill of mystery.

Bhayanaka Rasa (Fear): This *Rasa* refers to feelings of worry, anxiety, distress, paranoia, and disabling terror.

How can we use this information? Like an alchemist, we can take an emotion, such as fear, and turn it into courage. If we talked to many of our military heroes, we would likely find that they were very much afraid at the time they made their decision to act heroically. In confronting that fear they recognized their ability to help and a duty to do so. Without taking on their fear they may have remained frozen, regretting their inaction for the rest of their lives.

Fear can be a gift, alerting us that we are approaching a Midline, an opportunity to take a risk that can bring us closer to Spirit. On the other hand, we don't want to become so fearless that we make imprudent decisions.

Similarly, anger can be converted through contemplation to compassion. We see mistreatment of others and we become angry. We ourselves are mistreated and that, too, makes us angry. In these cases anger may give us the courage to take steps to resolve the problems we might have otherwise ignored. Much of the Viet Nam war protest arose out of anger, leading to an end to that war. Anger is important, in part because it provides a signal to us that something inside us has been deeply stirred. We know when we are angry that it is time to look deeper inside ourselves, fearlessly, and possibly with professional help, until we find the root cause of that anger.

Why look at our anger? Anger is so very powerful that it often drives us into action of some sort. Out of anger we lash out with stinging, harmful words or retaliatory, injurious conduct. If we wish to act with integrity, we don't want to unleash such energy into the world out of some misplaced sense of what triggered the anger. In fact, do we want to unleash such energies at all? Will it really do any good or will it just give the anger more power?

We learn from Richard Freeman that a great way to cultivate this ability to shift from anger to compassion is to start with how we feel about ourselves. Maybe I'm the only one like this, but I find that so often when my anger is triggered, what really triggered it was some unresolved issue I have with myself. The triggering event rubbed that unresolved issue a certain way, pulled the scab off of it, and brought it to the surface. Because I know this about myself, I take Richard's advice quite seriously. I do my own self-study and forgiveness tour, resolving as best I can those otherwise unresolved feelings of hurt and sadness that can remain a source of inappropriate action if I don't tend to them.

There might be a tendency to look at these *Rasas* and lump some of them into a "good" category and others into a "bad" category. For example, feelings of calmness (*Shanta* or Peace *rasa*), devotion (*Shringara* or Love *rasa*), humor (*Hasya* or Joy *rasa*), pity (*Karuna* or Compassion *Rasa*), heroism (*Vira* or Courage *Rasa*), and curiosity (*Adbhuta* or Wonder *Rasa*) at first blush appear to be "good" emotions. In contrast, feelings of repugnance (*Vibhatsa* or Disgust *Rasa*), hostile rage (*Raudra* or Anger *Rasa*), and worry (*Bhayanaka* or Fear *Rasa*) appear to be "bad" emotions.

While it is easy to see how the seemingly "good" *Rasas* can help us use our experiences for greater happiness, it is also true that the three *Rasas* that appear to be negative emotions can also serve us. For example, disgust can be a tool for realigning our life into a different direction. I remember a time when I looked in the mirror and saw that I had gained far more weight than I was used to carrying. I knew when I climbed stairs that I had lost some of my cardiovascular conditioning. Although I had committed myself to being healthy so I could fully participate in my grandkids' lives for as long as possible, I had lost that direction.

I was disgusted. That emotion operated to my advantage because it awakened me to some life-style changes I needed to make and I made them.

Similarly, we can all see how fear can aid us, as when we are walking down the street at night and see somebody coming toward us, a little bit of fear may well keep us safe. We may cross the street, pause under a light, or simply change our body posture in a way that deters trouble.

And not every seemingly favorable *Rasa* is always good for us. While being "calm in a storm" can be wise, sometimes it is important to get out of the storm. Too much contentment can lead to a lack of effort or passion, leading to eventual problems in our job or relationship. We can become out of balance with love, allowing our love to become possessiveness. Humor can be fun but can lead to hurtful, divisive sarcasm. Empathy can lead to enablement. Courage can be taken too far, leading to foolhardiness. Too much curiosity or thrill of mystery can cause us to make foolish choices.

When we learn to cultivate a greater sensitivity to our emotional flavors, we are better able to make choices that lead to a life of well-being. We taste each life experience more fully and with more discernment. We awaken to Midline as we learn how to better make selections in the candy store of life. ■

A MIDLINE PRACTICE

Notice when you feel angry about something. If it is safe to do so, sit with the anger for a few minutes and simply notice what thoughts arise.

CHAPTER 40
Fine tuning—the Gunas

My son and his wife were married a number of years ago on Georgetown Island, near Bath, Maine. I flew out and spent a week exploring Maine and fell in love with it. Maine is great! I love the harbors and the small towns along the coast, as well as the people themselves. Inland, the woods, lakes, and villages are welcoming and picturesque. It feels cozy driving along small, winding roads with large trees forming a canopy overhead, as if you are driving through a large green cave. Around the next bend in the road is often a small store, filled with knick-knacks as well as treats, tended by some friendly, helpful person with their own story to tell.

Many of Jeff and Cait's friends and family flew in for much of the week. That only added to my good mood. I spent quite a bit of time in Bath and liked it so much that I decided I would buy a home there. There is a big river flowing through town. Downtown is made up of old 19TH Century brick buildings, lovingly restored with bright colored trims, reds, greens, yellows, purples, and blues, to create a warm, welcoming place a person could call home.

I saw a house I liked so much I checked the price out and contacted a real estate agent. I toured the house; it was perfect and the price was great. This house was a large wood-framed structure built in the 1800's, with architectural details that gave it a Classic appearance, perhaps Italian, perhaps Greek. It sat on a hill about a block up from the main downtown street, close to the river. It had a big porch where a person could sit and watch people walk up and down the hill, waving at friends and making new ones.

Just as I was seriously considering making an offer my son said to me: "Dad, why in the world do you want to buy a home in Bath? You live all the way across the country. I'm taking your checkbook away!" He was probably right and I didn't buy the home, although I was so excited by the week, the beauty of the state, and the welcoming old-style river-front appeal of Bath, that it was a close call.

I tell this story as an introduction to the material or "Relative" world on the *Tattva* chart, Table 1. In the *Tattvas*, the category of the individual, Spirit as it resides in each of us as our "limited' spirit, is called *Purusha*. *Purusha* means the person who lives in the castle.[108] Our bodies are our castles and Spirit resides within us. I've talked at length about Spirit, so let's turn from *Purusha* to the next step in the *Tattva* chart, *Prakriti,* the actual matter out of which our whole world is created, including our physical bodies.[109]

According to yoga philosophy, *Prakriti,* matter, consists of three *Gunas,* each representing a general tendency of how we act. These three *Gunas* are: 1) activity (*Rajas*); 2) inertia (*Tamas*); and 3) purity or balance (*Sattva*). One *Guna,* or tendency, will be stronger in us at any particular time than the other two, with a different *Guna* taking over in another moment, asserting influence on our actions.

How do these qualities operate? Why is it helpful to know about them? The story about my almost-new hometown, Bath, Maine, helps answer this question and illustrates why we need to be aware of these three energies constantly at play within us. As tendencies, they can subtly nudge us into an action we might later regret or, conversely, cause us to miss out on opportunities, life's Midlines.

Rajas is considered an expanding, heating, accelerating upward energy. It is associated with activity, stimulation, and dynamism and with the elements of fire and air. When I was visiting Maine I was so charged up with the energy of the visit that it almost drove me to buy a house in a town over 2,000 miles away from where I live, nowhere near anybody I knew. I was "fired up." *Rajas* can give rise to agitation and passion.[110] As anybody knows who has spent time with me, I can be agitated, passionate, and intense. Too much agitation is problematic; such as we get caught in traffic and tend to freak out. On the other hand, passion when properly channeled is crucial to living a full life.

Another tendency of "matter" is *Tamas,* which has the quality of darkness. It is considered a cooling energy, a slowing and condensing energy and is associated with stillness and quiet and with the elements of earth and water. We all have the tendency at times to be dark, cool, slow, condensed, still and quiet. This can be good for us, but too much darkness can lead to all sorts of problems. We can get into a funk, withdrawing from the world and all Spirit offers. On the other hand, sometimes we need a touch of *Tamas.* My son's intercession was probably the type of cooling energy I needed to keep me from buying the house in Bath.

The third *Guna, Sattva,* is considered a balancing and optimizing energy. It is associated with light and luminosity. It gives rise to clarity and harmony and is the closest to our true nature as Spirit.[111] This is the energetic place that best allows us to find Midline and make the most appropriate choices in response to the invitations Midline offers. Choosing not to buy the house was, at the time, a balanced choice arising from a cooling of my fire to own a place in such a great spot, given the circumstances at the time. My son helped me bring clarity to the choice I was considering, helping me to be *Sattvic.*

We can use these energies of the *Gunas* in ways that help us to act appropriately. Sometimes we need stillness, *Tamas*. This is particularly the case when we live in a world of stress that builds up and stays with us. Life can get to the point where even the smallest issue can set us off. So, for people with this type of intense life style, scheduling quiet time-outs might be crucial to keep good health and to live skillfully.

When I mention this I can't help but think about my grandson Henry and his frequent time-outs. They seem to work. He goes from throwing food at his sister to helping her play a game. *Tamasic* energy also helps when we are tired and need a rest. Then, it is helpful to create an environment conducive to a settling feeling. Perhaps for people feeling stressed, a quiet out-of-the-way vacation might make more sense than a trip to New York City. A quiet evening listening to music might make more sense than watching episodes of "NCIS."

Other times we may be feeling cool, slow, a bit down in energy but circumstances require a more active, fiery energy (*Rajas*). For example, as a trial attorney I might wake up feeling low but have to conduct a jury trial or deposition that day. Maybe I don't feel well when I'm visiting the grandkids but I want to be upbeat and energetic to enjoy my time with them. In those cases, I might want to turn on some up-tempo music. In that regard, I suggest *Healing at the Speed of Sound,* a book by Alex Doman, and Don Campbell,[112] Their book, which discusses the role of vibration, sound, rhythms and music in the functioning of our brain, our body, and our health, includes suggestions about what types of music help us with our moods. They include links that lead us to music to calm us down or pep us up.

Because the *Gunas* are our tendencies, we will be prone to speak or act based on our mood at the time, whether those actions are beneficial or not. The *Gunas* have the power to distort our experience by affecting our moods, putting us in "high" moods or "dark" places. Knowing that these energies might be affecting our moods will make us more sensitive to whether what we are about to say or do might be mood-related and not the best choice in the moment. When Midline appears we want to be as balanced as we can, mood-wise, so we don't miss the opportunities it presents. ∎

A MIDLINE PRACTICE

Take a few moments to think about what songs or music tend to have an effect on your moods.

PART IV

A Road Map Of the Outer World—The Tattvas

C. Navigating the traffic jam of the mind

CHAPTER 41
Okay, I hear what you're saying: now what?— Manas *and* Buddhi

I went to Whole Foods and picked up a few things I needed. As I moved into the "15 Items or Less" line a guy cut in front of me, literally pushing me out of his way. He turned and looked at me with a "What are you going to do about it?" look and then looked away. About a million thoughts and feelings went through me. In my neighborhood growing up, that type of blatant rudeness is a direct affront to our manliness, requiring a response. I could feel my fists clench and muscles tighten, as I got ready to respond.

Here was a Midline for sure! How do I react: like a guy trying to be macho, or a rational mature person who had created a meaningful place in the community and is trying to live in connection to Spirit? I looked at him and saw a guy much shorter than me, only a few years younger, soft and out of shape. I was pretty sure, given my years sparring with Reggie, that I could "convince" this guy to get out of my way. I started thinking about how this would play out and the thought of going to jail and being sued for assault didn't fit into my plans for the future. Also, I'd been taking yoga by this time and meditating, and the longer I looked at this guy, the more I began to calm down. So, I waited in line until Mr. Bulldozer finished and it was my turn.

I use this example to introduce the next three levels on the *Tattva* chart, the three levels of the mind: *Buddhi, Ahamkara,* and *Manas,* Table 1. These three levels are collectively the processing center for our ability to experience the world. Together, this processing center, sometimes called "the psychic instrument," has three main functions: the ability to discriminate between experiences, the ability to personally relate to those experiences, and the ability to think.[113]

The first of these levels is the *Buddhi,* or intellect. This is where the ability to discriminate exists.[114] The *Buddhi* is the highest and most subtle aspect of the mind, where we perceive experiences and what they signify.[115] In addition to the ability to discriminate, the *Buddhi* is also where we find what we call our intelligence, judgment and intuition.[116] The *Buddhi* is our spiritual intelligence.

When the guy cut in front of me in line, the *Buddhi* is the place where I was able to figure out the proper course of action, given all the circumstances. I was an attorney, parent and grandparent, standing in Whole Foods, not some young guy back in my neighborhood where a reputation for being able to take care of yourself mattered. I knew the right thing to do, what best served Spirit and would keep me out of jail.

My ability to figure out the appropriate action, in this case, restraint, required that I have a functioning relationship with the other two levels of the mind, *Ahamkara* and *Manas*. *Manas* is where we store and process information and our linear, cognitive thinking occurs. Here is where we synthesize information from our senses and turn them into images and concepts.[117] The *Manas* explains to *Buddhi* what we have just seen and heard.

In my example from Whole Foods, the *Manas* identified the out-of-shape guy with a chip on his shoulder as well as a woman watching me to see how I was going to react after Mr. Bulldozer bumped me. [118] The *Buddhi* received this information and was able to sort out all these sense impressions to help me make the best choice.[119]

When this process works smoothly, we behave in a way that best serves us. However, as we have already discussed, my brain could have experienced a neural hijacking and I might have punched or shoved this guy before *Manas* and *Buddhi* had a chance to work things out. This is where I believe the lessons of yoga have helped make a difference for me. There are times in the past where I might have acted precipitously, getting myself in trouble. However, the hours and hours I've spent mindfully focusing on alignment in yoga poses, whether in fast-paced *Vinyasa* classes or slower classes focusing on pose alignment, as well as meditating and going for long walks have given my brain's system more capacity to choose the right path of action.

Had it been twenty years ago, perhaps the urge to shove this guy out of the way might have led to a different result. Had that occurred, this would have indicated that the third level of the mind, *Ahamkara*, ego, had overridden what the *Buddhi* knew was the right thing to do. ■

A MIDLINE PRACTICE

The next time something stressful arises in your interaction with others, whether somebody takes a parking place you want, cuts in front of you in line, or bumps into you, notice how your mind and body start to react.

CHAPTER 42
Yet another way to get hijacked—Ahamkara

As I admitted, twenty years ago, maybe even ten years ago, the guy cutting in front of me probably would have caused me to retaliate. My ego's desire to do so would have overwhelmed what the *Buddhi* knew was the right thing to do.

Most of us can think of times when we let our ego get in the way of good judgment. The first marathon I ran, on Madeline Island near Bayfield, Wisconsin, is a great example. I had trained pretty well but hadn't done the long, weekend 20-milers that the more serious runners do for about two months before a marathon. I ran religiously during the week with my training group but, come Saturday morning, I couldn't get out of bed to join them for their long run. Instead, I'd sleep in, drive to where I knew they would be at about the 10-mile mark, park my car, and finish the last 10 miles with them. I could always get somebody to drive me back to my car, after we had a fantastic breakfast.

So, when the race came I ran well until about mile 20 and then began to have problems. By mile 23 I was pretty much walking, with an occasional attempt to jog that would last about 10 feet. My legs were cramped and sore; I just wanted it to be over and I was already thinking about ice cream. Just as I hit the mile 25 marker I looked ahead and saw Linda, a woman I had been dating for some time. We had just broken up and I knew it was over, but it wasn't a result I had wanted. She was standing with a few people, including Mr. Soon-to-be-New-Boyfriend. Some of you can already see what comes next, since this is a chapter about ego.

Showing you how powerful ego can be, as soon as I saw them I took off running. I wasn't hobbling like I had been for three-plus miles. I was running, or at least I think I was. As I ran past them Linda and Mr. Hey-that's-MY-girlfriend cheered for me and asked how I was doing. "Fine" I replied in my most macho voice. There was no way I was going to let them know that my legs would require about $10,000 of massage work the following day, or so it felt. Lucky for me, there was a bend in the road and as soon as I figured I was out of their sight, I stopped, taking about a week (it seemed) to finish the last mile.

I paid the price for that little bit of ego-assertion and I suspect if I had it to do over again, I probably would do the same thing.

That is a bit of a glimpse of ego. On the *Tattva* chart, Table 1, this brings us to the subject of *Ahamkara,* our sense of ego or individuality. *Ahamkara* is where we individualize our experiences, making them about us: "How does this affect me?" "What's in it for me?" This is an important process. However, when we individualize our experience we risk losing the bigger picture of connection, our knowledge that we are all part of Spirit[120]

While the ego is a gift because it gives us our distinctiveness and personality, ego becomes a problem when, in making choices, we do dumb things, like running too fast when our legs are worn out. Worse, though, when we think the world is only about us we can fail to make connection to something other than ourselves.[121] In the line at Whole Foods I remembered that the world wasn't just about me. I felt that this guy must have enough problems to act the way he did. Also, if my goal is to be a kinder man and somebody who influences others to do the same, this was a good time to act like it, not just think about it.

We create our world through our thoughts.[122] If *Ahamkara* is allowed to appropriate an experience, hijacking it away from *Buddhi,* all sorts of consequences can arise.[123] This appears to be a yogic version of Dr. Goleman's neural hijacking. Yoga practices help us to develop the ability to observe everything that arises and make sound choices without letting our emotions get the better of us.[124]

This is another reason to consider the value of meditation or practicing mindfulness in other activities. My own personal experience is that the practice of meditation is crucial to living a life of well-being. It provides the spatial capacity to allow these three levels of the mind to appropriately and skillfully interact. Meditation buys our psychic processing center some much needed space and time so we can make the best choices. Meditation is like a free pass to Midline. ■

A MIDLINE PRACTICE

Recall the last time you became upset over something another person said or did. See if you can now view the event from what you imagine would have been that person's perspective.

CHAPTER 43
Meditation—the traffic cop of the mind

Speaking of meditation, here's a little story. My friend, student, and fellow-yoga teacher Roger and his wife Jenn were about to move to South America, Colombia, for an "adventure." Just before leaving Roger looked me in the eye and told me not to ever forget how many people I had helped through teaching yoga. I said all the right "Thank you" things to Roger but in reality my brain blew it off (I thought), saying to itself "Sure, sure; yeah yeah yeah." This is what many of us do when we are complimented; at least I know I do.

Several days later, I was meditating and, right in the middle of a thought about cutting the lawn before dark, Roger's face and words came back. Suddenly and unbidden, I began to see faces of students whom I'd helped. My brain had stored memories of my relationships with them and connected memories of these students to each other.

First to appear was my former student Mary. I talked about her earlier. Then she was joined by a series of other yoga students whom I had helped in one way or another to find a bit of their promise. Then, other faces and events appeared; all involving persons I'd assisted in some way, for no purpose other than trying to help them find themselves or, in some cases, so that they might feel better if just for a short while.

I remember at that point in the meditation a voice deep inside me whispered: "See, you're not a bad man," at the same time as scenes arose involving things I'd done that I had carried shame and guilt about for so many years. I felt a contraction in the area around my heart, followed by an expansive feeling in the same spot as it began to sink in that I really was a nice person. I began to cry.

Here's what I think was happening. Part of me had made the judgment decades ago that I was a jerk. Certainly I had done some things to warrant that suspicion and there always seemed to be somebody willing to confirm that view. Apparently that judgment sat inside me all those years, no doubt influencing everything I thought or felt about myself.

As I sat in meditation with this experience I'm describing to you, something else even more profound then happened. From way down deep inside me a warm, bright light began to shine, accompanied by a sense that I wasn't a "good" man because the nice things I had done for people finally outweighed the jerky stuff. Rather, I was a "good" man because I am Spirit, all of me: the part of me that has and does make mistakes as well the part that acts with kindness and generosity. Meditation had helped me remember not only the nice things I had done for people. It had also awakened me to a much more important realization: I am Spirit.

In a flash, I felt waves of forgiveness for myself, as well as an overwhelming sense of peace and happiness. Then, go figure, in the next moment, my granddaughter showed up in the meditation and gave me a giant hug, as if to seal the deal. Here's yet another strange fact about that meditation. After all this, I broke a rule and opened my eyes; there was 18 minutes left to go in a 25-minute meditation!

After that meditation things shifted for me. Roger's words had found a home. Neural connections had been made, linking positive memories with the experience of peace and self-love. This is what meditation does. Old positive connections are strengthened and new connections are forged as positive memories are given time and space to find themselves, causing less-helpful connections to lose their heavy influence.

The space provided by meditation allows us to create a context, to remember our Divine essence. Midline's invitations are all around us, with potential in every moment. Over time, these new and strengthened combinations of positive memories, combined with our more efficient spatial capacity, allow us to recognize and respond to Midline in ways that greatly enrich our lives.

Meditation is such a big help in successfully navigating life, with its *Kanchukas, Malas, Gunas* and other influences, including ego. We just need to give the circuitry inside our brain a fair chance to develop and be heard. I ask you to consider adding a meditation practice to your life, even if just for ten or fifteen minutes a day. ■

A MIDLINE PRACTICE

Find a quite, private place to sit for two minutes. Sit as upright as you can. Close your eyes and for that two minutes pay attention to your inhales and exhales and the pauses between them. As thoughts come up, simply notice them but don't dwell on them, don't chase them with your mind. For two minutes watch your breath like this.

PART IV

A Road Map Of the Outer World— The Tattvas

D. Spirit isn't hiding at all!

CHAPTER 44

There are all sorts of tools to find Spirit— the sense organs, Jnanendriyas, *action organs,* Karmendriyas, *and subtle elements,* Tanmatras

I recently did a meditation retreat with Dr. Paul Muller-Ortega in the California high desert. He held the gathering at a retreat center located in an oasis, with a gurgling brook, hundreds of trees of different varieties, flowers of all colors, fruit groves, green, soft grass that was nice to lay in, and even a Tai Chi practice arena with a bright blue training floor surrounded by red rocks and tall pines.

I spent part of my quiet time wandering around this beautiful retreat center, taking in some of the beauty and interesting things the desert offers, all of which were new to me. What really got to me was the sky, how open it was. Where I live, there are mountain peaks all around. At this desert retreat center, I sat in a meditation grove looking down at miles upon miles of open land, blending in a haze with the mountains far beyond.

There is an inviting spiritual openness to the vast sky, with mountains in the distance growing right out of the miles of sandy emptiness. Seeing that view invites deep thoughts, the type of thoughts one would expect or hope to have at a silent meditation retreat! Watching a small brook flowing over rocks into and through a pond, surrounded by shrubs, flowers, stone and benches, and listening to the gurgle of the water, seemed strange and out of place somehow.

That very strangeness drew my attention all the more. While in Minnesota or even in my Colorado mountain town, a river or flowing water is a normal sight I sometimes take for granted. Its presence in this desert caused me to focus on it and, in focusing, find a place of greater calm inside me.

It was hot every day, but in the evenings we experienced a cool breeze. The sudden appearance of that breeze so absent during the hot days, caused me to savor it. I could feel it brush across my face, refreshing me. My other senses were fully engaged as well. I walked around a bit late at night, using a flashlight in the dark to avoid stepping on snakes or stumbling over something. If I wandered too far away, the warm, inviting light of the main gathering hall helped me find my way to the always full chocolate chip cookie jar. I'd grab a few cookies, step back out into the dark, and enjoy the star-filled night sky.

Even though, where I live, it is easy to see a sky full of stars; this sky looked different, maybe because I was looking through eyes that had an easier time concentrating from being so relaxed. This retreat, although spent in silence, meditating on what lies within me, was a sensory bombardment of Spirit in so many different forms of expression, space, water, air, earth and light.

I tell this story to open a discussion about our senses. The senses are the vehicles for bringing our experiences inside us to the three levels of the brain. If Midline is the opportunity to connect to God at the deepest possible level, and if God exists everywhere, then the senses are truly gifts to aid us in that connection.

We are born with five sense organs, collectively called *Jnanendriyas*. The sense organs consist of the ears for hearing, the skin for feeling and touching, the eyes for seeing, the tongue for tasting, and the nose for smelling. These are the tools that make it possible for us to have experiences of Spirit in the world and begin to process them.[125] My experiences in the desert exposed me to so many things different than I was used to, serving as a great reminder of the gift of the senses, companions to help us experience Spirit.

Spirit has given us so much to consider and appreciate. Can we teach ourselves to listen for sounds that are pleasant, such as a gurgling brook as we walk past it? That is easy enough to do when we are at a meditation retreat, walking silently through beautiful gardens, but can we be this sensitive to sound when walking through a crowded shopping mall? Can we tune in to the sound of a child's laughter? Similarly, can we take time to use our sense of touch to feel not only a cool breeze on our face on a hot day, but also the tenderness of a loving touch?

The eyes offer numerous opportunities to find beauty. Can we allow them to see the beauty of nature? Can we use our eyes to find the amazing creativity in the way a building is designed, a yard is landscaped, or a house is decorated? Can we use our tongue not only to taste something yummy but also to distinguish all the different tastes of foods; savoring a juicy steak, then enjoying the contrast when we bite in to a piece of lemon meringue pie?

Similarly, our sense of smell offers us many opportunities to explore the countless ways Spirit manifests in this world. We probably all love the aroma of fresh bread but I have to confess a jolt of pleasure the other day when I walked down the alley behind a bar known for its pool tables and hamburgers. The commingling fragrance of the fries, grease and burgers was pretty seductive.

Spirit also created the organs of action, known as *Karmendriyas*. These include the mouth for speaking, the hands for touching, the feet for walking, the genitals for procreating, and the bowels for eliminating. These powers of action are gifts that allow us to explore and enjoy being alive. They are tools to manifest whomever we choose to be in the world. We have the freedom to speak in ways that create the possibility of greater connection. We have the ability to ask questions to learn something new. We have the opportunity to say things that inspire.

The hands provide us with the ability to touch in ways that generate love or offer comfort, and craft the many beautiful and useful things that make and fill our world. The feet give us freedom to discover, as I did in the desert oasis. Our powers of procreation and excretion serve us in ways that make life in our bodies pleasurable and functional.

From the sense and action organs we turn next to the subtle and gross elements on the *Tattva* chart, Table 1. We move from the body to nature's offerings. The five subtle elements are collectively referred to as the *Tanmatras*. These are: the energy of vibration or sound (*Shabda*); the energy of impact or touch (*Sparsha*); the energy of light and form (*Rupa*); the energy of taste (*Rasa*); and the energy of smell (*Ghanda*).

Why do we care about all this? When we develop, through practice and thoughtfulness, a capacity to differentiate all that life offers through these powers, we develop a greater capacity to find, maintain, and grow relationships. If we truly seek to live in Midline, connected to Spirit, the sense and action organs, along with the subtle and gross elements, are the tools we've been given as human beings to make this connection happen.

This isn't just some form of new age gibberish that sounds good. Try, some evening, taking extra time to taste the wine, the main course, the vegetables, and the dessert. Pay attention to how each tastes different from the other. Try to distinguish what you like and don't like about each different taste. Then, go outside and see if you can pick up the feel of the breeze on your face, the smell of a freshly cut lawn, and whatever else is in the air. Is it about to rain? What does that feel like? What do these feelings evoke within you?

Why bother? We're in a hurry. Who wants to stop what we are doing, go outside, and smell some fresh cut grass? Monday Night Football is about to start. The answer is important. Without even thinking about it, if you start to pay attention to these simple messages of life, you will discover that you now see the excitement in your little girl's smile when you praise her, the way she stands just a bit taller. You'll see that and eventually you'll feel it! Then you'll send the feeling of love in your heart right into her heart, a connection she'll never forget, ever. That's a gift of Spirit. ■

A MIDLINE PRACTICE

Walk outside or look through your window and notice all the different shades of colors. Spend two minutes picking out the subtle differences in the various colors, for example the different shades of greens and browns. See how many different variations of colors you can count.

CHAPTER 45
It is all elementary—the gross elements, Mahabhutas

Whenever I see a stream I am reminded of a time, years and years ago, when I sat by a creek every night with my dog weighing whether or not to get divorced. I took our collie out every night for a walk and we ended up at Minnehaha Creek in Minneapolis, sitting on the bank. Each night I listened to and watched the fast moving current in the moonlight. I took time to think about why I felt so unhappy and what I ought to do about it. Unfortunately, I didn't have a sufficient understanding of my own feelings to have an answer. I couldn't break through my sense of sadness and discontent and get to their roots. So, over time, sitting there each night, I ended up concluding that my marriage must be at fault.

At the time I thought divorce was the wise and only choice; now I see it was not a choice at all. This decision was simply a blind and uninformed reaction to years of unresolved, confusing and emotional turmoil having nothing to do with my marriage. It was a mistaken expression of a desire to be free, mistaken in that I hadn't a clue as to what was really causing my unhappiness and dissatisfaction with life.

Considering divorce was a Midline for me. Spirit invited me to a life of companionship and intimacy through marriage and family. Instead of taking the risk of doing the painful, deep introspective work necessary to identify the true source of my unhappiness—my own lack of worthiness—I stepped away from Spirit's invitation. I did so by choosing to remain in my emotional comfort zone, fed by the false notion that without any serious work on my part, things would nonetheless be better once the marriage ended.

Eventually, long after getting divorced, I saw how foolish and ill informed my choice was and that realization caused me a great deal of sadness. Every time I saw a running creek or stream I associated the water with those feelings of sadness. It got so bad that at times I didn't even feel like taking a shower. Eventually, yoga practices, meditation, and other mindfulness work helped me to shift my viewpoint. I eventually got another dog and during many long walks with my dog Riley I re-focused my attitude. I decided that if water was going to have this much of an impact on me, I wanted that impact to be positive.

Over time I've learned to associate a creek or stream with the positive memories I have resulting from the marriage. The marriage brought my son into the world and, with him, his wife and kids—my grandkids. I'm fond of my ex, her husband and family. Through consistent mindfulness work I taught myself to associate water with pride and ongoing meaningful relationships. Today, the sight and sound of water stirs joy within me.

I tell this story to introduce us to the gross elements located at the bottom of the *Tattva* chart, Table 1. The gross elements, the *Mahabhutas,* are those elements that make up the matter out of which our bodies and our world are made. These gross elements are: Space or Sky (*Akasha*), Air (*Vayu*), Fire (*Agni*), Water (*Ap*), and Earth (*Prithivi*). All of our memories consist of experiences involving this matter, the five gross elements. This means that every experience we have, either of the outside world or of memories within, are made from the elements.

So what? How does knowing this help things? This is where my story about my divorce and water comes in. We can learn to associate the elements with positive, even precious memories. Doing so makes those memories more readily available to us.

We can practice stimulating the brain to make associations between each element and positive, supportive memories, just as I described in my association with water. We can learn to associate memories of people we have always been able to depend on with the solid support of the earth. We learn to associate the vast openness of the sky with potential and hope; we look up and immediately the sight of the sky awakens us to our dreams. We see fire, or a bright light, and the brilliance of the flame or light prods our passions and desire to create an amazing life for our families, friends, neighbors, and ourselves. We feel air and are immediately motivated to make the offering of our lives as meaningful as we can make it. As we learned from our behavioral scientists, it is all in what we choose to focus upon.

The *Tattvas* invite us to flow with the elements in this way, using them as allies in embracing Midline. ∎

A MIDLINE PRACTICE

Bring to mind somebody who has supported you in your life and spend a few moments visualizing that person helping you. Now, keeping that vision in mind, stand up; feel the supportive floor or ground underneath you. Can you associate the support of the floor or ground with the support that person gave you? Whether you feel the association or not isn't important right now; it is the trying to make the association that matters.

CHAPTER 46
The sky is the limit—The Sky Element, Akasha

One of my favorite music artists is Bruce Springsteen. When I hear *Badlands* I feel I can do anything, simple as that. *Bobby Jean* brings me poignantly back to old relationships and *Fade Away*, if I let it, to sadness that I'm getting closer to having to say goodbye to everybody I cherish. *No Surrender* reminds me to remember what's important. *Working on a Dream*, by now is obvious: I want big things to happen, for me, for my family, and for you. Bob Segar touches me the same way, with *Against the Wind, Feel Like A Number,* and *Fire Inside*, getting to me one way, and *Old Time Rock and Roll* and *Katmandu* reminding me that life is supposed to include fun.

Other types of music stir me in different ways. Classical music can be so extraordinarily beautiful. Or, if you want to be moved deeply, listen sometime to the version of *Danny Boy* by Sir James Galway and Phil Coulter. There are times I like to listen to devotional yogic chanting, music by Krishna Das, Shantala, Satnam Kaur, and others. I often play this type of music, particularly the more fast tempo chants, when I'm on a cardio machine or bike at the gym. These chants will stay with me all day long and help me stay in a more upbeat mental state. They also can come to my aid, unbidden, when I need their messages.

I remember one morning going to the gym and listening to Shantala (Heather and Benjy Werthheimer). I listened to their cd *Sri* that includes the song *Om Namo Bhagavate.* They've constructed a translation of the main refrain that says: "Because the One I love lives inside of you, I get as close to you as I can." This translation reminds me of the idea that each of us is Spirit, so if we want to connect to Spirit, we get closer to each other. This chant can really rock out and so I played it over a few times while on the elliptical machine, not a particularly typical spiritual practice but that's what I did. Wait a minute—that is a big point in this book—everything is Spirit, so everything is Spiritual!

Later that day I went to a store and while I was trying to find a parking place, a guy cut right in front of me to pull in to a spot I was waiting for. I know it is beginning to sound like I attract such people, but these stories really are the exception. He got out of the car and without a glance, walked in to the store. I started to get angry, but up came the chant "Because the One I love lives inside of you, I get as close to you as I can." I didn't ask for it to show up in my mind; it just did. The song worked some magic on me. It's pretty hard to stay angry with somebody when you remember that they, just like me, are an embodied form of Spirit; perhaps in more of a hurry that me, but Spirit nonetheless.

This brings us to a discussion of what we refer to in yoga as the Sky or Space Element (*Akasha*). The Sky or Space Element represents unbounded freedom and is the home of possibility. When we pay attention to the sky, we are opening to Spirit, remembering we are part of a bigger whole. So, remembering that, I not only listen to music or recite *Mantra*, sometimes I spend time simply staring out at the sky, allowing its spaciousness to suggest to me what my future could be or reminding me of our connection to each other.

How does working with the Sky or Space Element work? When we focus on the expanse of space, which carries and includes things such as sound, we increase our mental clarity, enhance our creativity, develop greater perception, enjoy peace of mind, and calm our chattering mind that can create and sustain anxiety. When we still that chatter we allow ourselves to experience feelings of surrender, humility, equanimity, tranquility, freedom, peacefulness, acceptance, and love. We feel unlimited possibility. These are handy side effects of staring at the sky or listening to music with positive messaging.

Anodea Judith, a leading author on the subject of spirituality, writes that sound is a way to connect to Spirit. She suggests the use of *Mantra* practice, repetition of words or sounds, to connect to the resonant integrating rhythm that connects us all.[126] Dr. Judith suggests that when a *Mantra* is spoken aloud for a few minutes each morning, it can stay with us all day.[127] This is exactly what happened to me in the parking lot that day when the man on a mission took "MY" parking spot. By listening over and over to the *Shantala* chant while I worked out, I had received the message from that chant that we are all Spirit, reminding me that we don't destroy connections and create disharmony over parking spots.

There is a direct correlation between the bottom five *Tattvas*, the elements, and the top five *Tattvas* of the Absolute level, Table 1. Sky Element corresponds to *Shiva*. When we open to Spirit, we open to the light of our potential and connection to each other. It is in this connection that Midline can appear.

Let me give an example. When I finished my Masters' degree my advisor wanted me to take my graduate work, "The Role of Yoga in Personal Transformation" and turn it into a book for lawyers. I decided that would be a good idea and I started work on it. However, over a period of time I became bogged down, eventually putting it aside. A few years ago one of my primary yoga teachers, Madhuri Martin, asked me to teach philosophy to a group taking a 100-hour course, a yoga immersion, to learn philosophy and pose basics. I agreed to teach and prepared some written materials. In the course of that preparation, I started digging deeper and deeper. I wanted to know more than can be taught in an immersion and I wanted her students to know more. So, I prepared my written material and began to present it orally in the classroom.

I found that when I did this I was, indeed, in Seventh Heaven. I loved the research, the writing, and the dialogue with the students. I was happy when students saw me around town and thanked me for such a nice explanation of the philosophy. Madhuri suggested that perhaps the philosophy ought to be the topic of my book. As soon as she suggested it I knew she was on to something and so we have this book. This is a great example of how Spirit comes to us through all sorts of resources; we simply need to be open to the message, a primary lesson of the Sky Element.

Madhuri's suggestion created a Midline for me, an invitation to risk expressing myself in a meaningful way by sharing what I've learned from so many great teachers. My receptivity to that suggestion was Sky Element working its magic in my life. ■

A MIDLINE PRACTICE
Find a quiet place outside, clear your mind, and then simply sit and stare at the sky for a few minutes.

CHAPTER 47
Love is in the air, particularly if we put it there— The Air Element, Vayu

I remember one day when my granddaughter, Lucy, was about a year and a half old. I was staying at my son's house in Boston so I could attend a yoga teacher training. It was early morning and he was hurrying to get ready to go to work for an important meeting. He takes the train into work and I was going to take the train with him, continuing on to my training. As he sat in the living room hurriedly putting on his shoes, Lucy saw his urgency and asked "Lucy...help...Daddy's shoe?" in a sweet, tentative voice.

There was my son, this big, tough former hockey player turned MBA, sitting in a suit and quite capable of tying his own shoes. Here, too, was this little girl, not yet able to put a sentence together, but clearly capable of feeling love for her daddy and a desire to help him. My son was in a huge hurry to get out the door and yet he stopped tying his shoe and told his daughter he would love to have her help him.

Lucy's face beamed as she reached down and proceeded to put a knot in the shoe that perhaps is still there today. It took her a couple of minutes and never once could you tell that my son was frantic to get out the door to go to his meeting. Lucy finished, my son thanked her profusely for doing such a great job, kissed her, and off we went, leaving her bursting with pride and joy. She had taken the risk of bothering her daddy when he was in a hurry, and, in return, created an even deeper connection with him and an even greater sense of self.

I tell that story to introduce the Air Element, (*Vayu*). The Air Element represents courage, creativity and a willingness to be vulnerable. As you can see from my story about Lucy and her dad, these traits can manifest into connection and love. Lucy picked up on the fact that her dad was feeling stress and it took some courage for her to interrupt him with her offer to help. After all, she was just a little girl, not even able to put sentences together very well. That didn't stop her from creatively figuring out a way to pitch in. My son saw that his daughter wanted to help him and he recognized it was important to her. As a result of this brief moment with the shoes, both Lucy and her dad made their father–daughter bond even stronger.

This is an everyday example of stepping into Midline, thanks to Air Element. Creating a life that is flourishing involves the risk of making choices that move us closer to our own heart and to others; to Spirit. How do we respond to the many invitations we receive each day to take a risk for the possible reward of a more meaningful life? The Air Element helps us by allowing us to cultivate the creativity and courage we need to greet Midline as it arises. We don't become good parents simply by virtue of having a child. We don't taste connection and intimacy just because we want to do so. We have to create them. This is how the Air Element helps us in that effort.

The Air Element correlates with *Kriya Shakti,* the capacity to act. This element helps us to identify when and where our skills can contribute and then gives us the daring to make an offering of those skills. We can choose to do so in a way that creates more love, beauty, peace, and relationship, as was the case with Lucy helping her dad. This is how the world can work. Just think if each of us spent even a fraction of the effort to serve each other in some way, to create more beauty, that Lucy had to spend. ■

▌ A MIDLINE PRACTICE
Volunteer your time for something, even if it just for part of an hour.

CHAPTER 48
The fire of transformation—the Fire Element, Agni

I remember a play in the closing minutes of the 2008 Super Bowl when the New York Giants upset the New England Patriots, 17–14. The Patriots were favored, having gone a perfect 17–0 heading into the game. As the game moved toward its conclusion, Eli Manning completed an amazing pass play in the closing minutes for the win. New England had just gone ahead with about 2 minutes to play and the Giants got the ball 83 yards away from scoring.

On the play I have in mind quarterback Eli Manning dropped back to pass and was swarmed under by a horde of Patriot pass rushers. There were so many Patriot players around Manning that you couldn't see him. Being a Patriot fan, I breathed a sigh of relief that they had sacked Manning. Somehow, though, Manning wasn't tackled but, instead, found a way out of the pile and, scrambling for his life, saw teammate David Tyree way downfield.

No doubt exhausted, Manning still found the strength to launch a long pass to Tyree who was completely covered by a Patriot defender. Tyree jumped in the air, possibly the highest jump of his life, and, because the pass was so high, had to fully extend one hand way up in the air, somehow catching the ball on the tips of his outstretched fingers. As he was dragged down to the earth by the defender he pulled the ball into his facemask and held it there for dear life as he slammed to the ground. All with one hand! That completion led to the go-ahead and winning score for the Giants.

Every time I think of that play, I am reminded of the next *Tattva,* the element of Fire (*Agni*). Fire has characteristics of passion, enthusiasm, commitment, inspiration, and transformation. Fire Element helps us to sharpen our mental focus, giving us clarity of purpose. We feel a sense of self-affirmation, determination, intention, decisiveness, and responsibility. Watching Manning refuse to be tackled and Tyree's determination in catching the ball and then holding on to it is a classic example of the passion, commitment, and focus we need to reach the goals in our lives.

Fire is hot, penetrating, bright, and transformative. It illuminates our own potential as well as the potential in others. We see the potency in each moment, the Midlines of life. Like fire, this element correlates with the energy of *Jhana Shakti* because it shines a light on our hopes and dreams, illuminating how to reach our goals and giving us the dedication needed to attain them.

I know it is just sports but I will never forget how much fire, passion, longing, and resolve these two players showed. In the heat of the moment, they found the path they needed to win. I thought to myself that if only I applied that type of effort to fulfilling my dreams, what might my life look like? ■

A MIDLINE PRACTICE
What do you feel passionate about?

CHAPTER 49
Flowing into Midline—the Water Element, Ap

In graduate school I took a class in creativity and one of the books I read was *The Creative Habit*, written by Twyla Tharp.[128] Ms. Tharp is a world-renowned choreographer who for years operated her own dance company. In the course of her career she has choreographed crossover ballets featuring the Joffrey Ballet dancing to Beach Boys music, Mikhail Baryshnikov dancing to Frank Sinatra music (I saw that one), and a show featuring the music of Bob Dylan. She has created dance performances for famous companies such as the American Ballet Theater, the Royal Ballet, the Martha Graham Dance Company, among many others.

The story I want to share is in Chapter 11 of her book. In that chapter she discusses her show *Movin' Out*, set to Billy Joel music, as a prime example of her having to admit a big mistake and fix it on the fly. With a multi-million dollar budget she prepared the show for opening, auditioning dancers, hiring designers for the set and costumes, and assembling production staff. As is the custom, she arranged to have an out-of-town opening at the Shubert Theater in Chicago in July.

Unfortunately, the show didn't start off well. Something was missing and she couldn't figure out what to do. She writes about how her production designer happened to be shopping in a supermarket, walking down the aisle, when he noticed that the beat of a Bill Joel song playing over the store's speaker system matched the beat of a twenty-year-old dance she had created for another performance.[129]

Remembering that one of the big criticisms in the reviews of Act One of *Movin' Out* was the opening number, she made the musical changes necessary and then hurriedly taught the old dance to her dancers. And, she writes, with the new opening number, the rest was history.[130]

The first audience to see the performance with the new opening number was blown away by it, charged with electricity that carried through all of Act One. The entire musical was transformed by this one change. *Movin' Out* ended up running for over 1,000 performances on Broadway, went on national tour, and received ten Tony nominations, with Ms. Tharp winning "Best Choreographer."

I love this story. Isn't this how we dream about our lives—that it will rock with so much energy that we have the whole world dancing in the aisles? This story reminds me of the next *Tattva,* the element of Water (*Ap*). Twyla Tharp had to adapt on the fly. Like Twyla Tharp's creative mind, water has characteristics of adaptability and is liquid, clear, and assimilative. Engaging water characteristics gives us greater mental receptivity, enhances our creativity and adaptability, as well as increases our ability to express ourselves. Sometimes when life offers us the opportunity for greatness, a Midline, we have to be fluid and creative in order to overcome whatever obstacles might be in the way, including the obstacles dwelling in our mind.

Twyla Tharp's story shows how a person can resourcefully flow and adjust, just like water works its way around logs and rocks in a river as it inexorably moves downriver despite those impediments. This great choreographer, as she admits, was in trouble. She had tried everything she knew. However, her team was receptive enough to recognize a new option and she was alert and flexible enough to reach for it. At no point did she give up or lose faith; she remained fluid and open to what might work. She persisted in trying to find a resolution for the show's problem.

This is why the Water Element correlates with *Iccha Shakti.* The energy of *Iccha Shakti,* as we've discussed is that of will power, the creative urge to manifest. Ms. Tharp and her staff demonstrated such a desire as they engaged in the creative flow necessary to refine the play in a way as to make it their best expression.[131]

This is the Water Element; keeping an open mind and flowing with the possibilities that are presented to us. By honoring this element in our lives we will notice many opportunities, so many Midlines, as they present themselves to us. ■

A MIDLINE PRACTICE

Think of the last time you had a disagreement with somebody and you felt your solution was best. Now, quietly to yourself and just as a practice, create an argument demonstrating why the other person's solution, not yours, would have been better.

CHAPTER 50
A foundation that creates Midline—the Earth Element, Prithivi

I spent years training in Shotokan Karate, a Japanese style of karate emphasizing deep, stable stances that generate powerful kicks and punches. I focused on developing a "reverse punch," a punch using the arm opposite the front foot. The reverse punch is effective in part because the legs and hips drive the punch through the shoulders and fist, and into the opponent. The power comes from the connection of the upper body to the sturdy foundation of the legs.

In a tournament, a technique, to be given a point, has to be delivered with full power, just a fraction of an inch short of hitting the opponent. The reason for this is that the technique has to contain enough power that it would, on its own, disable the opponent. This dates back to Samurai times when the farmers weren't allowed to carry weapons. If they were attacked on the road by an armed bandit, for example, the farmer would get one chance to escape, one blow that would either disable the armed attacker or not. If that blow wasn't sufficiently powerful to put the attacker out of action, the farmer would likely lose his or her life or suffer severe injury.

Legendary Sensei Hidetaka Nishiyama was the test evaluator when I tested for my black belt. He decided who passed or not. Sensei was considered a pioneer of karate in the United States and when he died in 2008, he held the rank of 10th Dan. Talk about pressure, having to convince this man I was worthy of a black belt!

In preparations leading up to my test, my instructor told me to practice using my reverse punch. It was a reliable and valuable asset and would serve me well during the sparring portion of the test. The test consisted of performing various individual techniques, *Kata*, forms of choreographed patterns of movement against imaginary opponents, and then fighting with a live opponent. When it came time to fight in my test, I used my reverse punch as much as possible.

I passed. Later, one of the black belts told me that when he and a friend watched me during the fighting part of my test, his friend said: "How come that guy isn't kicking very much?" My black belt friend replied: "With a reverse punch like that, you don't have to kick." I also found out that Sensei Nishiyama was heard to comment that my punch was strong; it "was karate." This is something I deeply cherish.

Years later, a different karate school opened right near my house, more of a Tai Kwon Do school. I watched the students practice and loved the look of that karate. These fighters tended to be more up and bouncy on their feet than we were in Shotokan. From their position they could launch lightening-speed kicks, sometimes spinning, sometimes hooking their legs and feet in ways that looked like they belonged in the movies. I decided that I wanted to develop all those flashy kicks and I signed up at the local school.

I started all over as a white belt but within about two years had progressed to the point where I could test for black belt in that style. To qualify for the big test in front of the crowds, you have to make it through some very rigorous screenings in front of senior teachers. I did great until my last screening. During the last screening I was sparring another student in front of the whole group, including the senior teachers assigned to evaluate us. I was bouncing around, feeling like Bruce Lee in *Enter the Dragon*, throwing hook kicks and spin kicks and pretty much feeling like a big deal. Suddenly, John, a top internationally ranked kick boxer and one of the owners evaluating the screening, stopped the fight and called me over. I wondered what he wanted because my opponent hadn't been hitting me very much.

John whispered a question to me: "How long have you been taking karate?" I knew he knew the answer but I told him anyway: "About fourteen years." He said: "That's right; what do you think is your best, strongest technique; your "go-to" self-defense weapon?" "Reverse punch," I said. John looked at me, patted me on the back and said: "That's right; you're a Shotokan trained fighter; your punch could stop a truck. How come I haven't seen you use it once tonight? Go out there and use it."

So, I did what he said but that wasn't enough. The next Monday, when results were announced, my teacher told me that they had decided that I needed to break the habit of using the fancy kicks, things that didn't come natural to me. Instead, they wanted me to punch more, to use my real weapon. My teacher told me that because they were teaching me self-defense, they would be falling down on the job if they didn't teach me to make my best technique an "automatic response." To be sure that I learned the lesson, they insisted that for the next three months, until the next screening, I could not use any kind of kick or leg technique when fighting. I could only use hand strikes and punches.

That's what we did. Almost every night for three months my teacher lined up all the students in front of me, including Reggie and Paul, one of the top high school fighters in the country, and they attacked me any way they wanted. I could only respond by punching or striking with my hands. I couldn't even use the front-leg thrust kick we all use to keep an over-zealous or very fast opponent from charging us. If I wanted to stop these people,

I had to become so strong, so stable, so adept in my basic foundation that I could "feel" through the incredibly fast moving kicks and punches. I had to keep from getting hit, find an opening, and score a punch. We did this every day, person after person after person, on and on, for three months.

Not surprisingly, when I advanced to the black belt exam and fought another person in front of the big crowd, I never threw a kick. Every opponent that got near me got punched, in the head (we wear protective gear), the side, the ribs, the stomach, somewhere. They became wary and backed off, reluctant to attack. Even with pads, punches to the ribs hurt. When they began backing off I used my hands to set them up, throwing a feint to the head with my left hand, then scoring with a right to the ribs. I had returned to my foundation, the source of my abilities. Instead of trying to practice karate in a way that "looked good," I returned to my stable, strong, well-practiced methods, methods that utilized my own skills and training.

In doing so, I found success. I accepted Midline's offering: I cast aside my need to impress, to look like Bruce Lee, in order to achieve a real objective—my black belt from this school. Yet, obtaining the black belt wasn't the only success. Learning to put aside ego in pursuit of a dream was the true gift of this Midline. Creating a life that is flourishing sometimes requires such baby steps.

Life is no different than the karate test. If we want to live a life of success, we have to remember our foundation. This story serves as an introduction to the final of the five elements, the Earth Element (*Prithivi*). Earth is our foundation, with characteristics of integrity, stability, dependability, discipline, persistence, trust, and self-honor. The Earth Element represents the reliable base we must have in order to recognize life's Midlines and find the courage it takes to step into them. We create our lives out of this foundation and, as such, this element is associated with the creative energy of *Shakti*.

What is our foundation? I suggest that our foundation is our set of memories and sense of who we are. Our foundation includes knowledge of our strengths and how to use them in a way that is meaningful. Our foundation also includes the recognition of our connection to others and the joy that comes from offering our special skills in a way that helps expand Spirit in the world. Just like Earth, which serves as the source for the growth of all things, we are the source of growth for each other. That is why Earth Element has the characteristic of dependability and integrity. We count on Earth; we want to be somebody others can count on and trust.

Many of us learned basic life lessons from our parents, teachers, relatives, friends, and others, perhaps a minister, priest, sensei, or rabbi. Many people helped us get where we are today. In karate I developed a powerful reverse punch, capable of propelling me to black belts in three separate martial arts and points in tournaments. I achieved these results because I had a strong, stable, foundation through my training and thanks to the patience and instruction of my teachers, Joel, Anita, Sensei Fusaro, Dean, Carrie, and Reggie.

I forgot that foundation for a while, instead trying to look like somebody in the movies or on television. Eventually, once I remembered my foundation, I was able to achieve success with karate. Similarly, to achieve true success in life we have to remember our foundation. If we don't, we will get distracted in our efforts and goals, acting in ways that may look good or feel good but in reality, will lead away from success.

Yoga practices are a great way to remember our foundation. When we practice yoga poses and meditate, we learn to physically and mentally infuse the body and mind with a sense of boundary and stability, remembering our foundation, both literally and figuratively. This in turn gives us greater confidence and courage, and develops a greater sense of responsibility and commitment. We feel nurtured by our body's embrace, becoming more in touch with our own spirit. Out of this sense of self-honor and stability we become more confident, better able to recognize Spirit's invitations to the Midlines of life. ■

A MIDLINE PRACTICE

Identify something you know you are good at; a skill that you know you can rely on in the clutch to help yourself and others.

PART V

*Connecting the outer world
to the inner world*

CHAPTER 51
There's something in the air

The ski town where I live, Winter Park, Colorado, hosts some great summer outdoor concerts at Hideaway Park in the middle of town, next to the river. There's blues and jazz festivals and rock music on the weekends, with free concerts every Thursday night. People can buy seats up front for the bigger weekend concerts but most of us bring our lawn chairs or blankets and sit out on the grass on the big bowl facing down toward the band shell. Kids run around, beer flows freely, grills come out, and everybody says hello to everybody else. It's a great environment, listening to music, enjoying friends, and meeting new people, all with our pine trees and a 12,000-foot mountain backdrop.

I remember one summer showing up at a Saturday afternoon concert and grabbing an extra lawn chair in a group of friends. As usual, there were a number of families I knew sitting together with their kids. The kids were playing in a fort they'd made out of lawn chairs and blankets. It was a hot Saturday afternoon and it felt great to be sitting in the sun listening to music. Right after I sat down Drew brought me an ice-cold beer. Life was good.

Even though the music was great and the company pleasant, as I looked around, I began to feel a bit lonely, even in the midst of friends and hundreds of other people. It was one of those times that I felt a bit disconnected because I had no spouse or partner. Sometimes when I feel that way it brings up old feelings of not being good enough for anybody.

As I was sitting there, drifting into this melancholy "pity pot" mood, Abigail, the three-year old daughter of my friends Stef and Drew, glanced at me as she was about to crawl into the lawn chair/blanket fort. She jumped up, ran over to me, and put up her arms for me to lift her onto my lap. When I did, she gave me a big hug and pushed her head right into my chest and over my heart. Having done that, she immediately climbed down and ran back to play with her friends. Needless to say, my "pity pot" mood immediately flew away.

I was amazed at what had happened and mentioned it to her mom, Stef, who was sitting right by me. She smiled and said: "Yep, she's pretty special." I didn't realize I looked all that sad yet this little girl was so tuned in to the energy in the air that she seemingly had picked up on the fact that I was sad. She had seen me an hour before when I first arrived and given me her usual smile and hug, so it seemed pretty clear to me that the extra hug was a result of her having sensed somehow that I needed it.

We probably all know people who have this sense of knowing. They seem to sense when we need a phone call or a kind word. No matter how busy they are, they appear to pick up on other people's energy and are often able to intercede at just the right moment. They have learned to be receptive to the energies of the people they meet and have a genuine sense of caring for others. When we meet them and they appear interested in us, it is because they really are interested and are paying attention to us. They want to connect.

Imagine how much more pleasant and productive it would be to work in a business if the management developed a capacity to pay attention and respond to the body language, facial expressions and energies of their employees. It takes a boss about 30 seconds to slip in a compliment about an employee in front of the group during a meeting, yet the power of that public acknowledgement lasts forever. If you have somebody working hard for you and you know you can't pay them what they would like, what is so tough about at least paying a compliment now and then? Why doesn't senior management figure that out in more businesses? The effort doesn't cost a dime, and the rewards can be endless.

On a family level, imagine how much richer our family experiences would be if we learned to be more attuned when our own family members need an extra kind word or touch. I remember attending a large dinner party at a friend's home and watching as the wife hurried back and forth from the kitchen to the dining room trying to put everything together while the husband attempted to keep the kids in line. She looked stressed. Then, just after we all sat down, the husband looked at her and announced how beautiful and appetizing everything looked and how lucky he was to be with her. Her face started to glow. Again, that gesture took the husband about 30 seconds and is probably one of the reasons they are so happy together.

What is with these people? Is there something in the air for them? Actually, as we will see, in yoga philosophy and modern science the answer is "yes." There is something in the air for all of us. There is an overall energetic landscape within the universe, a vibrating living and powerful energy, and this energetic landscape pervades our body-mind since we are made out of that universe.

We are wired to connect to the universe and to each other. It is our desire at our deepest internal level to find intimacy, live happily, and share our happiness. It is our desire to recognize and avail ourselves of life's opportunities, the Midlines. That is our innate way of being. ■

A MIDLINE PRACTICE

Look around at home or in the office and see if you can notice if somebody looks stressed, happy, sad, or in some other particular mood. What are your clues?

CHAPTER 52
We are wired to connect

I was having a pleasant conversation with my friend Jennifer one day. As I was turning to leave, she asked if I wanted to take an apple with me. Just as she asked me the question, a pain shot down my leg from my injured hip, immediately making me angry; when will this heal? I was just starting to say: "No thanks" when the pain hit and, as I began to speak, the anger arose in my voice. This anger and the sudden shock of pain turned my face into a highly annoyed grimace. Instead of nicely responding by saying "No thanks" I spat out: "No!"

Jennifer looked as if I had slapped her. Even though she knew right away that I wasn't upset with her or intentionally yelling at her, down deep her mind and body had already registered the same emotional responses that would have arisen if I had threatened her. She read and felt the anger even though her higher brain knew it had nothing to do with her. The energy of the anger was in the room and had crossed in to her.

This is an example of how fast and efficient our internal emotional mirroring systems can work. I immediately apologized. Jennifer acknowledged that she knew I was only feeling some momentary pain. Sadly, though, her face still remained strained, her eyes were wide, and her body was tense. My emotions had crossed the neural bridge between us. Jennifer's energetic body, her nerves, muscles, and hormones, had already reacted as if somebody had attacked her.

This brings our discussion from the outer world; the many varied outer forms of Spirit we study through the *Tattvas,* to the inner world of the human being; our own internal circuitry. We explore this internal circuitry because it is a part of who we are and because it is part of what connects us to each other. It is a circuitry open and free to transmit the love, harmony and beauty within us to those lucky enough to cross our path. This circuitry is free to help us recognize and step into Midlines, finding greater joy, relationship and meaning as a result.

We begin by looking at what social neuroscience teaches us about our inner world and how it operates in the way we interact with others. Daniel Goleman, in his book, *Social Intelligence,*[132] a follow-up to *Emotional Intelligence,*[133] analyzes research in the field of social neuroscience, the study of how we engage with others. He describes our ability to connect with each other over a "neural bridge" between us that allows us to influence each other through our feelings.[134] Our feelings, because of this bridge, have an impact on each other even when we think we are keeping them hidden.

We've often heard the phrase that "what you think, you become." Dr. Goleman shows us that what we think and feel not only fashions what we become, it can be transmitted to others, affecting their emotions and biological functions. Knowing this, we have an extra incentive to engage in practices that are enriching to our inner selves so that there is a greater likelihood that what we feel inside, and, thus, what we transmit, is positive and uplifting. It's one thing to walk around being a mope but it's another thing if I'm transmitting that to my grandkids. That won't do!

Dr. Goleman attributes the strides made by social neuroscientists, such as the identification of this neural bridge, in part to the development of the functional MRI ("fMRI"). A computer creates what amounts to a video of the brain that a traditional MRI cannot provide. Neuroscientists are now able to map where the brain responds to a variety of emotions and, using the fMRI, can observe when such emotions are stimulated. From a fMRI scientists can see, for example, what happens in the brain when we gaze at a loved one or, conversely, when a bigot sees somebody of a group against which he carries a bias.[135] If Jennifer's brain was being filmed by an fMRI when I shouted "No!" in response to her offer of the apple, I suspect we would have seen the parts of the brain that register fear light up, recruiting stress hormones and all sorts of physical reactions she needed to protect herself.

Using fMRI scientists have been able to study how the brain reacts to outside stimulus in ways that before could only be the subject of speculation. Dr. Goleman's book discusses these studies and some of the amazing things they've found. For example, research utilizing fMRI led to the discovery of mirror neurons that allow us to sense another person's feelings. The mirror neurons instantly generate those same feelings within us; we "mirror" them and prepare for a response.[136] In the situation where Jennifer offered me the piece of fruit, I looked angry and like I might strike out. Jennifer's neural system picked up that image and, through her own mirroring of what I was feeling, activated her sense of being under attack. Great, huh?

Pause for a moment and think about the implications of this discovery. We can affect the feelings of people without even saying a word and even in spite of what we say. If you are watching a television show or reading a book and your young son walks in to share a story, and, for just a moment, you are frustrated by being interrupted, there is a fair chance that frustration will be communicated, no matter what you say or how well you try to mask it.

This is yet another reason to engage in mindfulness practices, such as yoga, meditation, walking the dog, or otherwise taking time daily to unwind. These mindfulness practices cultivate an internal environment that is more efficient in connecting to our own positive emotions. We become more efficient in remembering our Divine attributes such as goodness, fullness, self-awareness, and joy. In time, this becomes our default way of being, our natural internal state. This becomes the state we transmit to others.

I do yoga practices not only to make my life more full but also because I'm more aware of the harm I can cause others, even if unintentionally, by allowing myself to remain stuck in emotions such as anger, envy, or resentment. Why should we force people to have to expend energy emotionally correcting course or righting their emotional ship after interacting with us?

Imagine if we could all cultivate a way of living in which our natural state of being is recognition that Spirit resides in each of us. That is a nice neural message to send out. ■

A MIDLINE PRACTICE

Just before you walk in the door at home, at a restaurant, a co-worker's office, or wherever else you are going to meet somebody, think of something about that person you really appreciate. Then, keeping that thought in mind, walk in the door and great whomever you are meeting.

CHAPTER 53
Emotional bridges

One of my first yoga retreats was with a group of 40 or 50 people held at a beautiful retreat center in the mountains of Utah. I was pretty stressed out when I arrived and felt some anxiety because I didn't know many people there. I wanted very much to fit in but was afraid I wouldn't.

I got there early and as I walked in I saw this large, unshaven man walking through the hall. He was wearing white, so I assumed he was the cook. He saw me, stopped, and asked: "Are you here for the yoga retreat?" "Yes," I said, and he immediately came over and swept me into a huge hug. It was like getting hugged by a friendly bear. He introduced himself as "Moses" and helped me check in.

Not too many weeks afterwards, I met a woman named Shelly while taking another yoga workshop in Pueblo, Colorado. Shelly is a physician who had been traveling to hospitals around the country that needed her expertise. We became friends and she told me about an amazing Sunday morning yoga class she had taken back east with a teacher named Moses. We quickly figured out this was the same friendly bear—my words; not Shelly's—that I'd met in Utah. Shelly told me his Sunday class was so emotionally powerful that when it was over nobody could leave. They couldn't even get up. They just sat there, some with tears, others just caught up in the flood of feelings Moses had generated with his class.

I've since come to know Moses better. I recall one night in Iowa going out to dinner at yet another workshop and sitting in the car afterwards in front of my hotel while he discussed yoga philosophy with me, leaving me spellbound. Talking to him about yoga philosophy is like a combination of chatting with the Dalai Lama and Stephen Colbert. My brain goes into overdrive and there's no sense taking the smile off my face because he'll put a new one there in the next instant.

Moses is an example of a person whose energy reaches across to your heart and enlivens it. My whole spirit lights up just thinking about how funny he is, how he inspires me, and how he makes me feel good about myself. Who doesn't want to be around such a person?

We process emotional information from each other subliminally.[137] We catch each other's feelings, enabling us to literally feel the happiness in another's voice, see the anger in their face, or notice a change in attitude through their posture.[138] I'm certain Moses picked up on my feelings of insecurity when I showed up at the retreat and he immediately reached out to me to make me feel welcome. He knew I needed it. At the same time, he transferred to me his own feelings of welcome and worthiness.

We really do transmit energy to each other. This explains how we can stab somebody in the heart just with a glance. We may think when we are in a conversation that by biting our tongue, we have effectively hidden our real feelings from the person opposite us, yet by the time we reach that point of having to bite our tongue, you can bet that our feelings have already crossed the neural bridge into their heart.

Whenever I find myself stewing in anger, envy, or other such emotions, I recognize I am in Midline. These emotions are signals that I am getting in my own way by bogging me down in an emotional briar patch. Being stuck in that briar patch will limit my enjoyment of the day and certainly my ability to create healthy connection with others. Such emotions will reach out over neural bridges and disrupt people I meet. That is no way to build relationships.

It is in part for these reasons that we study the internal body, called the subtle body in yoga. We study the subtle body so we can carefully cultivate it, planting seeds of compassion, love, gratitude, and other emotions and attitudes we truly wish to transmit into the world. When we do this the neural bridges between others and us become pathways for the infusion of possibility and Spirit.

This is vital stuff! Whether we want to get along better in the business world, teaching classes, or hanging out with our partners, family and friends, it is crucial that we realize how easy it is for emotions to be transmitted. If I want my granddaughter to feel loved and honored, I don't have to necessarily read fifteen books on how to raise kids and remember every little suggestion. I can start by simply slowing down and embracing the love and honor I carry in my heart for her. Then, when we interact, these feelings transmit naturally.

If I want the young lawyers in my firm or the students I teach to feel valued, I simply have to value them. If I want somebody I know who has potential to live up to that potential, I can help her along the way by "seeing" her acting out of that potential. That vision will transmit. How amazing is this?

Lest there be any doubt that we have the neurological capacity to affect other people, Dr. Goleman discusses studies that demonstrate how influential these internal systems of social neurology are in our lives. He reports experiments in which observers were wired up so that their reactions, including heart rate, could be measured as they observed others.[139] As these volunteers watched tapes of couples having arguments, the physiology of the observers changed to mimic the emotions of the couples, with the strongest reaction, unfortunately, being to negative emotions such as anger.[140]

Dr. Goleman calls this a "feedback loop." He reports that as people interact, their brains link signals that tend to harmonize their feelings, thoughts and even actions. [141] We seek to match the signals of the person with whom we are interacting.[142]

Yoga teaches us to develop our capacity to get into our hearts, our inner self. We are then able to fill ourselves with worthwhile thoughts and emotions, while exercising the courage and discipline necessary to process and transmute negative emotions we don't want to transmit. When I realize I can send out emotions such as anger to others it makes me want to practice yoga and mindfulness more. When we learn to pay attention, and remember to watch the subtle body, we can send good and compassionate feelings over the neural bridges to each other. How much would that change our daily lives, and the world! ■

A MIDLINE PRACTICE

Notice the next time you interact with somebody and your mood changes as a result, becoming more like the mood of that person.

PART VI

The Inner Body

A. The *Koshas* and our inner circuitry

CHAPTER 54
The energetic garden—the Subtle Body

What if there is an afterlife, or a Heaven, but it doesn't look quite like we imagine: picnics in sun-lit, grassy meadows with baby deer grazing nearby, or parties with angels as wait-staff? There are no Lab puppies wandering around us, wagging their tails and licking us. We don't automatically get to lie in hammocks and look at a sun that never sets, with a slight breeze blowing across our face and our favorite drink always at the ready, with chocolate-dipped strawberries within an easy reach.

What if our Heaven or our Hell is made up of the thoughts, emotions, and attitudes we fill ourselves with? That grudge we choose to carry stays with us, constantly eating at us, forever and ever, and in this case I do mean forever! Doesn't this suggest yet another reason why we want to engage in practices that create within us the very environment we wish to transmigrate with when we step into the Afterlife?

What if at this very moment you are sitting there stewing because your law partner got the parking spot closer to the elevator than you (this does happen!) and suddenly, as Fred Sanford used to say: "It's the Big One" and, poof!—off you go, transmigrating to wherever? Then, instead of sitting in Heaven in a Lazy Boy recliner watching the Cubs win the world series each day, or losing a pound every time you eat a piece of cherry pie, two pounds if you add ice cream, you are wandering around some semi-lit, somewhat smelly and vast expanse of parking lot, viewing with seething envy all the great parking spots assigned to everybody in your life you didn't like.

No thanks. Not only do I want to cultivate a lovely garden within me that I can constantly access in this life and offer out to others over my neural bridges, I'm creating my own Heaven right now inside me, just in case.

If we have the ability to cultivate a heavenly garden within us that we can share energetically with others, why don't we? We saw at least a partial answer in our study of the various cloaks that put dust on the mirrors of our hearts, causing us to forget our connection to each other and to Spirit. These cloaks prevent us from seeing that we all win when we remember our connection. We all benefit when we help each other create beautiful gardens because we get to share energetically in that beauty.

Conversely, we all suffer when another's garden fills with weeds, sadness, suffering, frustration, despair, because our neighbor will be passing on those feelings to us across the neural bridges that link us. The other day I pampered myself to a "fluff and buff" massage, the kind where the therapist spends the whole hour making you feel good instead of digging her elbows into your tight spots. I floated out of there and, wouldn't you know, the first person I run into when I step outside is a guy screaming at somebody over his cell phone because the person on the other end of the call hadn't done something he wanted. Walking through his verbal energetic field was like driving through a giant mud puddle.

This is what I mean when I say that tending to our feelings is Midline. We affect not only ourselves but also others if we allow negative emotions to remain unresolved. When I remember that we are connected and affect each other energetically, I make choices to tend to not only my garden, but my neighbor's garden as well, as much as I am able. I water their flowers when they are dry, pitching in to weed if necessary and possible. I try not to spread more weeds.

Just like I want to look across the street and see a well-tended house and yard, everybody in one way or another is a neighbor because we share the same roads, the same stores, the same cities, the same national parks, and the same planet. My neighbor's garden creates part of the beauty in my life. I realize I may be sounding like Chauncey Gardner from the movie *Being There*—amazing movie, by the way, but it is true: we have a vested interest in the cultivation of each other. We not only provide environment for each other, we are also the inspiration for each other, each other's keeper.

These are some of the reasons I tend to the garden of my own emotions and attitudes. If I am going to live forever after, why not create that place right now just in case we are required, at the end of the day, literally, to schlep it with us to the Afterlife? Even if God picks the place for me, then maybe I can make the choice easier by having already hinted at a spot He'll know I like.

If there is no forever after, then I feel like a bit of a dummy if I don't make every moment here and now a garden filled with my favorite flowers and music. What am I waiting for? Certainly, if, as the scientists say, I really am transferring whatever I feel and think across neural bridges to people I care about, I'd rather be transferring a beautiful fragrance than the stench of anger, envy and other smelly stuff that I allow to fester inside me.

Just as modern science recognizes that neural systems interact between us to create connection, yoga has long recognized the human body-mind as a system that parallels the universe outside the body: "The 'deep structures' of the body share in the structures of its larger environment: the macrocosmic world we live in.[143] The late yoga historian Dr. Georg Feuerstein discussed how the universe exists in various vibratory frequencies and that every layer of us, including our mind, is part of this vibration.

Dr. Feuerstein compared yoga study to modern quantum physics, pointing out that we believe in things like electrons even though we can't see them.[144] He wrote that studies within quantum physics look upon reality as a "cybernetic network of circuits."[145] This means that our inner, or subtle body is part of the same cybernetic network of circuitry that exists within everyone as well as everything. Dr. Feuerstein explained that all esoteric traditions assume that there is a correspondence between inner and outer reality, citing Carl Jung's notion of synchronicity, the way, in apparent coincidence, events happen just as we are thinking about them.[146]

What exactly is the subtle body? Yoga identifies systems within our body that act as a counterpart to the energy of the entire universe.[147] These inner systems consist of five sheaths or *Koshas*, as well as energetic centers, the *Chakras*, and energy currents or pathways called *Nadis*. The energy that moves as a current through this subtle body is called *Prana*, or "life force."[148] The Chinese refer to this life force as *Chi*, or *Qi*; the Japanese refer to it as *Ki*. In yoga we sometimes hear the term *Shakti* used to describe this creative power as it pulses through our bodies as life force.

Our subtle body is made up of this energy and it is the energy of our emotions and thoughts.[149] It is this subtle body that is believed to leave our body to enjoy the Afterlife and, in some philosophies, join as energy in other physical bodies.[150] The subtle body also is the location of *Buddhi, Manas* and *Ahamkara*, the highest mind, the perceiving mind and the ego.[151]

There really is something "in the air." A circuitry connects us and it is in the refinement of our own internal circuitry through study and practice that we maximize this gift of embodiment, fully tapping into, sustaining and growing the universal vibrating energy of Spirit. ■

▌ A MIDLINE PRACTICE

The next time you make a call on your cell phone in some public setting, notice your surroundings and consider what energy from the call; i.e., stress, anger, humor, you are about to put into the air for those sitting or walking nearby.

CHAPTER 55
The Body Layer: the part we think is doing the Yoga—Annamaya Kosha

I think people who have known me well from the time I started my yoga practice through today will tell you that my entire outer body and my demeanor have softened over the years since I started practicing. Doing any kind of backbend was beyond me because the muscles that surround my heart were tight and hard, reflecting my way of dealing with the world. I had created a hard outer shell to protect my feelings. Years of counseling helped me to understand the events and feelings that led to that attitude but hadn't resulted in allowing me to fully let go or soften. My protective armor was keeping me from the nourishment of relationships.

Over time I listened to my yoga teachers talk about the value of the physical yoga practice as a means to cultivate our hearts. I decided that improving my backbends would be a way to soften myself, make me more approachable and also more sensitive. This was a huge Midline for me because it required that I confront how my behavior had affected others in the past. In addition, it required that I let go of the emotional protective mechanisms I had created to prevent being hurt. I had to be willing to endure rejection as I shed my armor.

I started working on using backbends to melt away the armor around my heart. I paid close attention to where within my body I was fighting my backbends. What muscles were clenching up? Why were they clenching up? I began to use my breath more mindfully.

One Sunday morning during a backbend practice Chris, a very popular Denver teacher, walked over to me as I lay on my back with my hands by my head ready to force myself up into a backbend. No doubt I was holding all sorts of tension in the muscles surrounding the very spine I intended to ask to bend. He stood over me, smiled, and told me to take a deep breath. He then softly coaxed me to use my breath to come up into a very deep (for me) backbend. I realized that he had tricked me into taking some of the tension out of the shoulder blade area so as to create a more open and fun pose.

This brings us to a discussion of the *Koshas*. "*Koshas*" means "layers" or "sheaths," and are the levels where Spirit resides inside us. The *Taittiriya Upanishad* discusses Spirit's existence in various forms both outside the human body and inside it, with Spirit moving increasingly from the most subtle, our heart, through layers of our body to the gross, the forms of all forces and objects of our material world.[152] The *Upanishads* recognize that God exists at all levels of the universe, most profoundly within our own hearts.

The *Koshas* are part of the cybernetic network of circuitry we discussed. The first of the five *Koshas* is *Annamaya Kosha*. In yoga we are taught that this *Kosha* is the physical body, our skin, bones, muscles, tissue, and organs. This first layer, *Annamaya Kosha*, is the outside body we can touch and feel, the form we use to exist in the world.[153]

As I prepared to do my backbend in Chris' class, I realized that my heart longed to have friends, to have connections with others that were fun and meaningful. My outermost layer, my *Annamaya Kosha* or physical body, was the first layer of protection I had created to protect me from the hurt of failed attempts at relationships. My teachers' advice, my practices, and then Chris' coaxing in class got me to soften that layer. The pathway into my heart became more navigable, as did my path outward and into Midline, the invitation for intimacy in my life. ∎

A MIDLINE PRACTICE

Several times in your day, stop for a moment and take an inventory of where, if anyplace, you feel you might be holding tension in your body.

CHAPTER 56
Identifying core patterns is itself a Midline

I talked to a dating coach once to help me figure out why I wasn't able to get a second date most of the time. She asked me to think about my last five dates to see what the common denominator might be. It wasn't so much about how I looked because these were on-line dates and I'd used current photos; I looked like the guy they expected to see. The women who didn't like my appearance had already screened me out. So, it had to be something else.

First I thought about where the dates had been, and realized that couldn't be the answer; each date had been at a different place. Then, I thought about what I'd worn on each of the five dates, but quickly dismissed that because some dates had been formal and some had been walks in shorts and a casual shirt. The dating coach shook her head: "No, that's not it; it's much simpler than that."

As I sat there trying to find the common denominator, the dating coach suggested the answer was easy: "Just think." So, I thought harder. Had I been sick all five times? No. Finally, after several more tortured attempts to figure it out, the dating coach said to me, gently: "Who was on each of those dates? Who was there?" I kid you not, for just a second I tried to remember if there was somebody who had been around for each date, interfering with my chance at romance, and then it hit me. The common denominator was me. I was the only one who went on all five dates. I was there each time, with all my habits, attitudes and patterns of behavior.

Once it hit me that it was about me and my habits (go figure), we were able to start discussing what I did on the dates to cause these women to say "No" to a second date. It didn't take much analysis. Just as if I were in front of a judge, I tried so hard to sell myself. Just like a backbend where I tried to force my spine to bend even as the muscles tensed to keep it from moving, on my dates I tried too hard.

I talked and talked about me, all my great experiences. I told jokes to show I was funny. I told stories about my accomplishments. However, in doing that I was creating no space for connection. These women no doubt felt totally invisible and could feel the energy of my insecurity and loneliness overwhelming them. Who wants to date that guy? My core patterns of trying to prove myself and avoid any meaningful conversation that might lead to connection were the "third wheel" I brought on each date.

Renowned yoga teacher Richard Freeman, probably not with my dating life in mind, writes that yoga practices allow us to observe the core patterns of how we think and feel.[154] He says that through practice we can build observational skills that help us to understand how we tend to act off the yoga mat. We see how we avoid dealing with some issues or cling to habits that interfere with the way we relate to the world.[155]

This has been my experience practicing yoga poses. Just as I typically tried to force my way up into backbends, so, too, I have tried for years to force results in my life. In my life off the mat I so much wanted connection that I tried too hard to make it happen. Yoga practices help us to wake up to these tendencies. Recognizing how much I was getting in my way was a huge Midline, offering me the chance to recognize and eliminate core patterns that diminished my enjoyment of life.

These are still tendencies for me. However, with practice focused on the outside body, I now teach my outward body to soften around the heart. This helps me carry myself in a more open and receptive way off the mat, approaching life in a warmer and more welcoming way. I am teaching myself to become more sensitive to others and, because I genuinely care about them, the path to my heart has an opportunity to open and connect to others. I ask questions of people I meet, so much so, that my dates have started to complain: "Whoa! I feel like I'm in a deposition. Tell me about you." Sounds like another trip to the dating coach might be in the cards.

At the same time, I meditate and do other things that focus on my inner self, fostering positive attitudes that lead to greater connection with others. I find time to relax. I take walks. I don't beat myself up all the time with ongoing, self-defeating internal chatter. I spend time with people who are positive and upbeat. These practices build new core patterns from the inside to the outside, creating and linking positive connections neurologically within me. Collectively, these practices have opened a pathway between my physical body and the tantalizing feelings inside me—feelings of peace, love, value, meaning, curiosity, and... Spirit.

There is work to do for many of us at this threshold *Kosha* that sits between the outer world and the inner world. *Annamaya Kosha* corresponds with the Earth element. As we navigate through life seeking connection, we find success along this path by being like earth: resolute, disciplined, stable, and self-honoring in our behavior. We are resolute when we stick to those practices that help us to find and refine our core patterns, whether the practice is yoga, meditation, running, hiking, walking the dog, visiting art museums, listening to music, knitting, sailing, long, peaceful drives, or any number of other activities performed mindfully.

To be effective, we must view our patterns of behavior with integrity, being scrupulously introspective, no matter how painful. This may well mean therapy if that is what it takes to break through our protective armor in order to make changes to our core patterns. Therapy may not be fun, but neither is it fun to be lonely. Believe me, it was no fun to have that discussion with the dating coach and realize I'd driven away nice people, but it opened my eyes and made that raw introspection worthwhile. Spirit is appearing in my world in the form of more relationships and a feeling of celebration as my heart's song begins to be heard. ■

A MIDLINE PRACTICE

Identify one or two core patterns in your life that you believe help serve you and your family.

CHAPTER 57
The highway to Spirit—Pranamaya Kosha

I started taking karate around 1978 in St. Paul at the Shotokan dojo. Shotokan is a Japanese style that emphasizes strong, powerful techniques. It is considered by many to be a "hard" martial art, as opposed to the more "internal" arts such as Tai Chi. At some point long after getting my black belt I began to train at a dojo closer to my home in Minneapolis that taught a different style of karate.

That studio was part of a large group of studios that regularly hosted point-fighting tournaments in which we participated, competing in divisions based on age, size and rank. Each division winner then moved on in the particular tournament until one overall champion prevailed. The scoring in point fighting was simple: we were awarded two points if we landed a kick and one point if we landed a hand strike. Obviously, we were padded but all the padding in the world doesn't keep you from feeling some pain when somebody lands a hard kick or strike. So, we learned to avoid getting hit, not just to win the competitions but also because it isn't fun to get smacked.

I competed in the tournaments and one year went to a national tournament, in fact the "Number 1" national karate tournament in the country, according to those who vote for such things. I fought some bouts and eventually somehow ended up in the championship match for my division. Before I knew what was happening officials rushed me to another ring and I found myself standing fully padded, mouth guard in, facing my opponent at the line, with the referee giving us our instructions. It was surreal.

All I could hear was this internal voice telling me that I didn't belong there, followed by another voice inside me saying: "Hey, good job: you're going to get second place!" There was no way, of course, that I would even think of winning; I didn't deserve that, I wasn't good enough. I was there by a stroke of pure luck; the better fighters were sick, injured or otherwise not competing that day for whatever reason. There was no chance I would win, but second place was fine for me. In other words, I was facing a huge Midline, a place where Spirit was inviting me to a new level of accomplishment but my fears, doubts, and feelings of unworthiness were holding me back, preventing me from going for it.

The referee waved us to start and even though I stood there in my fighting stance, I wasn't really "there." I was still back in my past, listening to every voice that had ever told me to "Be seen, not heard," "Don't bring attention to yourself," and "Who do you think you are?" Although my body was standing in the "present moment," I wasn't present.

Unfortunately, my opponent didn't suffer from any such illusion and it only took a moment for him to score.

My teacher immediately called a time-out and took me aside. He knew exactly where I was, stuck in my fear of being something more, my fear of really putting myself on the line. It seems strange: apparently I didn't have a fear of getting punched in the ribs or kicked in the head but I was terrified of exploring how good I really might be! Anyway, rather than try to psychoanalyze me, my teacher, after telling me I was capable of winning this match, gave this advice: "Take a deep breath ... Remember your training ... Breathe ... Use your hands ... Breathe."

He told me that it is so unusual to ever end up in a large national tournament division championship match that I might never get there again—in fact, I probably wouldn't. He told me to use my breath, wake up, and give it my best shot. He reminded me there was no harm in losing but he didn't want me to look back on this moment years later with regret for not having tried. Again, he told me, use the breath to center myself.

So, I took a couple of deep breaths (this "time-out" is quite short) and stepped back in. The transition was incredible. No longer was I listening to the choir from my past, the voices of unworthiness. I felt totally relaxed. My entire focus was now on my opponent. Maybe you know the feeling but when you are in that place of total connection to yourself, the brain processes information way faster than the blink of an eye. This is particularly true when you have practiced for hundreds of hours doing this very thing—fighting.

Free of all the chatter of my past, I could easily hear my brain telling me that if I stood just the same way, with the same hint of lack of confidence and commitment, my opponent would come at me with the same technique.

Sure enough, his body shifted ever so slightly as he began the process of launching his attack. In that instant I knew where he would be open and, without waiting or second-guessing myself, I shifted and shot out a reverse punch aimed directly at the place on his body that was now open once he made his move. Point for me! I started to feel myself get excited; maybe I did belong here. Maybe I could win. Immediately, though, I took another calming breath, taking myself back to that place of just being spacious, aware and available to the lightening-quick computer inside me that was processing information I needed to hear and feel.

The match went on and I remember seeing my opponent now a bit unsure of where to put his hands, what parts of his body to protect. His stance tightened, his shoulders tensed just a bit. Training took over. I faked a punch to his ribs, knowing it wouldn't score but also just knowing that the fake would cause him to start to lower his right arm closer to his ribs. In that same instant I kicked out at his open right side of the head and scored. Two more points for me; I was ahead. No time for mind chatter now; time to keep breathing. I was now so close to the five points needed to win, so close to winning. I had stepped into Midline; I was going all out to win without holding back, without leaving myself some excuse to fall back on later in life.

Having used my breath to calm my fears and quiet the voices of unworthiness, I now used my breathing to calm my rising excitement. I simply wanted to exist in these moments, watching for the scoring opportunities. I suppose real martial artists watch the opponent's eyes, but I was watching his body; it seemed to tell me what to do. Plus, I've never been kicked or punched by somebody's eyes.

I won the match.

That was pretty cool. More than that, though, I had stepped into a giant Midline. I had successfully overcome the deep-rooted messages that I wasn't worthy to be champion of anything. Instead, I made a full-on effort to prove those voices wrong. I think the real winning was in taking that risk, going all out without fear of failure, rejection, or any of the other things that so often hold us back. How could I live a life as full as possible, if I always stepped away from the most rewarding opportunities out of fear or a sense that I didn't deserve them? How could I genuinely inspire my students, my friends, my son or my grandkids to "go for it" in life if I couldn't even go for it in a sport tournament?

This tournament victory was a huge breakthrough for me. I won a trophy that, no kidding, was as tall as me. This outcome, interestingly, was due to one simple instruction: "Breathe."

All my teacher really did was remind me to connect to the vital energy of my breath. He knew from his own national championships that ultimately the breath is the tool in our arsenal that we must employ to access all our skills, all our possibilities. He knew that by focusing on my breath I would reconnect to a channel of energy that connects us to every piece of knowledge within us, and also with the flow of energy outside us, to Spirit. If we live in a cybernetic network of circuitry that exists both inside and outside us, then the breath is the Porsche—at least that's my choice—that helps us move along that highway of circuitry smoothly and effectively.

This brings us to the next step inward within the subtle body: *Pranamaya Kosha.* This is the *Kosha* of the breath, or *Prana,* and is considered our "vital force." Dr. William Mahony tells us that the breath is the "life of all things."[156] As far back as the *Upanishads* yoga philosophers recognized that there is a connection between us and the entire world and the breath is the linkage in that connection.[157] When we locate ourselves within our breath we find our linkage to everything. We find our access to that part of us that knows we are worthy, that knows we are Spirit. ■

A MIDLINE PRACTICE

Right now, pause for a moment and slow down your breathing. Lengthen the inhalations and exhalations, making them of the same duration. Do this for one to two minutes.

CHAPTER 58
Breath: the pranic *bridge to Spirit*

Once I decided to start doing tournament fighting I cranked my training up dramatically. We spent hours working on fakes where we would direct a punch or kick in one direction as a set-up to make the other person move their guard to deflect the attack they thought was coming their way. Then, when they made their adjustment, we would strike at the spot we had opened up through our fake. We all did this to each other, so the goal was trying to read the other person's fakes by whatever subtle clue the body gives. My friend Reggie was great at reading my every clue. There isn't a body part on me where he hasn't landed a kick or punch because I fell for one of his fakes or he didn't fall for mine.

This level of training, performed over a long period of time, made me a strong competitor. At the tournament I described earlier, my teacher knew how hard I'd trained and my level of talent. When he saw me falter in the match, he knew I had temporarily lost my connection to the knowledge I'd worked so hard to acquire. He knew that my breath would reconnect me to what I had trained to do.

How did breathing help me in the karate tournament? The breath, or *Prana*, is a connective power. It connects us to everything we know and also to the energy outside of us. It allows us to assimilate life's experiences. Recalling Dr. Goleman's discussion about neural bridges, it would seem that such bridges are made of *Prana* and carry the most precious of cargo—our emotions and the expressions of our hearts.

Perhaps because *Prana* carries such a precious cargo, Sally Kempton calls the *Kosha* of the breath, *Pranamaya Kosha,* the "vital sheath" because it provides the energy that powers our lives.[158] She says *Prana* was the name yoga sages gave to the life force that becomes sap in the trees, rays of sunlight, and nourishment in water.[159]

Prana is the energetic movement of our minds, providing for our awareness, perception, sensations, feelings, thoughts and emotions. If *Prana* becomes agitated or disturbed, the mind also will be agitated.[160] I can easily see the comparison between the karate tournament and life. Just like I found my most skillful action by reconnecting with my life force in the match, so too we can learn to use our breath to calm ourselves in any of life's situations. We can create a space where choosing our optimal behavior is possible.

Imagine, if you are at all like me, how many times you said something and wished it hadn't slipped out of your mouth. How many relationships would be stronger or how many feelings could be spared if we would all learn to consult our life force, our breath, before we communicate? Just like I could use my breath to read my opponent, I can use my breath as I read the face and energy of my friends. In doing so, I choose a different set of words, words that heal rather than hurt. What a gift of Midline; the ability to simply take a long breath and, in doing so, preserve and nurture a relationship.

This *Kosha* corresponds to the Water element. When we think of *Prana* in terms of being part of our ability to perceive and feel, then we see why this connection to the water element is made. It is through water's characteristic of adaptability that we cultivate our capacity to connect with others in mutually serving ways. Our very process of breathing serves as a tool for slowing down, becoming more receptive, softening and creating space for connection.

Sally Kempton recognizes the role of *Prana* as an "energetic bridge" connecting all the systems in our body with spirit.[161] When I think of the breath this way I am reminded about why I want the breath to flow freely. The breath is the bridge that connects me to all that I know and all that I am. It carries possibility for ever-more harmony, beauty and enjoyment in the world. It is the bridge over which deeper and more fulfilling relationships are created. Who wants to miss out on that? ∎

A MIDLINE PRACTICE

Notice your breath while having a discussion with another person. Before saying anything, take a deep breath, inhaling slowly and then exhaling slowly. Then, say what you wish. The person will then say something. When it is again your turn to respond, repeat this exercise, one slow inhale and one slow exhale, before responding.

CHAPTER 59
The pranic *highway—the* Nadis

I confess I am amazed by the effectiveness of acupuncture. I assume when something hurts in my hip, I'm going to get a needle in the hip. However, my acupuncturist constantly surprises me. She always tells me she has a plan for the day. Despite my skepticism, she puts a needle in my left shoulder and the insides of my feet and I immediately feel a twitching right where my right hip is sore. I ask her how that can be; you put a needle in here and I feel it way over there? She smiles and tells me to relax and concentrate on being a lawyer and teaching yoga. These experiences seem to happen pretty regularly. I can be stiff and sore someplace or have an ache, then 20 minutes later I feel great and quite often the pins never went near the place that ached.

This experience confirms for me yet again that life, and certainly my body, are indeed part of a cybernetic network of circuitry. Acupuncture is an art or science that uses this network for healing. When I personally experience this seeming mystery associated with acupuncture, it opens my mind to what other so-called New Age concepts, such as life force, are worth exploring. What does our internal network of life force look like?

Somewhat like Chinese medicine, yoga recognizes that our vital life force, *Prana,* moves through our subtle body by a system of *Nadis,* or channels. The number of *Nadis* varies from 72,000 to as many as 350,000, depending on what text you read. The *Nadis* originate at the *Kanda,* a bulb or nexus of energy located in the belly near the navel in the center of the body.[162] Whether Chinese medicine or yoga, these are the pathways or circuitry running through us at an energetic level.

The *Sushumna* is the central conduit in the circuitry for this flow of life force. It runs as a vertical channel through the Midline of the body from the base of the spine and through the spine to the crown of the head.[163] Think about that: the body's Midline is the central channel of our sacred life force just like life's Midlines are those places where we most powerfully and completely connect to Spirit.

In addition to the *Sushumna,* there are two *Nadis* considered to be primary conduits for *Prana.* The *Ida* starts at the left nostril, moving to the crown of the head and then down to the base of the spine.[164] The second of the two primary *Nadis* is *Pingala. Pingala Nadi* starts at the right nostril, moves to the crown of the head, then down to the base of the spine. Some say that these two *Nadis* cross *Sushumna* in a spiraling manner, crossing at each *Chakra.*[165]

What do we do with all this information? This information helps us understand how people are able to tap in to the universal energy. And certain people can pick up on the feelings of others and create harmony in their lives because of their receptivity, their ability to tap into this network of circuitry over which Spirit travels. They not only pick up on our energy, they seem able to transmute our moods, somehow sending us transformative and helpful energy.

That's how I want to live. I believe this internal energetic network exists, and because I want to experience life to the max, I want to have at least some understanding about the systems that carry life's vital force, *Prana*. Through yoga study and practices, we develop a capacity for awareness of how *Prana* flows in the world, carrying the information that we need to enter Midline. ■

A MIDLINE PRACTICE

Think of somebody you know who always seems to lighten the mood in the room, someone who leaves you feeling more upbeat after an encounter with him or her. Can you identify anything about their behavior that might account for this?

CHAPTER 60
Dancing with the breath

Yoga teachers sometimes caution their students about "*Pranic* leaks," or dissipating our *Prana* in ways that distract us from what we are feeling. These leaks occur from nervousness, fear, or simply habit. We say or do something unnecessary, a nervous utterance, perhaps a loud sigh, just to avoid dealing with whatever is inside us that is making us nervous or fearful.

I first heard of "*Pranic* leaks" at a workshop years ago. We were doing backbends and the room was buzzing with conversation. No doubt recognizing this as a learning opportunity, the teacher asked that after the next backbend we do nothing, say nothing, and make no motion with our body. He requested that we just lie there and pay attention to whatever feelings arose after our next backbend. I did the backbend, making it the very best I could do, and then finished by releasing to the floor.

The backbend was particularly deep for me and I immediately felt this urge to shout or make some noise or gesture, something to express how great I felt. Instead, in order to do what was asked, I had to lie there, retain the energy inside me, breathe, and experience it. In this space and silence I was able to notice what I was feeling: pride in my practice and persistence, and a sense of happiness and accomplishment.

Again we see that the breath is a powerful tool of Midline. Had I not remained still and silent, I would never have experienced those feelings. In a giant "*Pranic* leak," I would never have heard these heart messages because the energy would have been released into the air without my having experienced it fully. This is a value in paying attention to our breath. Recognizing its precious nature, we honor the breath and learn to pay attention to the messages it carries. We learn to appreciate the breath and view it with humility and care. Instead of trying to be in charge of the breath, we welcome it.

Understanding *Prana* and how to use it effectively helps me in how I interact with people. For example, I learned that the dynamics of *Prana* are associated with three forms of energy, or special powers: 1) *Laghima:* the ability to become light, even weightless; 2) *Anima:* the ability to become as tiny as an atom; and 3) *Mahima:* the ability to become as big as the universe.

When I first heard this I wondered how knowing this information could possibly make it easier to get along with my neighbor across the road? In time I learned to think of the breath as a vehicle for connection to others, as well as to our hearts. I remembered that we are in a dance of relationship with each other and so we want to behave in a way that makes the dance spicier.

These three powers are reminders of how to use our life force in ways that maximize our ability to get along with each other. For example, sometimes to create harmony at home or work we want to have a light touch, responding to problems with softness, in a peaceful manner that encourages a successful resolution. We want to be *Laghima*. What worked best for me as a young lawyer was when a supervising partner took time to tell me something they appreciated about me before suggesting how I might improve on something else. In such cases, the light touch was the way to create a more successful relationship.

There are times when we need to become small, to step away completely. We need to become *Anima,* as tiny as an atom. In my days as a young lawyer there came a time when my mentor, Bob, decided that rather than intercede regularly as the supervising partner, it was now time for him to step away so that I could develop the skills and confidence necessary to become a partner myself. While he quietly continued to monitor my work, he did so by being so "small," so invisible, that I really felt like I was in charge. In that way I was able to stand on my own feet, develop confidence, and, with that, my competency grew.

Finally, sometimes we need to step up large and powerful to create social change. Remember how the collective outrage of the Vietnam War protesters became a huge outcry that resulted in dramatic and necessary change? These protestors, each an individual who may at one time thought they were too small and insignificant to change anything, formed a collective voice that was *Mahima*, so large it could not be ignored. That voice became as loud as the universe.

Breath awareness leads to a more productive, meaningful life. Through the breath we access our deepest feelings and create space for more meaningful and richer relationships. We learn when to employ the soft approach. We know when to step into the background. We know when it is time to step up powerfully.

Through the breath each moment becomes a tingling, exciting opportunity to taste Spirit fully, to partake of life's gift completely, here and now. ■

A MIDLINE PRACTICE

Identify a situation at home or at work where you could step back a bit from your usual leadership role and allow somebody else to demonstrate his or her competency.

CHAPTER 61
Focusing on Spirit—
Manomaya Kosha *and* Mantra

At a Yoga Journal conference in Estes Park, Colorado I noticed that I was feeling a bit disconnected from everyone else. I don't know about you, but try as I might, this type of feeling happens to me from time to time. I thought it a bit ironic that I could feel this way in the middle of this beautiful high-mountain retreat center, surrounded by so many yoga practitioners but, for whatever reason, that's what I felt.

Sometimes at these large gatherings my competitive fire is stoked and I get frustrated that I can't do the amazing poses some of these people can drop into in the blink of an eye. One time I lamented to my friend Chris, a top teacher from Denver, that I wish I'd started practicing yoga full time when he did, as a very young man of high school/college age. I told him that if I'd done that, I'd be bendy like him. He smiled at me with that smile that is uniquely "Chris," kind and understanding, and promptly told me he wished that when he was bending himself into a pretzel "way back then" he had, instead, gone to law school like me so that he would have fewer money problems today.

He got me to laugh and I began to lose my feeling of disconnection to everybody. From that point on, for the rest of the conference, I remembered his comment every time I became envious or resentful that I wasn't the yogic star of the show, even if the only show was the one I imagined going on in my head.

This brings us to the third of the *Koshas: Manomaya Kosha*. This *Kosha* contains the rational or linear mind, our instincts and emotions, and corresponds to the element of Fire with its brilliant transformative light ready to show us the way to Spirit. This *Kosha* involves the mind's function of processing sensory input.[166] This is the place where *Ahamkara*, ego, seeks to assert itself over our thoughts and memories. Here the mind can become conflicted in what choices to make, driven by doubt and desire.[167] The fire of illumination helps us make the most appropriate choices. On the other hand, this is where, if we let it, ego can drive us into feelings of separation from everyone else, just as I felt in Estes Park. It is this separation that leads us away from Spirit.

One way to avoid these feelings of separation is to remember that we are all connected, each with our own special package of skills. In my conversation with Chris he reminded me that everybody at the conference had his or her own challenges, making us more similar than separate. As I continued through the rest of the conference, I kept repeating Chris's words, reminding myself that all of us there were connected by a common desire to learn more about yoga.

The practice of *Mantra*, the repetition of words infused with sacred or uplifting meaning, can help us in our struggle with ego and lead us to connection with others and ourselves. Words have powerful energy and their pure sound and vibration, regardless of what language the words are in, carry energy and meaning. Words communicate meaning not only to others, but also to ourselves.[168] We form thoughts using words and create labels made of words. Because of that fact, what we think and how we label our experiences are Midlines because we can choose how we create our world through this language of thought and labeling.

Since words are so important, it is worthwhile to explore the power of *Mantra*. How does *Mantra* work? We are each made of Spirit but the chatter of our mind causes us to forget that fact. When we introduce *Mantra* into our inner circuitry, we stabilize and focus on Spirit like a beam of light.[169] A beam of *Mantra* can illuminate, like fire, the presence of Spirit, helping us to make appropriate decisions. *Mantra Shakti* draws us toward the heart. The uplifting words of a *Mantra* can calm the mind when someone's words make us angry.[170] Gurumayi says listening to the sacred sounds of a *Mantra* allows us to hear God speaking to us.[171]

Later during that conference in Estes Park I approached meditation teacher Sally Kempton and told her I needed a *Mantra* that would help me remember my connection to Spirit. I wanted to get back in touch with my feeling of connection to others. She suggested a very popular *Mantra, Om Namah Shivaya*. This *Mantra* has been translated as "I bow to *Shiva*" or "I offer myself to *Shiva*." She suggested that reciting this *Mantra* would return me to a deep remembering of our universal connection to each other and to Spirit.

I found a quiet spot to meditate, more difficult than one would think at a yoga conference, and sat down to recite this *Mantra*. It didn't take very long before I was bathed in a feeling of peaceful connection, as Sally no doubt knew would happen.

Between Chris' comments and this *Mantra* the rest of my conference was fun and I made even more friends. I think this is probably a big reason why I like *Mantra* repetition. It always brings me directly to Spirit, particularly when I'm losing my way. ■

A MIDLINE PRACTICE

Select a word or sound that is important to you, sacred in some way. This word or sound can be from a prayer you've learned in your religious upbringing or current practice, or in your spiritual studies; it can be "Om," or it can be any word or sound you choose, infused with your intent to make it significant. Close your eyes and say the word or sound softly, to yourself. It simply has to be a word or sound you hold in personal reverence. Repeat the word or sound for a minute.

CHAPTER 62
Tinted sunglasses—
Vijnanamaya Kosha *and* Vikalpas

When I bought my home in Colorado years ago, the entire county, including Fraser Valley where I live, was full of tall, green and beautiful Lodge Pole pine trees. My own land was blanketed with these trees. Then the pine beetle arrived and within a few years there were thousands upon thousands of dead trees, all turning brown. I was devastated at the tree loss everywhere. When my son came to visit, we took a drive to a nearby town, Granby, and drove past mile upon mile of dead trees. Sure, there were patches where the dead trees had been removed, revealing glimpses of open green meadows, but mostly all I saw were miles of dead trees.

As we came down the mountain into Granby we were captivated by its high green rolling hills. My son said: "Dad, doesn't that look just like one of our favorite places in Ireland?" I agreed. The bare, beautiful green hills of Granby reminded me of one of the most beautiful places I've been lucky enough to visit, an old Dorigan (in this case, Doorigan) homestead in County Caven, Ireland. If you stand on the hill next to the house, you can see a number of counties all stretched out in vivid shades of green in every direction. It is a beautiful view. Jeff then said to me "Wow, when the dead trees get cleared your view at home is going to be just like this!"

He was right. The view from my home of the Continental Divide could easily be like that view I love in Ireland. Ever since that conversation, my entire attitude toward the dead trees changed. What I see when I look out the window has changed. My eye moves right past any brown trees, finding instead the emerald beauty becoming more expansive all the time as the dead trees are taken down on the mountainside across the valley from me. We now have an even more beautiful place to live and the pine trees that survived, and there are thousands of them, are even more stunning, more precious. It was all a matter of dissolving a perception and seeing the beauty that was really there.

This story introduces us to the fourth *Kosha, Vijnanamaya Kosha*. This *Kosha* is the sheath of the intuitive mind, the body of wisdom, and corresponds to the element of Air with its characteristics of curiosity, wonderment, joy, and wisdom. At this point on our journey inward through the subtle body, we are now close to our highest self, Spirit, and we can view our thoughts and emotions in terms of whether or not they serve Spirit.

To arrive at this place we dissolve conceptualization, *Vikalpa*. I've read and heard the term *Vikalpa* for some time and am grateful to authors and scholars such as B.K.S. Iyengar, Swami Shantananda, Dr. Paul Muller-Ortega, and Dr. Douglas Brooks for explaining what it means. From everything I've read and heard, a *Vikalpa* means the way we categorize and label our experiences. Unfortunately, sometimes the label we apply is inaccurate due to our limited, mistaken viewpoints or lack of knowledge.[172] When I look out at a beautiful view and categorize the view as unsightly because of the dead trees, my labeling is based on a false presumption. I am missing the beauty of the openness before me. I am missing Spirit; I'm missing Midline, the chance to connect to beauty in that moment based on my bias.

We hear about something called a *Vikalpa* and our brain goes into some sort of intellectual freeze. Oh boy, another Sanskrit New-age piece of jargon with no remote applicability to me. Yet, nothing could be further from the truth.

The way I viewed the dead trees is such a great example of how we tend to view so much in life, how we create a perception that misses the boat. Instead of seeing the potential beauty of what is right in front of us, we only see the dead trees of the situation. My impression that the Valley would be forever ugly was a conceptualization, a *Vikalpa*, based on incorrect assumptions. This is much like the way many of us tend to approach a challenge, convincing ourselves we aren't worthy or adequate, even though we actually are quite capable of handling the situation.

Vikalpa is a choice that separates and distinguishes one thing from another. It is how we make distinctions, or groupings. For example, we may see each other as separate from each other. We may see members of a different political party, religion, or ethnic group as also being separate from us. When we think "separate" we forget that we are all Spirit, connected, not separate.[173]

Like the way we create our world through our thoughts and words, we similarly create our world by these *Vikalpas*.[174] How? We perceive something and add our own label to it based on associations stored in our memory.[175] We perceive things but do so through whatever tinted lenses we are wearing in the moment. This tint can distort what we perceive. This tinted perspective causes us to miss the Midline of Spirit's offerings. I looked out my window and missed the beauty across the valley because my perception is tainted by my recollection of when all the trees were alive. I saw my sparring partner Reggie as not having something to offer me on the subject of art because I viewed him through the tinted perception that he didn't study art in college. How could he know as much about a painting I studied as me?

It is at this *Kosha* where we can dissolve those groupings of perceptions that are devoid of substance and full of fancy or imagination.[176] We see things through the clear lens of our own sense of Spirit, finding connection in difference, finding Spirit where before we saw separation. We take off the tinted glasses. ∎

A MIDLINE PRACTICE

Spend a few minutes people watching and find somebody that looks a bit different from your sense of normal, whether by virtue of their clothing or mannerisms. Without being obvious about it, watch this person and see if you can find something about him or her that reminds you of you.

CHAPTER 63
Embracing Spirit—Anandamaya Kosha

The other day I was feeling under the weather and decided to plop on the couch and turn on the television. I watched an episode of "Property Brothers" on HGTV and found myself drawn to the particular couple that the brothers were helping create their dream home. At the end of the show, during the big reveal of the new, beautiful design, I found myself moved to tears when the couple saw the home and the wife began to cry with happiness. I could actually feel her happiness.

Later that evening I found myself laughing long and hard at something talk-show host Stephen Colbert said. He cracked me up. The news came on and there was a story about a local tragedy and I felt such sadness over the senseless loss, almost moved to tears for the second time that night. I felt angry over a political ad I knew was false. I felt excitement pulse through me watching a replay of some Denver Bronco highlights.

As I got ready for bed I realized that I felt totally alive, completely pleased just to be. I had no plans for the next day, or even for the week. It just felt good to be so connected to my own emotions and to the world around me. Watching my own grandkids and their friends, I imagined that this must be what it is like for little kids. They can be totally present in each moment, alert for whatever comes their way next, ready to tackle it fully.

Little children often go about their day unclouded by worries and anxieties that seem to come to us as we grow up. These worries and anxieties prevent us from feeling or sensing loving connections with others. Healthy little children look and see with their hearts. They innately feel love and joy and freely offer these feelings to others. On the flip side, they readily sense our sadness and pain and are eager to help out. Living this way is a natural expression of who they are. This is the natural state of all humans, not just young children. We can all return to this state through study and practice.

This brings us to the fifth of the five *Koshas* called *Anandamaya Kosha*. Here is that carefree, peaceful place within us where we connect to our true Divine essence. This place corresponds to the Space or Sky element because here is where we have mental clarity and perception. Here is where we feel at home, comfortable, safe, and accepting of who we are. Here, the illusion of separation dissolves and we recognize the connection of each of us to the other and to the entire world.[177]

As I age, particularly in light of some humbling degenerative problems with my body, I am dropping the trappings of the various masks I've worn for years in order to project an image to the world. I'm finding that beneath these masks lies a deep sense of serenity, love, and joy. When I see a young woman whose life dream of a beautiful home for her family comes true when she didn't think it was possible, it directly touches my heart. When I see the grief of a family whose young daughter has been tragically taken from them, I feel that grief.

I've sought for years to connect to Spirit, to feel the mystical connection to God. I realize now that this connection doesn't require that we live a rigorous life of solitude in the forest or a monastery. To the contrary, I suggest that we attain our mystical connection to Spirit every time we allow ourselves simply to feel the energy of each other's experiences, as well as our own.

We become mystics each time we dissolve the illusion of separation, reveling in the awe-inspiring majesty of our diversity, and recognizing the Divine imprint in the entire material word and ourselves.

When the channel to our heart and soul is open and free flowing, we come to a place of *Paramananda*, the highest state of love.[178] This state is innately present within us.[179] In the fun and good times, the joy and excitement can be extraordinary. When the lousy things happen, we are deeply and painfully touched. At the appropriate time we then look at the situation from the perspective that we want to keep on going; we pick ourselves up off the floor, dust ourselves off, and enjoy life again. We want to revel in life. We want to serve Spirit. We want to be vigilant for Midline, vibrating with the intensity of a child to take on its challenge. ■

A MIDLINE PRACTICE

Notice the next time you truly laugh, a deep belly laugh. Spend some time enjoying how that feels.

PART VI

The Inner Body

B. The *Chakras*

CHAPTER 64
Spirit on computer disks—the Chakras

Today is another beautiful powder day in ski country. My skis are in my locker at the base of the mountain and I'm ready. However, if I want to finish this chapter today, I can't go ski. I have to stay grounded. Somehow, somewhere, I've learned the discipline to stay inside and work on this chapter. However, don't feel too sorry for me. I've found that writing these stories and sharing this philosophy with others is fun. I've learned how to liberate my gifts and talents in a way that matters. I am bringing information to people interested in this philosophy who haven't been blessed with as much time and access to the teachings as I have been given. So, this is my idea of a fun day.

Keeping this in mind, let's now talk about the *Chakras,* also spelled *Cakras,* the foundational structures of the subtle body.[180] Understanding the *Chakras* helps me figure out what I'm feeling in any particular experience and then link that feeling to its deeper meaning. This is a crucial function of living in Midline; the ability to pause in each experience and determine its significance.

So, when I feel antsy and want to ski: the feeling of being antsy tells me to ground myself. When I do ground myself and start to write, I feel free and fully engaged, and time flies by. This tells me I'm connected to Spirit. I'm engaged, expressing myself in a true and meaningful way.

The *Chakras* are vortices of our life force, our vital energy, *Prana*. They are circular wheels or lotuses of energy located inside the central channel of the *Sushumna,* arranged in descending order from the crown of the head, down through the central channel to the base of the spine.[181] They are considered to be organizational hubs in our body that receive, process, and manifest life force energy.[182] We use the *Chakras* in our yoga practices and in life as steps to connect to Spirit.[183] I will discuss a seven-*Chakra* model because that is the model that I have studied the most, although various teachers use different models, including, for example, a five-*Chakra* model.

To help us understand *Chakras* and their power to enrich our well-being, Dr. Anodea Judith points out that another translation of *Chakra* is "disk" and so we might think of our body as a bio-computer, with the *Chakras* as floppy disks. These disks contain "programs" for running the body, helping us make choices about issues such as eating, sleeping, spending, and even our basic survival.[184] Just like we buy programs to run in our home computers, we receive programs as children about things such as gender roles and, as adults, programs relating to social mores and proper behavior.[185]

In Dr. Judith's example, the body is the computer hardware, our programming is the software, and we are the user.[186] She tells us that the *Chakra* system can help us to reprogram our lives.[187] To me this is exciting news. I already have the computer, my body. And, yoga is my automatic software update. We just need to make sure our system is working virus-free. ▪

A MIDLINE PRACTICE

Think for a moment about how the various software packages you use in your computer or the applications you use on your cell phone make your life better and easier.

CHAPTER 65
Manifesting and liberating currents of connection

I attended a large public hearing for a client's project some time ago and one of the opposing lawyers, Barry, showed up early. He's a nice guy, mild and quiet. By then most of the lawyers I spent any time with had heard of my karate background. He told me he had been practicing Tai Chi for twenty-five years and liked that nice, soft style. I asked him if he could show me some of it and so we started to do something called "push hands."

We lined up facing each other, forearms to forearms. He smiled at me and told me to do whatever I wanted. I thought I had better be careful not to send too much power into Barry because he was a good guy, we were dressed in suits, and I didn't want to be a bully. Well, forget that. Sparring with him was like trying to move water around. No matter what I did, he stood in perfect balance, moving with me, smiling and chatting away. If I got frustrated and tried to sneak up on him by relaxing and then suddenly muscling him, he just flowed with it. If I tried to power him over, he kept me from falling on my face and getting dirt on my suit. I learned a new respect for "Eastern," "new age" practices.

The *Chakras* are hardly new age. In fact, they've been around far longer than many current behavioral therapy concepts we value so highly today. The *Chakras* were discussed as far back as the early Upanishads.[188] We're talking possibly over 2,000 years here. While being really old isn't necessarily a mark of credibility, the *Chakras* have been studied throughout history and have become an integral part of yoga philosophy.[189]

The seven *Chakras* exist in a vertical column along the *Sushumna,* serving as a primary route over which our energies travel,[190] connecting us with Spirit. [191] The *Nadis* emanate out of the *Sushumna,* circulating life force.[192] Because each *Chakra* is a center of organization for our life force as it moves within us, we must pay attention and make sure each is open and unblocked. [193]

When there is movement of energy downward through the *Sushumna,* this is called a current of manifestation as Spirit manifests as us. An upward movement of energy is a current of liberation as Spirit moves out through us and into the world. The liberating current gets its name in part because, as we travel through each *Chakra* upward toward greater connection with Spirit and Midline, we free ourselves from old habits that hold us back. It is the current that liberates us from *Maya,* the cloak of illusion that keeps us from seeing Spirit in each other and within ourselves.[194]

So much has been written about the *Chakras* by people who have made this subject their life work that I will provide just a brief summary of each, along with my perspective of how they work for me. ■

❙ A MIDLINE PRACTICE

Identify a habit you have that serves you well.

CHAPTER 66
*Our foundation—the First, or "Root" Chakra—*Muladhara Chakra

My mother and Grandmother had a way of expressing their disdain for something I was doing by making some sort of guttural sound in their throat: "Achhh!" or something like that. Jewish readers likely know this sound. I remember one time I was home from college and had a job in a steel mill. It was a hot, sweaty, filthy job and I was on the 11:00 PM to 7:00 AM shift. By the way, this was a union job, with two mandatory breaks, safety supervisors, and a pretty sweet per hour pay rate for a college kid. But...I digress...back to my story about my Mother and the steel mill.

I am getting ready to head out to my 11:00 PM shift at Inland Steel in East Chicago, Indiana when my sister's very cute friend calls me and says she wants to go hang out. Whew!! Anyway, if you had ever met this friend, you would understand that shoveling broken, hot bricks in the Number Two Blooming Mill suddenly looked even less appealing than before the phone call. I quickly changed my clothes and almost made it out the door when my Mother, who for sure should have been in bed reading but, unfathomably, was instead standing in the kitchen, says: "Don't you work tonight?"

I respond that I do but that my sister's friend had called and I thought she and I would get together; I would call in sick. "You need the money; see her on your night off," my Mother says. "But I have enough money saved, Mom, I can afford a night off." "ACHHH! You'll never amount to anything. There's no way any kid of mine is going to end up starving on the street or not able to buy clothes for their family. Get upstairs and put on your clothes and get to work."

By this time I am probably a junior in college, playing varsity football, and getting good grades. My ability to toe the line and make a living in the future was pretty well established, but my mom wasn't taking chances. So, the night with my sister's friend was postponed.

That was my mother. She was committed that I learn not to take the easy way out; she never wanted me to give up. She was the daughter of a Jew whose family had avoided persecution in Europe during World War II. Her parents built a nice life for my mother and her brother and sister, through hard work and this same attitude of "never give up." In turn, my mother passed my grandparents' example on to me. She wanted to be sure that I had a work ethic that would provide me with a strong foundation necessary for me to thrive as an adult. She knew from her own family that to survive took perseverance and dedication and she made sure to instill those qualities in me. She, along with my dad, my

Aunt Irene, my Grandma, and others helped me forge a strong, dependable foundation upon which I could launch a life of success.

I tell this story to introduce the first *Chakra, Muladhara,* located at the root of the tailbone. A sound foundation prepares us to be successful in life and on the spiritual path. Having a solid base understandably makes it easier to accept the invitations of Midline because we're receiving those invitations from a place of confidence and a feeling of being supported. Each of us has had support in our past, such as parents, family members, teachers, friends, and others and it is important to acknowledge those influences. They are part of our foundation, the first mirrors for our possibilities.

As in the story about my father and I, sometimes, maybe even quite often, we forget or refuse to consider the valuable contribution others have made to the building of our foundation. We harbor resentments that blind us to these contributions or perhaps we never bother to stop and think of all the help these people gave us. Taking a fresh look at these foundational relationships is the work of Midline. I say that because these wonderful people gave us a glimpse of what we could become, inspired us by their own behavior, and gave us the support we needed to stand on our own two feet. It is an important practice to contemplate our past this way and, as possible, let go of emotions that prevent us from feeling the gratitude owed to these people.

Every time we remember somebody who helped us, we remember our foundation and that memory infuses us with the confidence we need to respond to whatever is presented to us. When I forget any of these people and think that any success I had achieved was all my own doing, I can still hear my mother's voice: "Shame on you." That's probably not politically correct parenting these days but forgetting the people who gave us our foundation IS a shame. Failing to appreciate my mother when she was alive, I today never delude myself into thinking I've built this successful life on my own and without her help.

This brings us back to the first *Chakra, Muladhara.* This *Chakra* is associated with the earth element and its attributes of survival, trust, grounding and stability, as well as *Annamaya Kosha,* because we are made of earth and it is our foundation. This *Chakra* also relates to the creative energy of *Shakti* in part because this is the foundation out of which we create our life. This is where we have our "roots," the background in our life that we draw upon as we seek our own way. ∎

A MIDLINE PRACTICE

Bring to mind something you've done by way of study, work experience, or some other effort, to create the foundation in your life. Spend two minutes recalling that work.

CHAPTER 67
The flow of relationship—the Second Chakra—Svadisthana Chakra

When my son was in his senior year of college he had a number of choices. He had always thought of playing professional ice hockey and had the opportunity to join one of the NHL's teams, starting at the minor league affiliate. At the same time he had a severe shoulder injury and, after weighing all the options and talking to his college coach, decided to hang up his skates.

I was disappointed, in part because I knew how much he had dreamed about playing pro hockey, but I soon realized that it was really more my dream than his. I wanted to be able to walk around and gloat about my kid playing pro hockey. While Jeff felt really sad about his choice, he was also excited about his future and soon I joined in that excitement, even though we didn't know what that future would look like.

He thought he might become a writer and considered a Masters' in Creative Writing. At the same time, I found myself getting ready to leave for France on business. I decided to spend a week in Prague. While there I was reminded that Prague was the home of the famous author, Franz Kafka. I visited everything "Kafka" and began to look for something inspiring to give my son as part of his quest to become a writer. I found this amazing book in which somebody had taken photographs of some of the main scenes featured in Kafka's books, capturing the mist in a courtyard, or the gloom of the clouded sky over the river, and included the photos with pertinent excerpts from the books involving those scenes.

I was so excited about this book that I carefully carried it the rest of my trip and kept guard over it until the time when I next saw Jeff and could give it to him. When Jeff opened the book he immediately recognized the love and commitment I had for him. Even more, I could see in his eyes a sense of greater connection to me; a part of him relaxed, knowing that he could make his own choices and still have his dad's support and affection.

The book helps me make an important point in our study of the *Chakras*. The book represented to me an ability to love somebody enough so that I could let go of my personal plans for them and step into the flow of their dreams and desires. Stop for a second! Can you imagine how wonderful it would be to be in relationship with people who cared enough for you to sense and respect the flow of your heart? Who wouldn't want to spend time with such a person? Isn't that what we are all looking for, somebody in sync with the fact that we have dreams and desires and honors that fact? What a precious gift to have a relationship like that.

The ability to flow in relationship is part of the work of the second *Chakra, Svadisthana,* located in the pelvic area. The second *Chakra* is associated with water, relationship, sexuality, pleasure and a desire for enjoyment and gratification. This association with water arises because we must be adaptable like water in our interactions with others if we wish the relationships to be honoring and meaningful. My adapting to Jeff's dreams is an example of how we must be willing to adjust in order to nurture and grow important relationships. Because of the necessity of flow, give and take, in a relationship, this *Chakra* relates to *Pranamaya Kosha,* the energetic bridge by which we interact with each other.

If we have a stable first *Chakra,* we have the foundation we need to adapt and flow like water into relationships with others because we are confident enough in our foundation to see and respect others. Our understanding of our self includes an awareness of others.[195] Our desire to connect with others stirs emotions within us, including feelings of sexuality, all of which operate to enrich us as individuals, bringing us closer to our essence as Spirit.[196] There is a *Spanda* in relationships in which, for those relationships to survive and be meaningful, there has to be the dynamic movement back and forth of ideas, hopes, and dreams. Otherwise, the relationships become stagnant and don't serve us.

Had I not been willing to be open to my son's feelings and dreams about his future, my future with him might well have been limited to perfunctory, courteous exchanges at birthdays and a few holidays. Instead, my ability to adapt to his vision for his future set the stage for a rewarding ongoing relationship in which we can talk about dreams and plans, or simply have fun. His decision not to play pro hockey, his own Midline, presented me with Midline. I had to choose whether I should hold on to my own dogged determination for what his life should look like and try to force it on him, or step with him into the excitement of an unknown future he could create for himself out of his own heart. ■

A MIDLINE PRACTICE

Recall a situation in which you reevaluated your viewpoint in some way in order to allow a relationship with somebody to flourish.

CHAPTER 68
The Fire of desire—the Third Chakra— Manipura Chakra

I have a yoga teacher friend, Jane, who is well loved and very popular in the community. Her students love going to her class and being with her. She had been a yoga student for a long time before she decided to teach yoga. She wanted to teach because yoga had done so much for her and she wanted to share its gifts with others. Also, she is gregarious and loves people.

This decision made, she found a teaching slot for an evening class. On the day of the first class, she was so scared and unsure of herself that she decided to cancel the class. She had convinced herself that she wasn't good enough, that her teaching ability was inferior, and therefore, she couldn't go through with it. We could play "Name the *Mala*," right? She frantically and without success called around, trying to find a substitute. Somebody eventually convinced her to just show up and teach the class. That's what she did.

Quite some time later I stopped by a local yoga studio right next door to one of my favorite bakeries—I have many favorite bakeries—and I noticed that even though it was 3:30 in the afternoon, when the studio would normally be closed, the lights were on and the front door open. I was curious and walked inside, eating my brownie.

A woman sat behind the desk and I asked her what class was underway. She said that one of the local teachers had volunteered to teach yoga to incarcerated junior high and high school girls. This was their yoga day and the woman behind the desk was in charge of supervising their trip over to the studio and back. She told me the girls loved doing yoga mostly because they loved the yoga teacher. They liked her sense of humor and the way she inspired them to make better choices in their lives, all while having fun and without a lecture. She said the girls even practiced yoga on their own.

This woman told me the teacher was a "Godsend." I looked inside the studio and it was Jane, the woman who some time earlier had felt so unworthy, so unlike "real" yoga teachers, that she almost quit before even trying. Instead of quitting, she had used her desire to help others motivate her past her fear. She had stepped into Midline, developing into a well-loved yoga teacher in our community. Jane shared her gift of commitment and courage to this special group of young women who so needed a role model for those character traits. By overcoming her own fears and insecurities, Jane offered these women a bird's eye view of how Spirit can show up in the world; no doubt changing their lives in the process by showing them what is possible not just in a pose but also as a full participant in life.

Jane's path to transformation introduces us to the third *Chakra, Manipura*, located near the solar plexus. This *Chakra* is associated with fire, vitality, individual willpower, self-esteem, and personality. Here we have a desire to express our individuality. This is the place where our hunger to transform ourselves can catapult us out of our comfort zone and into Midline. When Jane chose to overcome her fears and doubts and show up to teach her first yoga class, this was an example of stepping into Midline. It was her yearning to serve others through her skills as a yoga teacher that burned away her fear and doubts.

The third *Chakra* is associated with *Manomaya Kosha* where the fire of illumination and the willpower for transformation guide us as we process our thoughts and feelings. Here is where we come into contact with our aspirations, our dreams and use the fire of our inner spirit, and its light, to illumine the best way to focus our will and then express ourselves artfully. We engage the power of the fire to burn away the resistance inside us that interferes with our transformation; i.e., feelings of unworthiness or the inability to see connection.

It is at this *Chakra* that we overcome inertia, freeing ourselves from old patterns of behavior as we create new habits that help us fulfill our vision of ourselves.[197] This reminds me of the story I told about my almost-date with my sister's friend. I couldn't understand at the time why my mother made such a big deal out of my skipping work that one night out of so many. She gave me heat about missing work because she understood that I needed to break a pattern, in this case the understandable pattern of the college kid who liked to party. She wanted me to forge a new pattern, that of being a responsible and dependable adult. She knew that I would need this new pattern to make it in life at the level of success she was determined I reach. She was right. Without that type of ongoing friction from my mother and father I would never have achieved what I have accomplished thus far.

We must develop some mastery at this level in order to recognize and step into Midline throughout our life. Otherwise, we remain on the safe side of Midline, the place where we may dance with all our emotions and desires, but the dance fails to be quite as much fun, not so rewarding; eventually somewhat empty.

It can be easy to stay stuck at the third *Chakra*, feeling the desire to expand but staying attached to those things that keep us feeling safe, remaining mired in the same place in our lives.[198] The challenge is to become proactive in seeking growth.[199] Yoga practices help us discover who we are and share it in service of something greater. Through these practices we learn how to create a life where we not only meet challenges head–on, we seek them out because we know that on the other side of the challenge is an even sweeter taste of Spirit.

I believe that some of our most rewarding relationships are those that provide friction in our lives from time to time. We need friction to create the sparks that start that fire of transformation. My Mother created friction by stopping me in the kitchen and telling me I would never amount to anything if, right then, I didn't turn around, go back upstairs, change into my work clothes and go to work at the steel mill. It wasn't that she didn't want me to have fun. She wanted me to learn that there has to be some willpower, some commitment in our lives if we are ever going to transform our dreams into reality. Similarly, Jane's desire to teach confronted her fear and those two energies rubbed each other until sparks flew, creating a fire of desire that burned through the fear. As a result, she showed up for her first class. Because she showed up, the community has been served in beautiful ways too numerous to count. ■

A MIDLINE PRACTICE

Think of an example where somebody pushed or prodded you to do something you felt resistance to doing, and now in hindsight you can see that your choice to do what they urged you to do has benefited you.

CHAPTER 69
Living out of the heart—the Fourth Chakra— Anahata Chakra

A few weeks ago I watched a man limping painfully along the street. He was disheveled and looked down and out. I felt sorry for him. I started to speculate as to why he wasn't able, like me, to simply access a doctor and get repaired. Then, rather than go down that road of wondering why this man couldn't take care of himself, I stopped speculating. My mind wouldn't even walk down that Judgment Avenue. It was not productive to do so and not even relevant. I didn't need to know this man's history, why he hadn't obtained good care, and if was due to his own fault. All I felt was a desire that he not be in pain.

I thought: "Who cares if somebody is not self-reliant when they are in pain? Does it really matter if the person is lazy, on drugs, smokes, or is otherwise hampered by his personal choices if he is hurting? Is it okay that someone live a pain-filled life everyday simply because they didn't study hard enough in eighth grade or, feeling despondent over losing a job, lost themselves in drugs or alcohol? What about people who try hard every day, live life by the rules, and still can't afford medical relief?" I'm all about personal responsibility, but—get real—we all are dealt different hands, many of them with no face cards.

How could somebody like me, somebody dealt a pretty good hand, ever possibly understand the difficulties somebody else has had to face? And, so what if I was up to the task and that other person was not? Does that make it acceptable that they suffer?

I've concluded, based on no evidence other than my own life's experience that many of us make these judgments about others because we have forgotten how lucky we've been and also because of a fear that if we are too free with our mercy and compassion, there won't be enough left over for us. When we remember our own good fortune and then let go of our fears and concerns about whether there will be enough for everyone, our innate empathy and compassion will cause us to open to the plight of others. When this occurs, we are then living out of the fourth *Chakra, Anahata*, located in the area of the heart.

The fourth *Chakra* is associated not only with compassion, but also a sense of equilibrium, love, and an open heart. Here we have a desire for love and self-acceptance. This *Chakra* relates to *Vijnanamaya Kosha* because our thoughts and feelings move through a tug of war with ego toward *Buddhi*, where we ultimately view the world as Spirit. We are better able to make the choices that lead to balanced and loving relationships with others and with ourselves. This *Chakra* is the center of love and our spiritual core.[200] If we are doing our personal work, engaging in self-study and other practices, our loving is not dependent on outside stimulation but, instead, becomes our natural state of being.[201] We begin to see the world in relationships and connection.[202]

On the day I saw the man limping in pain, in that moment at least, I was living in a state of concern for others, independent of what was in it for me. I looked at the man and experienced a desire that he feel the same peace and freedom I have been blessed with.

There is something blocked in our system when we either cannot or will not open to the plight of other people. I am thankful in part because I know that but for luck, *Lila*, along the way, I could be that down and out guy walking with the painful limp, seemingly resigned to spending his life in that pain. That could be me. Or, that could be a family member. Or, that could be a friend.

Where do we draw the line in terms of whether we care or not? I think as soon as we begin to draw lines we are creating categories to rationalize an argument that those in pain are somehow separate from us and therefore not worthy of help. When we do that we might as well be building dams to block the flow of loving possibility into and out of our hearts. When we become selective of whom we can or cannot love and feel empathy for, we diminish our capacity to feel love and, with that, to be loved. Ultimately, we're either love or we're not.

The step into Midline is to begin to view everybody, including the planet, as part of a collective whole, as Spirit in its many diverse forms. When I view another human being in this way, I return to Spirit. We feel connected with people we don't know because, ultimately, they are just like us, people trying to find happiness or at least some modicum of peace in their life. When we view each other like this, our choices become easier to make, our base-line motivation becomes that of connection and service, of love and support for each other. When we reach this state, Midline and the fourth *Chakra* become our home. ■

▌ A MIDLINE PRACTICE

Think back to a time when you saw a stranger in trouble and you helped or, conversely, when a stranger lent you a hand when you needed help.

CHAPTER 70
Spirit's communications—the Fifth Chakra— Vishuddha Chakra

Think back to my friend Jane the yoga teacher who almost quit without ever teaching a class. She felt unworthy and afraid. She has since become a very popular and valued teacher. One reason, of course, is that she studies and keeps working on becoming a better teacher. However, there is another reason that makes her so special. Somewhere in the course of her life she has learned how to communicate directly from her heart. When her students take her class they can feel her commitment. Then, on top of that, her teaching comes wrapped in humor and good nature. She views life as fun and she brings that attitude to her class. No wonder she is popular. Imagine knowing that you can go someplace for an hour and spend some time with a person that cares about you and will make you laugh. Learning yoga is a nice side dish.

Earlier I mentioned another yoga teacher, Chris, who is also very popular in Denver. He's popular for so many reasons but I've identified a particular ability that stands out to me. When we first sit down on our mats to begin class he tells us a story. Sometimes the story is out of his personal life. Other times the story is about an Indian God or Goddess. It really doesn't matter. What matters is that when Chris is telling the story, it comes right from his heart. I've seen his face well up with tears on occasion, perhaps recounting to us an article about something tragic that he read. I've heard him giggling as he narrates something funny he experienced. Once I could almost hear Chris' heart breaking as he shared a personal hurt.

By the time Chris finishes a story, we are already so in touch with our own spirit that it wouldn't matter what poses he has us do. His gift is to get in touch with Spirit and, through his sincere telling of the story, connect us to Spirit as well. When he teaches, he teaches from Midline because he is willing to risk sharing his vulnerabilities with us so that we can each feel free to explore our own feelings.

Jane and Chris's ability to communicate brings us to the fifth *Chakra, Vishuddha,* located at the throat and associated with sound, vibration, communication, and creativity. We desire to speak and hear the truth. This *Chakra* is associated with *Anandamaya Kosha* because we are now living out of the heart and able to make harmonious communication leading to connection, and enhancing Spirit in the world. At this point we have learned to engage in intimate and mutually serving relationships. This is a point where we are able to now make our deeper, more creative voice be heard.

The world benefits when each of us uses our skills of communication to coax each other beyond our perceived limitations.[203] Why? How can we not benefit when more and more people offer their unique talents, as for example, when Mozart decided to give us his music or our latest Olympians chose to develop their skills? Communication through such expressions of artistry cannot help but inspire us to higher expressions of ourselves.

We don't have to be Mozart or an Olympian. We just have to learn how to communicate as Spirit, creating pathways into and out from our heart for Spirit to travel as we move through life. Yoga practices are a great means for keeping those pathways clear and flowing. ■

A MIDLINE PRACTICE

Think of a time when somebody touched your heart by what they said or perhaps even how they said it. Why do you think this person was able to touch you this way?

CHAPTER 71
The Third Eye—the Sixth Chakra— Ajna Chakra

During the 2012 Olympics I saw a fascinating commercial. U.S. swimming competitor Rebecca Soni had just won the gold medal in the 200-meter breaststroke, breaking her own world record. She won in a time of 2 minutes, 19.59 seconds, the first woman to ever break 2 minutes and 20 seconds.

In a marvel of technology, just as I finished watching the race on my television in Colorado, the broadcast broke away from the time-delayed event in London to a commercial. The commercial shows a young woman looking at her phone and watching the race we just saw. Spellbound, she watches Ms. Soni win the race and set the world record. The girl in the commercial then puts her phone down, stands up, her face a picture of total contemplation. After a brief moment, her expression changes to one full of determination and she walks over to her chalkboard. She writes: "Goal: 2:19.59", which, of course, is Ms. Soni's brand new world record that we just watched. She then picks up her swim bag, and walks out the door, with the message "Here's to the new possible" at the bottom of the television screen.

This clever commercial, put together so rapidly, reminded me of the sixth *Chakra, Ajna,* our ability to experience something, and then visualize how we might create something new for ourselves out of that experience. This woman was obviously a serious swimmer and when she watched Ms. Soni set the new record, she immediately envisioned where she needed to take her swimming commitment, her "new possible." She was viewing this swimming event out of a healthy sixth *Chakra,* one that sees the promise inherent in each experience. What a great way to view the world.

This *Chakra,* located between the eyebrows, is associated with light, luminosity, intuition, psychic perception, clarity and wisdom. We see the unity in diversity. This sixth *Chakra* is located in the middle of the head. In India, Hindu women often put a red dot, a *Bindu,* at the location of this *Chakra,*[204] the location where telepathic communications are transmitted and received.[205] It is a place of clairvoyance and other similar paranormal abilities.[206]

When we engage with other people from this place, we are more likely to truly see or sense what is in their hearts. We see the promise residing within them. Here we perceive images and then creatively visualize the potential of what we just saw.[207] The swimmer watched Ms. Soni set a world record, assimilated that image, created a vision, and then headed out the door to train in order to break the new record, to fulfill the vision she just created for herself.

How much we are able to visualize and create is a function of how curious we are about the world and how willing we are to take the risks associated with Midline, to choose to reach out to a potentially rich new experience. With so much diversity in the world, there is an endless stream of stimuli, information from which we can envision dream after dream after dream.

Our ability to visualize and create is also dependent on how much self-study we do, Self-study opens us to see and prioritize our experiences clearly, uncluttered by bias, envy or other emotions. This allows us to make better-informed choices and expands our capacity to visualize more in each experience. Self-study helps us to honestly appraise our strengths and recognize areas we need to work on.

I recently read about high school super-star swimmer Missy Franklin's training before heading off to the Olympics. She added gut-wrenching box jumps to her routine; a series of jumps using an 18-inch box designed to help give her more explosion in her race starts. No wonder she had such a phenomenal Olympics. She was able to be honest with herself as to what she needed to do to become even greater at her sport. Imagine how many potential superstars could realize their full potential by doing some honest introspective study of where they might improve. We'd have to schedule more Olympics!

The more we meditate and practice yoga and other mindfulness activities, the more we slow down and mindfully participate in each moment, the better our brain becomes at connecting all the data we've gathered through our curiosity and self-study. As we assimilate what we've experienced, we begin to find patterns in everything we've seen and learned. We then attach meaning to this information through the wisdom of our memories, intuition and imagination.[208] Yoga practices help us develop the creative capacity located at this *Chakra*, enabling us to visualize a future built out of our dreams and swim for it! ■

A MIDLINE PRACTICE

Think of something you do each day on a regular basis, a hobby, your job, a sport activity, or something else, where the initial inspiration to try that activity came from watching somebody else.

CHAPTER 72
You really can't miss Spirit—
the Seventh Chakra—Sahasrara Chakra

I called my friend Hannah when I learned she had just undergone a highly invasive surgery. She had been feeling pain but presumed the pain was due to an injury. A routine visit to the doctor revealed a problem and during the surgery the doctors discovered a far more serious and unanticipated complication. Fortunately, due to some amazing medical devices that allowed for exploration, as well as the skill of the surgeons and staff, they were able to resolve everything during this surgery, leaving her healthy again.

As Hannah told me the story, I marveled at modern science. The doctors made a tiny insertion into her body, and then used some form of gas to gently separate tissue and see what was happening. Using a tiny light, they encountered the problem and were immediately able to treat it. Hannah gave me permission to tell this story.

Hannah's story is yet another wonderful example of how we can find Spirit by taking time to observe the many ways Spirit manifests in the world. It is easy to see Spirit in a beautiful rainbow. If we are aware, it is also easy to see Spirit in the skill of a surgeon, the inventiveness of a medical device manufacturer, or in countless other ways, all easily visible to us when we wake up. When we live out of the seventh *Chakra, Sahasrara,* we've awakened.

This *Chakra,* located at the top of the head, is associated with the bliss of pure consciousness and spiritual connection. We know the essence of ourselves, how Spirit resides in us, and that Spirit exists everywhere. The higher mental functions of *Buddhi* occur here and the full potential of this *Chakra* is mystical experience and illumination.[209] We no longer feel threatened by differences between us; instead, we immediately feel connection. When we awaken to this viewpoint, we find meaning, not only in our own lives but also the underlying order of everything.[210] At this *Chakra* we achieve the ideal interaction of *Manas, Ahamkara,* and *Buddhi,* making choices that bring us to Midline. We are Spirit in action.

At this point in our spiritual development the restricted vision imposed on us by the *Kanchukas,* while necessarily present within us by virtue of our being in human form, are reduced in their effectiveness. Our capacity to envision our future and, as we choose, create ourselves anew is at its highest level of development.[211]

Anodea Judith suggests that to find Spirit all we have to do is take a look around us, at the inventiveness of our own household furnishings, the design of our cities, or the treasures on our bookshelves.[212] Spirit, she says, exists not only in the amazing display of nature's diversity, but also in the unlimited creative expression of we humans.[213]

Dr. Judith urges us to be curious, fascinated, in wonder, to find meaning in metaphor and to explore. When we live this way, we may come to that place in our lives where we naturally find Spirit in everything. We seek, find, and choose the Midline at every turn. ■

A MIDLINE PRACTICE

Spend two minutes contemplating how many amazing things any modern invention of your choice does for you. Think of the thought and creativity that resulted in its existence.

PART VII

It takes practice—Patanjali's Yoga Sutras

A. Looking inside; becoming absorbed in Spirit

CHAPTER 73
A magical bike ride

On a beautiful fall morning I looked out the window and realized that because of my travels I hadn't taken my mountain bike out for a ride in far too long. Up where I live I can see the Devil's Thumb Ranch valley just below me, as well as the Continental Divide right across the way, rising far higher than the 9,000-foot elevation of my place. The sun was shining. It was a day that demands you go outside. Tall green lodge pole pine trees intermixed with fully turned aspens, their leaves flicking gold in the clear, crisp, brilliant light. It was a spectacular day.

I decided to take my bike out for a long, gentle ride and enjoy the fall color. The bright morning air was fresh and cool. My home is outside of town, truly out in the woods. Our roads outside of town are all hard-packed clay that twist and turn through the trees as they climb to well over 10,000 feet. A fast-running stream, fueled by snowmelt all season long, runs along a good part of the County road, and I love hearing it pour down the mountain.

Because I hadn't been riding much, I thought I would just take my time. As I rode along, my mind began a debate with itself. Even though I was in great shape and wanted to take off and ride fast to celebrate the day, some voice inside told me to hold back. The voice reminded me that I hadn't ridden in awhile, that I was getting older and that, because I wasn't a kid anymore, perhaps I should take it easy.

Inside me it was like the battle of the bands. One voice pleaded with me to take off, and the other voice told me to just play it safe and cruise along. As I rode, this internal debate went on and on. One voice argued that it was perfectly okay, given this elevation, to gently glide along and enjoy the colors, while the competing voice begged me to fly up and down the rolling terrain. This chatter was getting in the way of a beautiful ride.

Suddenly, a group of men and women came up from behind me and then sped by me on their bikes, moving hard along the County road. They shouted "Good Morning" in a friendly way and kept on going. Soon, they were way ahead of me. Watching them fly past and move off into the distance, I could feel the juices flowing in me even more. I wanted to pick up my pace and enjoy the raw pleasure that comes from biking hard and fast. My heart wanted to soar! However, again, there was that other voice, the voice of doubt, speaking to me. That voice kept telling me that trying to go fast might be beyond my reach. It told me to ignore the part of me that wanted to have fun and, instead, simply to take it easy.

I had been listening to that latter voice all morning. Suddenly, I told that voice to "take a hike!" I let that powerful desire to ride hard take over and I took off. By this time I had turned around and after heading downhill into the valley, I now had to ride uphill to get back to my place. It didn't matter. I was having fun, the cool wind in my face, my body and spirit alive. I could feel the blood pumping through my legs and my legs responding, driving me harder and faster, even as the incline became intense. Forgotten was the voice of doubt and in its place were feelings of sheer happiness and pleasure. Amazingly, I was surprised at how easy the uphill was.

I came to the final hill, the really steep incline I have to take to get back to my house. In the past, even when I was riding all the time, I could barely get up that hill. This time, though, I charged up the hill as if it weren't there, arriving at my house with energy to spare. I got off my bike and felt like dancing the way Rocky did at the top of the stairs in Philadelphia.

As I put my bike away, I felt high, a feeling of pleasure and contentment. There were no thoughts other than how great it was to be alive. I watched the tall pines sway gently in the breeze and enjoyed the sun glowing off the aspen, with my red chokecherry trees a brilliant contrast against the bright yellow aspen. I grabbed some water and sat in a chair on the deck and enjoyed the scenery as well as the feelings inside me. Instead of a battle of the bands inside my head, now I was listening to a beautiful symphony.

As I sat there, it eventually occurred to me that all the chattering of the mind, the self-doubts fighting with my desire to fully enjoy the ride, was a microcosm of how I lived so much of my life before yoga and before learning about Midline. Every time I had been offered something positive in my life, it seemed like one part of me would fight with another part of me, trying to decide if I was worthy enough or good enough to accept the chance being offered. Often times the "you are unworthy" voice won out. The opportunity walked away while my mind conducted its debate.

These inner conversations were all Midlines, inviting me to connect more fully with Spirit. When I think of these lost opportunities, the times I chose to play it safe, I feel sad, knowing how foolish it is for any of us to miss chances to deeply enjoy the gift of our time on earth. It is too bad that we let the self-limiting messages inside us overpower the other voice, the voice of Spirit, urging us to open to our potential. The chatter of our mind really can keep us from stepping into Midline, those opportunities to be happy, fulfilled and find meaning in our lives.

I include this story here to lead off a discussion of Patanjali's *Yoga Sutras*. We've discussed how yoga's lessons can help us create a life of well-being, a life in which we use our own special skills in ways that makes us feel engaged with life, creating harmony in our workplace, at home, and in our community. Just like we have to practice to get better at playing the piano or riding a mountain bike well, we have to do the practices taught by yoga, even if we never do yoga poses, if we want to live life well. Practicing is how we get better at life.

So, what are the practices yoga teaches? Where do we learn about them? One of the most highly regarded texts on the practices of yoga is Patanjali's *Yoga Sutras*, probably one of the most studied works in any yoga philosophy course. A *Sutra*, which literally means a "thread," is a short statement that conveys philosophical information concisely.[214] In these next chapters we'll get to take a short look at these *Sutras*. ■

A MIDLINE PRACTICE

Even if you have no intention of every doing a yoga pose, are you open to learning the value of paying attention to your breath, so that you can incorporate attentive breathing into your own choice of activities, such as bike riding, lifting weights, gardening, making a meal, or brewing coffee?

CHAPTER 74
A meaningful life takes practice

I played football in high school and college. As a seventh grader going out for the team, I gravitated to center and played that position all the way through college. Back in seventh grade my good friend Jim—Jim from the Introduction of this book and my "visitor" at Machu Picchu—was the punter. Sometimes during our junior high games I'd bounce the ball back to him, other times I'd send it sailing ten feet over his head. By the end of the seventh grade season I think he had lost ten pounds with all the running he had to do chasing after the ball or running away from tacklers after scooping up one of my low snaps.

At some point, a guy from our neighborhood, another Jim, a former state champion wrestler and all-state center for our state champion high school team, took pity on me, or more likely, my punter friend Jim. He showed me how to snap the ball properly so it would rocket back in a nice tight spiral to the kicker or holder. He taught me exactly how to hold the ball, how to snap my wrists, and even how to hit my inner thighs with my arms at just exactly the right spot, guaranteeing I would get the ball exactly where it was supposed to go. He also told me that hardly anybody knows how to snap the ball correctly and if I could learn to do it well, I would make the varsity team for sure when I was old enough.

I began to practice. I found people to catch the ball. If I couldn't find people, I'd go to an alley somewhere, stand about 15 yards away from a brick wall, and snap the ball, trying to hit the mark I'd scrawled on the wall.

I practiced and practiced and practiced. I bet I snapped the ball not just hundreds of times but thousands. By the time I got to the defending state champion high school, the coaches immediately saw my tight, fast spiral hikes from all the way across the field. The all-state center from my neighborhood had graduated and they were having a tough time finding somebody to snap to the kicker. At the high school level, punts, extra points and field goals mattered and a team couldn't do any of those things if the center couldn't get the ball back with speed and accuracy. I made the varsity as a sophomore, playing third-string as a center but serving as the number one snapper for all the kicks.

What a great experience. I got to play in every game throughout the season as we went undefeated again and were ranked first in the state. Toward the end of the season I got to play first-string for a while due to injuries to the other centers. We made it all the way to the Indiana state championship game, where we lost to Elkhart for our only loss that season. I got to play in the game, something so few players ever get to do.

Over the course of that season I played against incredibly talented opposing players: an eventual starting defensive end at Nebraska; another eventual starting linebacker at Illinois; and yet another linebacker who went on to star at Notre Dame. This player made the cover of *Sports Illustrated*, which captured him making a key interception during the famous 10 –10 national championship game between Notre Dame and Michigan State in 1966. What great experiences.

Being on the varsity football team as a sophomore greatly eased my transition into a large high school and helped set the stage for a successful time, leading to even more success and fun in college, where I also played center on the varsity team. Those thousands upon thousands of practice snaps paid off big time.

Yoga philosophy and proper technique, and I'm not only referring here to poses, if practiced diligently, reward us immeasurably. But we have to practice. Just like practicing hiking a football enriched my high school and college experiences, and beyond, it takes practice to shift behaviors. The lessons of yoga identify these practices.

Patanjali's *Yoga Sutras* identifies for us practices we can use, for example, as we navigate the *Tattvas*. Patanjali helps us learn how and where to look in every moment for the potential, whether it is another person, an event, or some act of nature. We learn to use our senses to look and listen for Spirit, and then to focus on Her. We learn to listen, speak and touch with more refinement. The *Yoga Sutras* identify meditation and self-study practices as means to cultivate and polish our ability to do these things. The *Yoga Sutras* also show us the importance of having a moral and ethical compass.

I think of all the hours I spent learning to hike or snap a football accurately and the rewards I experienced as a result. This one skill brought me greater confidence and social ease at school and the financial opportunity to attend college. This is a big lesson I get from the study of Patanjali's *Yoga Sutras*—practice! Just as I found that practicing the long snap in football paid dividends, so, too, can yoga practices pay dividends for all of us, regardless of the playing field. ■

A MIDLINE PRACTICE
Think of something you do well. Now, think of how much you've practiced doing that particular thing in order to become skilled at it.

CHAPTER 75
Where practice can take us

When I go to Denver I leave the Fraser River valley, drive through numerous high mountain switchbacks until I reach Berthoud Pass, at 11,307 feet, cross the Continental Divide, and then head back downhill through more switchbacks into Clear Creek County. The whole area, from bottom to top and back down again, is a top draw in the summer for biking and hiking and, in the winter, for backcountry skiers, snowboarders and people on snowshoes.

While a driver must pay strict attention to the steep and winding road, you can't help but be overwhelmed by the way every switchback reveals a scene more spectacular than the last one. Even though I take this road often, every time there is a slightly different blend of light and colors showing off the trees, rocks and vegetation in a way different from before. To me, it is like God saying: "Look what I want to give you today."

A few weeks ago I saw something new that really wowed me. As I was driving east toward the town of Empire, after coming over the pass, the wild grass along the road caught my attention. In November it has rich texture and colors: brilliant yellows, purples and reds. The wind was hitting the grasses just right, and they bent and lifted, moving in waves, not unlike the waves on the ocean. It was gentle, beautiful and rhythmic, as if the wind was playing a soft song.

Years ago, I never would have noticed the grass or been touched by its rhythmic comfort. My yoga practices have been teaching my mind to slow down, observe and appreciate. The practices have also taught me not to constantly dwell on the thoughts that used to drive me nuts. I'm learning to stay rooted in the present. My mind doesn't fly off into the future quite so often, imagining disasters that I can't stop anyway. I don't get so caught up in my inner chatter that I miss the most exquisite moment of all: the one right outside the car window, right now.

There is another point to this story and this is perhaps the most significant. It is so wonderful, so magical, such a blessing, to become more aware of nature and the fascinating, beautiful things around us. What would our lives be like if we could give the same engaged attention and wonder to our hopes, dreams and feelings on a regular basis? What would it feel like to live on the edge of our seats for our own lives, stunned, on a daily basis, at how much life offers us and how rich we are just by being on the planet?

When we engage in practices such as *Mantra,* yoga poses, methods of relaxed breathing, meditation, or when we exercise simple awareness as we go about our day, we become more mindful and increase our ability to recognize the feelings of others as well as our own. We don't miss the opportunities for connection so frequently. Our child comes in to the room all excited about something and we no longer tell them to come back later because we're on the phone or finishing a newspaper article. Our mind is spacious enough to readily sense our child is excited and proud of something they've figured out and they are offering us the chance to share in that precious experience. We recognize this very special invitation to connect with them and build their self-esteem with our focus and praise.

We are aware that our friends, partners and loved ones need to share the joy or pain they've experienced and so we give them our attention. As a result, we become closer to them, sharing in that joy or easing their burden. As we get older these are the memories and experiences we will most treasure, so why wouldn't we build our capacity to recognize and experience them in the moment they are offered? This is the level of attentiveness we must have to identify when Midline appears. If we don't even recognize a Midline, life's invitations to richer experiences and precious relationships, we can't possibly avail ourselves of those invitations.

What is it about Patanjali's *Yoga Sutras* that makes yoga teachers everywhere recommend we study them? B.K.S. Iyengar, highly renowned yoga teacher and founder of Iyengar Yoga, tells us Patanjali studied the human condition in depth and his *Sutras* explain how, through yoga, we can achieve a fuller, happier life.[215] Mr. Iyengar suggests if we follow Patanjali's teachings, and absorb their powerful insights into the depths of our inner selves, our lives will be filled with profound meaning and happiness.[216]

Mr. Iyengar tells us yoga practice, *Sadhana,* can help us overcome the limitations posed by certain of our *Samskaras,* the storehouse of our past perceptions, instincts and impressions built up over our entire life.[217] Through Patanjali we learn how to avoid the pitfalls in our conduct that get in our way while at the same time how to build the character necessary to meet life's challenges head-on.[218] This appeals to me! We can use yoga practices to develop not only the necessary awareness to recognize Midline, but also the strength and courage to do something about the opportunities Midline presents. ■

A MIDLINE PRACTICE

Go for a walk in a neighborhood of your choice, with plenty of houses to see. Select three of your favorite homes, whether due to the design of the house itself, the landscaping, or whatever else you find pleasant and appealing about the homes.

CHAPTER 76
Elevator music—Patanjali's Yoga Sutra 1.2; seeing through the chatter

The other night I started a Stuart Woods' novel starring the recurring character Stone Barrington. Barrington, a former New York homicide detective, is a well-to-do attorney living in New York City. Over the course of the novels, Stone Barrington has become a pretty sophisticated man. In the novel he and his friend Dino are having dinner at their table at Elaine's, a restaurant for the upper crust. In walks a beautiful woman and Barrington, having never met her before, nonetheless casually walks up to her at the bar and invites her to join him and his friends at their table. She agrees and the novel is off to the races—as is their relationship.

As I read that, marveling at Stone's easy and confident demeanor around women, I remembered one time when I was working late in our Minneapolis law office. I finally decided I had enough and needed to get to the gym for a workout. I liked working out because it was fun and made me feel good. There was, of course, another reason I worked out. I wanted to look good because I thought it would help me to be attractive to women.

I got in the elevator for the long ride down to the parking garage. The elevator stopped at a lower floor and a woman entered the elevator. She smiled at me and said hello and I responded in kind. She said something to the effect of "I'm worn out, I need to relax and have a drink downstairs." There was a nice restaurant/bar on our main floor, and I thought to myself that it would be nice to have a drink with her and get to know her, but I knew I needed to get to the gym, so I said nothing. Also, the thought went through my mind that she was good looking and I'm sort of a normal-looking guy, so she'd probably say "No" anyway.

As the elevator descended we chatted about the weather, always a safe topic in Minneapolis, and eventually we got to the main floor. The whole way down I sort of listened to her but also spent the time thinking of my next response. What could I say to impress her? How do I ask her for her name and number? Would she even give it to me?

When the door opened on the main floor, she looked at me and said that it was nice meeting me. Then, surprisingly, she asked me if I really needed to rush off or could I join her for a drink. Still convinced that she wouldn't find me interesting, and still thinking that I had to get to the gym, I declined. I said that I unfortunately had to get somewhere. She shrugged, smiled and got off the elevator to go have a drink by herself or with any friends she might find. I didn't have the nerve to even ask for her name or number.

I got in my car and hurried off to the gym. It took me almost a mile before it hit me: I was so obsessed with getting to the gym to make myself look good that I had just missed a chance to connect with a seemingly nice, pleasant, eligible woman expressing interest in me. Because my mind was so busy chattering, I'd missed the great opportunity Midline offered me, the possibility of a new and potentially great relationship. I missed the opportunity because my mind had been tied up trying to balance such thoughts as: 1) getting to the gym to look good to be attractive to women just like her; 2) fear of rejection; and 3) only half listening to her because I wanted to appear witty to impress her, tying up my brain with figuring out snappy retorts.

My brain was so preoccupied with all these disparate thoughts that I had no space to process what was happening in the elevator. Certainly there was no space for my heart to be heard: "You're lonely; she seems really nice, so have the drink." With my mind trying to handle so many churning thoughts, any possibility of finding a connection with this person was lost amidst the chatter. Unlike Stone Barrington, I was not very practiced at what it takes to make a connection with an appealing woman who seemed to be interested in me.

This embarrassing glimpse into my dating life, or understandable lack thereof, begins our study of selected *Sutras*. We start by looking at Patanjali Yoga *Sutra* 1.2, often translated to say that yoga is the controlling of the fluctuations of the mind. Possibly, in this *Sutra*, Patanjali has defined the entire system of yoga.[219]

If this *Sutra* is so important, why am I introducing it with a story about my dating life? I think the story fits: how can we recognize Midline when our minds race a mile a minute, trying to make sense from conflicting thoughts and emotions? This story reveals how the fluctuations of the mind, if allowed to run unabated at their whim, prevent or limit our ability to recognize and embrace Midline, to connect to Spirit. Even when we recognize Midline, our mind has to have enough space, enough clarity, to overcome the patterns of thought and behavior that hold us back from accepting the invitation Midline is offering.

The story shows how important it is that we engage in practices that cultivate the ability to slow down and mentally create space in the mind. This space allows us to properly process the thoughts and emotions that arise in any given situation. Here I am, going to the gym, in part, to make myself look appealing to potential dates. Yet, when a real live potential date walks right into my elevator and asks me for a drink, my mind is having so many conversations with itself there is no time for common sense to step in and say: "Excuse me...Duh!"

Patanjali's *Yoga Sutra* 1.2 tells us the practice of yoga, ultimately, involves learning how to deal with the activity of our mind so our mental commotion doesn't get in our way. There is already plenty happening in our minds when meeting a new person. Add to this mix the effects of the various energies we've already studied, such as the *Malas*, which can have an impact on how we think, feel, and respond in a conversation. In my elevator story above, we could play the game: "Name That *Mala*." The correct answer would be "All three." I felt unworthy. I felt separate from the type of guys I imagined she would be interested in. The result: I acted in a way that, motivated to try to fix these perceptions by impressing her with my wit, I actually created separation.

Yoga teaches us practices that give us the space we need to process the chatter and respond in a way that best serves Spirit. Such chatter, or fluctuations of the mind are called *Vrttis* in the *Yoga Sutras*.[220]

I suspect that many of you will see a little bit of yourselves in my elevator story. This is the way the human mind works. There is so much to process and so many conflicting energies at play. It is no surprise that Patanjali opens the *Yoga Sutras* by telling us the goal of yoga is to find ways to skillfully deal with this vibratory chatter so we can hear the underlying message of Spirit. Sometimes those messages are a simple as: "Hey Bill! Your biceps are fine; nobody cares. She looks fun and the margaritas in this bar are fantastic." ■

A MIDLINE PRACTICE

The next several times you engage in a conversation with somebody, notice if and when your mind begins to chatter, thinking about other things and taking you away from the conversation.

CHAPTER 77

My senior partner practices Yoga; who knew? — Patanjali's Yoga Sutra 1.12; detachment

A number of years ago I was working on a very large case, defending one of our law firm's biggest clients, an international manufacturer. There had been an explosion that killed a number of people. The explosion left even more workers severely burned or otherwise injured. Our client made a very small computer control product that was used in the system of processing equipment involved in the explosion.

I was taking depositions to determine exactly what had caused the explosion. As I took the depositions it became clear that our client's product had worked just like it was supposed to work and had nothing to do with the accident. The plaintiff's lawyer, not knowing what had caused the explosion, had, as a matter of course, sued almost every manufacturer whose product has been incorporated in this system of processing equipment.

My partner in charge called me in to his office after reading the depositions and suggested a strategy that was brilliant, innovative, and something I don't think I would have ever thought of myself at that point in my career. I implemented the strategy in the next series of depositions. That part was pretty easy. Any of my partners could have done that. As a result, we achieved a shocking early settlement. It was shocking both in terms of how little money our client had to pay and how early in the proceedings we were able to negotiate this arrangement.

As part of the settlement we obtained our client's dismissal from the case, not only potentially saving our client millions of dollars as well as the cost of a trial, but also exposing the previously unrevealed reckless conduct of others that led to the explosion. This, in turn led to far greater compensation for the victims because of the "deep pockets" of those really at fault that suddenly became part of the mix. It was a sweet result. The client was quite pleased.

The end of the year rolled around and our law firm's Executive Board awarded bonus compensation: a discretionary amount paid in addition to each partner's share of firm profits based on ownership interest. I received a bonus far beyond anything I had ever received before, way beyond the bounds of what I reasonably expected to earn. Then, as icing on the cake, one of the named partners stopped by my office to chat.

I was surprised to see him for a number of reasons. Although he knew me and was always pleasant to me when I occasionally ran into him, I didn't remember his ever visiting our floor before and I didn't think he knew where to even find my particular office. Certainly he'd never sought me out to chitchat. In any event, there he was at my office door. He stepped in and told me he had visited the client and they were so pleased with the result in the explosion case they had just given our firm significant additional work. This senior partner told me he wanted to stop in and thank me for all of "my" great work in the case.

I was stunned. A visit of this nature from one of our most senior partners was, for me, unheard of and, from my interpretation of what happened in the case, hard to figure out. The partner in charge of the case had been the one to come up with the brilliant strategy and I had simply carried the ball the way any number of my partners could have.

Eventually, I figured out what I think happened: my partner had shifted the credit to me. He had been comfortable enough in his status in the firm and his income that he hadn't felt any need to claim credit. He later told me he felt I had been doing a great job for a long time and deserved some praise. He felt this was a way he could say "Thank you" for everything I had done to help him serve our firm's clients so effectively. He seemed genuinely happy at my good fortune and told me it made him feel good to see me get this credit. How often do we see that in the business world? Wouldn't it be great if we saw it more? Patanjali tells us how we can become like that partner.

Patanjali's *Yoga Sutra* 1.12 tells us that we control the fluctuations of the mind through practice and dispassion. Some commentators suggest that another term for dispassion in this context is detachment.[221] My law partner's behavior shows us what a person who regularly engages in yogic practices looks like when he or she is able to detach from the usual temptations for more in the everyday stressful business world, as well as in life in general. Like my partner, when we are offered an opportunity to share our fortune with somebody deserving, we face Midline, the chance to risk some sacrifice in order to spread the seeds of good fortune and see how they might bloom.

My partner became a success by studying and practicing what it takes to reach and sustain a high level of accomplishment. He engaged in self-study for years and seemed to always find the courage to acknowledge when he needed to refine his behavior. I remember conversations with him when he shared some of these experiences with me. It was no surprise to me, then, to see a product of that self-study appear in the form of his kindness and graciousness towards me. He had a spiritual practice and took it seriously. As part of his practices he learned to be generous and openhearted with the fruits of his success.

My partner also cared about the firm and wanted to encourage its growth by taking care of younger lawyers he felt deserving. Through his practices he developed the courage, confidence and freedom of heart needed to detach, in this case to shift credit away from him and onto another, and to gift the economic rewards that accompanied that credit. His behavior truly reflects what it looks like when a person, through practice and dispassion, harmonizes the conflicting chatter in the mind and acts for purposes of creating more expression of Spirit in the world.

What practices does Patanjali suggest for us? How do we become people who behave in the best interest of everyone, not just themselves? Mr. Iyengar identifies committed and ongoing practices, *Abhyasa*, to be those contained in the Eightfold Path of *Astanga* (*Ashtanga*) *Yoga: Yamas, Niyamas, Asana, Pranayama, Pratyahara, Dharana, Dhyana,* and *Samadhi*.[222] When engaged in these practices Patanjali tells us we must also practice *Vairagya*, detachment, which means the discarding of thoughts and actions that interfere with our practice.[223]

Through these eight practices, we develop discrimination: the ability to discard ideas and actions that keep us from Midline.[224] Through these practices we connect to Spirit. We'll have a look at them next. ■

A MIDLINE PRACTICE

Think of a time when you were so interested in somebody else's success that you put that person's opportunities ahead of your needs and desires.

CHAPTER 78

Learning to trust—Patanjali's Yoga Sutra *1.20; learning to "bring it"*

A number of years ago I was at a large yoga workshop. Several hundred people were in the room. Late on Sunday afternoon, toward the end, we were all in a lunge pose. Suddenly, as the teacher walked down one of the rows, he stopped, asking one woman to hold her pose while telling everybody else to come around and observe. He turned to me and asked: "Bill, what do you see in her pose?" I responded that I saw a strong, powerful woman who was committed to using her gifts to be a force in the world. The woman's pose was strong, of course, and I'm sure I could have found something to enhance it; some slight shift of her shoulder or foot, perhaps. However, what I chiefly saw was a feeling of power and commitment flowing out of this woman. So, that is what I said.

The teacher looked at me for a moment and then told the group when a person is trained to teach yoga, that person over time and with committed practice learns to look first for the highest, the most beautiful expression. To paraphrase, we learn to first look for Spirit's finest expression, whether in a yoga pose or whatever else appears in life. We don't ignore the junk, but we start from the foundation of connecting to Spirit.

He went on to say when a person is trained this way it would be impossible not to feel the woman's strength, power and determination. It was that pronounced. Afterwards, the woman came up to me and said she had to thank me; what I had said was one of the nicest things anybody had ever said about her and it meant a great deal. She had tears in her eyes as she said it and she gave me a huge hug.

Yoga Sutra 1:20 says that connection to Spirit requires faith, courage, memory, concentration, and wisdom. When I first started practicing yoga regularly I had despaired that I would ever be able to interact with others, particularly women, in a way that left them feeling respected, recognized and honored. I held on to the hope that there had to be a way to change my behavior. And, after spending time studying yoga I decided to put my faith, *Sraddha*, in yoga study and took the plunge to become a certified yoga teacher. I did so because I had faith in the yoga philosophy I'd studied.

Based on my graduate work, I could clearly see that over time, becoming immersed in the method of learning to feel heart qualities such as love, compassion, gratitude, kindness, patience, and other such emotions, and then teaching students from that place of feeling, would help me to become those qualities myself. I wanted to *be* love, compassion, courage, and all those other beautiful heart qualities we were asked to teach. It was this clarity of purpose, or faith and trust in this process, that has in fact led me to become at least at times, this type of person.

I studied consistently and with "courage," *Virya*, getting up every time I fell down, literally and figuratively, and kept learning, studying the entire Eightfold Path of yoga, as suggested by Patanjali.[225] Even though I was embarrassed at how stiff and tight I was and a bit ashamed of how my uptight behavior was so off-putting to others, I found the courage to stay on the path because it was too painful to consider the alternative—that I would remain the uncon-nected and insensitive guy that made people uncomfortable. It was the memory, *Smrti*, of what my life had been like before yoga that kept me going.

These practices fueled my passion to transform myself. I concentrated on retaining all the teachings I could and cultivating and applying them in my life. I put aside whatever con-flicted with my goals, wherever I could. My concentration, *Samadhi*, was full: I bet I racked up a world record number of study hours learning more and more about yoga.[226]

After I saw how much I had touched this woman's heart at the workshop, I thought: "It's a miracle." I'm actually connecting out of my heart with another person, a woman no less, and in a way in which my motivation was to serve her, helping her to see her greatness. Wow! I was able to see others as Spirit. This was the discernment or wisdom, *Prajna*, I had been seeking. I could find Spirit in others as a first impulse, at least this one time.[227]

We probably have all seen the P 90X commercials, with the before and after stories of men and women who have transformed their bodies by doing the workouts each day. The secret, they say, is to "bring it" each day: do the workout with commitment, follow the diet, and just keep showing up. I've tried the program and was pleased with the results. There is amazing value in finding a program you can trust and then sticking with it. My whole life has changed for the better because of my consistent yoga practices, and this book is a tribute to that, and a gift back to my teachers, to the teachings, and to learning how to trust. ■

▌ A MIDLINE PRACTICE

Bring to mind a person whom you've trusted and, over the years, that trust has proven to be well placed.

CHAPTER 79
Everything becomes clear— Patanjali's Yoga Sutra *1.33;* compassion and the joy of connection

I spent a tremendous amount of energy throughout my life trying to project whatever image I thought would impress others or allow me to fit in. I tried to be a tough guy in my neighborhood so I'd be left alone, yet I also sought to be a witty, nice guy so people would like me. I attempted to be the smart guy in the college-prep history class so my fellow classmates would respect me for being bright. I had to be careful, though, not to be too much the intellect lest I appear the wimp, conflicting with the tough guy persona I kept trying to portray. Keeping track of who I was could be a tough proposition, wearing me out every day.

Later, as a lawyer I did the same thing. It was a ton of work to try to impress everybody all the time. It makes me tired even writing about that fruitless goal. I wanted to impress partners so they would think I was partner material. I wanted to impress the women I met so I could get dates. That was a whole subcategory of challenges: This woman seemed to like the intellectual; that one was attracted to jocks. Good grief! Trying to find out who I was inside, my own unique strengths and gifts, was not even on my radar screen.

Over a period of time this approach to living not only wore me down physically, it wore me down emotionally and spiritually. Not realizing I was engaged in a futile mission, trying to please everybody all the time, I became angry and depressed. I lost track of my foundation. The idea of stopping long enough to ask myself: "Who am I, really?" was foreign to me. Who cares who I am since I need to be somebody else every ten minutes, often several different people at the same time? My earlier hunger to connect to God, to lead a mystical life of union with Spirit, was buried in an avalanche of frustration and confusion. Not surprisingly, this type of behavior took its toll on people around me causing hurt and confused feelings, resentment and even in some cases provoking open hostility toward me.

Fortunately, certain people showed up right when I most needed them. One particular person was Jerry, my Al-Anon sponsor way back then. I had joined Al-Anon initially at the suggestion of my wife at the time, Cyndi. Al-Anon is a Twelve-Step program for people who have, for one reason or another, been affected by another person's drinking. Cyndi wasn't a problem drinker, but she knew I had some exposure in my past to alcohol-related issues. She had heard that Al-Anon works for people in a way that might resonate with me. In these meetings people don't give each other advice but, instead, learn from each other how to get along in life by sharing their own personal experiences. Perhaps knowing how tired I was of being told what to do, she thought such a safe, non-judgmental environment might, over time, help me find lessons applicable to me.

I met Jerry when I first started attending Al-Anon meetings and immediately warmed to him. He was so friendly and kind. Jerry was a big guy and his hugs felt like I was being drawn into a cozy, safe cocoon of large jovial Teddy bears. Over a period of several years I grew to trust him more and more and eventually decided to ask him to be my sponsor.

The sponsor in these groups is the person "there for you" when you need it. They walk a fine line. They don't feed you a line of babble and let you get away with deceiving yourself about your shortcomings, but neither do they let you lose yourself in your dark places. Believe me, when you join these groups, if you are like me, your dark places can get pretty dark. It's easy to stay in denial about how much harm you are causing in the world but once you get real about changing your attitudes and behaviors, you can easily get lost in some truly nasty stuff on your way to Spirit. Sponsors often are true lifelines of support because you are deep into Midline when you work the twelve-step programs. You are rooting and digging through all that makes you vulnerable because you've found your desire to connect to Spirit, to live life full-on.

Jerry agreed to be my sponsor and over time our relationship became closer. I felt free to talk with him about the confusion and pain I was experiencing. I would make a mess at work and be angry about it. He would listen and then help me sort out the underlying issues, gently prodding me to own my behavior while at the same time letting me feel my worth and value as a person.

I felt I was a failure as a father, as a husband, and as a lawyer. I didn't think I was much of a man. There were times when these failures weighed so heavy on me that I didn't think I could take another day. Jerry would always answer his phone and always knew where some place was open that had hot coffee ready. My faith and trust in him became a crucial pillar of support. Over several years of coffee, restaurants, and even trips together, we became fast friends.

After some time in this relationship we both knew it was time for me to do the "Fifth Step" of AA and Al-Anon: "Admit to God, to myself and to another human being the exact nature of my wrongs." As you can imagine, in the course of trying to be all things to all people I caused harm. I got angry with people, shouting sometimes for no reason. I gossiped in order to fit in. By this time I was no longer married and my dating life was filled with hurt and disappointments I inflicted on women because I didn't have the courage to be honest with them—I wasn't ready or courageous enough to commit.

This Fifth Step is a big deal. So many of us, including me, "game" ourselves. We think we are being introspective and honest about our motives, yet we really are not being honest. It is awful sometimes to acknowledge the harm we've caused others and what we've cost ourselves in terms of lost love and friendship. Yet as hard as it is to dig deeply and honestly within ourselves, it is excruciating agony to risk a friendship with somebody you love and cherish in order to do your Fifth Step, to come fully clean with all the harm you've caused.

I sat down with Jerry and came clean. I shared with him the details of everything I write about in this book, and even more: all the emotional havoc I'd wreaked, the hearts I'd stomped on, the dreams I'd crushed—all in my attempt to be something other than the man Spirit created. In the true sense of an honest and complete Fifth Step: I shared every ugly detail, holding nothing back.

As I disclosed these very private, personal things to Jerry, my face burned in shame. Tears flowed down my face, as I knew that I was likely forever losing this dear friend. I feared I had now lost not only my lifeline but the one person in the world who I thought saw the value deep inside me that even I usually doubted was there. This was Midline in its most serious moment: risking my whole sense of self out of a burning hunger to be a nice man. After all, if I couldn't stand myself, how could I expect anyone else to tolerate me? Jerry was a strong, powerful man of integrity who would no doubt want nothing further to do with me after we finished.

Filled with fear and self-disgust, I looked up and all I could see in Jerry's face was love and acknowledgement. The process is private so I won't elaborate, but I knew that all he saw in me was Spirit. Seeing his compassion, sympathy and acceptance of me as somebody of worth, I knew I was ready to do what it took to change. I knew Spirit, through this man and in other ways, would be there to see that change through. And so it has been.

I tell this story to introduce us to Patanjali's *Yoga Sutra*: 1.33. This *Sutra* tells us that by cultivating attitudes of friendliness toward the happy, compassion toward the suffering, sympathetic joy toward the virtuous, and equanimity toward the non-virtuous, the mind becomes lucid. Mastering the teachings of this *Sutra* is considered necessary groundwork for connection to Spirit.[228] Here is where we learn practices to develop the clarity of mind required to connect to Spirit amidst the mind's chattering and the challenges of the world that create separation rather than connection.[229]

If you really want to connect to Spirit, if you really want to live in Midline where you refuse to let fear and insecurity keep you from joy and fulfillment, take time to study this *Sutra*. Become this *Sutra*. Become like Jerry. As far as I am concerned, until I become the person Patanjali describes here, I am not fully joined in Spirit.

Let's break this *Sutra* down a bit. As vital as it is, the lesson is really pretty simple. First, lucidity means clarity of the mind. To be fully absorbed in Spirit we have to clearly identify and then work through the many challenges life throws at us. A big challenge is the way we judge others so harshly, forgetting to find Spirit within them. Sure, we judge all the time, if for no other reason than to honor what we really like in life and to keep ourselves safe. It's part of life to decide that I don't care for pea soup no matter how good it might be for me and no matter how many times people urge me to try their recipe. It makes good sense to decide that after I've loaned money to Edwina and she blows me off, I might choose not to loan her anything else. Also, it's wise to keep boundaries with people whose behavior could put us in some danger.

These judgments are different from the type of thinking we engage in where we create separation; refusing to see and honor the Spirit in another because of something they've said or done. Clarity of mind means that we find and honor Spirit no matter how She is on display because we recognize everything is Spirit. Can we, like Jerry, find Spirit even in the mess of whatever behavior we are judging? Can we be *Sattvic*, pierce through whatever is hiding Spirit?[230] Can we do this regularly so we are able to make choices in our day-to-day affairs and social interactions that connect us to Spirit?[231]

How do we do this? The four attitudes listed in the *Sutra* show us the way.[232] The first two of these teachings are to practice cultivating an attitude of friendship toward those who are happy, as well as an attitude of joy toward those who are virtuous. The notion here, perhaps based on Buddhist wisdom, is that if we can learn to be genuinely friendly and happy around others who are doing well, we leave no space for thoughts that lead to envy or other such emotions.[233]

Most of us can be happy when our kids succeed; it is tough sometimes to be happy when somebody we are jealous of achieves success. I have to admit to a touch of resentment every time Stone Barrington attracts yet another beautiful, wealthy, sexually liberated woman. Patanjali asks us to learn how to be friendly and happy as part of our natural state, not reserving it only for those we happen to prefer or who don't threaten our status in the group.

The other two practices identified in this *Sutra* are that of cultivating compassion toward those in distress and equanimity toward the non-virtuous. This was how Jerry dealt with me at that most pivotal moment when I totally came clean with him in my Fifth Step process. I knew him well enough to understand that some of what I told him probably surprised him and was distasteful. I knew I'd behaved on occasion in ways that violated his sense of values. That was the purpose of the process but it was also the underlying basis of my terror that by revealing these things to him I would lose the one person in my life who I thought saw the real me—Spirit as me. That was my Midline.

Look at how Jerry handled it. That's what I believe Patanjali is asking us to do with each other. I strongly suspect Jerry felt appalled at some of what I disclosed to him. The temptation for him to harshly judge me and categorize me as a *persona non grata* for the rest of his life must have presented itself. Yet his depth of compassion and composure was so complete that when I looked for the disgust in his face and eyes, it wasn't there! Instead of mirroring back to me my own self-defeating viewpoint of myself, he chose to shine back Spirit.

Jerry was so committed to finding Spirit in me that all he could see in front of him was Spirit. He certainly heard the bad, I can tell you that for sure, because we had many, many discussions over the years after that night. But, in that moment, when it most counted, when he could be of the greatest service, he sat as Spirit, looking only for the good, looking only at the way we were connected to Spirit.

When we exercise compassion and equanimity, we leave no room for thoughts that create separation, judgments that create harm.[234] Such attitudes can't survive alongside true compassion and equanimity, in a heart absorbed in Spirit.

How do we develop this deep sense of compassion and state of poise so valuable in serving each other? Richard Freeman points out that we are far less inclined to be so quick to judge another who has behaved in a way we believe less than ideal, when we take time to study our own slip ups and, in doing so, forgive ourselves.[235] Suddenly, we can see another's mistakes from the perspective of the same kindness and understanding we have learned to show ourselves.

This *Sutra* teaches us practices that provide us the clarity we need when Spirit offers us Midline. We have the opportunity to truly serve another as Jerry served me that night. We are able to recognize Midline and welcome it, without envy, fear, or anger high jacking us away from embracing our potential, able to show up for others and ourselves with total love and absolute acceptance. ■

A MIDLINE PRACTICE

Think of something a friend or relative said to you in the last week or so that hurt your feelings. Close your eyes and spend a minute or two seeing if you can find something positive about that person.

PART VII

It takes practice—Patanjali's Yoga Sutras

B. It takes practice to look inside—
so how do we practice?

CHAPTER 80
Time for a change—Patanjali's Yoga Sutra *2.1; the nuts and bolts for connection to Spirit*

Eventually, after my divorce, I began to date. After a time, some of my dates began to turn into relationships. Occasionally, the relationships moved from casual to serious; "serious" meaning that we started to talk about a future together, including starting a family. When this would happen the same nagging voice I heard while I was married would return, telling me I wasn't worthy or competent enough to be part of any woman's dream. When the relationships reached this point I typically created some mess to cause my girl friends to flee as far away from me as possible.

This pattern continued until one night when I was sitting on the couch with my girl friend at the time. She began to share her dream about us: our future family, even the kind of house we'd live in. As I looked into her eyes I saw her excitement about our future together. This was the breaking point for me. I told her I wasn't the guy for her; I wasn't the guy for anybody. I could see the hurt in her eyes. I saw a lovely human being's heart shatter like a fine, beautiful piece of china casually thrown to a hard and cold tile floor.

Later that night as I lay in bed feeling ashamed of myself, I began to re-live, viscerally, the hurt, shame, and anger I felt in the past when others treated me badly. Feeling again those awful emotions, I realized I inflicted them on others. I was, in that moment, in Midline, willing to risk confronting those patterns of thought and behavior that kept me emotionally safe in order to accept life's nudge that I become a nicer, more honest and sensitive man. I made a choice to do what it would take to change.

I don't think we can make much progress on any spiritual path without a commitment to look with serious and honest introspection at ourselves and how our patterns of thought and behavior affect others; no holds barred. This is what Patanjali teaches in *Yoga Sutra*: 2.1: austerity, self-study, and devotion to the Lord form the practice of yoga. In this *Sutra* Patanjali gives us the nuts and bolts of what it takes to meaningfully practice yoga in a way that leads us to Spirit.

First, this *Sutra* tells us we must practice austerity, which typically means rigor or discipline. From my experience, living a life that honors Spirit within others and within ourselves does require rigor and discipline. Sometimes we need to make dramatic and painful changes. It takes guts to even reach the point where we can acknowledge that some change is necessary, the gut-wrenching, honest introspection I mentioned. Once we identify what changes in our attitudes and patterns of conduct are needed, we have to be rigorously disciplined in order to make those changes. This rigor is necessary because it can be easier to stand pat in our cozy old way of seeing the world and our habit-forming patterns of acting in it.

The word in the *Sutra* used to describe this commitment is *Tapah*, referring to *Tapas*: "a burning desire."[236] It takes serious fire to get past the self-serving rationalizations we use to blame others when things go awry. It sometimes requires a giant inferno of commitment to say to ourselves: "Yes, I occasionally and needlessly hurt and diminish others as well as myself."

Patanjali calls this deep, honest introspection *Svadhyaya*, which means self-study or to reflect on our selves.[237] I was so stubborn in my refusal to deal with my harmful attitudes and behavior that I eventually adopted a practice to break through that stubbornness. Instead of rationalizing my behavior every time I get into a disagreement, I assume I likely contributed to it in some way. Instead of spending my energy evaluating how the other person is wrong, I spend my energy trying to figure out how my attitudes and behavior play a role: "What unresolved junk inside me did this situation trigger?" "How could I have headed off this problem?" "What could I have said differently?" "Should I have kept my mouth shut or keyboard quiet?"

Sure, the other person may well have been a total jerk, but for the sake of this exercise my interest is in transforming me, not them. This is tough. It takes *Tapas*, a burning desire to dig deep, identify my own issues, and where necessary, create change. At the same time, it takes determination to do this while at the same time avoiding going to a dark and unworthy place inside myself. Therapists may be necessary as loving and understanding guides.

We derive the rigor and fire we need for this introspection from *Ishvarapranidhani*—devotion to Spirit. When we remember that we are all Spirit, our motivation to treat each other with integrity and respect will increase of its own accord. Remembering my connection to something bigger gives me the extra juice I need to stay on the path of change. All I have to do is think about the precious friends I've made over the last number of years and the joy and spontaneity that has become available to me because I stayed on this path.

Midline presents itself every time we interact with another. Even if we choose not to establish a relationship with that person, the very fact that we risked meeting them with an open and honest mind, seeking to connect to Spirit within them, brings us a step closer to living as Spirit. ∎

▌ A MIDLINE PRACTICE

Recall a recent disagreement you had with somebody. As you think of that person, identify an aspect of Spirit within that person.

248   *Finding the Midline*

CHAPTER 81
Let's dance some more—Patanjali's Yoga Sutras *2.3; Kleshas; and 2.5; ignorance*

My girl friend Nancy loved dance. She pleaded with me to go with her to a dance performance on the campus of the University of Minnesota. Mr. Macho here kept saying "No way." I knew nothing about dance but figured "Who needs it?" Nancy tried everything, including telling me how much I would appreciate dance because it would remind me of karate. Finally, a friend of mine suggested the obvious: "If she loves it so much, and you care for her; go. Don't be a creep!" So, I agreed to go. Nancy was thrilled. She got us tickets in Row 7 for a performance featuring Mikhail Baryshnikov, one of the greatest ballet dancers in history.

The night arrived. There was a live orchestra and, as the music began, a group of female dancers wearing beautiful white costumes floated gracefully on stage across a subdued mostly blue backdrop. Suddenly, the music became louder and faster. A male dancer "flew" from off stage, appearing to hover about ten feet off the ground, one leg in front and one behind in a full split. The move made Michael Jordan look earth-bound. He returned to earth at center stage, landed on one foot and began rapidly spinning around with arms extended, one foot about waist high. I gasped, as it did the entire audience. Nancy leaned over to me and whispered: "That's not even Baryshnikov. Wait."

Needless to say, I was spellbound and hooked. Nancy had been totally right! The combination of this beautiful music, the costumes and set design, and athleticism and grace in movement, was something I'd never seen. I knew from my karate training how difficult it was for these men and women to be so flexible yet strong and elegant. I knew I was watching Spirit in full play. Also, as you can imagine, Nancy was delighted that I had kept an open mind and found such an appreciation for something she loved, something we could now share.

I use this story to introduce us to Patanjali's *Yoga Sutra* 2.3, which tells us that on the path of yoga we will be challenged by ignorance, ego, desire, aversion, and clinging to life. These afflictions are known in yoga as the *Kleshas*.

The *Kleshas* are the more influential and detrimental chattering of the mind, the *Vrittis*, we contend with all the time. Such chattering is considered detrimental to us, *Klista*, when it leads us away from our hearts, away from Spirit and Midline.[238] My ignorance of dance reflected an overall ignorance about things that were not familiar or which didn't comport with my image of how I needed to show up in the world. I was a macho lawyer/jock who wouldn't dream of being seen attending a dance performance.

Such ignorance can prevent us from seeing the potential in the moment and certainly can blind us to Spirit. In this case the potential was that of creating a deeper relationship with Nancy, as well as a new passion for dance. This was also an opportunity for me to deepen my connection to Spirit by experiencing yet again another form of Spirit at play.

Vrittis can also be helpful, *Aklista*.[239] Helpful *Vrittis* are those thoughts that awaken us to Spirit and help us navigate Midline, opening us to the poetry of our hearts and the magic of life.[240] My love and respect for Nancy and underlying curiosity about life (and my wise friend who told me to go!) created a conversation in my mind that helped me meet a Midline: I risked my safe but limited viewpoints to accept the invitation from Nancy to a deeper, richer and intimate connection, as well as discovery of something new—dance.

The first of the five *Kleshas*, challenges, is *Avidya*, ignorance. The most significant type of ignorance is when we forget that we are all part of something bigger than just ourselves, Spirit.[241] *Yoga Sutra* 2.5 elaborates: We forget we are all forms and expressions of Spirit born with special skills that can make this world a better place for all of us. We forget we are mirrors for each other's possibility and potential for joy. It is this ignorance that serves as the breeding ground of the other *Kleshas*.[242]

Think back to my conversation with my friend in Costa Rica, the wealthy man who owned businesses in Costa Rica and paid so much of his income to support health care for others. He saw Spirit from all perspectives, feeling pride and honor in helping others less blessed. He saw the world through pure knowledge, *Vidya*, connection to Spirit. ■

A MIDLINE PRACTICE

Take a walk down a street with which you are familiar and identify three examples of Spirit that you've not identified previously, such as, for example, the interesting and pleasant combination of colors a neighbor has selected to match lawn chairs to house trim, or the beautiful arrangement of flowers in a pot by the front door, or a unique and enjoyable design of a room addition.

CHAPTER 82
You mean I don't have to Be perfect?—Patanjali's Yoga Sutra 2.6; ego

From time to time I take Gyrotonic training with Sara, working with equipment to stretch and move my body. This training is great for strengthening joints, muscles and connective tissues, as well as coordinating movement. As I go through the various exercises, Sara regularly, and I do mean "regularly," corrects me. She constantly tells me to relax my shoulders, sit up taller, or any number of other instructions. Sara's nice and very competent. No matter. I find myself getting irritated with all the corrections even though I know each is important. After about the third or fourth time she tells me to relax my shoulders I am ready to scream. After the tenth time, I almost burst into tears of frustration. Why can't I do this right? Am I stupid?

This is my all-too usual reaction to criticism. I'm a competent man, able to do more than a few things very well. Give me a giant multi-million dollar mine collapse case and I'll take depositions that'll knock the socks off the opposition. Put me in charge of witnesses in the tobacco litigation and I'll handle it smoothly. Ask me to speak to a room of 1,000 people on almost any subject and I'll gladly grab the microphone. But...ask me to relax my shoulders more than twice and I feel like a dumb, worthless piece of yuck. What gives?

"What gives" is the challenge of the second *Klesha, Asmita*, which means "ego. *Asmita* is discussed in *Yoga Sutra* 2.6. Ego becomes a problem when we forget our connection to each other through Spirit. We think of ourselves, which is fine, but grow indifferent to our impact on others.[243] Thinking everything is all about us, we get wrapped up in having to put on a good show, being perfect no matter what. If the show doesn't win the applause we seek, we react with frustration and disappointment, forgetting this greater connection.

I forget that my flaws are mirror reflections of my strengths. Lifting my shoulder blades comes from an intensity that has driven me to great results for clients who were injured. Would I want to give up that fire? No way. I just need to cut myself some slack. Rather than constantly trying to gain approval by trying to outdo everybody else, a totally futile effort, by the way, I serve Spirit by being Spirit. I do so by being the unique and special person that came with my body when I was born. I use my ego to develop and offer my skills. The world needs that person.

I'm glad there is ego. I enjoy the way we each, through ego, develop and celebrate our skills for all of us to enjoy. As a Denver Bronco fan, am I happy Peyton Manning has ego?

You bet. Me, I enjoy being a good lawyer and yoga teacher. I'm a devoted dad, a supportive grandfather, and loyal friend. This is Spirit living through me when I am not distracted trying to be something I'm not. ■

A MIDLINE PRACTICE

Bring to mind a friend who has a great talent for something that you aren't particularly competent at doing; perhaps he or she plays the piano well or can build a back deck blindfolded, by way of example. Now, remind yourself of something you do particularly well and this same friend might struggle a bit if he or she attempted to do this thing you can do. Close your eyes and reflect for a moment that you both still enjoy each other despite these differing skills.

CHAPTER 83
Our heart's desire—
Patanjali's Yoga Sutra *2.7; desire*

We all loved going to Mama Bosso's for pizza when we were in college. We couldn't get enough of the place. Our top priority each day would be deciding when we would meet to head over for pizza. Being college guys, most of us athletes, we didn't have much money but we did have huge appetites and enjoyed our beer. More than a few of us were fairly large in size; all of us were strong and fit.

Being hungry young men, broke, hungry, young men, we soon saw opportunity. Mama Bosso's pizzas were huge. Inevitably, some unwary couple or family would order way more pizza than they could eat. We watched these people enjoy their meals at nearby tables and booths, much the way a pack of coyotes watch potential prey, waiting for just the right moment. More often than not, given the size of the pizzas, these customers would depart, leaving precious slices of pizza and unfinished pitchers of beer just sitting there waiting for the staff to clear the table.

Our reflexes became so sharpened that we would sweep in, taking any remaining slices and beer back to our table even before the customers made it out the front door. The only problem was, once in awhile, the customers would stop at the front counter and ask that their leftover pizza be boxed up for them to take home. You can see the problem.

Before long the owners worked out a deal with us—leave the customers alone and buy our own beer. If we did that and promised to wait until the customers cleared the establishment we could then take whatever pizza they left behind. What a great deal for broke, growing college boys!

We started to go to Mama Bosso's with great frequency, in fact, with such great frequency that we drastically cut our study time. This threatened to affect our grades; we were too active to have problems with our waistlines back then. Eventually, we all figured out that as much as we liked Mama Bosso's, we had to curtail the number of visits we made each week.

This leads us to the third *Klesha* or challenge: *Raga*, desire for sensory gratification, discussed at *Yoga Sutra* 2.7. At a workshop Roger Pressman and I gave in Denver, a theology Ph.D candidate in attendance asked us if desire is viewed as a bad thing in yoga. This question comes up frequently at yoga workshops dealing with philosophy. While some yoga philosophies urge us to disengage from the world in order to find Spirit, other philosophies, such as the one I write about here, tell us that it is *in the world* that we find Spirit.

If we believe that the material world is a manifestation of God or Spirit, we want to cultivate a healthy desire to connect to that world and its many forms so we will experience more of Spirit. Sensory gratification, pleasure, *Sukha*, is part of life. Only when we let the memories of such gratification, and the desire for more, drive our actions to the detriment of Spirit do we run into problems.[244]

My pizza story helps demonstrate the balance this *Sutra* asks of us. I have no interest in avoiding the world and its pleasures. But we all recognize, as we did back then in college, that indulging in pleasures to the detriment of what is important to our overall well-being is a challenge. We are given these bodies to enjoy, but balance is so important. We can enjoy the world and experience the pleasures of our desire, but with the caveat that we do so with common sense. As my father told me: "Too much of anything is not good." Remembering that wisdom, we take pleasure in the world, mindful of honoring Spirit as we do so.

It is out of desire that ballet dancers practice and practice, eventually offering us the gift of their desires. It is out of desire that our artists create, the inventors invent, and the scientists discover. Desire is what ultimately drives all of us to express our gifts. It is our desire to manifest ourselves that prompts us to express Spirit as He appears through us. It is this desire that prompts us to take the risks that invite the potential rewards of Midline. ■

A MIDLINE PRACTICE

Think of some skill or talent you've developed for the sheer pleasure of it and how you use that skill or talent today to bring enjoyment into your circle of family, friends, or workmates.

CHAPTER 84
Give it a try—Patanjali's Yoga Sutra 2.8; aversion

I had a bit of time before a meeting and walked into an ice cream store. Wearing a suit and tie, I looked like what I was, a lawyer coming from court. The clerk was a young guy in his 20's with a huge tattoo covering his whole right arm and body piercing all over his face. I immediately judged him as somebody of no interest to me, other than selling me a cookie. I had no desire to interact with him. He apparently must have felt the same way and maybe read my energy because, looking over at my suit and tie, he almost glared at me.

When he was finished with his other customers, he walked over and said with as little courtesy as he could muster: "Can I help you?" All of a sudden I noticed the artwork in his tattoos. The tattoos consisted of, among other things, some beautiful renditions of several spiritual icons, including an angel with a sword, at least two Hindu goddesses, and other amazing symbolism. The colors were brilliant.

I asked him to explain the meaning of the tattoos and, with enthusiasm, he did. It turned out that this was a deeply spiritual man very well studied and holding views quite like mine. He had done the tattoo work himself, so he was also artistic. In fact, he was practicing how to do tattoos with his off hand so he could eventually do the other arm. He was a really interesting guy.

We had a great talk. When it came time to sell me the cookie, he told me to wait a minute and brought out fresh chocolate chip cookies right from the oven. Then he reached for a hot cookie, deliberately broke it and said: "Whoops, looks like this one's broken. Here, have it for free." You can't beat that! Ten minutes before there would have been no way he would have given me the hot, fresh cookies from the oven or a free cookie. No way would we have considered each other interesting company.

This situation once again reminded me of how important it is to keep an open mind, even when we are sure we want nothing to do with whoever is in front of us; even though the person or situation we are involved with appears off-putting and a bit distasteful to us. This is a typical Midline; a moment when somebody interesting crosses our path and we either allow our attitudes and judgments to prevent any interaction, thus cheating ourselves out of a potentially rich experience, or, conversely, we risk a few minutes of our time to open our mind and learn something new.

I use this story to introduce our next challenge: *Dvesha*, which means aversion or repulsion, found in *Yoga Sutra* 2.8.[245] When we allow ourselves to think our way is the only way, choosing to stay attached to our known pleasures, we risk losing out on amazing new opportunities because they appear unappealing. We can become so focused on what we think is cool or hip that we create separation from everything else. We can become unhappy, even grief-stricken, *Dukha*, if we don't keep getting more of that to which we've become attached.[246] All the while we miss out on new opportunities to expand our experience of the world, to connect to Spirit in fresh ways.

We may not think we have these attitudes but if we check our behavior we will see that we make choices every day that serve as rejections of other possibilities. We steer clear of meeting new people who don't fit the profile of somebody we think would be fun to know. We avoid places that are different from our favorites. We avoid new things, such as ballet, thinking the experience will be unpleasant. In doing so we miss opportunities to enrich ourselves. We pass up the chance to step into the Midline of risk that might lead to a greater reward—a new and enriching life experience or relationship. ■

A MIDLINE PRACTICE

Recall the last few times somebody asked you to try something different, perhaps a new restaurant, a different type of movie, an author you haven't read, a short road trip to a town you've yet to visit; and you said "no." Pick one of the invitations and tell the person who made the suggestion that you've changed your mind and try out whatever it is they suggested.

CHAPTER 85
We can't buy love—Patanjali's Yoga Sutra *2.9; clinging to life*

After inserting the acupuncture needles Cheryl dimmed the lights, put on some music, and left me alone in the comfy room. In under a minute I became overwhelmed with sadness and tears began to flow down my face. Seemingly out of the blue I realized that I didn't want to die.

I'd been dealing with some parts of my body beginning to wear out, "degenerative" they call it, and maybe that was causing me to feel mortal. It was a bittersweet type of sadness as I recognized I'm aging. Despite my efforts to deny that fact, I won't be here forever. The things that matter so much to me will eventually go away or, rather, they won't go away; it will be me that goes away.

Different memories passed through my mind. I remembered the delighted smile on my granddaughter's face, when not quite two years old, she heard my son walk in the door of the house. I saw how happy she was to see him and how much excitement there was in her voice when she yelled "DADDY!!" and jumped up and down in her high chair. My wish that day was that my son would catch a glimpse of how much love she felt for him.

Then I recalled a hockey game when Jeff was in high school and, although heavily favored in a playoff game, his team almost lost because so many players had the flu. Because of that and some penalties, they had to play the whole third period with only eight skaters. I don't think my son and a couple of his teammates sat for even a minute during the last part of the third period, something almost impossible to do if you know hockey. What I'll never forget is when he stood there, exhausted but proud, savoring a 5-4 win, and how he looked at me on the bench—I was an assistant coach—and, without a word, an amazing bond was forged. I'll never forget that, ever.

I remembered when I was in a relationship and in love and my girl friend reached across the car seat and fondly touched the back of my neck; or another time when she took my hand. Those simple touches remain in my heart. As I lay on the acupuncture table I remembered so many things and the sadness came, coming from knowing that at some point I'll have to say goodbye.

None of these things would ever make the book: "Fifty Things to Do Before You Die." In those moments on the table I had no memory of a wonderful travel destination—although

I've been to more than a few—of a thing I owned that cost a bunch of money to buy, or a recollection of basking in somebody's approval. Instead, standing out was this: these precious memories all involved relationships. They each involved intimate connection. Every time I chose to enjoy those relationships instead of pursuing unnecessary material gain, I had answered Spirit's call at Midline, the beckoning to a dazzling and wondrous life I decided I wanted for myself, the flourishing life Dr. Seligman writes about.[247]

I share this story to introduce the fifth *Klesha* or challenge: *Abhinivesah*, clinging to life, or "fear of death," discussed in *Yoga Sutra* 2.9.[248] I asked myself what in the world Patanjali meant by this. To me, "clinging to life" means spending time and energy on things that don't foster deeper connection or otherwise resonate with my heart. Why work extra hours to buy a new car I don't need if it takes time away that I could spend with people I care about? Sure, I want to do things on the Top Fifty list. I expect it would be fun to bungee jump into some amazing canyon or be an "extra" in a movie. However, I won't regret for a moment skipping these things because I spent time creating the memories I share in this story. I've lived a great life. ■

A MIDLINE PRACTICE

Identify someone precious to you or something fun you love to do and ask yourself if you are engaging in any behavior that unnecessarily keeps you from spending time with that person or doing that thing you love to do.

CHAPTER 86

We can all get along—Patanjali's Yoga Sutras *2.29 and 2.30—the Eightfold Path and the* Yamas

One of the things I enjoy about visiting Boston is picking up my granddaughter Lucy at the end of her school day. She attends a Boston public school and each day, when class lets out, the kids play. The older kids shoot baskets while little ones climb all over the elaborate playground structure, the thing with a huge, curvy slide, climbing bars, rings to swing from, and other stuff I can't figure out. While some of the kids are climbing, sliding, or swinging from every imaginable part of this equipment, others are racing all over the place.

My grandson, Henry, who is three as I write this, comes with us to pick up his sister and immediately joins in races with the older boys, the kindergartners, first, and second graders. He probably runs about twenty miles—exaggerating a bit here—but the point is that he never stops moving and never stops laughing. Well, almost never. Occasionally he falls down on the asphalt. Inevitably, when he falls down, like most three year olds, he starts to cry; usually he has scraped his hands or his knee.

What is pretty cool is this: when he falls down, the older boys stop, come over, and before any adult can get there to soothe him, the boys do the job, sometimes with the help of a young girl walking by. These kids are only five, six, or seven years old, but they care that the little kid is crying. They forget about their racing and they help Henry out.

These kids work hard all day, focusing on their studies, taking language, music and art classes, but also learning how to play together, respect each other, and get along. From time to time one of them gets in trouble, breaking a rule. For that they are not humiliated; instead, they are gently but firmly taught not to hit, not to talk out of turn, not to bully. I'm really happy with this school. I think Lucy is getting just the foundation she needs in terms of socializing and becoming a meaningful member of her community.

Just like the children's school, Patanjali shows us the path necessary to create a life of relationships and meaning. *Yoga Sutra:* 2.29 states that the Eightfold Path, or practice, of yoga is: ethical precepts in relationship with others and oneself, physical postures, breathing exercises, turning inward, concentration on an object, meditation, and spiritual absorption. Here Patanjali spells out for us "the" spiritual path, the practices we must employ to create the ultimate life experience, one in which we live absorbed in Spirit.[249] He gives us a manual, so to speak, for finding the flourishing life of well-being that yoga can provide, helping us find, appreciate, and revel in life's Midlines.

The first of the Eightfold Path, the *Yamas*, is identified in *Yoga Sutra* 2.30. That *Sutra* teaches that the five guidelines for healthy relationships with others are: non-violence, truth, abstention from stealing, self-restraint, particularly in sexual matters, and absence of greed.[250] How important are these *Yamas* to our practice? *Sutra* 2.31 tells us the *Yamas* are timeless and universal vows we all make to each other and to Spirit, regardless of our status in life, whether we are rich or poor.[251] These vows are absolute and "nonnegotiable."[252]

We now turn to a discussion of this critical framework for finding meaningful and honest connection with each other. By remembering these teachings, and bringing their practice into our daily lives, we will be able to find and connect to Spirit no matter the temptation or crisis.[253] Stepping into life's Midlines means we do so with integrity, in ways that not only express the poetry of our hearts, where every line is composed by Spirit, but also honors, respects, and encourages the poetry of others. ■

A MIDLINE PRACTICE

The next time you are stopped in your car at a very busy intersection, ask yourself if you are glad that society has figured out some rules about how to govern traffic movement on busy streets.

CHAPTER 87
A yogic golden rule—Patanjali's Yoga Sutra *2.35; non-harming*

At one point when I was in high school I wanted to join the military as soon as I graduated. It wasn't because I wanted to be a soldier and patriotically serve my country. Rather, I wanted to vent my anger and frustration with my parents and at life. Even though I had already been admitted to college and had a scholarship, I decided to join the army and go to Viet Nam.

I was walking down the hall at school one day when one of the teachers called me over. He told me he understood I was going to join the army and skip college. He pointed out with a war going on, there was a good chance I might not make it back alive or in any condition to go to college. Then he leaned in close to me and whispered to me in a soft but powerful voice. He told me he knew I was angry but I had a lot to offer and it would be a real shame for me to skip college. He said by avoiding college out of anger I was really ripping off any number of people down the road whom I could serve as a coach or teacher or something. He suggested I go to college first, develop my potential and then, if I were still angry, join the army later. With that, he walked away.

This had a strong impact on me. Other than hurting my family I hadn't thought about the implications for anyone else of running off to the army. It was a personal mini-version of the movie *The Five People You Meet in Heaven*; the teacher gave me a glimpse of what I could be and the harm it could cause if I didn't pursue that path. My anger had hidden from me the potential I had to do some good in the world. I changed my mind and went to college. This was a tremendous Midline. I not only took a serious look at my anger but also had the courage to admit I had value and worth. I decided it was time to get off the self-destructive path I had selected for myself.

Joining the military is an honorable choice, one of the most honorable things we can do. However, in my case I wasn't joining to be honorable, to serve my country. I was joining to vent my teenage angst. There's no honor in that. We have to really think about the reasons for what we are doing and then consider as best we can the cause and effect of each choice. When doing so we have to think about whether we are setting into motion the possibility of harm, broadening our perspective on what constitutes harm.

The first of the *Yamas* is *Ahimsa*, nonviolence or non-harming through thoughts, words, or action.[254] *Ahimsa,* discussed in *Yoga Sutra* 2.35, governs all the other *Yamas* and the goal of the other *Yamas* is to achieve *Ahimsa* and enhance it.[255] This is the importance Patanjali placed on non-harming; it should be the ultimate gateway for our thoughts, words and behavior. For example, while truth is one of the underpinnings of successful relationship with others, truth must be tempered by passing the test of whether it creates more harm than any good we think it might serve.[256] If truth cannot pass this test, then it is *Ahimsa*, a violence to Spirit.

This *Sutra* specifically pertains to potentially harmful thoughts and emotions. Anger is one example. Understanding emotions such as anger is a necessary step to our healing and can also lead to vital change in the world. While anger can serve us, it is often a leading cause of harm because, being so volatile, we often act out of anger before understanding its cause and without thinking of the ramifications of our behavior. Since this is the case, nonviolence necessarily includes working through anger instead of allowing it to fester into words and deeds of retribution. Practicing non-harming also includes working through thoughts of prejudice, malice and hatred because these thoughts too can lead to action that causes harm.[257]

Because Spirit resides in all things, *Ahimsa* applies to all things. Being awake to Spirit in everything, we understand that when we do harm to the earth, we are also harming humans and all other living creatures. We only have to think of the Amazon Rain Forest to appreciate that as it is cut down, habitat crucial to a host of living creatures is destroyed.

Swami Paramahansa Yogananda wrote *Ahmisa* arises from our recognition of the Divine in everything and everyone.[258] Out of this recognition our natural urge is to be of service to each other. Doing harm occurs when we can be of service, but choose not to do so.[259] One way we serve our community is living as the *Sutra* itself asks: being a "presence" that inspires others to abandon harmful thoughts, words, and actions.[260]

Richard Freeman reminds us that *Ahimsa* also applies to the way we treat ourselves. Practicing personal non-violence helps us to find Spirit both inside us and outside us.[261] First, needlessly criticizing ourselves or downplaying our successes diminishes our potential to make great things happen. When we diminish ourselves or don't appear to respect ourselves very much, we undermine our credibility to inspire other people.

As I sit here today and review the good I've done as a lawyer, I believe that the teacher in the hallway had a point. Had I joined the military I may not have returned and gone to college and law school. I would not have developed my strengths in a way that best serves others. When we refuse to think of ourselves in terms of our potential greatness, always backing away from embracing that greatness, we really do rip off the world. We rip off ourselves; we rip off Spirit. ■

A MIDLINE PRACTICE
Think of the last time somebody gave you a compliment and you brushed it off, refusing to take credit where credit was due.

CHAPTER 88
Can we handle the truth?— Patanjali's *Yoga Sutra 2.36; truth*

I recall handling a lawsuit against a developer for his defective construction of some town-homes south of Denver. The damage ranged from leaky roofs and windows to the biggest problem, cracked walls, foundations and concrete due to expansive and settling soils. The developer had built the entire project on landfill and ignored the soils reports that warned about these problems.

Unfortunately, the developer was out of business and had no assets other than his insurance, which was insufficient to cover all the repairs. After discussing this bad news with our clients, we agreed with the developer's lawyer to settle the case for the entire amount of all the insurance policies, leaving our clients about half a million dollars short.

Several weeks later, as we were getting all the settlement papers ready, we received a call from the developer's lawyer. On instinct he had asked his long-time client to take him to the client's warehouse to dig through dirty boxes filled with old records. Based upon what he knew of his client's normal business practices over the years, the lawyer felt there had to be additional insurance. While digging they found an extra insurance policy that applied to our client's project.

After getting authority from that insurance company, Counsel called us to let us know that he now had an additional one million dollars to give us. Our client was made whole and we received that portion of the fees we had agreed with our client to reduce when we thought there was no more insurance money available. Everybody was happy and I came away with an elevated sense of respect for the integrity of that lawyer. We were experts at finding insurance coverage to pay for our clients' damages, but at some point, the system requires that we rely on each other's honest and full disclosure. This lawyer had gone beyond what many lawyers would have done, out of a sense of wanting to do the right thing.

This brings us to the second of the *Yamas*, the ethical rules that guide us in our relationships with others. This second *Yama, Satya*, found in *Yoga Sutra* 2.36, means truth and honesty.[262] As this story illustrates, honesty requires something more than giving a truthful answer to a question, or simply parroting facts. This *Sutra* requires that we commit to conducting ourselves with integrity as the lawyer did in my story. He lives in integrity, earning a special regard among his peers.

To be truthful also means understanding the limits of what we know, and how our limited knowledge shapes the way we perceive things.[263] We need to acknowledge when we don't know all the facts or when our perspective is biased. We might be jumping to inaccurate or ill-informed conclusions because we are uninformed or simply because, out of prejudice, we feel like it. Mr. Iyengar cautions us to analyze and investigate not only the truth but also our motives, allowing us to recognize when our mind is caught up in our own personal motivation to hurt another.[264]

Even if what we say about somebody is true, do the circumstances warrant the damage we will cause to a reputation? If the real motive for gossiping was for retribution, haven't we just done violence upon ourselves as well, by churning up and keeping alive anger and other emotions that block or inhibit our ability for loving connection? Rather than expressing our Divine freedom, haven't we in reality just acted as a prisoner of our anger and desire to lash out? Haven't we just fueled those emotions rather than benefiting from what they have to teach us?

Every time we are tempted to speak out on a subject we face a Midline: are we speaking out in order to truly serve a greater good or is that just our rationalization because we are angry or hurt? There are two age-old tests about truth that serve as wonderful guides. One test is to apply this old adage: Is what you are about to say true? Is it necessary that it be said? If so, what's the kindest way to say it? Finally, is this the right time to say it? This leads to the second test: would we want this done to or said about ourselves? That gauge, the "golden rule", always seems to bring us back to the ultimate truth; we are Spirit and our life is most meaningful when we honor Her in words and action. ∎

A MIDLINE PRACTICE
Have you or somebody you know and care about ever been hurt in some way by a rumor or gossip?

CHAPTER 89
Honesty pays—Patanjali's Yoga Sutra 2.37; non-stealing

I wanted to build my own private yoga studio for years. My land overlooks the Continental Divide and a beautiful valley down below, home of Devil's Thumb Ranch, 5,000 acres of meadows, woods and streams. This ranch resort is home to top cross-country skiing in the winter, and mountain biking and horseback riding all summer long. The view is amazing. I knew I could create a very special place to meditate and practice yoga and karate.

I spent several years trying to figure out exactly where to put the studio and finally selected a spot. I had plans drawn up and submitted them to various contractors. In response, I received bids in differing amounts, all from very reputable and well-regarded local builders. Watching this process, my friend and landscaper, "tree guy," Jay, kept urging me to use his friends Dave and Mitch. Jay and I had known each other for a number of years, his work was superb, he always stuck to the price quotes, and I trusted him.

Based on Jay's recommendation, I decided to go with Dave and Mitch. What a great choice! They finished ahead of schedule and right on the dime, with the only extra costs being for upgrades I asked them to do. Their work was so good and reasonably priced that I immediately decided to hire them to do some long-needed structural repair to my home and then tear down my old decking and rebuild new ones before I put my foot through them again. By this time my neighbor up the road caught wind of the caliber and trustworthiness of these guys and asked them to do a large addition on his home. That's how reputations are made up here in the mountains.

This leads us to the third *Yama: Asteya,* or non-stealing. We know that we ought not walk out of the restaurant without paying or grab somebody's purse or wallet when they aren't looking. *Yoga Sutra* 2.37 provides some additional interesting commentary on non-stealing, saying when a person is known as a non-stealing person, "all jewels manifest."[265] What? How do you get jewels from not stealing stuff?

Dr. Edwin Bryant suggests when a person refrains from stealing, that person's honest attitude attracts the trust of his neighbors, leading to material and spiritual wealth.[266] Dave and Mitch are great examples of this in action. They do a great job and people are drawn to them because of their reputation for honesty. They carry themselves with integrity and you can sense it when you first meet them and discuss a project. They want you to get exactly what you want. Dave, Mitch, and Jonesy, their associate, are busy every day, even in a tough economy. It's no surprise they've also each carved out an active and satisfying social life: "jewels" are clearly manifesting in their lives.

If we want our life to be as rich as it can be, full of jewels, then we can take a lesson from this *Sutra*: when a Midline appears, offering us a chance to behave as Spirit, it is wise to do so because that honest behavior will attract more Spirit to us. ■

A MIDLINE PRACTICE

Do you have some business you use regularly, such as car repair, for example, that you use in part because you trust that businessperson to be honest with you?

CHAPTER 90
Strings attached—Patanjali's Yoga Sutra 2.38; sexual restraint

My friends Tom and Marcia sat on either side of me late one Friday night at a Bennigan's in the Twin Cities, relaxing after a night of dancing. I knew Tom from the gym where we worked out and I knew Marcia because she worked with me for years at the law firm. We were part of a large group of friends who met almost every Friday night to dance at any number of local live-music venues in the Minneapolis area. The Minneapolis live music scene really "rocks," no pun intended. For example, we knew of Prince when most people had yet to hear of him.

Some of the folks in the group shared romances. Tom married somebody from our group. Marcia and I, though, had always been just friends. But that night at Bennigans she and I were looking at each other a bit differently. We'd both had a fun night. We must have really started to send out some vibe because Tom leaned over to me and whispered: "Billy, don't go there. She's your friend and...you work together. Leave it alone. Let's split." So, I told Marcia I was leaving and would see her Monday.

When Monday arrived, Marcia walked into my office, closed the door and we had a discussion. She told me she was interested in taking the relationship beyond friendship and wanted to discuss what I thought. Reluctantly, I told her that I didn't want to be in a relationship with anyone. I told her I had to keep working on myself and knew I'd screw up this important bond we had with each other. The conversation was painful; tears were shed. But, in this case, the bond remained and in fact not long ago, well over twenty-five years later, I helped her and her family with a legal matter.

This leads us to the fourth *Yama* of *Brahmacarya*, sexual restraint, discussed in *Yoga Sutra* 2.38. Patanjali says the path to Spirit requires such restraint.[267] I think of Marcia when I read this *Sutra*. Restraint in that case was the right thing to do. I was seeing a therapist to help me break through attitudes and behavior that were keeping me from committing my heart in dating relationships. Her advice was to avoid sexual entanglements because she felt that such energy could confuse me, keeping me from opening to my feelings. This was part of my commitment to myself to stop hurting others and so I followed this advice. I knew that I had to create a boundary with Marcia. I cared about her friendship and her feelings, so we kept our relationship on the friend level. I stood in Midline by making the choice that best served Spirit in both of us.

Brahmacharya does not mean celibacy and in fact sexual relationships can provide significant love and happiness.[268] I don't offer an opinion here about the value of "no-strings" sexual liaisons. What I suggest is that Patanjali's teachings encourage us to view situations with integrity. Mr. Iyengar suggests the test is whether we use our sexual power with a courageous mind, honoring Spirit in everybody.[269] What are the hopes and dreams of our partner? What are the real world strings that are attached, even as we pretend there are none? Who gets hurt? Who loses out on the energy we take from our partner if that person has other commitments?

We need to be particularly careful we don't interject an uncomfortable sexual energy into the workplace. We must remember everybody, including those we work with, have dreams and visions of professional success. I know from my own experience how easy it is to create confusion and hard feelings. I've caused both, never intending to do so but rather, by being oblivious to the delicacy of the situation at work. Out of desire for relationship and by having my own share of sexual energy I made mistakes. I sent out sexual energy to women who simply wanted to do their jobs and either had no interest in me whatsoever or, even if they did, didn't need to add more workplace stress to their lives. Seeing our workmates the way I saw Marcia, as a precious person whose feelings and dreams mattered to me, is a great start to handling these situations. We have to pay very close attention to this dynamic, or staying on the side of the angels can get away from us fast. ■

▌ A MIDLINE PRACTICE
Remember the hopes and dreams you brought with you when you began your career.

CHAPTER 91
It's all about the love—
Patanjali's Yoga Sutra 2.39; lack of greed

When I first told Cyndi I wanted a divorce, she knew I had no real sense of what was going on inside me emotionally. This was when she suggested I start attending Al-Anon, the "Twelve-Step" program for people who have been affected by another person's drinking. She knew I had some exposure in my past to alcohol-related issues. Cyndi didn't have a drinking issue, but she knew my history and felt this would be a good start.

It took me a number of tries before I ever walked in the door. To be honest, I was terrified. I didn't want to confront my history. I knew I had hurt so many people by the way I treated them: people at work, people I loved, and on and on. I knew I was creating problems for myself by my need for approval and the way criticism, even if delivered gently, shattered my sense of self and obsession with trying to be perfect. I could continue but even I'm getting tired of this list! Yep! The idea of attending Al-Anon was a sound one.

I think it took me five separate trips before I finally walked in to a meeting. In fact, I was sitting in the parking lot at the church when a kind woman walked up to my car and knocked on the window. She smiled at me and I rolled the window down to hear what she had to say. She asked: "Are you here for the meeting?" I said, "Yes" and she responded: "I thought maybe you were. I saw you sitting here in the parking lot the last few weeks at the same time. Come on in with me. We don't bite, except the cookies." What a saint this woman was! There was something safe about her and, because she had the nerve to walk up to my car, she may have saved my life.

I followed her in and took a seat in a circle of chairs. Everybody else had already arrived. I didn't say anything other than mumbling my name and trying to follow along when the group recited the Twelve Steps. I capitalize this because these Twelve Steps are Spirit; they are guideposts to the flourishing life we all seek, first published by Alcoholics Anonymous. For me, and for thousands of others, they are not only guideposts; they can literally be lifelines. A "lifeline" was precisely what I had been handed when Cyndi suggested Al-Anon and when the woman knocked on my car window. I just didn't know it yet.

I'm sitting in this first meeting and checking out everybody. I don't know what I expected. I knew the group wouldn't be made up of a bunch of obvious down and outers with rags for clothes and who hadn't bathed. I guess, though, I didn't expect that everybody would look so...normal...like my law partners, my neighbors, my car mechanic, or my pharmacist.

There was one guy there, "Bob," who was dressed in Brooks Brothers, great tie, shined shoes, and who looked like the guy all women want to date. He was nice, kind, and open. He was a lawyer at another huge law firm and he immediately made me feel relaxed and welcome. I confess wondering to myself: "What's HIS problem? Why is HE here?"

For about a month I didn't hear anything from Bob about his own personal life, nor did I say a word about me. But I did show up. I watched the others, including Bob, treat each other with honesty and compassion. The energy of empathy filled the room. Then, after about a month, Bob chose to share some feelings. Something had happened with his dad and he felt the need to discuss it. As it turned out, we could have been brothers the way he felt anger and resentment toward his father.

Our similarity didn't end there. Like me, Bob never felt anything he did was good enough. Although quite successful, he couldn't enjoy anything he had attained. He never stood up for himself at law firm meetings, letting people tease him or, in some cases, take credit for his work without his uttering a single protest. He ran away from sweet, loving women.

About this time he began to sob uncontrollably, his body racking as he completely broke down, telling us he wanted to end this pain; he wanted to die. Everybody gathered around him, men and women, holding him, letting him experience his agony but also letting him know they were there and they wanted him there. Eventually, he calmed down and even smiled. I am happy to say, he is alive today, thriving, married with kids, and a joy to his neighbors, family, and friends.

I went home stunned. Bob was the very man I wanted to be, so totally together, hip, cool, competent. How could this be? Then it hit me: Bob is each of us. We each have our history, our experiences, and our ups and downs. Everybody is different but, in the deepest understanding, we are each the same. We are each Spirit, carrying Spirit's attributes in endless diverse and valuable ways. Most of us, though, forget this important truth, just like Bob had forgotten.

By having the opportunity to truly know Bob, and, more importantly, by his courage in letting us experience his experience, I became infused with hope. I was able to see, despite my tainted view of myself, despite my fears, and despite my "conviction" of unworthiness; I was in fact a lovable man, a man with value. Like Bob, I have Spirit in me, and it is always present and ready, powerfully, to offer itself in service.

This brings us to the fifth of the ethical precepts for our relationships with others, *Aparigrahah*, non-possessiveness, lack of greed. What does my story about Bob have to do with greed? Isn't greed associated with hoarding our possessions, refusing to share? Of course it is, but you already know that so I won't waste your time telling you stuff you already know. Of course we know to share. This book is about finding Spirit and Patanjali gives us a huge clue here as to what other meaning we can give to the concept of greed.

In *Yoga Sutra* 2.39 Patanjali teaches when we learn to live without more than we need and without greed, we realize the true meaning of life.[270] This whole book has been about finding Midline, which, as we now know, means finding the opportunity in each moment for greater connection to Spirit and, whenever we possibly can, taking the risks required to seize that opportunity. When I read this *Sutra* it makes me think about what my most precious possession might be. I conclude that it is the fact that I am Spirit and I know that you are too. To me, there is nothing I own that is more treasured.

Each time I hold back, whether it is my ability to help somebody, my ability to share an experience the way Bob shared, or simply by using my special God-given strengths, I am being greedy. I am hoarding something Grace gave me. I am not sharing my version of Spirit walking through the world.

What Bob didn't know that night when he decided to share his soul with us was that I was in the same place. I don't know if I would have made it back the next week if he hadn't chosen that moment to offer himself fully to us. I don't know that I would have had a "next week" because I was in deep despair. His choice to share himself moved me so deeply, opening me to a completely different view of who I was and could become.

It is really all about love, about offering love, offering Spirit. When we remember that, the other stuff you already know about greed becomes easy. You don't need a book for that. ■

▌ A MIDLINE PRACTICE
Identify a part of you that benefits others when you share it.

CHAPTER 92
Time to clean house—
Patanjali's Yoga Sutra *2.32; Niyamas*

During an advanced course in a personal development program I took, we had a group interaction that has influenced me every day, all these years later. We lined up chairs in a "U" shape, with one chair for each of the 68 participants in the course. Five of us sat, while the other 63 got up, formed a line, and began to walk, one at a time, past the five who were seated.

Each person in line stopped in front of each seated member of the group and then turned to face that person. Immediately, the person standing in line had to give a "gut" response, labeling the seated person as either a "giver" or a "taker." Even a moment's hesitation counted as a "taker" vote.

The person in the chair entered each "vote" into their notebook in either a "giver" or "taker" column. The line progressed through all five seated people, and then the seated people got up, joined the line and were replaced. This continued until we had each evaluated every member of the group, face to face, one choice or the other.

As I sat there, most of the group told me I was a "giver." Hearing this feedback was pretty shocking. This starkly contrasted with my own view of myself. I could feel a physical aching inside as this new information fought so hard to be heard over the voice of self-disgust within me. Then one friend, a guy I spent quite a bit of time with in this group, stopped, turned, looked at me and told me I was a "taker." Initially, it was like somebody slapped me hard across the face, only much worse. But, of course, that viewpoint immediately found a home within me. It was what I expected.

He was one of only three people who labeled me a "taker" out of 68, yet for most of the time the exercise continued I kept thinking about why he saw me that way. I thought: "that one night when we were preparing our homework and he told me about his daughter's school play and I didn't pay attention—I bet that's it!" Completely forgetting all the other wonderful affirmation from everybody else, all I could do was dwell on why these three people felt I had failed them.

The exercise ended and the trainer told us to get up and stand away from the chairs. Then she said: "Who has 68 giver votes? Nobody? I didn't think so; not with this selfish group. You only think about yourselves!" The trainers could be tough. She went on to lecture us about how we were all so self-centered. She continued: "67?...66?...65?" At that point I raised my hand and she said, gruffly: "Sit down in that first chair."

Eventually we all took our seats, based on the number of "giver" votes we had. The trainer launched into an expletive-filled lecture on selfishness and then said: "Who wants to share? Who wants to tell us why they take, take, take?" I raised my hand; anxious to share why I was such a louse for not listening to my friend and all the other things I do to take from people.

The trainer looked at me aghast. "Sir!" she literally screamed. I swear saliva spewed out of her mouth. She went on: "How many giver votes did you have?" I answered: "65." She responded: "That's right...65 out of 68 and you get up here and whine about being a taker." I nodded. Then, she went off, and I'll leave the expletives out—about every other word—of what she said. In a loud, angry, almost blaring voice she got right up in my face and said: "Sir, I'll tell you how you take. Every time you play small, every time you play victim, every time you play cautious, trying to impress somebody, trying to look good, trying to avoid making waves, you take from me. You take from your friends; you take from your family. Every time you are too weak to stand up and be a man and offer what God gave you—you steal from God, you rip off every one of us; you take a piece of soul out of our world!" She concluded: "So, sit down, shut the &#@% up! and think about that for awhile. SIT DOWN!"

As you might expect, I remember this moment well; every "F-bomb" directed in disgust at me. Every word landing like a sharp knife was being rammed into me. Eventually the course ended. This trainer, eyes full of tears, warmly hugged me when we "graduated" and told me she expected to hear about me doing amazing things. I think these trainers cared deeply about making a difference for us and, regardless of the wisdom of their methods, this worked for me.

I later met with the therapist I was seeing. It is always good, I suggest, having a therapist at hand when taking such courses. Together we went through what had happened and began to "clean house" so to speak, emotionally. We started the process of working through all the excuses I used to play small in the world. As we did our emotional cleansing, I remembered that I was a competent man, capable of helping others not only through my job but also in other ways. I again saw the guy that teacher in the hall had seen back in High School when he talked me out of going to Viet Nam.

This was a huge Midline for me. In taking the course and then working with the therapist, I was taking the risk of confronting comfortable patterns of behaviors that held me back from fully engaging in life, ways of viewing myself that I relied upon to avoid taking risks and being hurt and disappointed.

I spent so much of my life doing precisely what the trainer had accused me of doing: I played small in the world, refusing to offer my opinions out of fear of looking silly or not fitting in. I often failed to step up when the circumstances required my strength and experience because I didn't want to hurt somebody's feelings. Of course there were times when I did enter the fray in order to help others but, all too often, I tended to hold back. The work in the course and with the therapist showed me how much I diminished my own spirit by not fully participating in life. It made me see how using my gifts not only enriched my friends and community, but also afforded me full freedom of expression and a sense of purpose.

Out of this experience I volunteered to be an assistant high school ice hockey coach for my son's team and spent the next three years helping boys on the team grown into young men. I found ways to share my experiences with them so that they might not stumble quite as much as I did. I helped a few of them form a vision of their future. I loved that time I served as a coach and a national magazine even wrote a story about it—the lawyer/hockey coach! Later, I began to teach yoga where there is an opportunity in each class, and even between classes, to serve and share what I've learned.

I tell this story to introduce us to the *Niyamas*, the second of the Eightfold Path of Patanjali's yoga. The *Niyamas,* found at *Yoga Sutra* 2.32, is a set of ethical precepts to guide our relationship with ourselves. These five ethical rules are: cleanliness (*Sauca*), contentment (*Santosa*), burning desire, (*Tapas*), study of the self (*Svadhyaha*), and devotion to God (*Isvara Pranidhanani*).[271]

We start with *Sauca*. *Sauca* is discussed in *Sutra* 2.40, which teaches that we increase our ability to connect to Spirit, by not only keeping the outside of our body and personal space clean, but also making sure we "clean up" the inner body.[272] We undertake the hard work of sorting out the clutter of false impressions we have about others and ourselves that keeps us from fully participating in the world. This means we learn to process through all internal contamination, including emotions such as unworthiness, jealousy, pride, hatred, and unhealthy attachments.[273] The Midline work I did with the course I described, and the therapy afterwards, helped me clean up those patterns of thought and behavior that prevented me from offering my value to my family and community.

I eventually found that practicing yoga poses, *Asana*, was important in helping me find a place of clarity and balance as I cleaned out disruptive attitudes, replacing them with an outlook allowing me to look at others and myself more open-mindedly and with greater kindness and understanding.[274] Meditation has been critical because it gives my mind the opportunity to remember my own special strengths. This allows me to create a meaningful life in which I share those gifts in relationship with others. *Mantra* practice works for me not just because it stops useless chatter in the mind, but also because it infuses my thoughts with feelings such as joy and peace, creating a fresh focus that helps keep me on my path to Midline and to Spirit.[275] I find that activities such as enjoying the creativity of a First Friday art walk, strolling through the woods or a park, or enjoying a good book, similarly bring me to this uncluttered, peaceful and clear state of mind. ∎

A MIDLINE PRACTICE

Find a closet or drawer somewhere that is cluttered and put it back in order, cleaning out what is necessary to do so.

CHAPTER 93
It feels good to be me— Patanjali's Yoga Sutra 2.42; contentment

It surprises me a bit that as I get older I feel more content. The surprise comes from the fact I haven't done anywhere near the number of cool things I thought I might do or been to as many places I was sure I would visit. I think this contentment comes in part from remembering my connection to Spirit and that I have the same attributes as Spirit. I remember I am a worthy being, unique and special in my own way. I take time to remember the ways I contribute meaningfully to the world: I've been a high school coach; I'm a good yoga teacher; I can usually make people smile or laugh; I generally have a way of helping people sort through their problems; all those years of being a lawyer, I guess.

I find ways to engage in satisfying and fun activities. I like to sneak in stories during yoga classes that sometimes make the students laugh, and ultimately makes them think and feel. I find there are many people interested in yoga philosophy so I give talks or workshops to help explain it. I go for hikes or bike rides, sometimes finding a creek I didn't know was there. Discovering, and then using my signature strengths, as Dr. Seligman calls them,[276] has made a huge difference in the quality of my life.

I talk here of contentment because the second of the *Niyamas* is *Santosa*, contentment. In *Yoga Sutra* 2.42 Patanjali says happiness flows from contentment.[277] Without contentment in our lives, how can we be open for Midline? How can we hear Spirit's voice and make choices that honors that voice?[278]

When I spent all my energy thinking about the things I would do when I was older, I couldn't concentrate on what was in front of me in the moment. I was free back then to enjoy a bike ride, a hike, or a book. Yet when I engaged in those activities there was always an undercurrent of rushing or hurrying, even if I had no appointment. I think I was hurrying to get to a time when I would be happy, not realizing all I had to do was choose to enjoy that moment, instead of waiting for some future moment. No wonder I didn't understand the *Wizard of Oz* until much later in life. Home can be pretty nice and all I had to do was click my heels to be there. We need to learn to be content with whatever we have and stop thinking we can only be happy when we get everything we desire.[279]

Shifting our attitude in this way leads to contentment. Why couldn't I have figured this out when I was 30, 40, or 50? Fortunately, you will, and it is never too late. A Midline is just ahead on our road, all the time. ■

A MIDLINE PRACTICE
What do you greatly appreciate that you already have in your life?

CHAPTER 94
On fire with desire—
Patanjali's Yoga Sutra *2.43; discipline*

I was working on a large case, the case I mentioned at the beginning of this book, against a large chemical manufacturer. Our argument, simplified, was the defendant's product, a chemical additive, caused steel embedded in brick and mortar walls of buildings to rust. The rust, according to our theory, created additional volume within the mortar and over time this extra rust exerted enough force to crack the brick walls. This product was used in high-rise residential construction, schools, hospitals, and other types of buildings. We alleged that this problem could result in hunks of bricks, or maybe portions of walls, falling, in some cases, many stories to the street below.

The defendant scoffed at our theory, arguing first the chloride released by their product doesn't rust steel and, second, any rust that might develop could not exert enough force to crack anything. The defendant hired experts from top universities and they were very persuasive. They continually tried to show that the severe cracking in our clients' buildings was due to structural flaws or design errors, certainly not the chemical additive. We kept thinking of ways to try to prove our point and kept coming up flat in terms of a winning argument to discredit the defendant's experts. It looked like it was going to be the "battle of the experts" pitting one PhD against another.

I was sitting in a large hotel conference room near the defendant's corporate headquarters reviewing hundreds of boxes of documents. It was depressing to sit in this conference room with no windows and know there still remained in nearby rooms many, many boxes full of documents yet to be reviewed, stacked floor to ceiling. The boxes contained all sorts of stuff with no seeming relevance to our case, including box after box of chemical formulas which even if we had figured them out, we'd never get a jury to understand. My partner Dave and I spent weeks and weeks at this place. Eventually things began getting testy and Dave and I almost came to blows, we were so bored, irritated, and stressed.

Then, one day, right in the middle of a box of some sort of strange chemical charts, we found a set of brochures for a totally different product by this same company. The product was a bridge deck overlay; a product placed on top of bridge decks to prevent them from cracking.

Ah Ha!!

We read through the brochures and were immediately rewarded by a bold headline admitting that chloride was the "enemy" of rebar. Rebar referred to steel reinforcement put inside the concrete bridge deck and brick walls to make them stronger. To make them stronger against what, you ask? There's where the "Ah Ha" comes in: The brochure talked about how deicing salts are dumped on the bridge deck and then permeate the concrete, turning to raw chloride. This chloride, our defendant clearly pointed out to its potential customers, rusts the steel. The rust then creates "expansive forces" which crack the concrete, causing millions of dollars of repairs. This was a huge problem well known in the highway construction industry so the message was clear: to prevent cracking of concrete from chloride, buy their product to keep chloride away from the steel.

I don't have to tell you how finding this brochure, a virtual needle in the haystack, changed the case to our clients' benefit. This is an example of the self-discipline it takes to be a good trial attorney: no matter what, we don't quit.

It is also an example of the commitment and dedication we must have if we truly want to experience success at anything, including connecting to Spirit. Not every Midline shows up as a dynamic, earth-changing event. In reality, life's Midlines offer themselves every day when we go about our business. This is true whether we are reviewing documents as a lawyer, helping the kids with homework when we're tired, or biting our tongue and listening to our spouse or partner when we are mad at them. We resist the temptation to slack off and, instead, do the task before us fully and with integrity.

This leads us to a discussion of the third *Niyama*, *Tapas*, burning desire or discipline. In *Yoga Sutra* 2.43 we learn rigorous self-discipline (*Tapas*) burns away those attitudes and habits that block or impede us from connecting with Spirit.[280] Gurumayi says *Tapas* provides us with the burning commitment necessary to stick with our yoga practices in order to better connect to Spirit.[281]

We build our capacity to connect with Spirit every time we set a worthy intention to do something and then stick to our intention regardless of the trouble and inconvenience it might bring. This intention may involve representing a client with all our skills and effort. It might involve being the best parent or partner humanly possible.

When we open to our true heart's desire and find our dreams, we work it and nourish it and don't back down. This is how we develop the ability to make our dreams a reality. We infuse the world with our dedication to finding and creating beauty and basic good. We do this with such a fire and passion the world notices and we create a quantum shift in that direction. ■

A MIDLINE PRACTICE

Identify a time in your life when you were so passionate about bringing about a result that you stuck with your efforts in the face of challenges until, one day, you achieved the result you sought.

CHAPTER 95
Put a cork in it!—
Patanjali's *Yoga Sutra 2.44; self-study*

One of my favorite yoga teachers, Desiree Rumbaugh, challenged us to see if we could avoid complaining for even just a month. Desiree said it would reap great results. She wasn't talking about the formal complaints we need to make when, for example, you tell the airline your bag didn't arrive. She was talking about the gossipy, whiney complaining we tend to do from time to time. Before we know it we are saying something negative about somebody who isn't there, just to get it off our chest. Or, we whine about our bills, our health, or who knows what else. There have been times when I'm talking to my son on the phone and I'm complaining about something. In the middle of my sentence I find I'm even boring myself. Even I don't want to listen to me!

I tried Desiree's suggestion and it works. While venting our frustrations can be helpful or even necessary on occasion, I've found that I enjoy life more when I keep the venting to a minimum, when it will be productive. Generally, though, I make better connections with people when I'm offering a positive energy to the conversation, something that provides some value to the interaction. Talking to another gives us a chance to get to know each other better and explore ideas. Why fill the conversation with negativity?

This brings us to the fourth *Niyama, Svadhyaha,* study of the self. We've discussed self-study quite a bit already; so let's see what Patanjali adds in *Yoga Sutra 2.44.* Traditionally, this *Sutra* refers to study of sacred scriptures and recitation of *Mantra* to better know Spirit.[282] When we read scripture and recite *Mantra* we find inspiration for creating patterns of attitudes and behavior that honor and connect to Spirit.

This *Sutra* also refers to introspection, finding God inside us.[283] We find Spirit when we observe how people of integrity carry themselves; they provide us examples of speech and behavior that enhance Spirit in the world.

We also find Spirit through the tragedies of life. Tragedies are Midlines because we have a choice as to how to respond. When we witness tragedy we receive Spirit's invitation to step up and offer our strengths in service of others. We grieve or take other appropriate action, but then we choose to move on, accepting life's invitations to its potential rather than remaining stuck in the remnants of the tragedy. Responding to tragedy in such a way is an example of how to successfully navigate Midline.

If Spirit resides as us, then self-study to connect to Spirit requires serious introspection. When our introspection reveals patterns that don't serve others or us, we have an obligation to change those patterns, remembering that we are all part of something bigger than just us.[284] If our objective is to live a meaningful life, then these habits need to be cast aside because they get in our way. Each time we confront such a habit we are at Midline, with the opportunity to let go of an old attitude or behavior in order to more richly connect to God.

I believe in getting back to the basics, the advice Desiree gave us that day in class: stop whining and figure out, through self-study, what we can do to change the situation for the better. When we stop whining we discover what's left—the uplifting aspects of our thoughts and feelings, the part of us that will recognize, embrace, and expand Spirit. ■

A MIDLINE PRACTICE

Identify one of your habits that helps you connect to Spirit, in whatever form you believe Spirit exits or, alternatively, a habit that helps you better connect to your family, friends, and workmates.

CHAPTER 96

Be in the flow of Spirit—Patanjali's Yoga Sutra *2.45; surrender to Spirit*

There is a legend I heard floating around for years in Minneapolis-St. Paul about an elderly top trial lawyer. Apparently, around the age of 72 he took on a personal injury case, representing the injured party. He prepared the case thoroughly and developed a theory on how to win. His entire case strategy depended on doing a cross-examination of the defendant's doctor that would end with the doctor being forced to agree with him.

The trial began and when it was time to cross-exam the opposing doctor, this elderly but feisty trial lawyer conducted his cross-examination so everybody in the courtroom, including the judge and jury, could see a mile away he was pinning the doctor down, preparing for a "Yes" answer from the doctor to the final cross examination question. Question by question he built toward the grand finale: "And, Dr., isn't it true_____?"—he asked with a self-assured, knowing tone in his voice. Ok, I'm embellishing here: I wasn't there and it isn't likely this lawyer used the television phrase: "Isn't it true?"—but you get the gist.

He had done such a masterful job everybody in the courtroom was primed for the doctor to meekly reply "Yes." However, the doctor threw a curve ball. Looking distastefully and smugly at the lawyer he answered with a mocking: "No, of course not."

Undaunted, this legendary trial lawyer proved once more why he is a legend. Without batting an eye and without even a moment's hesitation, he slammed his file down on his table with a disgusted flourish, looked right at the doctor for just a moment with a sneer, and then, turning to the jury, said, quite loudly and triumphantly: "I thought not!"

The Legend won the trial. He took what the Universe offered him.

The fifth *Niyama*, found in *Yoga Sutra* 2.45, says we will find full absorption in, or connection with Spirit, by surrendering to God, *Isvara Pranidhanani.*[285] How does this story about a very clever trial attorney illustrate this point?

We truly become absorbed in Spirit when, like the legendary trial lawyer, we become clearly and intensely connected to our strengths and how those strengths serve Spirit. We are then in flow with Spirit. In this case, the Legend was in this flow when he put the obstinate doctor in line, using his considerable skill so an injured person could receive just compensation. Nothing could disrupt that flow.

When we connect to Spirit we stop trying to force our way through the world and, instead, step into the flow of the world. We find the place where we are being asked to offer our strengths in service of a greater whole. Such moments are Midlines because we take the risk of letting go of, surrendering, what we think we want and, instead, take what Spirit is offering us. Yoga practices help us find the clarity needed for this surrender and absorption.[286]

Spirit is offering possibility to us all the time. Every day She offers us invitations to step into a place of greater success, whether by deeper intimacy with those close to us, creation of new healthy relationships, opportunities to manifest our dreams, or perhaps just a brief glimpse of Spirit in full flourish—the smell of fresh-baked cookies, the sound of a song we love playing in the background, the humor of a stranger. These invitations are life's Midlines. Can you recognize and connect to Spirit right in this moment? This is a reason why I practice yoga, so I can recognize Midlines and surrender to the flow of Spirit's offerings. ■

A MIDLINE PRACTICE

Right this moment, right in front of you—what is Spirit offering you?

CHAPTER 97
Lining up body and heart— Patanjali's Yoga Sutras 2.46 to 2.48; poses

I dreaded backbends when I started doing yoga. I've always been tight in my upper body. At first I thought it was because I lifted weights but after watching really muscular guys like Desiree Rumbaugh's husband, Andrew Rivin, bend in the upper body like pretzels, there went that excuse. Eventually I realized what contributed to making me stiff and tight in the upper body were attitudes I carried inside me.

At an early age I noticed the tough guys in my neighborhood walking with their chests puffed out like they were daring everybody to "lip off." It was a survival posture: you show people you are tough and confident and they take somebody else's lunch money. I lifted weights early in my life not just to get strong for football, but also to build an image of being the wrong guy to pick on.

Later, as a trial lawyer I adopted the same posture, hoping to intimidate other lawyers and portray an air of confidence to juries. These life-long habits and attitudes didn't always serve me too well, but did succeed in funneling tension into my upper back and chest muscles. No wonder I didn't like backbends. How can you suddenly bend a spine locked for years in a Vulcan Death Grip of tensed muscles and tissue?

And honestly, I was afraid to get hurt emotionally. I steeled myself early on against being hurt and disappointed in my desire for affection and love. I created a mental and physical wall around my heart so nobody could ever really get in and hurt me. Unfortunately, for a guy who wants to do a backbend, the spine runs right through that steel fortress.

My teachers told me that through yoga I could learn to soften the muscles around the spine, and this would eventually cause me to also soften those attitudes getting in the way of my relationships. Backbends are great for this, they said. I didn't really like feeling vulnerable, but I was getting tired of experiencing everything alone, sitting in restaurants alone, going on trips alone. It's a drag always laughing at *Saturday Night Live* by myself. I longed for connection: we all do.

At long last I decided to start doing backbends. Sure enough, after some time, my muscles began to soften and my posture became far more relaxed. Even my facial expressions relaxed. My body began to let go of some of the tension holding the fortress together. All this softening allowed me to go deeper into my poses and even made me stronger physically. At the same time I was becoming more approachable and likeable as a person.

This takes us to the next part of the Eightfold Path identified by Patanjali: *Asana,* poses, a posture, a seat, discussed by Patanjali in *Yoga Sutras* 2.46 to 2.48. We learn from Patanjali that performing a yoga pose in proper alignment helps connect us to Spirit.[287] The practice of doing yoga poses is possibly unique in its ability to show us every time where our attitudes could use some shaking up. I learned to do entire marathons with a tight upper body and became effective with martial arts while holding unnecessary tension in my shoulders.

Yoga, though, doesn't allow for this: I couldn't do a backbend without relaxing the very muscles I had used for years in an attempt to browbeat the universe into giving me what I felt I should have. Practicing yoga caused me to soften the outer body and I found I needed to soften my inner self as well in order to make that happen. Practicing this way has helped me to change my approach to life, minimizing my counterproductive and misdirected efforts. As a result, I am experiencing deeper relationships in my life, simply by softening both the outer and inner "me" and become more receptive to others.

Mr. Iyengar eloquently says: *Asana* should be "nourishing and illuminative."[288] Rather than trying to force our body into a pose, we calm down, connect with our breath, and place the body into its proper position for doing the pose. We set a heart-felt intention and then create space within our system for the pose to unfold, aligned with that intention. We mindfully create space to allow the muscles, joints and ligaments to properly coordinate.[289] This is how we allow the body to be nurtured by the pose.

Practicing poses this way, is illuminative because we are, at the same time, paying attention to our body's feedback. What adjustments does our body tell us are needed? This mindfulness also teaches us to be spacious off the mat, to take these practices of attentiveness into all our daily activities. Just like when we do a pose, we can take time to thoughtfully line up our words, our actions and our thoughts with the world around us by paying attention to the world and our response. Just as we line up with Spirit by paying attention to how we line up our body in a pose,[290] we can use this same mindfulness and process of alignment in our interactions with others. How many times have we said something in haste, wishing too late we had taken a moment to align our brain, mind and intelligence to gauge the appropriateness of what just popped out of our mouth?

By taking time to line up the little things in our poses, such as our wrist creases or our thighbones, we are developing the habit of mindfulness. Off the yoga mat this same habit will cause us to look into the eyes of our spouses and partners and see through to their hearts. It will cause us to truly listen to the words of our children and feel the love in the touch of a friend.

Mindfulness opens the door to finding Spirit and Her invitation to a rich experience of Midline in each moment.

This is why it is so important for us to set the stage for our *Asana* practice with a heart-oriented intention that seeks greater alignment with Spirit: focusing today on tranquility and peace, tomorrow on courage, the next day on gratitude. We align our inner sheaths, our *Koshas,* to harmonize with each other as we become infused with these intentions.[291] Our outer body, the *Annamaya Kosha,* is in constant communion with the innermost body, working together to make a truly heartfelt expression of Spirit as only our heart and body can uniquely make.[292] We learn to pay attention to what is going on inside us. Through this constantly checking in to see if something feels right or not, we learn there is an "us" inside. This "us" has dreams, hopes, desires, and needs. This "us" wants to sing its song to the world.

It is this awareness that develops our ability to find Midline in life, whether we do poses or not. Through learning to line up our heart with our body—what we say, what we do, what we think—we align our dreams with Spirit. ■

A MIDLINE PRACTICE

Set an intention that the next time you speak to a person you enjoy knowing, you will pay attention not only to the words the person says, but also to the look in his or her eyes, their facial expression, their body posture—all the clues as to how Spirit can shine through that person.

CHAPTER 98
Pathway to the heart—
Patanjali's Yoga Sutras 2.49 to 2.53; breath

Thanks to a top Denver yoga teacher Crystal and her sister Chanda, I attended a workshop taught by Matthew Sanford. Matthew is a yoga teacher, an author, and a nationally recognized public speaker on the subject of mind-body relationships. He is a very powerful man with a powerful message, made even more so because he is paralyzed from the chest down as a result of an auto accident when he was young. He has drawn upon his experiences learning to live with physical challenges, to become a leader in adapting yoga for people with disabilities.[293]

During the workshop, Matthew worked with a young college-age man in a wheelchair who had developed a forward leaning contracted posture in which his chest, shoulders, and upper back rounded forward. This even drew his face into a downward position. Matthew and Crystal took some pillows and together helped him sit upright so his chest, chin, and face all lifted and his heart area opened up and out.

As he did this, there was a giant release of energy literally palpable in the room, as if all the emotion in this young man found release. I looked around through wet eyes and noticed everybody around me was in tears. Matthew hadn't said anything other than describing how to place the pillows and where and how he and Crystal were placing their hands. The young man hadn't said anything, yet his freed heart energy spoke volumes.

This brings us to the next part of Patanjali's Eightfold Path of yoga, *Pranayama. Pranayama* involves creating a meaningful relationship with our breath, our life force, *Prana*. We discussed *Prana* and breathing in the section pertaining to *Pranamaya Kosha*. In *Yoga Sutras* 2.49 to 2.52 Patanjali identifies the practice of *Pranayama* as a specific part of our pathway to reaching Spirit.[294] Resources that teach these practices include Mr. Iyengar's books, *Light on Pranayama*,[295] and *Light on Yoga*,[296] and Donna Fhari's *The Breathing Book*.[297]

Pranayama is the doorway to our thoughts, a pathway directly to the heart.[298] This is what I think happened with the young man in the wheelchair: his life force had been stuck in the contracted position his body had adopted over the years confined in that chair. By placing him in an open position, Matthew literally unplugged that life force, allowing it once again to freely flow through him and then out into the world in full expression.

Our life force, *Prana*, is in constant contact with our thoughts, so when we calm the breath, we are able to calm our mind's chatter, allowing us to find the steadiness we require in any given moment.[299] Calming the breath is an essential step in finding and embracing Midline because the stilling of our mind's chatter allows us to be receptive to life's invitations. It also allows us to evaluate those invitations unfettered by negative patterns of thoughts that can interfere with our choices in response to the offer of Midline.

Prana connects us directly to Spirit.[300] Think back to my karate tournament. My mind's chatter had completely separated me from what I knew in my body and mind. By following my teacher's advice and taking some deep breaths, I re-connected to those thoughts and memories that best served me.

This sudden connection reminds me of a time during the fall when I flew to New York, via White Plains. I remember looking forward to the airplane's slow descent over the Hudson River so I could enjoy this bird's-eye view of all the trees in their colorful autumn majesty. Unfortunately, it was cloudy and I was disappointed as I looked out from my window seat in vain. Clouds completely covered the spectacular scene hidden below. Suddenly, as we descended, the clouds lifted! Before me was this magnificent brilliant splendor.

This is what the simple act of paying attention to our breath does for us. It clears away the clouds and connects us to Spirit. Richard Freeman says that in our meditation we allow our breath to unravel the associations our mind has made over the years that don't serve us, breaking them up so as to free us to create healthy new connections.[301] Just like the clouds broke up that day on my flight, attention to the breath breaks up the clouds that sometimes can hide Spirit from us.

My experience attending the class with Matthew Sanford, Crystal, and Chanda that day demonstrated to me the power of *Prana* and the need for a proper foundation to facilitate connection of the breath to Spirit. When Matthew and Crystal used pillows to help the young man sit up, they moved his spine into a position to maximize flow of breath, opening his heart space. When this happened the power of this man's life force literally surged into his heart and, from there, into the room, touching each of our hearts.

Now I get what Senior Iyengar teacher Gabriella Giubillaro was doing when she spent a good portion of a *Pranayama* workshop making sure we were sitting just right. Magic happens when we fully connect to *Prana*. We maximize the opportunity for that magic to occur by setting the best foundation we can. We open as fully as we can to invite Spirit to flow within us. ∎

A MIDLINE PRACTICE

Please get comfortable on a chair, sit "tall," lift your chin and look straight ahead. Place your palms flat on your thighs. Notice how alive this posture makes you feel.

CHAPTER 99
Going within—Patanjali's Yoga Sutra 2.54; withdrawing the senses

I sat in a meditation workshop outside Sedona, Arizona. We were in a room with large windows looking out into a beautiful garden, with red rock formations in the background as far as the eye could see. It was impossible not to notice the birds, the lush and diverse high desert, and the beautiful landscaping just on the other side of the windows. I was designing my own retreat area for my home in Colorado and so my attention kept moving away from the instructor so I could take in the view through the windows. I was searching for ideas I could use for my own land. I saw the shrubs, the trellises, and the trees and began to wonder what would grow at my place at 9,000 feet.

Dr. Paul Muller Ortega must have noticed this because he mentioned the importance of closing the eyes in meditation practice. With the eyes closed we can't be as distracted by what is happening around us. Normally as we move about our day, we want our eyes open as we engage in the world. In meditation, it is time to turn inside so we can best process our experiences.

A vast array of memories is stored inside us, awaiting our attention. Meditation is an opportunity to make associations between different sets of memories. Closing our eyes focuses our attention on what we might find inside where we process emotions, create context, and even forge new neural connections. Our hopes and dreams lie inside.

Closing our eyes allows us access, without distraction, to all these great resources. It's like going to a fantastic movie, with no idea what's playing but knowing it will be interesting—and all without having to buy a ticket. If we allow the senses to take over, our amazing access to Spirit can slip out of view.[302]

This process of looking inside is the next part of the Eightfold Path of yoga, *Pratyahara*. *Yoga Sutra* 2.54 says that *Pratyahara* involves withdrawing the senses, mind, and consciousness from external objects so that we can direct them towards Spirit within. [303] Yoga philosophers compare the relationship between our senses and the mind to the way bees follow the Queen Bee around. If the Queen flies off, so do the bees. If the Queen settles down, the bees settle down.[304] Similarly, if our senses fly all over, the mind will follow, but if the senses take a rest, then the mind will rest. This is reason enough to withdraw the senses and let the mind relax. We go where the honey is—inside! ∎

A MIDLINE PRACTICE

Close your eyes and spend the next minute noticing whatever thoughts and images arise.

PART VII

It takes practice—Patanjali's Yoga Sutras

C. Absorption in Spirit—
the path to real freedom

CHAPTER 100
Here's the play—Patanjali's Yoga Sutra 3.1; focus

As a college football player I had the privilege of playing center for quarterback Ken Anderson, who was also, by the way, my pledge brother and who went on to become a repeat Pro-Bowl quarterback in the National Football League. He guided the Cincinnati Bengals to a Super Bowl and set several NFL passing records during his career. The guy was a leader.

I recall a game when we were behind, which didn't happen too often. We were driving down the field, needing a touchdown. On the play I have in mind, somebody, one of the other linemen or me, missed a block and our running back was stuffed for no gain. Walking back to the huddle, my teammate and I began shouting at each other. He yelled, "Dorigan: you've got to get that guy!" My response was to yell: "#$@% you, Gordie!"

In the midst of this shouting and finger pointing, Ken Anderson steps into the huddle and says loudly: "Knock it off. Here's the play." Talk about getting our attention. Suddenly you could hear a pin drop as he immediately shut us up and brought our attention right back to the moment, the next play. We listened to what he wanted us to do. The arguments and frustrations of just a moment ago were forgotten as we focused on him with all our attention.

This story illustrates the next part of the Eightfold Path of yoga, *Dharana,* which *Yoga Sutra* 3.1 defines as the fixing of our consciousness on one point.[305] Here, having asserted ourselves over our senses, we begin to create a union or connection with some object of focus as we further reduce the mind's chatter.[306]

When Ken Anderson stepped in to the huddle as our leader, we were a textbook example of single-pointed concentration. Gone were the chatter, the arguing, the yelling, and the finger pointing. Not one spark of energy was spent stewing that my friend had blamed me for missing the block or I had swore at him. Nothing distracted us from our focus on Ken and what he wanted us to do right then.

This is exactly how we focus as we seek to connect with each other. This is the Midline in our every day interactions with each other. Rather than thinking of other things, glancing around the room or down at our phone, we focus on the other person fully so we can absorb what they are saying and even what they are feeling. This is how intimacy is created. We can practice this focus simply walking down the street. Remember how Anodea

Judith challenged us to find God in some amazing architecture? We can focus on the building's design, trying to imagine the designer's creative mental process. From that focus we may even become absorbed in contemplation of that designer's likely creative process.

We practice this focus when we do a yoga pose, concentrating totally on the precise action of our rear leg, for example, and what physical and emotional feeling that action generates. We focus on our breath or *Mantra* in mediation. We focus on our friends when they speak to us so that a true connection takes place.

By focusing solely on the object of our concentration, we are able to create space to join with the music in our heart; the poetry it is reciting all day long. It is through this practice that we recognize Midline; our focus on Spirit is so strong that we don't miss Her when she beckons.

This sets the stage for *Dhyana*. ■

A MIDLINE PRACTICE

Become totally focused on the next person you speak with, directing your attention solely to that person.

CHAPTER 101
Flowing with Spirit—
Patanjali's Yoga Sutra 3.2; ongoing focus

Years ago I attended a fantastic weeklong workshop at the Omega Institute in upstate New York. It was a beautiful autumn week and the Omega campus was an artist's palate of colors, with trees in their full fall costumes of red, gold, orange, and shades in between. The air was crisp, the people were warm and friendly, and anticipation was high.

Krishna Das, a singer and musician known for Indian devotional chanting, was there to play music during yoga class and lead *Kirtan* each night. *Kirtan,* if you've never been to one, is call-and-response sacred chanting with music. When Krishna Das does *Kirtan,* the music starts slow but often builds to a fast tempo where you have no choice but to get up and dance. His music reaches out to you like a potential dance partner holding out a hand, and your body feels compelled to take the offered hand and rock out.

I had other reasons for looking forward to the week with eager anticipation. At an earlier yoga workshop I had connected with a woman who really appealed to me. Toward the end of that workshop I sensed that she was interested in me but, even with my yoga practices, I still hadn't had the courage to let her know I was interested. Instead, I had acted with some indifference, not wanting to risk being mistaken and then getting embarrassed and hurt. In other words, out of these fears I'd missed a Midline, a chance for a heart connection.

I knew she was attending the Omega retreat and when I showed up at Omega, I immediately looked for her. I found her, told her that I'd been thinking about her all these months, and was hoping we could see where we might take our relationship. She smiled at me and then broke the news: she really had been interested but, in the ensuing eight or nine months had met somebody else and was now in a steady relationship she wanted to pursue.

I wished her the best and went my way, heartbroken, to tell the truth. It had taken me quite a bit of nerve to approach her and once again, I felt I'd really screwed up. This was the pattern in my life. I showed up too late for my dad and my mom; I'd messed up being married; I'd let other good relationships slip away and now I'd done it again. "What a loser," I thought, not a great way to talk to yourself but that is what I felt like back then.

Deflated and sad I walked over to the Omega Café, paperback novel in hand. I walked in, bought a chocolate chip cookie and coffee, and sat at a small table against the wall. I sat out of the traffic pattern, to my way of thinking at the time, an appropriate place for me—by myself.

I started to escape into my mystery novel when I sensed a presence at my table. I looked up and saw a man standing at my table, smiling at me. It was Krishna Das. I hadn't met him before but recognized him. When I stood up to introduce myself he swept me into a hug. All he said was: "Don't worry; things are going to be great" and, with that, he walked away.

I was shocked. The Café was full and it's not like I was sitting there all teary-eyed. How in the world did he know that I was in pain? One possible explanation is that he has a connection to Spirit that is so strong he literally lives in that connection. Maybe his years and years of *Mantra* and meditation have so filled him with Spirit he was able to immediately sense when there was even a subtle disruption to Spirit's flow in the room.

I tell you this story to introduce the next part of Patanjali's Eightfold Path, *Dhyana,* meditation. *Dhyana* is described in *Yoga Sutra* 3.2 as a steady and continuous flow of our attention directed toward a single point.[307] Through practice we develop an ability to hold our focus despite the mind's chatter and the world's endless distractions. If we are meditating, then we find and stay with Spirit's voice while in the meditation. For me, there is a point during meditation where I forget that I'm reciting a *Mantra* and become totally absorbed in that *Mantra* in a constant flow of attention. Mr. Iyengar compares this uninterrupted attention to the smoothness and consistency of oil pouring out of a jug.[308]

Remember: we practice so that we can become absorbed in Spirit in each moment as we go about our activities. By practicing with our focus on a building's design, for example, and trying to imagine the creative spark of the designer, we teach ourselves how to become absorbed in the object of our focus. If we focus on finding the expression of Spirit in the design, we become absorbed in Spirit.

At some point, this ability to focus on Spirit becomes who we are, how we live and flow through life. I suspect that Krishna Das' commitment to sacred chanting infuses him with this capacity. We too have the potential, like him, to enter a room, sense that some stranger is hurting, and walk over and offer a reminder of Spirit to a soul hungry to know some love. Imagine how much potential we have to make a difference in the lives of our friends and family as we develop our ability to focus on Spirit. ■

A MIDLINE PRACTICE

When you walk into a crowded place, whether a locker room, a conference room just before a meeting, a grocery store, or some other place where there is a number of people, look around and select a person to smile at or say hello to. You can then continue the conversation or simply go about your business. Later, ask yourself why you chose that person.

CHAPTER 102
Union with the heart— *Patanjali's* Yoga Sutra *3.3; total absorption*

I visited a friend in his office on the top floor of a ten-story building overlooking a residential neighborhood in Denver. He was on the phone and I stared out the window while I waited for him to finish his conversation. My attention was drawn to a man who was pruning his hedges in the backyard of his home, ten stories below me. I had to really concentrate to even see that it was a man. I could see his house, and a little attached patio. There was a nice patch of green lawn, tiny from way up high. A little line, a sidewalk, ran from the patio out to the garage at the back of the property.

I watched the man trimming the hedge and imagined how much he cared about his yard, how he likely wanted it to be clean and welcoming. Maybe he planned to have visitors later and they would all sit out on the patio and talk about their day. The whole scene reminded me of my own yard and how much fun it is when friends visit.

As I stood there, absorbed in watching him trimming his hedge, I began to take in the houses on either side of him. They looked mostly the same from that height. The house on one side of his was more a yellow, the one across the street a light green and, next to it, another white house. Each house had different landscaping, each a distinct expression of the owner.

While I continued to focus on this one man, my vision expanded to take in the whole block, the homes across the street, and then the next block, and the next. I knew that to each homeowner, the homes were different; the lives of each person inhabiting those homes were certainly different. Yet, from this perspective everything was really the same: a commingling of colors, shapes, and fellow human beings all joining together.

We all go about our daily lives, each with our own apparently unique problems and challenges yet, at the end, all each of us wants is to feel at home, safe, happy and feeling that we are valued. Focusing first on this man and then his neighborhood, I began to drift into a warm, all-encompassing sensation of connection to everyone and everything. There was no "I" or "they." There was, just for a moment, a calm sense of being and a serene union with Spirit.

The final part of the Eightfold Path of yoga is *Samadhi,* perfect absorption: union with the heart, connection with Spirit. *Yoga Sutra* 3.3 describes *Samadhi* as a feeling of being engulfed by Spirit, losing any self-awareness, as we become Spirit.[309] Mr. Iyengar describes it this way: *Dhyana* flows into *Samadhi* as when a musician loses himself or herself by becoming completely engrossed in the music.[310] *Yoga Sutra* 3.4 says that the combination of these last three limbs, this process of absorption, *Dharana, Dhyana* and *Samadhi*, is called *Samyama,* which means integration.[311]

The more we engage in yoga practices, and by this I mean seeking to pay mindful attention to Spirit in each moment, the more we cultivate the discipline and fire necessary to become absorbed in Spirit, anywhere and anytime. We develop an ability to draw our attention to Spirit, focus on Her, and then step into Her flow. *Yoga Sutra* 3.56 says that when we arrive at that place where our default way of being is to find Spirit everywhere and become absorbed in Her, we have reached perfection in yoga, called *Kaivalya.*[312]

Since Spirit is in everyone and everything, doesn't this mean that we can become absorbed in all the sad stuff too? I think the answer is "Yes." Sadness, tragedy, evil action; these are all part of Spirit since they are expressions of Spirit existing as man and nature. Since we all share Spirit's attributes of abiding love and joy, I don't know how we avoid feeling sadness when sad things happen. In fact, I suspect the failure to feel sadness is an indication that we are not really fully absorbed in Spirit; we are missing the empathy of true connection to others and to Spirit that comes from the heart. When we live out of the heart, as pure Spirit, we use our freedom to return to love and joy, particularly the joy of serving others in times of sadness.

This profound way of living in the world is, to me, the ultimate mystical experience, the supernatural connection to God I've always dreamed of having. *Patanjali,* at the very end of his teachings, *Yoga Sutra:* 4.25, brings it all home as he addresses the possibility for such an experience for each of us. He says when our thoughts are of Spirit, we will necessarily only find Spirit in everyone and everything.[313]

When we fully understand at our core that we are each a unique expression of God, we become absorbed in Spirit, able to see connection. We can't miss finding Midline because, absorbed in Spirit, we are now living in Midline. ■

A MIDLINE PRACTICE
The next time you read or watch a news story about some tragedy, pause for a moment and notice if you feel any sadness or anger.

PART VII

It takes practice—Patanjali's Yoga Sutras

D. You want mystical?
Some real Yoga magic

CHAPTER 103
It's magic!—Patanjali's Yoga Sutra 4.1; supernatural powers

When I was younger my favorite sport was basketball. I loved playing. I grew to about 5'11" in junior high and that added to my ability to make a difference in games, making basketball even more fun. Since my father was much taller, I expected I would continue to grow and eventually be a big star in high school and college, maybe go all the way to the pros. I played pick up games constantly, several a day when weather allowed, at different neighborhood courts.

That was a junior high dream. I never grew any taller. I ran into some significant challenges when I tried out for the basketball team as a sophomore at Hammond High School in Indiana, right smack in the middle of a real high school basketball hot bed. I tried out against players who went on to star in the Big Ten and other conferences. They even made a movie about some guys over in Gary, Indiana, part of our conference, who won a national basketball championship when they moved on together to college in Texas. All wasn't lost. I ended up doing well at football. Still, I loved basketball.

I have never forgotten those times and my dreams about making it big in basketball. I guess it must have been a really powerful dream because it is the only explanation I have for what I'm about to share with you. Back in 1962–63, before I figured out that I wasn't going to be 6'5" and a pro basketball star, I followed the University of Cincinnati. A player from my high school who was that size played for them and they were a dominant team. They won the NCAA national championship in men's basketball in 1961 and 1962 and were playing Loyola of Chicago for the championship in 1963. I could think of nothing else but that game. Talk about total absorption!

The night of the game arrived and for some reason I couldn't watch it on television. I think my parents must have invited company over to the house and they were in the room with the only television. Anyway, I figured I would just go to bed right away so when I woke up the game would be done and I could read all about it in the newspaper. I crawled into bed and didn't even bother to read a book. I wanted to go right to sleep so the night would pass and the suspense would be over. I knew when I woke up I could read about my Bearcats winning a third straight title.

Here's the strange part of the story. I woke up that morning and as I woke up I "saw" the newspaper headline in my mind even before getting out of bed: Loyola had beaten

Cincinnati 60—58. I'm not kidding: I saw the score in my head. I went downstairs, opened the door to get the paper, and, sure enough, Loyola had won by that exact score.

Here's yet another interesting thing: at the time I didn't give much if any thought to the fact that I'd seen the score in my head. Back then "seeing" a thing ahead of time apparently wasn't that big a deal to me. I've since learned to anticipate a variety of things in my career as a lawyer, but don't recall any other more recent examples of such a clear, precise vision of what was about to happen.

I know people have psychic capabilities and experiences but if I do, the only evidence I remember was this basketball game involving nobody I really even knew! I wonder why this special talent hasn't shown up for more productive uses. Why couldn't I tell that we were going to have a boy and not a girl until the ultrasound told us? What is the reason I couldn't see ahead and make better relationship choices or at least smarter real estate decisions? Do you have any idea how much my former house in Denver's Hilltop neighborhood is worth today? I do, but it's not mine; it should be, but it isn't. I didn't see into the future on that one.

My instincts suggest that seeing the basketball score ahead of time had something to do with a kid's ability to tap into the cybernetic network of circuitry the way little Abigail and Lucy did. Maybe as a young boy, unhampered by all the worries that befall us as we age, I was able to "see" things that the chattering mind of an adult misses. Also, since I feel silly telling this story, maybe society puts out a subtle message to us that it isn't wise to acknowledge such abilities and so we ignore them to the point where they fade into the background.

Maybe if we really master Patanjali's practices whatever psychic gifts we've been given would be more readily apparent. So long as I keep missing the obvious invitations God offers through Midlines, either because my mind is chattering with a hundred different thoughts at the same time, or I'm afraid, feeling unworthy, or for whatever other reason, it shouldn't surprise me that I might miss the more subtle messages delivered at the psychic level.

When I read *Autobiography of a Yogi*,[314] I was enthralled with the stories, particularly those stories of miracles and saintly supernatural powers. Similarly, I find Patanjali's discussion of mystical powers to be absolutely riveting. Rather than assume that they are made-up yarns, I believe that there are possibilities for connection to each other, to Spirit, we simply don't understand. Perhaps we have too many distractions, particularly now with a cell phone able to instantly connect us to endless streams of emails, tweets, and other forms of information. Maybe we haven't yet become open-minded enough to fully explore other connective possibilities. Or, maybe it is a combination of all these things. Whatever the reason, I've decided it's more fun to stay flexible and available to what my possibilities might be as I continue on my journey of becoming intimate with Spirit.

Why, you may ask, am I talking about supernatural powers? We've followed Patanjali to the point where he teaches us about *Samadhi* and we see that *Samadhi* is attainable for all of us. In *Yoga Sutra:* 4.1 Patanjali tells us that when we reach this state of *Samadhi,* we may in fact experience one form or another of supernatural powers.[315] Just what are these supernatural powers, often referred to as *Siddhis*?

The eight specific *Siddhis,* as identified by Mr. Iyengar, are: 1) *Anima* (to become as minute as an atom, even invisible); 2) *Mahima* (to grow in magnitude, acquire immense power); 3) *Laghima* (to become light, capable of becoming any creature); 4) *Garima* (to become heavy, immovable); 5) *Prapti* (to dominate and obtain anything desired; accessing all places); 6) *Prakamya* (freedom of will and attainment of wishes; the ability to fly); 7) *Isatva* (supremacy over all, including the elements); and 8) *Vasitva* (power to subjugate anyone or anything).[316]

Patanjali tells us in *Yoga Sutra* 4.1 that there are ways other than *Samadhi* that might lead us to one or more of these supernatural powers: use of herbs, *Mantra* repetition, past lives in which we practiced yoga, and rigorous practice in this life.[317] I've already discussed *Mantra* and rigorous practices. Discussion of how past lives and use of herbs might bring us to realization of one or more of these powers is beyond the scope of this book.

These particular powers are derived from *Yoga Sutra* 3.45 (3.46 in Mr. Iyengar's commentary) and the *Sutras* that follow.[318] Let's talk about them. ■

▌ A MIDLINE PRACTICE
Recall a coincidence, perhaps receiving a phone call from somebody you were thinking about or some other seemingly unexplained and unanticipated event.

CHAPTER 104
Playing big and playing small

When I was a young lawyer, early in my career, I pestered my mentor all the time. I asked him to review every little thing I sent out. I wanted my work to be perfect and I wanted to hear him tell me how perfect my work was and how amazing I was. I am sure I drove him nuts.

One day he called me into his office and said to me: "If you ever want to be a partner, you've got to start treating every work project like you own it; like you're already a partner. Try to forget I'm even here. What would you do if I weren't here and this project had to get done? What if I was not around and the court or client demanded an immediate decision? What would you do? If you think this way and handle the files I give you just this way, you will grow into being a partner."

What a Midline for me. I was terrified that I would make a mistake. Rather than acknowledge I was feeling insecure, I instead became angry with him for putting me on the spot. I even thought about quitting and joining another firm. Pretty quickly, though, I saw the fantastic opportunity he was giving me: the chance to become a really great trial lawyer like him. So, rather than quit, I faced my fears and followed his advice. I pretended each file was mine. I started handling the files as if he were not around. I wrote letters when I thought I should and said what I thought needed to be said. I set and took depositions. I hired and used expert witnesses as I thought fit. Eventually I became a partner.

Later he told me he watched everything I did during that entire period of time, going to the files to see what I had written, how I had conducted the depositions, and what I'd spent money on. He did this to be sure the client was well represented; he just didn't tell me he was doing it. He said a few times he shuddered a bit at how I'd handled issues, but saw things were turning out well so he left me alone. At the same time, he continued to show me how he handled matters he was working on so I could watch and learn. I would then go back and copy his habits because I wanted to practice like him.

Sometimes we need to "play small." By my mentor playing small, I grew "big." I grew into being a partner. To play small we learn to let go of ego and become almost invisible on occasions when necessary. This is a version of the first supernatural power, *Anima*. We can choose to become so small, other people in the room get the attention they deserve.

The workplace is a great opportunity to use this power. When my partner gave me credit for his ideas on the large explosion/fire case, he was being *Anima*, minute, so I would appear large in contrast. We might be part of a team at work, and on the team is a shy person with great talent who remains under the radar of management, never getting noticed. By becoming small we allow light to shine on that deserving person. Similarly, we can look within our family or community and see when it is time for somebody else to get the spotlight.

Alternatively, sometimes we need to be large, *Mahima*. The occasion might call for us to step up and use our power. Again using the office story, we may wish to intercede on behalf of an unnoticed co-worker, using our prestige to support that person's advancement. Just as my partners in the stories played small, they also on other occasions played big, making sure the firm was aware of the talents of those who worked with them, including me. They guided the firm through tough issues, and otherwise shared their experience and wisdom to help us all become better lawyers.

When we are in a group and gossip starts, we become large when we speak up and put a stop to it or, if we can't, we express our distaste for such activity and, if necessary, walk away. The same holds true when the discussion turns into a conversation of separation—gay bashing, racial slurs or other types of divisive talk. We become large when we challenge such behavior. At home we become large when we provide constructive and necessary criticism to our children in a kind and loving way, instead of stepping back and not saying anything just to avoid an argument. We become large when we own our own greatness and celebrate it, offering our gifts even at the risk of rejection and embarrassment.

There is an endless number of ways we can use these two powers to create a happier world. ■

A MIDLINE PRACTICE
Look around your workplace, family, or group of friends and identify a way you can, by playing small, boost the confidence and image of another at work, within the family, or within the group.

CHAPTER 105
More supernatural powers!

I had an expert witness, Ed, who was a brilliant engineer with an almost photographic memory. He took great pride in how he put together his files for claims on construction projects we were handling. We could count on him to have every detail properly photographed and documented. We represented plaintiffs whose property had failed due to construction defects and the defendant builders and other contractors would pick us apart if we couldn't prove every single defect. Ed was our guy who could do that.

I remember sitting through dozens of depositions in which lawyers tried to find mistakes in Ed's files or testimony. Because he didn't make many mistakes, some of these lawyers tried to browbeat him into submission, thinking if they shouted or bullied him, he would cave in and say something he didn't really mean. That strategy never worked with him. Ed had not only a quick mind but also a rather large and healthy ego; nobody was going to push him around.

We had a case involving roof flashing, a material that diverts water away from openings. He testified about a flashing failure he had seen on ten different buildings in a multi-family project. One of the developer's lawyers, a large guy with a booming voice, demanded during a deposition in an insulting tone that Ed prove those failures really existed on each building by showing us the photos of those flashing mistakes at each location. The photos were in 15 or so binders of photographs Ed had brought to the deposition.

Ed, probably in a hurry to finish, and also no doubt just to tweak the loud badgering lawyer, said he couldn't readily find the photos; it would take too long. He knew he was under no legal obligation to look because he had made them available for inspection before the deposition and it was the badgering lawyer's job to have located them. The lawyer kept pushing and Ed kept digging his heels in. Eventually the lawyer finished his questions and passed the witness to Mari.

Mari is a very bright, friendly woman who also wanted Ed to show her the photos he had referred to. However, instead of trying to push Ed around, she tried the light touch. She smiled at Ed, said "Hi," and asked him how he was doing and whether he wanted a break. Then, after a few questions, she said sweetly: "Ed, I know you said you couldn't find the photos of the flashing and I know I'd never be able to keep track of them, if it were me. But, I know your mind; I know how smart you are, how hard you work, and I know you know exactly where those pictures are in those binders"—all the while smiling and talking softly and kindly. "Would you help me out and find them for me, pleeeeaaase?" Ed smiled back meekly and replied "Sure," putting his hands on the photos in about 30 seconds.

This is an example of the third *Siddhi*, *Laghima*, to become light. How can we use this power in our lives? In this case, Mari was successful by being light. Her demeanor stood in stark contrast to the lawyer who had preceded her, who played the heavy but without success. Sometimes we have to be light, and use a light touch.

Over my career as a trial lawyer I've marveled at how some lawyers adjust to the circumstances and get the job done while others, like the loud, badgering lawyer, can't seem to let go of habits that, from my experience, seldom work. This is an example of Midline. The heavy-handed lawyer had attended enough of these depositions to see that his style never produced maximum results, but that others, by being at least somewhat courteous, obtained far more information from Ed and other witnesses. This lawyer's refusal to look at his behavior prevented him from true success, at least in these depositions. Watching these displays of style over the years caused me to frequently examine my own patterns of behavior to see what worked and what didn't.

There are times when we need to play the heavy. I attended a Catholic school and in fourth grade got in trouble one day. That night, while I was studying, my father came in to my room. In an angry voice, he said: "Do you know who that was on the phone?" He then proceeded to tell me how the head nun at the school had called to let him know I was being a behavior problem. He told me he promised her it wouldn't happen again. He glared at me, face red, towering over me, and said in a voice I will never forget: "And I don't want that nun to EVER call here again!"

My dad walked out the door and there was no way in the world I would ever get in trouble at that school again. In fact, I was careful not to even do something particularly good or praiseworthy out of fear the head nun might call my dad again: better to leave well enough alone! Who knows these days whether this was good parenting or not but it worked for me. My dad was *Garima*, the fourth *Siddhi*—to become heavy.

Prapti is the fifth *Siddhi* and is the power to dominate and attain what one wants. Even though Mari was light in her approach to Ed, she also dominated and got what she wanted. She knows how to be successful. Notice, though, she wasn't dominating by trying to be pushy or the heavy. She got what she wanted by understanding the person in front of her and creating relationship. In my experience as a lawyer, and as the story with Mari shows, trying to dominate by force usually doesn't work and, in fact, often fails because it makes the other person resist even harder. While sometimes being the heavy is the appropriate choice, to truly be dominant, we often need to soften, finding the flow of connection.

I've used the soft approach to great success in my career, although it is easy for me because I'm curious about people. In the tobacco litigation I was asked to defend our client in depositions taken by lawyers from the tobacco industry. This was serious high-stakes litigation, hardly a love-fest. I remember on the first morning I got to the deposition early and saw this giant guy in the conference room, dressed in a suit. I introduced myself and found out that he was the lead attorney for one of the tobacco companies and would be the first questioner that day. At first he was pretty abrupt with me, wearing the same very tough guy posture I tried to wear. The only problem was this guy was easily half a foot bigger than me and perhaps a good 50 or 60 pounds heavier, mostly muscle.

Without thinking about trying to dominate this guy—that would be a futile effort—I instead asked him the obvious question on my mind: "Where did you play football?" It turned out that he was a former college athletic star and that got us talking about my own football days as well as his sports career. Before long we were laughing at some stories, which was a bit disconcerting to my client as she walked in the door and saw us having a good time.

Once the deposition started this man either found it impossible or was otherwise unwilling to try to intimidate my client, apparently one of his normal tactics. Without even trying, I had become dominant in this lawyer-to-lawyer contest. I had done so not by trying to overwhelm him with toughness but, rather, by connecting with him legitimately in a common interest. He still conducted a tough deposition but the energy of intimidation was missing. The soft touch worked. ■

▌ A MIDLINE PRACTICE
How do you react when somebody tries to browbeat you into doing something?

CHAPTER 106
And even more supernatural powers!

One time I represented employees of a clothing store in a lawsuit against the former storeowner who had invested the employees' pension and retirement funds in a speculative real estate venture, a subdivided ranch out west. The former owner, on a tip from a friend, bought a partnership interest thinking it was a "can't lose" venture. As with many "can't lose" ventures, it was losing badly. In order to shore up this investment he had taken the company's pension and retirement funds and bought an interest in the ranch for the employees. Back then, that was a huge legal no-no.

While I was able to prove my case against him, the problem was recovering the money he had taken out of the fund to invest in the ranch. The ranch didn't have value sufficient to recover against. This didn't look like a winner for us but we took the case anyway. We were outraged at the owner's conduct and really liked the employees we knew. The situation would have dissuaded quite a few lawyers, but, stepping into Midline, we kept at it, facing the risks of no recovery head-on as we explored ways to get our clients' money back.

I spent hours talking with this man and his lawyer, digging through all his deals, and finally we hit upon a settlement plan. The former storeowner was also a part owner of a gold mine somewhere out west and, unlike the ranch deal, could sign over an interest in the mine to us that might someday be worth something. It looked like a total pie-in-the-sky possibility, but we were out of options. We took a risk on the mine eventually paying off and settled the deal, with my clothing store employees becoming the proud part owners of a gold mine.

Several years later, the gold mine paid off! Because of the willingness of my clients to take that risk, and because of our willingness to stick with them to get their retirement funds back, we "struck pay dirt."

This is an example of *Prakamya*, the sixth *Siddhi*, freedom of will and the ability to be unobstructed in our desires. We were committed to recovering our clients' investments and were able to do so, obtain our desire, by learning how to sense the flow of a situation and then, through hard work and commitment, create our own success.

Obtaining our desires, despite intimidating obstacles, is often Midline work. In this case, my firm's desire and commitment to help our friends overcame our financial concerns about the cost of chasing this defendant all over the place. Willpower paid off for my clients. By remaining undaunted in our determination, we overcame every obstacle, unobstructed in gaining our objective. Even we, the lawyers, were paid. Along with my psychic preview of the Loyola—Cincinnati score, getting my clients' money back was supernatural power at its best!

The seventh *Siddhi* is *Isatva,* supremacy or Lordship. We see every moment through our heart and there is no longer a question of competition or envy. We view every person and every act, whether it is something we label good or bad, as an expression of Spirit. We look for the potential in the person or event. When we have practiced the Eightfold Path of yoga we can develop such an absorption in Spirit that we will be able to find Spirit in everything. We see the Midlines offered by life and readily step into them, constantly enriching our lives. We surrender to Spirit, no longer demanding He give us what we want, but instead, being happy to receive what He offers. We become Lord over our lives because we can't lose; we are happy to be in flow with Spirit.

The eighth *Siddhi* is *Vasitva,* the power to successfully engage anyone or anything, including the elements. As we become skilled yoga practitioners, this power appears as a deep appreciation of every moment we live in embodied form. Ultimately, we exercise control over others and events because they have lost any power to disrupt our nature; they can't control us. We no longer define winning as defeating somebody. Instead, we define success as engaging others or circumstances in such a way as to expand Spirit. Where we can, we seek win–win situations. I recently participated in a large negotiation with another lawyer involving a property damage insurance claim. We got along so well and treated each other with such regard we were able to effect a fair settlement that made everybody happy. The insurance company felt what it paid was fair and my client was happy with what he was paid.

This result surprised everyone. My client and the insurance company were convinced we would fail. I remember picking up the phone and this lawyer would say hello and ask me how my trip to Boston went. Then he would listen and make a comment or two before ever getting to the business at hand. I did the same thing. We probably spent, cumulatively, less than an hour extra over the course of our relationship than we would otherwise have spent without the chit–chat. However, as a result, we reached this great result. We both exercised the gift of *Vasitva,* successfully engaging each other and enjoying that engagement for its own sake—that of mutually enriching connection. ▪

A MIDLINE PRACTICE

Think of somebody you know whom you consider successful, who seems to be well-liked, and gets along with people, even when there are disagreements. What are some of this person's people-skills that are most obvious to you?

CHAPTER 107
Whoa! There's still more!—
Patanjali's Yoga Sutra 3.16; psychic power

When I think back to my one-time meeting with Krishna Das I realize what a gift it is to be able to feel when other people, even strangers, are a bit down and can use a small dose of kindness. When he left my table I felt a warm glow, a certainty that life would be okay.

Aren't you a bit curious about what powers you might have? Was Walt Disney simply stubborn or was Spirit whispering, "Dwarfs, Dwarfs" in his ear, giving him a vision of the millions upon millions of people he would thrill over the years if he didn't give up? What guides scientists to discover wonderful, life-saving vaccines and medical techniques even when they weren't looking? How can a little girl look up from a game in the park and immediately know that an adult needs a hug? How can a man walk into a busy coffee shop and instantly feel that somebody is sad and needs a touch of kindness?

What might happen to our world if we found a way to educate kids so that they never forget how to sense the feelings of others as they grow up and never lose track of the music playing in their own hearts? Did I know the score of the game because of special psychic skills? I think, "Yes," in part. I also suspect I knew the score because at that young age I knew so many facts about the teams, the scores of their games, and the relative match ups of the players. My brain was allowed to work freely and had figured out the result ahead of time based on what I knew. Psychic skills or not, ultimately, who cares? Patanjali teaches us that we all can become absorbed in Spirit's flow if we are willing to practice.

Isn't it fun to experience what we are capable of if we fully step into the flow of Spirit, easily discerning Spirit in the chatter and distraction of the world? Fortunately, yoga practices, including meditation, give us the clarity to make logical connections most people would miss. Patanjali's *Yoga Sutra* 3.16 and those that immediately follow it introduce an additional array of mystical powers, *Siddhis*.[319] I discuss two of them to provide you with a hint of their flavor. These powers are crucial to Midline because they sharpen our ability to sense Midline's invitations to a richer experience of life.

Yoga Sutra 3.16 says that we can develop knowledge of the past and the future.[320] According to Dr. Bryant, Patanjali might have meant that by looking clearly at the facts, one can figure out what must have happened in the past and what will likely occur in the future.[321] Maybe I really did have the two basketball teams so thoroughly analyzed that my subconscious had figured out the score in advance, down to the very points scored. If that is the case, then what if I applied that passion and intensity to my commitment to the happiness and well-being of others, including me?

I know in my law practice I've had enough experience and skill to know in advance what the likely outcome of a situation will be. Although I can't predict with certainty what a jury will do, I can usually tell that certain things are going to happen in a case ahead of time. By knowing a certain lawyer's behavior, I can predict how he or she will act in a deposition, what questions will be asked. I can often figure out way ahead of time how to get a witness in a deposition to say something important for our case. It is really just like the karate tournament I described earlier. We prepare, we stay spacious, and we use the breath to access our life's experiences stored inside us. Those experiences, memories, help tell us what will likely happen next.

Yoga Sutra 3.19 provides another example: we can figure out what others are thinking.[322] Dr. Bryant echoes what we learned from Dr. Goleman. When we pay attention really well, we pick up the emotions and thoughts of others. We become fully attuned to the neural bridges between us.

Dr. Bryant suggests what Dr. Goleman and others have proven through fMRIs: we can detect fear, desire, anger, or other emotions from a person's facial expressions.[323] In addition, we can develop a capacity to understand enough of how the mind works to predict what another is thinking.[324] Again, in my karate tournament I knew that if I faked a punch to my opponent's side, he would drop his arms to defend against that attack. This of course left his head wide open for a kick. Similarly, in the deposition, Mari knew that if she flattered Ed about his photographic memory, he would respond to the flattery by helping her. It isn't rocket science here; though to me, rocket science is pretty supernatural in and of itself.

Dr. Bryant acknowledges that the notion of supernatural powers may seem outlandish to us today.[325] Many philosophers and scholars assume these powers have no substance whatsoever, suggesting the possibility Patanjali included these *Siddhis* out of deference to expectations of his day regarding yoga.[326] Apparently, people believed yogis had mystical powers and, for their part, yogis probably encouraged those beliefs because it brought them power and safety, as in: "Let's not mess with that guy!"

Dr. Bryant responds by saying he personally believes Patanjali was too much the intellectual to have dedicated such a large portion of his text to this subject of supernatural powers simply out of such deference.[327] He cites, for example, *Sutra* 3.37 (38 in Mr.

Iyengar's numbering system) in which Patanjali warns these *Siddhis* can be an impediment to *Samadhi*. He says Patanjali would not likely issue this warning if he felt the *Siddhis* were fanciful or imaginary.[328] So, given the wisdom of everything else Patanjali has to say, Dr. Bryant persuades me there is value in exploring these particular powers. I'm inclined to believe these powers are available to us in their most mystical form but with all our technology today and our many distractions, we've somehow lost touch with some of our most enticing possibilities.

Besides, I've had enough of a taste of psychic skill and incredible coincidences to convince me these powers are accessible to us. Even if you don't believe in such things, I've demonstrated here the metaphorical value of knowing about these powers. Even if you can't fly through the air, you can use the airwaves to telephone an aging and dear relative that longs to hear from you. Even if you can't freely exert your will over the masses, you can use your powers of persuasion to shift conversations into something of value. Even if you can't make yourself tiny as an atom, you can learn to step out of the limelight so it can shine on another who could use the honor of the moment. Even if you can't make yourself so heavy and immobile that you can't be budged, you can stand strong and with conviction for those things that matter to you.

It is important to contemplate these powers and consider their potential in our own lives. If our objective is greater connection to our heart and to Spirit in the world, what's there to lose by exploring these ideas? If our desire is to live in the Midlines of life, how better to recognize and evaluate Midline's invitations than to be fully attuned to all our mind's skills? ■

A MIDLINE PRACTICE

Engage in a conversation about current events with a friend or family member. Notice how often you will know what the other person is going to say, just an instant before they say it.

CONCLUSION

CHAPTER 108
Spirit really is all around us!

My son went to a small high school in Windom, Minnesota, a town of about 4,500 people in the southwest part of the state. Sports are huge in Windom, as they are in many small towns across the nation. When Jeff, was a sophomore, Windom H.S. had a great football team. In fact, up until the very last game of the season Windom was not only undefeated, it was "un-scored upon." Nobody had scored a touchdown or even a field goal against them the entire season. Windom was ranked near the top of the state's small school football poll. The last game of the year was at home against conference rival Pipestone. As luck would have it, Pipestone was also undefeated and right up there with Windom in the small school state rankings.

Windom's football stadium was jammed that Friday night, standing room only: people were lined up in row after row all around the field. The town itself was empty; everybody from miles around was somewhere in or around the stadium. This was probably the biggest high school football game in that part of the state for years, maybe ever.

The game lived up to every expectation. Sometime during the first half, Pipestone scored a touchdown, the first time anybody had scored a point against Windom all year. Pipestone missed the extra point but it was a huge emotional moment in the game. Windom hadn't been able to move the ball at all and it looked like the dream season might come to an end. It looked even bleaker for Windom when, toward the end of the first half Pipestone drove down the field, heading for another score. Windom held and Pipestone lined up for a chip shot field goal at around the 10-yard line, only a minute or so to go before Halftime. The Windom crowd was depressed and silent; Pipestone's fans were screaming so loud you could hear it all across town.

The Pipestone center snapped the ball and the kicker kicked it. A Windom player, Mike Piper as I recall, broke through and blocked the kick. The ball bounced off to the side where my son Jeff, one of the only sophomores starting for Windom, playing cornerback, scooped up the ball and ran it all the way back, finally running out of steam and getting tackled on the one-yard line. No matter. Totally awakened, Windom slammed it in for the tying touchdown. Jeff kicked the extra point: Windom 7—Pipestone 6. Windom held on in the second half to win. If I remember correctly, the only scoring in the second half was a field goal Jeff kicked. The undefeated season was saved!

Following the game I was bursting with pride. I hugged Jeff, congratulated those team-mates I knew, and celebrated with all the happy parents. Cyndi and Chuck were beaming. I eventually got in the car to head back to Minneapolis, about a three-hour drive. As soon as I was alone, it hit me: I really wanted to call my dad. My father lived for football. He would be ecstatic, envisioning Jeff in a Chicago Bear uniform. This was a moment he would savor, letting everybody in Chicago know about his grandson. There would be nobody from Rockford, Illinois to South Bend, Indiana that wouldn't know the Windom—Pipestone score and Jeff's role in it. The urge to reach him right away was overwhelming.

Then, in the very next instant, I realized dad was dead. This was the very experience I'd most wanted to share with him and it wasn't going to happen. This is what I'd told him about in his hospital room right before he passed. He would have been so proud of his grandson and so thrilled to watch him, just as I was proud and wanted to share the experience with my dad.

I sat there crushed as I realized again how I'd let some real joy in my life slip away by creating the rift between my dad and me. The pain of his loss, and mine, arose again and I broke down in the car. It wasn't just that I couldn't share this moment with him. It was the bitter reminder I'd had chances to share my son with my father and I'd blown those chances. By the time I figured out I wanted a relationship and made the connection, his health gave out and he died without ever watching Jeff play. Eventually I composed myself somewhat and took off for Minneapolis, feeling sad and empty.

Even as I drove home from the game, knowing dad was gone; I was, for some reason, still bursting to share this experience with him. After a while, I stopped at a gas station near St. James to buy the ever-important bag of Fritos and Pepsi. It was about midnight. The place was empty except for a high school–aged girl behind the counter. She looked up from whatever she was reading and smiled at me before turning back to her book.

I found my provisions and went to the counter to pay. The girl looked at me for a moment, then, furrowing her eyebrows, asked me if I was all right. Suddenly, it all gushed out of me. I told her I had an amazing night and had to tell somebody about it. She smiled as if inviting me to go on and so off I went, re-living for what must have felt to her every play of the entire game.

She listened, appearing to even be fascinated. From time to time she nodded, smiled and I swear she even pumped a fist when I told her about Jeff scooping up the ball and running it back. For a second I thought she must be a Windom H.S. cheerleader, she seemed so excited.

I finished my story and, as I did so, my eyes filled with tears. I told her all that was missing was my dad didn't get to see it; he'd recently passed on. I told her how proud he would have been. I apologized to her for bending her ear, and told her I had to share with somebody. She looked at me, her face full with compassion. Then she reached over, touched my arm and said: "Oh don't worry—he saw it." I thanked her and left.

I spent all of about five minutes with this young woman. Yet, in that five minutes she outlined for all of us a path to Spirit, a way to dwell in the wonderfully full connection to life and Spirit that is Midline, the place where we come into communion with the nature of our true self, with Spirit. This place is always present, awaiting us to risk stepping into this Knowing. I practice my yoga with the intention that I can live a life as engaged, as sincere, and as kind as this young woman was that night. To me, this girl was an expression of Spirit in Her highest form.

Look at the path she followed that night. First, she paid attention to me. To her I was more than just a customer; I was another human being, standing right there in front of her at midnight with a bag of Fritos and a Pepsi. No matter what she was doing when I walked in—homework, reading a novel, whatever—she became open and attentive to me. She was receptive to how the moment offered an opportunity to connect to another person. At the same time she was sensitive to her own heart, her own ability to serve—and I'm not talking about selling me my junk food—I'm talking about her willingness to listen, to connect from her heart.

These moments of engagement, whether it is meeting another person or experiencing whatever life is handing out, is Spirit's whispered invitation to Midline. No matter what our occupation, we can all live a life of engagement when we choose to take a moment and engage out of the heart, offering our unique abilities to bring kindness, understanding and peace to another. That is a strength we all have. That is a sense of accomplishment we always can attain.

Once we open to Midline, Spirit's beckoning to us; we take on the moment fully. Like the young woman at the gas station, we pay attention, watching, listening, and feeling. We become absorbed. This is how good lawyers take depositions, interview clients, or talk with witnesses. We become immersed in the conversation, attentive to every nuance, so that we can maximize the encounter in order to enrich our case. If we only commit halfway, we will miss something important. In fact, these are the hallmarks of how anybody who leads a flourishing life, a teacher, a parent, a partner, a friend, interacts in the world. They do so with full engagement, full connection.

Look at how this young woman listened to me: she was so fully attuned to my excitement that she seemed to be as thrilled as me when she heard how Jeff turned the game around, pumping her fist in the air like it was her school who won, her kid who was the star. Her attention was a reflection back to me that I was significant to her; I mattered. Think about that. What a gift we give to each other when we simply do that—infuse another with a sense that they matter. This is how we can be authentically present for each other. We see and feel the potency of that moment. We pick up on the often very subtle cues that are opportunities to forge a deeper relationship. Paying attention, full engagement, leads to the deeper, richer relationships we all long for.

We assimilate the information we are receiving, including the subtlest energetic gradations of our encounter, the non-verbal information crossing the neural bridge. We don't just listen with our ears and watch with our eyes, we feel with our whole being. We then shine the light of our knowledge and experiences on what we've taken in, formulating what, if any, response is appropriate.

Many times all that is needed is the listening. Mindful of our own strengths, we craft an appropriate and, where possible, caring, gracious and helpful response that best serves the situation. I don't know what went through this young woman's mind as she listened to me but it seemed pretty clear to me she processed my words and emotions through her heart, and out of that process formulated a kind, effective and highly refined way to reply to me.

The young woman's final expression to me was not only sweet, sincere, and kind, it was loving and compassionate, infused with Spirit. It was such a beautiful response, not necessarily because I believed, or wished, my dad was floating around somewhere watching all this but, rather, because my heart wanted connection to Spirit and that is what she offered. This girl was absorbed in Spirit and engaging with me as Spirit.

This book has been about finding Midline, connecting to Spirit. Probably nobody knows they want to find a Midline, but many people know they want to find a path to Spirit. Following the path through life discussed in this book, and so simply illustrated by my friend in the St. James truck stop, will bring us to that flourishing life possible for each of us. Finding the deep, full connection to Spirit, the absorption of *Samadhi*, and then the *Kaivalya* of living as Spirit, requires practice. Practice provides an ability to awaken to the whispered invitations, the sometimes subtle, sometimes not so subtle beckoning of Spirit to come play. Always alert to that whisper, we then take the risk of engagement, to gain the potential reward of a sweeter life.

Where is Midline, then? It is where those invitations are offered and the risks confronted. It is that place where we can choose to make our deepest connection between our own spirit and God, the Spirit connecting us all. Ultimately, we are each Spirit. Living in recognition of this is the only roadmap we ultimately need. ■

A MIDLINE PRACTICE

Sit down for a chat with somebody you really care about, somebody that truly matters to you. Listen to that person in such a way that, without having to say so with words, your very process of listening to them conveys to them how much they matter.

ENDNOTES

CHAPTER 2

1   Seligman, Dr. Martin E.P. (2011). *Flourish A Visionary New Understanding Of Happiness And Well-being.* New York, NY: Free Press, at 2; 16–21.

CHAPTER 4

2   Millman, Dan (1980). *Way of the Peaceful Warrior.* Tiburon, CA: H.J. Kramer, Inc.
3   Goleman, Dr. Daniel (1995). *Emotional Intelligence.* New York, NY: Bantam Books. This book was a New York Times bestseller for a year-and-a-half, with over 5 million copies in print in 40 languages.
4   *Id.,* e.g., at 5–8.
5   *Id.* at 4–8.
6   *Id.*
7   *Id.* at 6.
8   *Id.* at 60–62.
9   *Id.* at 14.
10 *Id.*
11 *Id.* at 17–20
12 *Id.* at 60–62.

CHAPTER 5

13 Lewis, Drs. Thomas, et al. (2000). *A General Theory Of Love.* New York, NY: Random House, at 128–132.

CHAPTER 6

14 *Emotional Intelligence, supra,* at 5–8.
15 *Id.*
16 Siegel, Dr. Daniel J. (2007). *The Mindful Brain.* New York, NY: WW Norton & Company, Inc., at 30–31.
17 *Id.* at 31. See also, Siegel, Dr. Daniel J. (2010). *Mindsight: The New Science of Personal Transformation.* New York, NY: Bantam Books, at 55–59.
18 *A General Theory of Love, supra,* at 141–144.
19 *Id.*

CHAPTER 7

20 I use numerous Sanskrit terms in this book and provide a Glossary at the end for your use. Sanskrit is a beautiful, refined language using various diacritical marks to identify, among other things, proper pronunciation of letters and words. These marks are not used in this book, including the Glossary at the end.
21 Shantananda, Swami (2003). *The Splendor of Recognition.* South Fallsburg, NY: SYDA Foundation, at 27; Marjanovic, Dr. Boris (2004 ed.); *Abhinavagupta's Commentary on the Bhagavad Gita Gitartha-Samgraha.* New Delhi, India: First Impression, at 15.
22 Muktananda, Swami (1981 ed.). *Where Are You Going?* South Fallsburg, NY: SYDA Foundation at 31; *See generally,* Brooks, Dr. Douglas R. (1992). *Auspicious Wisdom.* Albany, NY: SUNY Press, at 122; for further exploration of the topics discussed in this book, consider Dr. Brooks' on-line study courses found at www.srividyalaya.com.

CHAPTER 9

23 See, e.g., Mahony, Dr. William K. (1998). *The Artful Universe.* Albany, NY: SUNY Press, at 14, discussing the *Upanisadic* view of *Brahman.*
24 *Where Are You Going?, supra,* at 28–29.
25 *The Splendor of Recognition, supra,* at 16.
26 *Where Are You Going? supra,* at 64.
27 *Flourish, supra,* at 16–20.
28 For further exploration of the topics discussed in this book, consider Dr. Muller-Ortega's courses offered through www.bluethroatyoga.com

CHAPTER 10

29 Gurumayi Chidvilasananda, Swami (1997). *Enthusiasm.* South Fallsburg, NY: SYDA Foundation, at 29.
30 Kempton, Sally (2011). *Meditation for the Love of It.* Boulder, CO: Sounds True, Inc., at 43. For further exploration of the topics discussed in this book, consider Sally Kempton's on-line study courses offered through www.sallykempton.com

31 *Id.*
32 *Id.* at 43–46.
33 Brooks, Dr. Douglas Renfroe. Public Lecture. Howard, Colorado. July 14, 2011.
34 *Flourish, supra,* at 16–17.
35 *Id.* at 10–12.
36 *Id.*
37 Seligman, Dr. Martin (2002). *Authentic Happiness.* New York, NY: Free Press, at 260.
38 *Id.*

CHAPTER 12
39 *Enthusiasm, supra,* at 10.

CHAPTER 13
40 Muller-Ortega, Dr. Paul (1989). *The Triadic Heart Of Shiva.* Albany, NY: SUNY Press, at 50.
41 *The Splendor of Recognition, supra,* at 35.

CHAPTER 14
42 *Flourish, supra,* at 11; 16–17.

CHAPTER 15
43 Mahony, Dr. William K. (2010). *Exquisite Love.* The Woodlands, TX: Anusara Press, at 20.
44 Feuerstein, Dr. Georg (2001 ed.). *The Yoga Tradition.* Prescott, AZ: Hohm Press, at 459.
45 *Meditation for the Love of It, supra,* at 36–37.
46 *Id.*
47 *Id.* at 36–37.
48 Aaron, Rabbi David (2004). *The Secret Life of God.* Boston, MA: Shambhala Publications, Inc.
49 *Id.,* at 12–13.
50 *Flourish, supra,* at 12. See also, *Authentic Happiness, supra,* at 260.

CHAPTER 16
51 *Meditation for the Love of It, supra,* at 143–144.
52 *Authentic Happiness, supra,* at 260. See also, www.authentichappiness.org). (Signature strengths test)

CHAPTER 17
53 *Exquisite Love, supra,* at 90.
54 *Flourish, supra,* at 11–17.
55 May, Dr. Rollo (1975). *The Courage to Create.* New York, NY: W.W. Norton & Company, Inc., at 39–40.
56 *Id.* at 40.
57 *Id.* at 134; 140.

CHAPTER 18
58 *The Triadic Heart Of Shiva. supra,* at 120.
59 *Id.* at 121.
60 *Meditation for the Love of It, supra,* at 89.
61 Dyczkowski, Dr. Mark S.G. (1987). *The Doctrine of Vibration.* New York, NY: SUNY Press, at 136.

CHAPTER 19
62 Brooks, Dr. Douglas Renfroe. Public Lecture. Howard, Colorado. July 14, 2011.
63 *Id.*
64 *Id.*
65 *Flourish, supra,* at 20.
66 Csikszentmihalyi, Dr. Mihaly (1990). *Flow. The Psychology of Optimal Experience.* New York, NY: HarperCollins Publishers, at 3; 164.
67 *Id.*

CHAPTER 20

68 Brooks, Dr. Douglas R. (Lecturer—Audio Tapes). (2010). *The Tattvas: Understanding the Principles of Reality.* Berkeley, CA: Brooks and YogaKula; *see also,* Bryant, Dr. Edwin F. (2009). *The Yoga Sutras of Patanjali.* New York, NY: North Point Press, at 121–128; 428–431; Iyengar, B.K.S. (1996 ed). *Light on the Yoga Sutras of Patanjali.* London, England: Thorsons, at 85; 261–262.
69 Brooks, *The Tattvas, supra.*
70 *Id.*
71 *Id.*
72 *The Splendor of Recognition, supra,* at 92.

CHAPTER 21

73 Brooks, *The Tattvas, supra.*
74 *Id.*
75 Doniger, Wendy (1981). *The Rig Veda.* New York, NY: Penguin Group, at 25–26.
76 *Id.*

CHAPTER 22

77 Brooks, *The Tattvas, supra.*
78 Brooks, *The Tattvas, supra.*

CHAPTER 23

79 *The Splendor of Recognition, supra,* at 94.
80 *Meditation for the Love of It, supra,* at 32.
81 *The Splendor of Recognition, supra,* at 16.
82 *Id.*

CHAPTER 24

83 Sears, Harold and Meredith. "Smile – Dancing Is About the Relationship." *American Dancer* 7 Aug. 2008: 13:16–17.
84 *Id.*

CHAPTER 25

85 *The Splendor of Recognition, supra,* at 95.
86 *Id.*
87 Brooks, *The Tattvas, supra.*
88 *Splendor of Recognition, supra,* at 94–95.
89 Brooks, *The Tattvas, supra.*

CHAPTER 26

90 *Splendor of Recognition, supra,* at 96–97.
91 *Id.*
92 Feuerstein, Georg (1998). *Tantra The Path Of Ecstasy.* Boston, MA: Shambhala Publications, Inc., at 62.

CHAPTER 27

93 *Splendor of Recognition, supra,* at 96–97.
94 *Id.,* at 97.

CHAPTER 30

95 *Triadic Heart of Shiva, supra,* at 138.

CHAPTER 31

96 *The Doctrine of Vibration, supra,* at 131.

CHAPTER 37

97 *Splendor of Recognition, supra,* at 203.
98 *Id.* at 204
99 *Id.*
100 *Id.*
101 *Id.*

CHAPTER 38
102 *Splendor of Recognition, supra,* at 182.
103 *Id.* at 183.
104 *Id.* at 185–186.
105 *Id.* at 186.

CHAPTER 39
106 *The Yoga Tradition, supra,* at 289.
107 *Enthusiasm, supra,* at 2.

CHAPTER 40
108 *Splendor of Recognition, supra,* at 99–100.
109 *Id.,* at 99; 143.
110 *Splendor of Recognition, supra,* at 143.
111 *Id.* at 143.
112 Campbell, Don and Doman, Alex (2012). *Healing at the Speed of Sound.* New York, NY: Penguin Group.

CHAPTER 41
113 *Splendor of Recognition, supra,* at 100.
114 *Tantra The Path to Ecstasy, supra,* at 64.
115 *Splendor of Recognition, supra,* at 136–137.
116 *Id.* at 137.
117 *Tantra, The Path of Ecstasy, supra,* at 65.
118 *Splendor of Recognition, supra,* at 100; 137.
119 *Id.* at 138.

CHAPTER 42
120 Brooks, *The Tattvas, supra.*
121 *Id.*
122 *Splendor of Recognition, supra,* at 118.
123 *Id.* at 139–142.
124 *Id.*

CHAPTER 44
125 *Splendor of Recognition, supra,* at 100.

CHAPTER 46
126 Judith, Dr. Anodea (2004 ed). *Wheels of Life.* St. Paul, MN: Llewellyn Publications, at 246–248.
127 *Id.* at 258–260.

CHAPTER 49
128 Tharp, Twyla (2003). *The Creative Habit Learn It And Use It For Life.* New York, NY: Simon & Schuster.
129 *Id.* at 225.
130 *Id.*
131 *Wheels of Life, supra,* at 108–109.

CHAPTER 52
132 Goleman, Dr. Daniel (2006). *Social Intelligence.* New York, NY: Bantam Dell
133 *Emotional Intelligence, supra.*
134 *Social Intelligence, supra,* at 4–5.
135 *Id.* at 10.
136 *Id.* at 9.

CHAPTER 53
137 *Social Intelligence, supra,* at 15–16.
138 *Id.* at 16.
139 *Id.* at 25.
140 *Id.*
141 *Id.* at 39–40.
142 *Id.*

CHAPTER 54

143 Feuerstein, *The Yoga Tradition, supra* at 350.

144 *Id.* at 348–350.

145 *Id.*

146 *Id.*

147 *Id.* at 348–356.

148 *Id.* at 351–352.

149 *Meditation for the Love of It, supra,* at 198–199.

150 *Id, citing Brihadaranyaka Upanishad* 4.4.3–6.

151 *Id.* at 199.

CHAPTER 55

152 *The Artful Universe, supra,* at 179.

153 *Tantra The Path Of Ecstasy, supra,* at 141.

CHAPTER 56

154 Freeman, Richard (2010). *The Mirror Of Yoga, Awakening the Intelligence of Body and Mind,* Boston, MA: Shambhala Publications, Inc., at 31.

155 *Id.*

CHAPTER 57

156 *The Artful Universe, supra,* at 179, quoting *Taittiriya Upanishad* 2.3.1.

157 *Supra.*

CHAPTER 58

158 *Meditation for the Love of It, supra,* at 199.

159 *Id.*

160 *Id.* at 199–203.

161 *Meditation for the Love of it, supra,* at 200.

CHAPTER 59

162 Iyengar, B.K.S. (2004 ed). *Light on Pranayama.* New York, NY: The Crossroads Publishing Company, at 32.

163 *Id.*

164 *Id.* at 269.

165 *Tantra The Path of Ecstasy, supra,* at 162.

CHAPTER 61

166 *Tantra The Path of Ecstasy, supra,* at 141.

167 *Id.*

168 Muller-Ortega, Dr. Paul (2009). *Siva Sutra Pravesana.* The Woodlands, TX: Anusara Press, at 39–40.

169 *Where are you Going?, supra,* at 90.

170 Chidvilasananda, Gurumayi Swami (1996). *The Yoga of Discipline.* South Fallsburg, NY: SYDA Foundation, at 105.

171 *Id.*

CHAPTER 62

172 *Light on the Yoga Sutras of Pananjali, supra,* at 56–57.

173 *The Splendor of Recognition, supra,* at 117.

174 *Id.* at 117–121.

175 *Id.*

176 *Light on the Yoga Sutras of Patanjali, supra,* at 56.

CHAPTER 63

177 *See, e.g., Enthusiasm, supra,* at 29.

178 *Exquisite Love, supra,* at 217–221.

179 *Id.*

CHAPTER 64

180 *Tantra The Path of Ecstasy, supra,* at 149.

181 *Id.* at 148–149; 159.
182 Judith, Anodea (2004 ed). *Eastern Body Western Mind.* Berkeley, CA: Celestial Arts, at 4.
183 *Id.*
184 *Id.* at 8–13.
185 *Id.*
186 *Id.*
187 *Id.*

CHAPTER 65
188 *The Yoga Tradition, supra,* at 317.
189 *Wheels of Life, supra,* at page 10.
190 *Id.* at 17.
191 *Id.*
192 *Id.*
193 *Id.* at 24.
194 *Id.* at 32.

CHAPTER 67
195 *Wheels of Life, supra,* at 108.
196 *Id.* at 108

CHAPTER 68
197 *Wheels of Life, supra,* at 151–152.
198 *Eastern Body Western Mind, supra,* at 182.
199 *Id.*

CHAPTER 69
200 *Wheels of Life, supra,* at 192.
201 *Id.* at 193.
202 *Id.* at 198.

CHAPTER 70
203 *Wheels of Life, supra,* at 236–237.

CHAPTER 71
204 *Tantra The Path of Ecstasy, supra,* at 152.
205 *Id.* at 152–153.
206 *Id.* at 153.
207 *Wheels of Life, supra,* at 281–284.
208 *Eastern Body Western Mind, supra,* at 344.

CHAPTER 72
209 *Tantra The Path of Ecstasy, supra,* at 151–152.
210 *Wheels of Life, supra,* at 319.
211 *Id.* at 323.
212 *Id.* at 322.
213 *Id.*

CHAPTER 73
214 *The Yoga Sutras of Patanjali, supra,* at xxxv.

CHAPTER 75
215 *See, generally, Light on the Yoga Sutras of Patanjali, supra,* Prologue and Introduction.
216 *Id.*
217 *Id.*
218 *Id.* at 135.

CHAPTER 76
219 *The Yoga Sutras of Patanjali, supra,* at 10.
220 *Light on the Yoga Sutras of Patanjali, supra,* at 52.

CHAPTER 77

221 *Light on the Yoga Sutras of Patanjali, supra,* at 61–63.
222 *Light on The Yoga Sutras of Patanjali, supra,* at 62.
223 *Id.*
224 *Id.*

CHAPTER 78

225 *The Yoga Sutras of Patanjali, supra,* at 73–75.
226 *Id.*
227 *Id.*

CHAPTER 79

228 *Light on the Yoga Sutras of Patanjali, supra,* at 86.
229 *The Yoga Sutras of Patanjali, supra,* at 128–130.
230 *Id.*
231 *Id.*
232 *Id.* at 129.
233 *Id.* at 129–130.
234 *Id.*
235 *The Mirror of Yoga, supra,* at 165.

CHAPTER 80

236 *Light on The Yoga Sutras of Patanjali, supra,* at 108.
237 *Id.*

CHAPTER 81

238 *The Yoga Sutras of Patanjali, supra,* at 27–31, citing Yoga Sutra 1.5.
239 *Id.*
240 *Id.*
241 *Id.* at 178–179.
242 *Id.,* at 177.

CHAPTER 82

243 *The Yoga Sutras of Patanjali, supra,* at 187; discussing *Yoga Sutra* 2.6 at 185–188.

CHAPTER 83

244 *The Yoga Sutras of Patanjali, supra,* at 189–190; *Light on the Yoga Sutras of Patanjali, supra,* at 115.

CHAPTER 84

245 *Light on the Yoga Sutras of Patanjali, supra,* at 116.
246 *Id.* at 116–117.

CHAPTER 85

247 *Flourish, supra.* For a fun exploration of how life, under any circumstances, can truly be dazzling and wondrous, *see* Hill, Judyth (2013). *Dazzling Wobble.* Mineral Bluff, GA: Futurecyle Press.
248 *The Yoga Sutras of Patanjali, supra,* at 191–192.

CHAPTER 86

249 *Light on The Yoga Sutras of Patanjali, supra,* at 140–142.
250 *Id.* at 142–143.
251 *Id.* at 143.
252 *The Yoga Sutras of Patanjali, supra,* at 248.
253 Iyengar, B.K.S. (2005). *Light on Life.* Emmaus, PA: Rodale Press, at 250–251.

CHAPTER 87

254 *Light on the Yoga Sutras of Patanjali, supra,* at 149.
255 *The Yoga Sutras of Patanjali, supra,* at 243.
256 *Id.* at 245–246.
257 *Id.* at 244–245.

258 Swami Paramahansa Yogananda (2005 ed.). *The Second Coming of Christ,* Los Angeles, CA: Self-Realization Fellowship Publishers, at 1228.
259 *Id.*
260 *The Yoga Sutras of Patanjali, supra,* at 261–262; *Light on the Yoga Sutras of Patanjali, supra,* at 149.
261 *The Mirror of Yoga, supra,* at 173.

CHAPTER 88
262 *Light on The Yoga Sutras of Patanjali, supra,* at 150.
263 Main, Darren (2002). *Yoga and the Path of the Urban Mystic,* Findhorn, Scotland: Findhorn Press, at 89–92.
264 *Light on The Yoga Sutras of Patanjali, supra,* at 145.

CHAPTER 89
265 *The Yoga Sutras of Patanjali, supra,* at 263.
266 *Id.* at 263–264.

CHAPTER 90
267 *Light on The Yoga Sutras of Patanjali, supra,* at 151–152.
268 Iyengar, B.K.S. (1979 ed). *Light on Yoga.* New York, NY: Schocken Books, at 34–35.
269 *Light on The Yoga Sutras of Patanjali, supra,* at 151–152.

CHAPTER 91
270 *Light on The Yoga Sutras of Patanjali, supra,* at 152–153.

CHAPTER 92
271 *Light on The Yoga Sutras of Patanjali, supra,* at 144–145.
272 *The Yoga Sutras of Patanjali, supra,* at 252–254.
273 *Id.* at 253.
274 *See, e.g., Light on Yoga, supra,* at 36.
275 *The Yoga of Discipline, supra,* at 29.

CHAPTER 93
276 *Flourish, supra.*
277 *Light on The Yoga Sutras of Patanjali, supra,* at 155.
278 *Light on Yoga, supra,* at 37–38.
279 *The Yoga Sutras of Patanjali, supra,* at 253.

CHAPTER 94
280 *Light on The Yoga Sutras of Patanjali, supra,* at 155–156.
281 *The Yoga of Discipline, supra,* at 32–33.

CHAPTER 95
282 *Light on The Yoga Sutras of Patanjali, supra,* at 156; *see also The Yoga Sutras of Patanjali, supra,* at 273–279.
283 *Light on the Yoga Sutras of Patanjali, supra,* at 156.
284 *Light on Life, supra,* at 261.

CHAPTER 96
285 *Light on The Yoga Sutras of Patanjali, supra,* at 157.
286 *Id.*

CHAPTER 97
287 *Light on the Yoga Sutras of Patanjali, supra,* at 157–160; *The Yoga Sutras of Patanjali, supra,* at 283–290.
288 *Light on The Yoga Sutras of Patanjali, supra,* at 157.
289 *Id.* at 158.
290 *Id.* at 157–158.
291 *Light on Life, supra,* at 28–33.
292 *Id.*

CHAPTER 98

293 www.Matthewsanford.com

294 *Light on the Yoga Sutras of Patanjali, supra,* at 160–167.

295 *Light on Pranayama, supra.*

296 *Light on Yoga, supra,* at 429–461.

297 Fhari, Donna (1996). *The Breathing Book,* New York, NY: Henry Holt and Company, LLC.

298 *Light on The Yoga Sutras of Patanjali, supra,* at 160–167.

299 *Id.* at 160–164.

300 Iyengar, B.K.S. (1988). *Tree of Yoga.* Boston, MA: Shambhala Publications, Inc. at 60.

301 *Mirror of Yoga, supra,* at 177–178.

CHAPTER 99

302 *The Yoga Sutras of Patanjali, supra,* at 297–298.

303 *Light on the Yoga Sutras of Patanjali, supra,* at 168–170.

304 *Id.; The Yoga Sutras of Patanjali, supra,* at 297.

CHAPTER 100

305 *Light on the Yoga Sutras of Patanjali, supra,* at 178–179.

306 *Id.*

CHAPTER 101

307 *Light on The Yoga Sutras of Patanjali, supra,* at 179–180.

308 *Id.* at 180.

CHAPTER 102

309 *Light on the Yoga Sutras of Patanjali, supra,* at 180–181.

310 *Id.*

311 *Id.* at 182.

312 *Id.* at 237–238.

313 *Light on The Yoga Sutras of Patanjali, supra,* at 274–275.

CHAPTER 103

314 Swami Paramahansa Yogananda (1946). *Autobiography of a Yogi.* Nevada City, CA: Crystal Clarity Publishers.

315 *Light on The Yoga Sutras of Patanjali, supra,* at 246–247.

316 *Id.* at 175–177.

317 *Id.* at 246–247.

318 *The Yoga Sutras of Patanjali, supra,* at 383–405.

CHAPTER 107

319 *The Yoga Sutras of Patanjali, supra,* at 329.

320 *Id.* at 329.

321 *Id.* at 337–338.

322 *Id.* at 345

323 *Id.* at 346.

324 *Id.* at 345–346.

325 *Id.* at 331.

326 *Id.* at 333.

327 *Id.* at 334.

328 *Id.*

BIBLIOGRAPHY

Aaron, Rabbi David (2004). *The Secret Life of God*. Boston, MA: Shambhala Publications, Inc.

Brooks, Dr. Douglas R. (1992). *Auspicious Wisdom*. Albany, NY: SUNY Press, at 122.

Brooks, Dr. Douglas R. (Lecturer – Audio Tapes). (2010). *The Tattvas: Understanding the Principles of Reality*. Berkeley, CA: Brooks and YogaKula.

Bryant, Dr. Edwin F. (2009). *The Yoga Sutras of Patanjali*. New York, NY: North Point Press.

Campbell, Don and Doman, Alex (2012). *Healing at the Speed of Sound*. New York, NY: Penguin Group.

Chidvilasananda, Gurumayi Swami (1996). *The Yoga of Discipline*. South Fallsburg, NY: SYDA Foundation.

Chidvilasananda, Swami Gurumayi (1997). *Enthusiasm*. South Fallsburg, NY: SYDA Foundation.

Csikszentmihalyi, Dr. Mihaly (1990). *Flow. The Psychology of Optimal Experience*. New York, NY: HarperCollins Publishers.

Doniger, Wendy (1981). *The Rig Veda*. New York, NY: Penguin Group.

Dyczkowski, Dr. Mark S.G. (1987). *The Doctrine of Vibration*. New York, NY: SUNY Press.

Feuerstein, Georg (1998). *Tantra The Path Of Ecstasy*. Boston, MA: Shambhala Publications, Inc.

Feuerstein, Dr. Georg (2001 ed.). *The Yoga Tradition*. Prescott, AZ: Hohm Press.

Fhari, Donna (1996). *The Breathing Book*, New York, NY: Henry Holt and Company, LLC.

Freeman, Richard (2010). *The Mirror Of Yoga, Awakening the Intelligence of Body and Mind*, Boston, MA: Shambhala Publications, Inc.

Goleman, Dr. Daniel (1995). *Emotional Intelligence*. New York, NY: Bantam Books.

Goleman, Dr. Daniel (2006). *Social Intelligence*. New York, NY: Bantam Dell.

Hill, Judyth (2013). *Dazzling Wobble*. Mineral Bluff, GA: Futurecyle Press.

Iyengar, B.K.S. (1979 ed). *Light on Yoga*. New York, NY: Schocken Books.

Iyengar, B.K.S. (2004 ed). *Light on Pranayama*. New York, NY: The Crossroads Publishing Company.

Iyengar, B.K.S. (1988). *Tree of Yoga*. Oxford, England: Fine Line Books, Ltd.

Iyengar, B.K.S. (1996 ed). *Light on the Yoga Sutras of Patanjali*. London, England: Thorsons.

Iyengar, B.K.S. (2005). *Light on Life*. Emmaus, PA: Rodale Press.

Judith, Dr. Anodea (2004 ed). *Wheels of Life*. St. Paul, MN: Llewellyn Publications.

Judith, Anodea (2004 ed). *Eastern Body Western Mind*. Berkeley, CA: Celestial Arts.

Kempton, Sally (2011). *Meditation for the Love of It*. Boulder, CO: Sounds True, Inc.

Lewis, Drs. Thomas, et al. (2000). *A General Theory Of Love*. New York, NY: Random House.

Mahony, Dr. William K. (1998). *The Artful Universe*. Albany, NY: SUNY Press.

Mahony, Dr. William K. (2010). *Exquisite Love*. The Woodlands, TX: Anusara Press.

Main, Darren (2002). *Yoga and the Path of the Urban Mystic*, Findhorn, Scotland: Findhorn Press.

Marjanovic, Dr. Boris (2004 ed.). *Abhinavagupta's Commentary on the Bhagavad Gita Gitartha-Samgraha*. New Delhi, India: First Impression.

May, Dr. Rollo (1975). *The Courage to Create*. New York, NY: W.W. Norton & Company, Inc.

Millman, Dan (1980). *Way of the Peaceful Warrior*. Tiburon, CA: H.J. Kramer, Inc.

Muktananda, Swami (1989 ed.). *Where Are You Going?* South Fallsburg, NY: SYDA Foundation.

Muller-Ortega, Dr. Paul (1989). *The Triadic Heart Of Shiva*. Albany, NY: SUNY Press.

Muller-Ortega, Dr. Paul (2009). *Siva Sutra Pravesana*. The Woodlands, TX: Anusara Press.

Sears, Harold and Meredith. "Smile – Dancing Is About the Relationship." *American Dancer* 7 Aug. 2008: 13:16–17.

Shantananda, Swami (2003). *The Splendor of Recognition*. South Fallsburg, NY: SYDA Foundation.

Seligman, Dr. Martin (2002). *Authentic Happiness*. New York, NY: Free Press.

Seligman, Dr. Martin (2011). *Flourish A Visionary New Understanding Of Happiness And Well-being*. New York, NY: Free Press.

Siegel, Dr. Daniel J. (2007). *The Mindful Brain*. New York, NY: WW Norton & Company, Inc..

Siegel, Dr. Daniel J. (2010). *Mindsight: the New Science of Personal Transformation*. New York, NY: Bantam Books.

Tharp, Twyla (2003). *The Creative Habit Learn It And Use It For Life*. New York, NY: Simon & Schuster.

Yogananda, Swami Paramahansa (1946). *Autobiography of a Yogi*. Nevada City, CA: Crystal Clarity Publishers.

Yogananda. Swami Paramahansa (2005). *The Second Coming of Christ,* Los Angeles, CA: Self-Realization Fellowship Publishers.

GLOSSARY

Abhinivesah: Clinging to life, fear of death, discussed by *Patanjali* in *Yoga Sutra* 2.9; one of the five afflictions or challenges that can interfere with connection to Spirit; these afflictions or challenges are called *Kleshas* and are identified by *Patanjali* in *Yoga Sutra* 2.3; the *Kleshas* also include: *Avidya* (ignorance; *Yoga Sutras* 2.3-2.5); *Asmita* (ego; *Yoga Sutra* 2.6); *Raga* (attachment, desire; *Yoga Sutra* 2.7); and *Dvesha* (aversion; *Yoga Sutra* 2.8).

Abhyasa: Ongoing, committed practice or study; *Patanjali* teaches in *Yoga Sutra* 1.12 that regular, informed practice of the Eightfold Path of yoga, along with detachment, *Vairagya*, from thoughts and actions that distract us from progress on the yoga path, are the means to optimize the mind's ability to connect to Spirit.

Adbhuta Rasa: Wonder; one of the *Rasas*, the emotional flavors or tastes of life; *Adbhuta Rasa* pertains to feelings of curiosity, astonishment, and the thrill of mystery; the other *Rasas* discussed in this book are: *Shanta Rasa* (Peace); *Karuna Rasa* (Compassion); *Vibhatsa Rasa* (Disgust); *Shringara Rasa:* (Love); *Vira Rasa* (Courage); *Raudra Rasa* (Anger); *Hasya Rasa* (Joy); and *Bhayanaka Rasa* (Fear).

Agni: Fire; one of the five gross elements, the *Mahabhutas*, identified in the *Tattvas*, the categories of existence identified in chart form in Table 1; the five *Mahabhutas* are: *Akasha* (space); *Vayu* (air); *Agni* (fire); *Ap* (water); and *Prithivi* (earth).

Ahamkara: Ego; pride; sense of self; one of the *Tattvas*, the categories of Spirit's existence; *Ahamkara*, along with *Buddhi* (Intelligence; higher intuitive mind), and *Manas* (Mind; organizer of information received from the senses), are part of the *Tattvas*, the categories of Spirit's existence identified in chart form in Table 1, and collectively form the mental processing center for our ability to experience the world.

Ahimsa: Non-harming, discussed by *Patanjali* in *Yoga Sutras* 2.34 and 2.35; first of the five *Yamas* identified by *Patanjali* in *Yoga Sutra* 2.30 as five rules for ethical behavior towards others, along with *Satya* (truth, honesty; *Yoga Sutras* 2.35-2.36); *Asteya* (non-stealing; *Yoga Sutra* 2.37); *Brahmacarya* (self-restraint, particularly in sexual matters; *Yoga Sutra* 2.38), and *Aparigrahah* (non-possessiveness, lack of greed; *Yoga Sutra* 2.39).

Ajna: Energy center located between the eyebrows; associated with intuition, clarity and psychic wisdom and telepathy; the "Third-eye;" the sixth *Chakra* in the seven *Chakra* system discussed in this book: First *Chakra, Muladhara Chakra* (root of tailbone—our foundation); Second *Chakra, Svadisthana Chakra* (pelvis—relationships with others); Third *Chakra, Manipura Chakra* (solar plexus—expression of our personality); Fourth *Chakra, Anahata Chakra* (heart – love and self-acceptance); Fifth *Chakra, Vishuddha Chakra* (throat—communication); Sixth *Chakra, Ajna Chakra* (between the eye brows—intuition and psychic perception; wisdom); and Seventh *Chakra, Sahasrara Chakra* (top of the head—absorption in Spirit).

Akasha: Space; one of the five gross elements, the **Mahabhutas**, identified in the *Tattvas,* the categories of existence identified in chart form in Table 1; the five **Mahabhutas** are: *Akasha* (space); *Vayu* (air); *Agni* (fire); *Ap* (water); and *Prithivi* (earth).

Aklista: Movements of the mind, **Vrttis**, non–detrimental to connection to Spirit; discussed by *Patanjali* in *Yoga Sutra* 1.5.

Anahata: Energy center located in the heart; associated with making decisions in harmony with Spirit; the fourth *Chakra* in the seven *Chakra* system discussed in this book: First *Chakra*, *Muladhara Chakra* (root of tailbone—our foundation); Second *Chakra, Svadisthana Chakra* (pelvis—relationships with others); Third *Chakra*, *Manipura Chakra* (solar plexus—expression of our personality); Fourth *Chakra*, *Anahata Chakra* (heart—love and self–acceptance); Fifth *Chakra*, *Vishuddha Chakra* (throat—communication); Sixth *Chakra*, *Ajna Chakra* (between the eye brows—intuition and psychic perception; wisdom); and Seventh *Chakra*, *Sahasrara Chakra* (top of the head—absorption in Spirit).

Ananda: Joy, bliss, delight.

Ananda Shakti: Power of bliss.

Anandamaya Kosha: Sheath of bliss; one of the five *Koshas*, or layers of a human being, along with *Annamaya Kosha* (Sheath of the physical body); *Pranamaya Kosha* (Sheath of the breath); *Manomaya Kosha* (Sheath of the mind); and *Vijnanamaya Kosha* (Sheath of the intuitive mind).

Anava–Mala: Feeling of being disconnected, inadequate, or imperfect; one of the three *Malas,* three impurities, cloaks, or veils that keep us from fully experiencing Spirit; the other two *Malas* are *Mayiya–Mala* (feeling of being different), and *Karma–Mala* (actions based on these feelings).

Anima: Power to become as minute as an atom, even invisible; one of the eight supernatural powers, the *Siddhis*, along with *Mahima* (to grow in magnitude); *Laghima* (to become light); *Garima* (to become heavy, immovable); *Prapti* (the power to dominate and obtain anything desired); *Prakamya* (the freedom of will and attainment of wishes); *Isatva* (supremacy over all, including the elements); and *Vasitva* (the power to subjugate anyone or anything); *Patanjali* discusses mystical powers and accomplishments in Part Three of his *Yoga Sutras, Vibhuti Pada*, and explains in *Yoga Sutra* 4.1 how they can be acquired; *Patanjali* warns in *Yoga Sutra* 3.38 (3.37 in some commentaries) that these powers and accomplishments can inhibit our ability to connect to Spirit.

Annamaya Kosha: Sheath of the physical body; one of the five *Koshas*, or layers of a human being, along with *Pranamaya Kosha* (Sheath of the breath); *Manomaya Kosha* (Sheath of the mind); and *Vijnanamaya Kosha* (Sheath of the intuitive mind); and *Anandamaya Kosha:* (Sheath of bliss).

Anugraha: Revelation; Divine Grace.

Ap: Water; one of the five gross elements, the *Mahabhutas*, identified in the *Tattvas*, the categories of existence identified in chart form in Table 1; the five *Mahabhutas* are: *Akasha* (space); *Vayu* (air); *Agni* (fire); *Ap* (water); and *Prithivi* (earth).

Aparigrahah: Non-possessiveness, lack of greed, discussed by *Patanjali* in *Yoga Sutra* 2.39; one of the five *Yamas* identified by *Patanjali* in *Yoga Sutra* 2.30 as five rules for ethical behavior towards others, along with *Ahimsa* (non-harming; *Yoga Sutras* 2.34 and 2.35); *Satya* (truth, honesty; *Yoga Sutras* 2.35-2.36); *Asteya* (non-stealing; *Yoga Sutra* 2.37); and *Brahmacarya* (self-restraint, particularly in sexual matters; Yoga Sutra 2.38).

Asana: A seat; yoga poses, discussed by *Patanjali* in *Yoga Sutras* 2.46 to 2.48; *Asana* is one part of *Patanjali's* Eightfold Path of yoga; the eight parts of this path are identified in *Yoga Sutra* 2.29 as: *Yamas* (ethical rules for treatment of others); *Niyamas* (rules for treating ourselves); *Asana* (a seat; poses); *Pranayama* (breathing practices); *Pratyahara* (drawing senses inward); *Dharana* (concentration), *Dhyana* (meditation); and *Samadhi* (absorption in Spirit).

Asmita: Ego, discussed by *Patanjali* in *Yoga Sutra* 2.6; one of the five afflictions or challenges that can interfere with connection to Spirit; these afflictions or challenges are called *Kleshas* and are identified by *Patanjali* in *Yoga Sutra* 2.3; the *Kleshas* also include: *Avidya* (ignorance; *Yoga Sutras* 2.3-2.5); *Raga* (attachment, desire; *Yoga Sutra* 2.7); *Dvesha* (aversion; *Yoga Sutra* 2.8); and *Abhinivesah:* (Clinging to life; *Yoga Sutra* 2.9).

Astanga (Ashtanga) Yoga: Eightfold Path of yoga identified by Patanjali in his *Yoga Sutras*

Asteya: Non-stealing, discussed by *Patanjali* in *Yoga Sutra* 2.37; one of the five *Yamas* identified by *Patanjali* in *Yoga Sutra* 2.30 as five rules for ethical behavior towards others, along with *Ahimsa* (non-violence; non-harming; *Yoga Sutras* 2.34-2.35); *Satya* (truth, honesty; *Yoga Sutras* 2.35-2.36); *Brahmacarya* (self-restraint, particularly in sexual matters; *Yoga Sutra* 2.38), and *Aparigrahah* (non-possessiveness, lack of greed; *Yoga Sutra* 2.39).

Avidya: Spiritual ignorance, discussed by *Patanjali* in *Yoga Sutras* 2.3-2.5; one of the five afflictions or challenges that can interfere with connection to Spirit; these afflictions or challenges are called *Kleshas* and are identified by *Patanjali* in *Yoga Sutra* 2.3; the *Kleshas* also include: *Asmita* (ego; *Yoga Sutra* 2.6); *Raga* (attachment, desire; *Yoga Sutra* 2.7); *Dvesha* (aversion; *Yoga Sutra* 2.8); and *Abhinivesah* (clinging to life, fear of death; *Yoga Sutra* 2.9).

Bhagavad Gita: "The Lord's Song;" perhaps the most famous yoga scripture; contains *Krishna's* teachings on yoga practices in the form of a conversation with Arjuna taking place just before a giant battle between two warring families.

Bhayanaka Rasa: Fear; one of the *Rasas*; the emotional flavors or tastes of life; *Bhayanaka Rasa* pertains to feelings of worry, anxiety, distress, paranoia, and disabling terror; the other *Rasas* discussed in this book are: *Shanta Rasa* (Peace); *Karuna Rasa*

(Compassion); *Vibhatsa Rasa* (Disgust); *Shringara Rasa:* (Love); *Vira Rasa* (Courage); *Raudra Rasa* (Anger); *Hasya Rasa* (Joy); and *Adbhuta Rasa* (Wonder).

Brahmacarya: Self-restraint, particularly in sexual matters, discussed by *Patanjali* in *Yoga Sutra* 2.38; one of the five *Yamas* identified by *Patanjali* in *Yoga Sutra* 2.30 as five rules for ethical behavior towards others, along with *Ahimsa* (non-violence; non-harming; *Yoga Sutras* 2.34-2.35); *Satya* (truth, honesty; *Yoga Sutras* 2.35-2.36); *Asteya* (non-stealing; *Yoga Sutra* 2.37); and *Aparigrahah* (non-possessiveness, lack of greed; *Yoga Sutra 2.39*).

Buddhi: Intelligence; the higher intuitive mind; one of the *Tattvas*, the categories of Spirit's existence; *Buddhi*, along with *Ahamkara* (Ego; pride; sense of self) and *Manas* (Mind; organizer of information received from the senses), are part of the *Tattvas* identified in chart form in Table 1, and collectively form the mental processing center for our ability to experience the world.

Chakras: Energy centers, "wheels" of energy, existing along the spinal column; this book discusses a seven *Chakra* system consisting of: First *Chakra*, *Muladhara Chakra* (pelvis—our foundation); Second *Chakra*, *Svadisthana Chakra* (below navel—relationships with others); Third *Chakra*, *Manipura Chakra* (solar plexus—expression of our personality); Fourth *Chakra*, *Anahata Chakra* (heart—love and self-acceptance); Fifth *Chakra*, *Vishuddha Chakra* (throat—communication); Sixth *Chakra*, *Ajna Chakra* (between the eye brows—intuition and psychic perception; wisdom); and Seventh *Chakra*, *Sahasrara Chakra* (top of the head—absorption in Spirit).

Chit (Cit): Pure awareness; self-awareness.

Dharana: Concentration; fixing our consciousness on one point, discussed by *Patanjali* in *Yoga Sutra* 3.1; *Dharana* is one part of *Patanjali's* Eightfold Path of yoga identified in *Yoga Sutra* 2.29 as: *Yamas* (ethical rules for treatment of others); *Niyamas* (rules for treating ourselves); *Asana* (a seat; poses); *Pranayama* (breathing practices); *Pratyahara* (drawing senses inward); *Dharana* (concentration), *Dhyana* (meditation); and *Samadhi* (absorption in Spirit).

Dharma: This word has many meanings; as used in this book the word means a sense of structure; also the nature of a person or thing; duty, virtue.

Dhyana: Meditation; steady and continuous flow of attention focused on a single point, discussed by *Patanjali* in *Yoga Sutra* 3.2; *Dhyana* is one part of *Patanjali's* Eightfold Path of yoga identified in *Yoga Sutra* 2.29 as: *Yamas* (ethical rules for treatment of others); *Niyamas* (rules for treating ourselves); *Asana* (a seat; poses); *Pranayama* (breathing practices); *Pratyahara* (drawing senses inward); *Dharana* (concentration), *Dhyana* (meditation); and *Samadhi* (absorption in Spirit).

Dvesha: Aversion, discussed by Patanjali in *Yoga Sutra* 2.8; one of the five afflictions or challenges that can interfere with connection to Spirit; these afflictions or challenges are called *Kleshas* and are identified by *Patanjali* in *Yoga Sutra* 2.3; the *Kleshas* also include: *Avidya* (ignorance; *Yoga Sutras* 2.3-2.5); *Asmita* (ego; *Yoga Sutra* 2.6); *Raga* (attachment, desire; *Yoga Sutra* 2.7); and *Abhinivesah*: (Clinging to life; *Yoga Sutra* 2.9).

Dukha: Unhappiness, grief, distress due to desires unfulfilled or memory of past pleasures; discussed by *Patanjali* in *Yoga Sutra* 2.8; can lead to aversion, *Dvesha*.

Eightfold Path of Yoga: *Patanjali's* Eightfold Path of yoga is identified in *Yoga Sutra* 2.29 as: *Yamas* (ethical rules for treatment of others); *Niyamas* (rules for treating ourselves); *Asana* (a seat; poses); *Pranayama* (breathing practices); *Pratyahara* (drawing senses inward); *Dharana* (concentration), *Dhyana* (meditation); and *Samadhi* (absorption in Spirit).

Gandha: Energy of cohesive attraction; smell; one of the five subtle elements, the categories of Spirit's existence identified in chart form in Table 1; the five *Tanmatras* are: *Shabda* (energy of vibration—sound); *Sparsha* (energy of impact—touch); *Rupa* (energy of light—form); *Rasa* (energy of viscous attraction—taste); and *Gandha* (energy of cohesive attraction—smell).

Garima: Power to become heavy or immobile; one of the eight supernatural powers, the *Siddhis*, along with *Anima* (Power to become as minute as an atom, even invisible); *Mahima* (to grow in magnitude); *Laghima* (to become light); *Prapti* (the power to dominate and obtain anything desired); *Prakamya* (the freedom of will and attainment of wishes); *Isatva* (supremacy over all, including the elements); and *Vasitva* (the power to subjugate anyone or anything); *Patanjali* discusses mystical powers and accomplishments in Part Three of his *Yoga Sutras*, *Vibhuti Pada*, and explains in *Yoga Sutra* 4.1 how they can be acquired; *Patanjali* warns in *Yoga Sutra* 3.38 (3.37 in some commentaries) that these powers and accomplishments can inhibit our ability to connect to Spirit.

Gunas: Qualities or tendencies of *Prakriti*, matter; general tendencies of how we act, discussed by Patanjali in Yoga Sutras 1.16, 2.15, 2.19, 4.32 and 4.34; the three primary *Gunas* are: *Sattva*—balance, lucidity; *Rajas*—action, heating, dynamic energy; and *Tamas*—inertia, dark, slow, cooling energy.

Hasya Rasa: Joy; humor; one of the *Rasas*; the emotional flavors or tastes of life; *Hasya Rasa* pertains to feelings of humor, comic happiness, satire, sarcasm, and exuberance; the other *Rasas* discussed in this book are: *Shanta Rasa* (Peace); *Karuna Rasa* (Compassion); *Vibhatsa Rasa* (Disgust); *Shringara Rasa:* (Love); *Vira Rasa* (Courage); *Raudra Rasa* (Anger); *Adbhuta Rasa* (Wonder); and *Bhayanaka Rasa* (Fear).

Iccha: Willpower or desire

Iccha Shakti: Power of Divine will; our desire to know and then fully express ourselves.

Ida: One of three conduits, *Nadis*, of life force, *Prana*, along with *Pingala* and *Shushumna*.

Isatva: Power to hold supremacy over all; one of the eight supernatural powers, the *Siddhis*, along with *Anima* (Power to become as minute as an atom, even invisible); *Mahima* (to grow in magnitude); *Laghima* (to become light); *Garima* (to become heavy, immovable); *Prapti* (the power to dominate and obtain anything desired); *Prakamya* (the freedom of will and attainment of wishes); and *Vasitva* (the power to subjugate anyone or anything); *Patanjali* discusses mystical powers and accomplishments in Part Three of his *Yoga Sutras, Vibhuti Pada,* and explains in *Yoga Sutra* 4.1 how they can be acquired; *Patanjali* warns in *Yoga Sutra* 3.38 (3.37 in some commentaries) that these powers and accomplishments can inhibit our ability to connect to Spirit.

Ishvara Pranidhani: Surrender to God, discussed by Patanjali in Yoga Sutra 2.45; one of the five *Niyamas* identified by *Patanjali* in *Yoga Sutra* 2.32 as five rules for guiding our relationship with ourselves, along with *Sauca* (cleanliness, purity; *Yoga Sutra* 2.40); *Santosa* (contentment; *Yoga Sutras* 2.41-2.42); *Tapah* (*Tapas*) (burning desire, self-discipline; *Yoga Sutra* 2.43); and *Svadhyaya* (study of scripture and of the self; *Yoga Sutra* 2.44).

Isvara: Lordship; one of the *Tattvas*, the categories of Spirit's existence identified in chart form in Table 1; a name for Spirit.

Iyengar, B.K.S.: Yoga pioneer, author and scholar; founder of Iyengar Yoga.

Jhana: Knowledge.

Jnanendriyas: The five sense organs identified in the *Tattvas*, the categories of Spirit's existence identified in chart form in Table 1; the five *Jnanendriyas* are: ears, skin, eyes, tongue, and nose.

Jhana Shakti: Power of Divine knowledge.

Kaivalya: Living in a state of total absorption in Spirit; liberation; discussed in Patanjali's *Yoga Sutra* 4.34.

Kala Kanchuka (Diacritical mark on second "a"): Limitation of our power of action; one of the five *Kanchukas* of the *Tattvas*, the categories of Spirit's existence identified in chart form in Table 1; the five *Kanchukas* are: *Kala* (limitation of our power of action); *Vidya* (limitation of our ability to know); *Raga* (limitation of our experience of fullness, wholeness, and completeness, hiding us from our willpower and desire to make our mark in the world); *Niyati* (limitation of our experience of natural law, the law of cause and effect); and *Kala* (limitation of our experience of time).

Kala Kanchuka (Diacritical mark on first "a"): Limitation of our experience of time; one of the five *Kanchukas* of the *Tattvas,* the categories of Spirit's existence identified in chart form in Table 1; the five *Kanchukas* are: *Kala* (limitation of our power of action); *Vidya* (limitation of our ability to know); *Raga* (limitation of our experience of fullness, wholeness, and completeness, hiding us from our willpower and desire to make our mark in the world); *Niyati* (limitation of our experience of natural law, the law of cause and effect); and *Kala* (limitation of our experience of time).

Kanchuka: Five ways Spirit, through the power of *Maya*, steps down into diversification in order to make our world; in the myth of creation, Spirit uses these five *Kanchukas* to conceal Herself through all the diverse forms on our planet; the five *Kanchukas* are: *Kala* (limitation of our power of action); *Vidya* (limitation of our ability to know); *Raga* (limitation of our experience of fullness, wholeness, and completeness, hiding us from our willpower and desire to make our mark in the world); *Niyati* (limitation of our experience of natural law, the law of cause and effect); and *Kala* (limitation of our experience of time).

Kanda: Point of origin of the *Nadis*, channels for our life force, *Prana*; located near base of spine.

Karma-Mala: Actions based on feelings arising from the *Malas*, impurities, cloaks, or veils that keep us from fully experiencing Spirit; these two *Malas* are *Anava-Mala* (feeling of being incomplete, inadequate, or imperfect) and *Mayiya-Mala* (feeling of being different, disconnected).

Karmendriyas: The five action organs identified in the *Tattvas*, the categories of Spirit's existence identified in chart form in Table 1; the five *Karmendriyas* are: mouth, hands, feet, genitals, and bowels.

Karuna Rasa: Compassion; sadness; one of the *Rasas*; the emotional flavors or tastes of life; *Karuna Rasa* pertains to feelings of pity, empathy, and a light sadness; the other *Rasas* discussed in this book are: *Shanta Rasa* (Peace); *Vibhatsa Rasa* (Disgust); *Shringara Rasa:* (Love); *Vira Rasa* (Courage); *Raudra Rasa* (Anger); *Hasya Rasa* (Joy); *Adbhuta Rasa* (Wonder); and *Bhayanaka Rasa* (Fear).

Kirtan: Call and response sacred chanting.

Kleshas (Klesas): Afflictions or challenges that can interfere with our connection to Spirit; *Patanjali* identifies five *Kleshas* in *Yoga Sutra* 2.3: *Avidya* (ignorance; *Yoga Sutras* 2.3-2.5), *Asmita* (ego; *Yoga Sutra* 2.6), *Raga* (desire; *Yoga Sutra* 2.7), *Dvesa* (aversion; *Yoga Sutra* 2.8) and *Abhinivesah* (clinging to life, fear of death; *Yoga Sutra* 2.9).

Klista: Movements of the mind, *Vrttis*, detrimental to connection to Spirit; discussed by *Patanjali* in *Yoga Sutra* 1.5.

Koshas (Kosas): Five layers or sheaths of a human being; the five *Koshas* are: *Annamaya Kosha* (Sheath of the physical body); *Pranamaya Kosha* (Sheath of the breath); *Manomaya Kosha* (Sheath of the mind); and *Vijnanamaya Kosha* (Sheath of the intuitive mind); and *Anandamaya Kosha*: (Sheath of bliss).

Krishna: Name for Spirit; Spirit appeared in human form to engage in conversation with Arjuna in *Bhagavad Gita*.

Kriya Shakti: Power of Divine action.

Laghima: Power to become light; one of the eight supernatural powers, the *Siddhis*, along with *Anima* (Power to become as minute as an atom, even invisible); *Mahima* (to grow in magnitude); *Garima* (to become heavy, immovable); *Prapti* (the power to dominate and obtain anything desired); *Prakamya* (the freedom of will and attainment of wishes); *Isatva* (supremacy over all, including the elements); and *Vasitva* (the power to subjugate anyone or anything); *Patanjali* discusses mystical powers and accomplishments in Part Three of his *Yoga Sutras*, *Vibhuti Pada*, and explains in *Yoga Sutra* 4.1 how they can be acquired; *Patanjali* warns in *Yoga Sutra* 3.38 (3.37 in some commentaries) that these powers and accomplishments can inhibit our ability to connect to Spirit.

Mahabhutas: The five gross elements identified in the *Tattvas*, the categories of Spirit's existence identified in chart form in Table 1; the five *Mahabuhutas* are: *Akasha* (space); *Vayu* (air); *Agni* (fire); *Ap* (water); and *Prithivi* (earth).

Mahima: Power to grow in size; one of the eight supernatural powers, the *Siddhis*, along with *Anima* (Power to become as minute as an atom, even invisible); *Laghima* (to become light); *Garima* (to become heavy, immovable); *Prapti* (the power to dominate and obtain anything desired); *Prakamya* (the freedom of will and attainment of wishes); *Isatva* (supremacy over all, including the elements); and *Vasitva* (the power to subjugate anyone or anything); *Patanjali* discusses mystical powers and accomplishments in Part Three of his *Yoga Sutras*, *Vibhuti Pada*, and explains in *Yoga Sutra* 4.1 how they can be acquired; *Patanjali* warns in *Yoga Sutra* 3.38 (3.37 in some commentaries) that these powers and accomplishments can inhibit our ability to connect to Spirit.

Mala: Three impurities, cloaks, or veils that can inhibit us from fully experiencing Spirit; the three *Malas* are: *Anava-Mala, Mayiya-Mala,* and *Karma-Mala.*

Manas: Mind; organizer of information received from the senses; *Manas*, along with *Ahamkara* (Ego; pride; sense of self) and *Buddhi* (Intelligence; the higher intuitive mind), are part of the *Tattvas*, the categories of Spirit's existence identified in chart form in Table 1, and collectively form the mental processing center for our ability to experience the world.

Manipura: Energy center located in the area between the navel and solar plexus; associated with self-expression, fire, vitality, individual willpower, self-esteem, and personality; the third *Chakra* in the seven *Chakra* system discussed in this book: First *Chakra*, *Muladhara Chakra* (root of tailbone—our foundation); Second *Chakra, Svadisthana Chakra* (pelvis—relationships with others); Third *Chakra, Manipura Chakra* (solar plexus—expression of our personality); Fourth *Chakra, Anahata Chakra* (heart—love and self-acceptance); Fifth *Chakra, Vishuddha Chakra* (throat—communication); Sixth *Chakra, Ajna Chakra* (between the eye brows—intuition and psychic perception; wisdom); and Seventh *Chakra, Sahasrara Chakra* (top of the head—absorption in Spirit).

Manomaya Kosha: Sheath of the mind; one of the five *Koshas*, or layers of a human being, along with *Annamaya Kosha* (Sheath of the physical body); *Pranamaya Kosha* (Sheath of the breath); *Vijnanamaya Kosha* (Sheath of the intuitive mind); and *Anandamaya Kosha* (Sheath of bliss).

Mantra: Repetition of words infused with sacred or uplifting meaning.

Maya: Differentiating power of the Universe; illusion.

Mayiya-Mala: Feeling of being different; one of the three *Malas,* three impurities, cloaks, or veils that keeps us from fully experiencing Spirit; the other two *Malas* are *Anava-Mala* (feelings of being disconnected, incomplete, inadequate or imperfect) and *Karma-Mala* (actions based on these feelings).

Muladhara: Energy center located in the perineum, base of spine; associated with the earth element and its attributes of survival, trust, grounding and stability; our "root" or foundational *Chakra*; the first of the seven *Chakras* in the seven *Chakra* system discussed in this book: First *Chakra, Muladhara Chakra* (root of tailbone—our foundation); Second *Chakra, Svadisthana Chakra* (pelvis—relationships with others); Third *Chakra, Manipura Chakra* (solar plexus—expression of our personality); Fourth *Chakra, Anahata Chakra* (heart—love and self-acceptance); Fifth *Chakra, Vishuddha Chakra* (throat—communication); Sixth *Chakra, Ajna Chakra* (between the eye brows—intuition and psychic perception; wisdom); and Seventh *Chakra, Sahasrara Chakra* (top of the head—absorption in Spirit).

Nadis: System of channels in our physical and also our subtle body, through which the *Prana*, our vital life force, moves.

Niyamas: Five rules for guiding our relationship with ourselves, discussed by *Patanjali* in *Yoga Sutras* 2.32-2.45; the five *Niyamas* are: *Sauca* (cleanliness, purity; *Yoga Sutra* 2.40); *Santosa* (contentment; *Yoga Sutras* 2.41-2.42); *Tapah* (*Tapas*) (burning desire, self-discipline; *Yoga Sutra* 2.43); *Svadhyaya* (study of scripture and of the self; *Yoga Sutra* 2.44); and *Isvara Pranidhanani* (surrender to God; *Yoga Sutra* 2.45); the *Niyamas* are part of *Patanjali's* Eightfold Path of yoga identified in *Yoga Sutra* 2.29 as: *Yamas* (ethical rules for treatment of others); *Niyamas* (rules for treating ourselves); *Asana* (a seat; poses); *Pranayama* (breathing practices); *Pratyahara* (drawing senses inward); *Dharana* (concentration), *Dhyana* (meditation); and *Samadhi* (absorption in Spirit).

Niyati Kanchuka: Limitation of our experience of natural law, the law of cause and effect; can limit our appreciation of our creative potential; one of the five *Kanchukas* of the *Tattvas*, the categories of Spirit's existence identified in chart form in Table 1; the five *Kanchukas* are: *Kala* (limitation of our power of action); *Vidya* (limitation of our ability to know); *Raga* (limitation of our experience of fullness, wholeness, and completeness, hiding us from our willpower and desire to make our mark in the world); *Niyati* (limitation of our experience of natural law, the law of cause and effect); and *Kala* (limitation of our experience of time).

Panca-Krtya: *Five Divine Acts of Shiva* or five cosmic actions: *Srsti* (creation, birth), *Sthiti* (maintenance, sustenance), *Samhara* (dissolution, death), *Vilaya* (concealment), and *Anugraha* (revelation).

Param: Supreme.

Paramananda: High state of love.

Paramshiva: Supreme Lord or Supreme Goodness, Benevolence.

Patanjali: Author of the *Yoga Sutras*, a compilation of yoga philosophy likely written sometime between 150 B.C.E. to 200 C.E.

Patanjali's Yoga Sutras: Highly regarded texts on the philosophy of yoga; one of the most studied works of yoga philosophy, teaching a pathway to Spirit.

Pingala: One of three conduits, *Nadis*, of life force, *Prana*, along with *Ida* and *Shushumna*

Prajna: Wisdom, lucidity; discernment.

Prakamya: Power to have wishes fulfilled; one of the eight supernatural powers, the *Siddhis*, along with *Anima* (Power to become as minute as an atom, even invisible); *Mahima* (to grow in magnitude); *Laghima* (to become light); *Garima* (to become heavy, immovable); *Prapti* (the power to dominate and obtain anything desired); *Isatva* (supremacy over all, including the elements); and *Vasitva* (the power to subjugate anyone or anything); *Patanjali* discusses mystical powers and accomplishments in Part Three of his *Yoga Sutras, Vibhuti Pada,* and explains in *Yoga Sutra* 4.1 how they can be acquired; *Patanjali* warns in *Yoga Sutra* 3.38 (3.37 in some commentaries) that these powers and accomplishments can inhibit our ability to connect to Spirit.

Prakasha: Pure light of Spirit, present at each and every level of creation.

Prakriti: Nature or matter; the material world; one of the *Tattvas,* the categories of Spirit's existence identified in chart form in Table 1.

Prana: Vital life force; breath.

Pranamaya Kosha: Sheath of the breath; life force; one of the five *Koshas,* or layers of a human being, along with *Annamaya Kosha* (Sheath of the physical body); *Manomaya Kosha* (Sheath of the mind); *Vijnanamaya Kosha* (Sheath of the intuitive mind); and *Anandamaya Kosha* (Sheath of bliss).

Pranayama: Breathing practices, discussed by Patanjali in Yoga Sutras 2.49-2.53; *Pranayama* is one part of *Patanjali's* Eightfold Path of yoga identified in *Yoga Sutra* 2.29 as: *Yamas* (ethical rules for treatment of others); *Niyamas* (rules for treating ourselves); *Asana* (a seat; poses); *Pranayama* (breathing practices); *Pratyahara* (drawing senses inward); *Dharana* (concentration), *Dhyana* (meditation); and *Samadhi* (absorption in Spirit).

Prapti: Power to dominate and obtain what one wants; one of the eight supernatural powers, the *Siddhis,* along with *Anima* (Power to become as minute as an atom, even invisible); *Mahima* (to grow in magnitude); *Laghima* (to become light); *Garima* (to become heavy, immovable); *Prakamya* (the freedom of will and attainment of wishes); *Isatva* (supremacy over all, including the elements); and *Vasitva* (the power to subjugate anyone or anything); *Patanjali* discusses mystical powers and accomplishments in Part Three of his *Yoga Sutras, Vibhuti Pada,* and explains in *Yoga Sutra* 4.1 how they can be acquired; *Patanjali* warns in *Yoga Sutra* 3.38 (3.37 in some commentaries) that these powers and accomplishments can inhibit our ability to connect to Spirit.

Pratyabhijnahrdayam: Key *Kashmir Shaivite* text, dating somewhere around 1025 CE, written by *Kshemaraja.*

Pratyahara: Drawing the senses inward, discussed by *Patanjali* in *Yoga Sutra* 2.54-2.55; *Pratyahara* is one part of *Patanjali's* Eightfold Path of yoga identified in *Yoga Sutra* 2.29 as: *Yamas* (ethical rules for treatment of others); *Niyamas* (rules for treating ourselves); *Asana* (a seat; poses); *Pranayama* (breathing practices); *Pratyahara* (drawing senses inward); *Dharana* (concentration), *Dhyana* (meditation); and *Samadhi* (absorption in Spirit).

Prithivi: Earth; one of the five gross elements, the *Mahabhutas*, identified in the *Tattvas*, the categories of existence identified in chart form in Table 1; the five *Mahabhutas* are: *Akasha* (space); *Vayu* (air); *Agni* (fire); *Ap* (water); and *Prithivi* (earth).

Purnatva: Fullness, wholeness, peace, perfection.

Purusha: Spirit; the soul; the true Self; one of the *Tattvas*, the categories of Spirit's existence identified in chart form in Table 1.

Raga: Attachment, desire; discussed by Patanjali in *Yoga Sutra* 2.7; one of the five afflictions or challenges that can interfere with connection to Spirit; these afflictions or challenges are called *Kleshas* and are identified by *Patanjali* in *Yoga Sutra* 2.3; the *Kleshas* also include: *Avidya* (ignorance; *Yoga Sutras* 2.3-2.5); *Asmita* (ego; *Yoga Sutra* 2.6); *Dvesha* (aversion; *Yoga Sutra* 2.8); and *Abhinivesah*: (Clinging to life; *Yoga Sutra* 2.9).

Raga: Limitation of our experience of fullness, wholeness, and completeness, hiding us from our willpower and desire to make our mark in the world; one of the five *Kanchukas* of the *Tattvas*, the categories of Spirit's existence identified in chart form in Table 1; the five *Kanchukas* are: *Kala* (limitation of our power of action); *Vidya* (limitation of our ability to know); *Raga* (limitation of our experience of fullness, wholeness, and completeness, hiding us from our willpower and desire to make our mark in the world); *Niyati* (limitation of our experience of natural law, the law of cause and effect); and *Kala* (limitation of our experience of time).

Rajas: Heating, dynamic energy; one of the three *Gunas,* the tendencies of *Prakriti*, matter, discussed by Patanjali in Yoga Sutras 1.16, 2.15, 2.19, 4.32 and 4.34; the three primary *Gunas* are: *Sattva*—balance, lucidity; *Rajas*—action, heating, dynamic energy; and *Tamas*—inertia, dark, slow, cooling energy.

Rasa: Energy of viscous attraction; taste; one of the five subtle elements identified in the *Tattvas*, the categories of Spirit's existence identified in chart form in Table 1; the five *Tanmatras* are: *Shabda* (energy of vibration—sound); *Sparsha* (energy of impact—touch); *Rupa* (energy of light—form); *Rasa* (energy of viscous attraction—taste); and *Gandha* (energy of cohesive attraction—smell).

Rasas: Taste, essence, the emotional flavors or tastes of life; the *Rasas* include: *Shanta Rasa* (Peace), *Karuna Rasa* (Compassion), *Vibhatsa Rasa* (Disgust), *Shringara Rasa* (Love), *Vira Rasa* (Courage), *Raudra Rasa* (Anger), *Hasya Rasa* (Joy), *Adbhuta Rasa* (Wonder), and *Bhayanaka Rasa* (Fear).

Raudra Rasa: Anger; one of the *Rasas*; the emotional flavors or tastes of life; *Raudra Rasa* pertains to feelings of fury, irritation, violence, and hostile rage; the other *Rasas* discussed in this book are: *Shanta Rasa* (Peace); *Karuna Rasa* (Compassion); *Vibhatsa Rasa* (Disgust); *Shringara Rasa:* (Love); *Vira Rasa* (Courage); *Hasya Rasa* (Joy); *Adbhuta Rasa* (Wonder); and *Bhayanaka Rasa* (Fear).

Rta: Absolute Reality; truth and order.

Rupa: Energy of light; form; one of the five subtle elements identified in the *Tattvas*, the categories of Spirit's existence identified in chart form in Table 1; the five *Tanmatras* are: *Shabda* (energy of vibration—sound); *Sparsha* (energy of impact—touch); *Rupa* (energy of light—form); *Rasa* (energy of viscous attraction—taste); and *Gandha* (energy of cohesive attraction—smell).

Sadashiva: Always *Shiva*; one of the *Tattvas*; a name for Spirit.

Sadhana: Practice.

Sahasrara: Energy center located at the top of the head; associated with the bliss of pure consciousness and spiritual connection; the seventh *Chakra* of the seven *Chakra* system discussed in this book: First *Chakra, Muladhara Chakra* (root of tailbone—our foundation); Second *Chakra, Svadisthana Chakra* (pelvis—relationships with others); Third *Chakra, Manipura Chakra* (solar plexus—expression of our personality); Fourth *Chakra, Anahata Chakra* (heart—love and self-acceptance); Fifth *Chakra, Vishuddha Chakra* (throat—communication); Sixth *Chakra, Ajna Chakra* (between the eye brows—intuition and psychic perception; wisdom); and Seventh *Chakra, Sahasrara Chakra* (top of the head—absorption in Spirit).

Samadhi: Absorption in Spirit, discussed by Patanjali in Yoga Sutras 3.3-3.15; Samadhi is one part of *Patanjali's* Eightfold Path of yoga identified in *Yoga Sutra* 2.29 as: *Yamas* (ethical rules for treatment of others); *Niyamas* (rules for treating ourselves); *Asana* (a seat; poses); *Pranayama* (breathing practices); *Pratyahara* (drawing senses inward); *Dharana* (concentration), *Dhyana* (meditation); and *Samadhi* (absorption in Spirit).

Samhara: Dissolution, death; one of the five Divine Acts of *Shiva*.

Samkhya: Division of philosophy identifying the categories of Spirit and matter.

Samskara: Storehouse of our past impressions.

Samyama: Integration; a continuous practice of *Dharana* (concentration), *Dhyana* (meditation), and *Samadhi* (total absorption), discussed by *Patanjali* in *Yoga Sutras* 3.4-3.15.

Santosa: Contentment, discussed by *Patanjali* in *Yoga Sutras* 2.41-2.42; one of the five *Niyamas* identified by *Patanjali* in *Yoga Sutra* 2.32 as five rules for guiding our relationship with ourselves, along with *Sauca* (cleanliness, purity; *Yoga Sutra* 2.40); *Tapah* (*Tapas*) (burning desire, self-discipline; *Yoga Sutra* 2.43); *Svadhyaya* (study of scripture and of the self; *Yoga Sutra* 2.44); and *Isvara Pranidhanani* (surrender to God; *Yoga Sutra* 2.45);

Sat: Being; truth.

Sattva: Pure; an optimizing, balancing energy, lucidity; one of the three *Gunas*, the tendencies of *Prakriti*, matter, discussed by Patanjali in Yoga Sutras 1.16, 2.15, 2.19, 4.32 and 4.34; the three primary *Gunas* are: *Sattva*—balance, lucidity; *Rajas*—action, heating, dynamic energy; and *Tamas*—inertia, dark, slow, cooling energy.

Satya: Truth, honesty, discussed by *Patanjali* in *Yoga Sutras* 2.35-2.36; one of the five *Yamas* identified by *Patanjali* in *Yoga Sutra* 2.30 as five rules for ethical behavior towards others, along with *Ahimsa* (non-violence; non-harming; *Yoga Sutras*

2.34-2.35); *Asteya* (non-stealing; *Yoga Sutra* 2.37); *Brahmacarya* (self-restraint, particularly in sexual matters; *Yoga Sutra* 2.38), and *Aparigrahah* (non-possessiveness, lack of greed; *Yoga Sutra* 2.39).

Sauca: Cleanliness, purity, cleanliness, discussed by *Patanjali* in *Yoga Sutra* 2.40; one of the five *Niyamas* identified by *Patanjali* in *Yoga Sutra* 2.32 as five rules for guiding our relationship with ourselves, along with *Santosa* (contentment; *Yoga Sutras* 2.41-2.42); *Tapah* (*Tapas*) (burning desire, self-discipline; *Yoga Sutra* 2.43); *Svadhyaya* (study of scripture and of the self; *Yoga Sutra* 2.44); and *Isvara Pranidhanani* (surrender to God; *Yoga Sutra* 2.45).

Shabda: Energy of vibration; sound; one of the five subtle elements identified in the *Tattvas*, the categories of Spirit's existence identified in chart form in Table 1; the five *Tanmatras* are: *Shabda* (energy of vibration—sound); *Sparsha* (energy of impact—touch); *Rupa* (energy of light—form); *Rasa* (energy of viscous attraction—taste); and *Gandha* (energy of cohesive attraction—smell).

Shakti (Sakti): Name of Spirit's feminine, creative power; one of the *Tattvas*, the categories of Spirit's existence identified in chart form in Table 1.

Shanta Rasa: Peace; one of the *Rasas*; the emotional flavors or tastes of life; *Shanta Rasa* pertains to feelings of calmness, fulfillment, contentment, and relaxation; the other *Rasas* discussed in this book are: *Karuna Rasa* (Compassion); *Vibhatsa Rasa* (Disgust); *Shringara Rasa:* (Love); *Vira Rasa* (Courage); *Raudra Rasa* (Anger); *Hasya Rasa* (Joy); *Adbhuta Rasa* (Wonder); and *Bhayanaka Rasa* (Fear).

Shanti: Peace.

Shiva (Siva): Name of Spirit's masculine power, good, benevolent, the Divine light; one of the *Tattvas*, the categories of Spirit's existence identified in chart form in Table 1.

Shri (Sri): Benevolence, creative power; abundance.

Shringara Rasa: Erotic love; one of the *Rasas;* the emotional flavors or tastes of life; *Shringara Rasa* pertains to feelings of erotic love, desire, devotion, divine beauty, and admiration; the other *Rasas* discussed in this book are: *Shanta Rasa* (Peace); *Karuna Rasa* (Compassion); *Vibhatsa Rasa* (Disgust); *Vira Rasa* (Courage); *Raudra Rasa* (Anger); *Hasya Rasa* (Joy); *Adbhuta Rasa* (Wonder); and *Bhayanaka Rasa* (Fear).

Siddhis: Supernatural powers; these powers include: *Anima* (to become as minute as an atom, even invisible); *Mahima* (to grow in magnitude); *Laghima* (to become light); *Garima* (to become heavy, immovable); *Prapti* (the power to dominate and obtain anything desired); *Prakamya* (the freedom of will and attainment of wishes); *Isatva* (supremacy over all, including the elements); and *Vasitva* (the power to subjugate anyone or anything); *Patanjali* discusses mystical powers and accomplishments in Part Three of his *Yoga Sutras, Vibhuti Pada,* and explains in *Yoga Sutra* 4.1 how they can be acquired; *Patanjali* warns in *Yoga Sutra* 3.38 (3.37 in some commentaries) that these powers and accomplishments can inhibit our ability to connect to Spirit.

Sparsha: Energy of impact; touch; one of the five subtle elements identified in the *Tattvas*, the categories of Spirit's existence identified in chart form in Table 1; the five *Tanmatras* are: *Shabda* (energy of vibration—sound); *Sparsha* (energy of impact—touch); *Rupa* (energy of light—form); *Rasa* (energy of viscous attraction—taste); and *Gandha* (energy of cohesive attraction—smell).

Spanda: Pulsation or vibration between contrasting or polar energies; opening and closing; contraction and expansion.

Sraddha: Faith.

Srsti: Creation; birth; one of the five Divine Acts of *Shiva*.

Sthiti: Sustenance; maintenance, one of the Five Divine Acts of *Shiva*.

Subtle body: Systems within our body that act as a counterpart to the energy of the entire universe, including the five sheaths (*Koshas*), energetic centers (*Chakras*), and energy currents or pathways called *Nadis*, as well as *Prana*, or "life force."

Suddhavidya: Pure knowledge; one of the *Tattvas*, the categories of Spirit's existence identified in chart form in Table 1.

Sushumna: Central *Nadi*; one of three conduits, *Nadis*, of life force, *Prana*, along with *Pingila* and *Ida*.

Sutra: Thread; a short statement that conveys philosophical information concisely.

Svadhyaha: Study of scripture and of the self, discussed by *Patanjali* in *Yoga Sutra* 2.44; one of the five *Niyamas* identified by *Patanjali* in *Yoga Sutra* 2.32 as five rules for guiding our relationship with ourselves, along with *Sauca* (cleanliness, purity; *Yoga Sutra* 2.40); *Santosa* (contentment; *Yoga Sutras* 2.41-2.42); *Tapah* (*Tapas*) (burning desire, self-discipline; *Yoga Sutra* 2.43); and *Isvara Pranidhanani* (surrender to God; *Yoga Sutra* 2.45).

Svadisthana: Energy center located below the navel in the lower abdomen, genitals, womb; associated with water, relationship, sexuality, pleasure and a desire for enjoyment and gratification; the second *Chakra* in the seven *Chakra* system discussed in this book: First *Chakra*, *Muladhara Chakra* (root of tailbone—our foundation); Second *Chakra*, *Svadisthana Chakra* (pelvis—relationships with others); Third *Chakra*, *Manipura Chakra* (solar plexus—expression of our personality); Fourth *Chakra*, *Anahata Chakra* (heart—love and self-acceptance); Fifth *Chakra*, *Vishuddha Chakra* (throat—communication); Sixth *Chakra*, *Ajna Chakra* (between the eye brows—intuition and psychic perception; wisdom); and Seventh *Chakra*, *Sahasrara Chakra* (top of the head—absorption in Spirit).

Svatantrya: Freedom.

Tamas: Cooling, slowing and condensing; one of the three *Gunas*, the tendencies of *Prakriti*, matter, discussed by Patanjali in Yoga Sutras 1.16, 2.15, 2.19, 4.32 and 4.34; the three primary *Gunas* are: *Sattva*—balance, lucidity; *Rajas*—action, heating, dynamic energy; and *Tamas*—inertia, dark, slow, cooling energy.

Tanmatras: Five subtle elements identified in the *Tattvas*, the categories of Spirit's existence identified in chart form in Table 1; the five *Tanmatras* are: *Shabda* (energy of vibration—sound); *Sparsha* (energy of impact—touch); *Rupa* (energy of light—form); *Rasa* (energy of viscous attraction—taste); and *Gandha* (energy of cohesive attraction—smell).

Tapah (Tapas): Burning desire, self-discipline, discussed by *Patanjali* in *Yoga Sutra* 2.43; one of the five *Niyamas* identified by *Patanjali* in *Yoga Sutra* 2.32 as five rules for guiding our relationship with ourselves, along with *Sauca* (cleanliness, purity; *Yoga Sutra* 2.40); *Santosa* (contentment; *Yoga Sutras* 2.41-2.42); *Svadhyaya* (study of scripture and of the self; *Yoga Sutra* 2.44); and *Isvara Pranidhanani* (surrender to God; *Yoga Sutra* 2.45).

Tattvas: Categories of Spirit's existence; a principle; "that-ness;" listed in chart form in Table 1; referenced by *Patanjali* in *Yoga Sutras* 1.32 and 4.14.

Vairagya: Detachment from thoughts and actions that distract us from progress on the yoga path; *Patanjali* teaches in *Yoga Sutra* 1.12 that regular, informed practice of the Eightfold Path of yoga, *Abhyasa*, along with detachment from thoughts and actions that distract us from progress on the yoga path, *Vairagya*, are the means to optimize the mind's ability to connect to Spirit.

Vasitva: Power of supremacy over all, including the elements; one of the eight supernatural powers, the *Siddhis,* along with *Anima* (Power to become as minute as an atom, even invisible); *Mahima* (to grow in magnitude); *Laghima* (to become light); *Garima* (to become heavy, immovable); *Prapti* (the power to dominate and obtain anything desired); *Prakamya* (the freedom of will and attainment of wishes); and *Isatva* (supremacy over all, including the elements); *Patanjali* discusses mystical powers and accomplishments in Part Three of his *Yoga Sutras*, *Vibhuti Pada*, and explains in *Yoga Sutra* 4.1 how they can be acquired; *Patanjali* warns in *Yoga Sutra* 3.38 (3.37 in some commentaries) that these powers and accomplishments can inhibit our ability to connect to Spirit.

Vayu: Air; one of the five gross elements, the *Mahabhutas*, identified in the *Tattvas*, the categories of existence identified in chart form in Table 1; the five *Mahabhutas* are: *Akasha* (space); *Vayu* (air); *Agni* (fire); *Ap* (water); and *Prithivi* (earth).

Vibhatsa Rasa: Disgust; repugnance; one of the *Rasas*; the emotional flavors or tastes of life; *Vibhatsa Rasa* pertains to feelings of repugnance, self-loathing, and heavy depression; the other *Rasas* discussed in this book are: *Shanta Rasa* (Peace); *Karuna Rasa* (Compassion); *Shringara Rasa:* (Love); *Vira Rasa* (Courage); *Raudra Rasa* (Anger); *Hasya Rasa* (Joy); *Adbhuta Rasa* (Wonder); and *Bhayanaka Rasa* (Fear).

Vidya: Discriminative knowledge; knowledge of Spirit, discussed by *Patanjali* in *Yoga Sutra* 2.3 and 2.4.

Vidya: Limitation of our ability to know; one of the five *Kanchukas* of the *Tattvas*, the categories of Spirit's existence identified in chart form in Table 1; the five *Kanchukas* are: *Kala* (limitation of our power of action); *Vidya* (limitation of our ability to know); *Raga* (limitation of our experience of fullness, wholeness, and completeness, hiding us from our willpower and desire to make our mark in the world); *Niyati* (limitation of our experience of natural law, the law of cause and effect); and *Kala* (limitation of our experience of time).

Vijnanamaya Kosha: the sheath of the intuitive mind, the body of wisdom; one of the five *Koshas*, or layers of a human being, along with *Annamaya Kosha* (Sheath of the physical body); *Pranamaya Kosha* (Sheath of the breath); *Manomaya Kosha* (sheath of the mind); and *Anandamaya Kosha* (Sheath of bliss).

Vikalpa: Conceptualization; the way we categorize, label, and distinguish our experiences based on doubt, indecision, hesitation, fancy, imagination, day-dreaming or other ways that create detrimental chatter in the mind; discussed by Patanjali in *Yoga Sutra* 1.6.

Vilaya: Concealment; one of the Five Divine Acts of *Shiva*.

Vimarsha: Capacity for Spirit to reflect upon its light and then to consider it and give it meaning.

Vira Rasa: Courage; one of the *Rasas;* the emotional flavors or tastes of life; *Vira Rasa* pertains to feelings of heroism, confidence, pride, and fiery disappointment; the other *Rasas* discussed in this book are: *Shanta Rasa* (Peace); *Karuna Rasa* (Compassion); *Vibhatsa Rasa* (Disgust); *Shringara Rasa:* (Love); *Raudra Rasa* (Anger); *Hasya Rasa* (Joy); *Adbhuta Rasa* (Wonder); and *Bhayanaka Rasa* (Fear).

Virya: Vigor; courage.

Vishuddha: Energy center located in the throat; associated with sound, vibration, communication, and creativity; the fifth *Chakra* in the seven *Chakra* system discussed in this book: First *Chakra*, *Muladhara Chakra* (root of tailbone—our foundation); Second *Chakra, Svadisthana Chakra* (pelvis—relationships with others); Third *Chakra*, *Manipura Chakra* (solar plexus—expression of our personality); Fourth *Chakra*, *Anahata Chakra* (heart—love and self-acceptance); Fifth *Chakra*, *Vishuddha Chakra* (throat—communication); Sixth *Chakra*, *Ajna Chakra* (between the eye brows—intuition and psychic perception; wisdom); and Seventh *Chakra*, *Sahasrara Chakra* (top of the head—absorption in Spirit).

Vrttis: Movements of the mind; *Patanjali* describes in *Yoga Sutra* 1.5 how *Klista* movements are detrimental to connecting to Spirit while *Aklista* movements are non-detrimental to connection to Spirit.

Yamas: Five rules for ethical behavior towards others, discussed by *Patanjali* in *Yoga Sutras* 2.30-2.39; the five *Yamas* are: *Ahimsa* (non-violence; non-harming; *Yoga Sutras* 2.34-2.35); *Satya* (truth; honesty; *Yoga Sutras* 2.35-2.36); *Asteya* (non-stealing; *Yoga Sutra* 2.37); *Brahmacarya* (self-restraint, particularly in sexual matters; *Yoga Sutra* 2.38); and *Aparigrahah* (non-possessiveness, lack of greed; *Yoga Sutra* 2.39); the *Yamas* are the first part of *Patanjali's* Eightfold Path of yoga identified in *Yoga Sutra* 2.29 as: *Yamas* (ethical rules for treatment of others); *Niyamas* (rules for treating ourselves); *Asana* (a seat; poses); *Pranayama* (breathing practices); *Pratyahara* (drawing senses inward); *Dharana* (concentration), *Dhyana* (meditation); and *Samadhi* (absorption in Spirit).

Yoga: Joining, yoking, connecting; path of connection to Spirit

More praise for *Finding The Midline*

"This book makes me smile. I want to pass it on to everyone I know who is curious about growing and feeling more satisfied in life and relationships. Bill shows you simple steps to becoming fulfilled, aware and happier from day to day. It is told through his lovable, fallible, and inspiring life experiences, and it is a joy to read. This is not a traditional philosophy book, but rather an honest account of the challenges we face as humans in a fast paced culture. It is a great story that you can apply to your life right now. Anyone, with any background, can pick up this book and discover how ancient Yoga concepts have real life benefits—today. Prepare to be inspired."
—KELLY LARSON, M.A., PhDc, CYT, Director, Center for the Study of Yoga and Health; Founder of the Power Yin Yoga tradition

"As a young professional, early in my career, I am often seeking a mentor's guidance to teach me everything he/she has learned that can help me be great at what I do. Bill Dorigan is a great mentor in *Finding the Midline*. Reading *Finding the Midline* was like having my own life coach speaking directly to me, with personal stories that I could relate to and learn from, directly benefiting my career, my personal life, and my yoga practice."
—ASHLEY POLLOCK, Esq., Attorney (Denver, Colorado)

"As a yoga instructor and practitioner, I've struggled to find readable, relate-able books about yoga philosophy. Finding the Midline is fresh, funny and fills that void in current yoga literature. Dorigan's masterful understanding of yoga principles is exhibited with humor, wit, humility and enthusiasm. This book serves as an invitation to find our best selves and live our best lives—a must-read!"
—RACHEL M. RANNOW, MA, RYT (Winter Park, Colorado)

"If you happening to find yourself stuck in the Lima airport for a day due to mechanical difficulties, this is a great book to have in your hands. Bill's lessons on how to turn life's follies from disasters into learning experiences are invaluable."
—DALE S. ROTHMAN, Ph.D, Educator and yoga student (Denver, Colorado)

"Bill's humor and love of life are met with intelligence and compassion in this book. A perfect blend of yogic philosophy and great writing that leave you inspired and energized. Each chapter lifts the reader up, encouraging them with each lesson to live the best life they can live. He unravels the mystery of yoga and threads it through our everyday life scenarios."
—ANGIE WOYAR, Certified Iyengar Yoga Instructor (Denver, Colorado)

"If you are serious about finding the connection between outer world to the inner world of your life or learn how to look inside and find the path to real freedom, or just looking to find true relationship and deeper spiritual connection, then this is a book that you need to read. *Finding the Midline* is easy reading and a well researched guide to your physical and spiritual well being. Listen to this man!"

—MARINE KARYAN, Certified BodyMind Sport Nutritionist (Denver, Colorado)

"As a high school counselor for nearly 40 years, I pursued my doctorate in order to be prepared to rise to the challenge of integrating affective experiences into school curricula.

In a catholic school, it's easy to utilize spirituality in creating a healthy school climate. But what of our public schools? As an educator, I focus on youth and school, but what Bill offers is a path that can provide a spiritual connection to our everyday lives. More and more the research is telling us that being smart may not be enough. We need emotional smarts to integrate information with our own feelings and reach for a more effective mode of living.

Bill deftly shows the reader where to find those places in life; "midlines", where we can connect our daily life experiences with a new perspective and vision. He speaks from his own experiences and own heart, and gives us some real-life examples of becoming aware of these moments through the lessons of Yoga.

The book appeals at several levels: the newcomer can easily relate and understand, and the truly curious can proceed to high levels of practice and philosophy. Bill describes in appealing vignettes moments where he learned to cast aside old ways of thinking for a new, more gentle, perspective. A hopeful, positive, and generous book."

—LAUREL ZIMMERMAN, Ed.D. (Minneapolis, Minnesota)

"Always intensely passionate and intensely curious about life, Bill Dorigan, gifted intellectually and athletically, a successful lawyer, knew that something was missing—some unifying purpose/exercise/concept to help him understand himself and his life, his strengths and especially his weaknesses.

Dorigan's *Finding the Midline* is his highly personal, detailed description of his discovery of his most important and enduring life tool—the philosophy and practice of yoga. Through *Finding the Midline*, Dorigan offers us his "light." He encourages us to take advantage of the myriad opportunities to step out of our comfort zones and embrace the potential of the moment (the Midline). With a multitude of his own life examples, he demonstrates for us how to take the risks necessary to create a richer, sweeter life of meaning and engagement—a life full of relating experiences and relationships that we treasure. These Midline experiences allow us, as they have Bill Dorigan, to connect with our own Spirit and the Spirit that is in everyone and everything.

One cannot help being seduced by Dorigan's passion and exuberance for yoga. The profound effect that yoga has had on his life can be found on every page of this remarkable book of transformation. With a plethora of memories, examples and exercises, Bill introduces and connects us to the concepts of yoga philosophy and practice in every chapter. In *Finding the Midline*, Bill Dorigan's openness and vulnerability to life and use of yoga as his life tool, allow one to yearn to learn more about yoga and the possibility of its seemingly endless effects on our own lives!"

—HOWARD PRESSMAN, M.D., Adult and Child Psychiatrist (Edgewater, Maryland)

"Dorigan uses his ability to talk to us in a language we can understand to convey the beauty and depth of yoga philosophy and practice.

I've found this book helpful in both my professional and personal life. First, as a Pharmacist, it is important for me to focus as I handle the many tasks involved in being a health care provider. Even though I've been performing these duties well for years, I find this book increases my effectiveness. Second, I've been a yoga student for many years and am, in fact, the "Jim" that introduced Bill to yoga back in the 90's. I find that as much as I practiced and studied yoga, this book opened doors to a far deeper understanding of yoga and how it can lead us to a richer life."

—JIM CLAUSIUS, Pharmacist and yoga student (Wyomissing, Pennsylvania)

"*Finding the Midline* is a wonderful compilation of heartfelt stories and life experiences that will enlighten anyone who is searching for a way to find balance and transform their life using the philosophy and spirituality of yoga."

—LISA ROCKERS (Durango, Colorado)

"Salon energy can be both hectic and exciting all day long due to stylists, clients and the atmosphere itself. Reading this has reminded me to slow down, smile, breathe, and enjoy every moment, everything and everyone who sits down in my chair. I am a newbie at yoga and so learning more about the philosophy was fascinating. I am able to take some 'Midline exercises' that were taught in the book and incorporate them into my crazy day at work, the next time I dabble in a yoga class, or while doing my yoga DVD at home. I think *Finding the Midline* is a book I will reference to throughout my life. There are lessons that pertain to my life now and I know I will be able to relate to it later. Who doesn't love a good read that's entertaining, makes you smile, tear up, giggle and inspires you to be a better person?"

—SARA COLLISHAW, Hairstylist and small business owner (Pine, Colorado)

"What a gift this book is! As a yoga instructor and practitioner for over 25 years, I found Bill's depth and understanding to be both profound and refreshing. The way that this book weaves yoga philosophy with personal stories is an inspiration and a reminder that true yoga is about taking our experience off of the mat and into our lives.

Also appreciated is the importance placed on meditation as a regular practice. Bill continually shows that meditation can be a tool that we can use to manage our usual erratic responses to life. With meditation as a partner to our yoga practice, Bill has shown us the value of connecting ourselves to ourselves, mind, body and spirit.

Easy to read and understand, the language of this book is accessible to all levels of readers. Can't wait to share this amazing book with my students, family and friends!"

—MARY ANN CAIRO, ERYT Yoga Instructor (West Reading, Pennsylvania)

"In *Finding the Midline* Bill Dorigan shares personal stories of Midline not to recount a come-from-behind epic, or an underdog's triumph, but to grant access to a philosophy and way to view the world that has long been viewed as the realm of those living on a higher plane of consciousness. Dorigan, not only simplifies and contextualizes this philosophy, but his stories about his life provide an easily relatable understanding of what it means and how it can be applied to ones' own life. If ever there were a compilation that offers such a clear understanding of an ancient and powerful source of happiness and wellness through humor and light-hearted stories—*Finding the Midline* is it."

—ROGER MARTIN-PRESSMAN, Yoga Instructor, teacher and trainer (Denver, Colorado)

"As a tradesman with little yoga experience, I wasn't sure what to make of this offering from Mr. Dorigan, but as I began to read the book it quickly became obvious that it contains a great deal of useful insights for me. I've felt for a long time that God is everywhere you choose to see Him, and there are countless opportunities for us to serve ourselves and each other by realizing this. I've known for a long time that my "being" doesn't stop at the ends of my fingers and toes, but, like most folks it's easy for me to forget about that in the daily effort toward food, clothing, shelter, and whatever else I think I need. The truly exceptional people I've known seem to remember it more often, but Dorigan has a practical way for any of us to remember who we really are and make better lives with the information. He weaves together varied and interesting stories from his own life with some of the lessons he took from them to paint a picture of what a conscious, happy, and meaningful life can look like if we choose to step into it. This book shows how a yoga practice (or a meditation practice) might start out as a physical experience but then often leads to ways of thinking that can take us a long way toward who and what we were put here to be. If you're thinking you're not cut out to be a yogi, no worries- as he says near the beginning, the book is "intentionally written so you can apply the lessons of yoga in your life without ever having to balance on one foot, or do a "Down Dog." This is a really inspiring read."

—PETER STOKES, owner Peter's Car Clinic and SQR Electric (Boulder, Colorado)

"This book is an invitation to craft a richer, fuller, more joyful life through the practice of yoga. Drawing on non-dualist Tantric philosophies and recent insights from behavioral psychology, Dorigan suggests that every moment offers the potential to create a more meaningful life, one steeped in loving relationship with oneself, with others, and with the universe. Through disarmingly honest and often moving stories from the author's own life, it illustrates how the practice of yoga—which may or may not include physical poses—can foster greater awareness of our internal makeup and its role in shaping the world in which we live. In so doing, yoga gifts us with the choice to construct the world we want. An easy-to-read road map of yoga philosophy and how-to manual of some of its key practices, this book will be invaluable to yoga teachers, students, and anyone wishing to more fully participate in creating a life of purpose and meaning."

—ROSARIO MONTOYA DEL SOLAR, Ph.D., Yoga Teacher and student;
Anthropologist, Historian (Denver, Colorado)

"*Finding the Midline* beautifully blends yoga philosophy with real life experiences to bring the teachings alive in a practical and understandable way. It not only speaks to the inquisitive mind but also speaks directly to the heart and soul. This book educates while inspiring one to live a more full and present life. The balance between the humorous antidotes and the gut wrenching facts of life stories, adds character and perspective to how life experiences can be perceived."

—LYNN HANGER, Yoga teacher (Denver, Colorado)

"*Finding the Midline* is an invitation to discover one's authentic Self, like the proverbial needle in the haystack, buried among the seeming-ordinariness of everyday life. It is a clarion call to awaken and begin listening to the creative voice that whispers in our ears, telling us to stop living such small, anxiously predictable lives. This very readable book combines the modern findings of Western Brain Research with ancient Eastern spiritual philosophies. Dorigan's entertaining stories mingle beautifully with his informative instructions on how to practice living life as a yogi—whether or not we are interested in putting our feet behind our head."

—LIZA M. SHAW, MA, Author; Licensed Marriage and Family Therapist
(Hickory, North Carolina)

"In this refreshingly honest and captivatingly clear account of his application of the integration of ancient yoga philosophy in to day to day life, Bill Dorigan hooks the reader immediately in to a mind-opening experience. With both wisdom and humor, Dorigan shares knowledge from his years of studying Ancient Yogic philosophy from both the original sources as well as contemporary teachers. In this work, we are treated to hearing of how even a aggressive trial lawyer can evolve to open his heart, mind, and life path to a deep sense of purpose, connection, and satisfaction. Dorigan's stories are endearing, his insight sharp and thought-provoking, and his joyful wit comes through this book with genuine humility and benevolence."

—MICHAEL POLON, Certified Advanced Rolfer, Rolf Institute Faculty Member
(Denver, Colorado)

"*Finding the Midline* is a helpful guide to understanding the value and grace of yoga. What is most impressive to me is how through story and experience, Bill Dorigan brings the principles and teachings of yoga to life. Those of us who study yoga, whether it be pranayama, asana practice, Ayurveda or otherwise, know that yoga is truly practiced in our lives and 'off the mat.' Our time on the mat, holding yoga poses and breathing, is merely the practice that enables us to embody the principals and grace of yoga in our lives. We hold the poses on the mat so as to better show up in this world. Bill's book is very effective in conveying how yoga enhances your everyday life. As a former trial attorney, Bill Dorigan brings a unique and helpful worldview to the practice of yoga. His knowledge of yoga and passion for the practice is evident. Being a practicing attorney and yogi myself, Bill's application of yoga in his life and career really resonated with me. *Finding the Midline* is a great read for anyone interested in learning how the practice of yoga can enrich all facets of life."

—CHRIS JORGENSON, Attorney (Jackson, Wyoming)

"Part memoir, part yoga philosophy, Bill invites his readers to join him in a conversation about the ancient philosophy as applied to the life of a Midwestern football player, a trial lawyer, a father, and a spiritual seeker. *Finding the Midline* explores the transformational experience a deeper exploration of yoga can offer. The philosophy is made accessible and relatable to the yoga novice through heartfelt stories and practices. For the more seasoned yoga student, *Finding the Midline* is a springboard to the abundant resources referenced in the book."

—VALERIE LANI (Denver, Colorado)

"Such a joyous read. Bill reaches deep into his heart to tell a true story of yoga by sharing personal experiences mixed about with his unique sense of humor. Thank you Bill, for continuing to be my teacher."

—STEFANIE NELSON (Winter Park, Colorado)

"Engaging and Accessible. Bill Dorigan artfully weaves yoga philosophy with anecdotes from his personal life to offer insights into how yoga can enhance anyone's life. Dorigan courageously shares his own shadow side to explain how yoga philosophy and practice taught him to become a more caring, thoughtful and compassionate person, transforming his own life and deepening his connection with others. I highly recommend *Finding the Midline* for any yoga enthusiast who wants to understand how basic concepts in yoga translate into practical wisdom."

—EMMA KOHN, Yoga Practitioner and Teacher, Yoga Studio Sadhana (Quito, Ecuador)

"As I read this manuscript the smile on my face kept getting brighter and brighter. With what I know was a Herculean effort Bill Dorigan has assembled an enormous amount of information in one volume. Whether you are a yoga teacher, serious student, new student, or even if you've never heard of yoga, this book is for you."

—MURRAY GREEN, Yoga Teacher at Meta Yoga Studios (Breckenridge, Colorado)

ABOUT THE AUTHOR

BILL DORIGAN is a highly successful trial attorney, a certified yoga teacher, lecturer, and published author in the legal field. Following a career as an equity partner in one of the nation's leading law firms, Bill completed a Master's Degree studying the correlation of yoga philosophy with Western behavioral psychology. Bill has combined his extensive experience litigating high profile lawsuits with his deep understanding of yoga philosophy to create a book, *Finding the Midline—How Yoga Helps a Trial Lawyer Make Friends and Connect to Spirit.* In his spare time Bill has been awarded three black belts in martial arts and enjoys all that the mountains of Colorado, his home, have to offer. Bill can be contacted through his website www.findingthemidline.com.

Made in the USA
Lexington, KY
31 July 2015